Blackstone's Guide to the
CRIMINAL JUSTICE ACT 1991
Second Edition

Blackstone's Guide to the

CRIMINAL JUSTICE ACT 1991

Second Edition

THE 1991 ACT IN THE COURTS

Includes a copy of the 1991 Act (as amended by the Criminal Justice Act 1993)

Martin Wasik, LLB, MA, Barrister
Professor of Law, Manchester University

and

Richard D. Taylor, MA, LLM, Barrister
Forbes Professor of English Law and Head of Department of Legal Studies
University of Central Lancashire

BLACKSTONE
PRESS LIMITED

First published in Great Britain 1991 by Blackstone Press Limited,
9–15 Aldine Street, London W12 8AW. Telephone 081-740 1173

© M. Wasik and R. D. Taylor, 1991

First edition 1991
Reprinted 1992
Reprinted 1993
Second edition 1994

ISBN: 1 85431 304 5

British Library Cataloguing in Publication Data
A CIP catalogue record for this book is available from the British Library

Typeset by Style Photosetting Ltd, Mayfield, East Sussex
Printed by Ashford Colour Press, Gosport, Hampshire

Contents

Maximum Penalties
1.1 Custodial sentences: maximum penalties: theft and burglary 1.2 Custodial sentences: maximum penalties: other offences 1.3 Custodial sentences: young offenders: detention in a young offender institution 1.4 Custodial sentences: young offenders: custody for life 1.5 Custodial sentences: young offenders: default and contempt 1.6 Custodial sentences: young offenders: grave crimes

Criteria for Custody
1.7 Justifying the imposition of custody 1.8 The exceptions 1.9 The 'seriousness of the offence' criterion 1.10 The 'public protection' criterion 1.11 Giving reasons for imposing custody 1.12 Pre-sentence reports 1.13 Other information required before imposing custody: mitigation and aggravation 1.14 Previous convictions

Criteria for Sentence Length
1.15 Fixing the length of custodial sentences 1.16 Justifying sentence length under s. 2(2)(a) 1.17 Combination with other offences 1.18 Exemplary sentencing, offence prevalence and local conditions 1.19 Justifying sentence length under s. 2(2)(b) 1.20 Giving reasons for sentence length 1.21 Pre-sentence reports 1.22 Other information required on length of

Preface

Within two years of enactment and only a matter of months after commencement, 'the most fundamental review of the Criminal Justice System for 50 years' had turned into one of the most pilloried pieces of law reform during the whole of that time. The inclusion of amending sections at a late stage in the passing of the 1993 Criminal Justice Act, to remedy the perceived worst aspects of the 1991 Act, seemed to be an appropriate opportunity to update this guide to the 1991 Act (as amended) and to explain and discuss the many developments there have been via case law, practice directions, statutory instruments, government circulars and other administrative actions. The 1991 Act is printed as amended by the 1993 Act and a new Appendix has been added containing substantial extracts from the important new Home Office National Standards.

We have been gratified by the numbers of those involved in the Criminal Justice System who have bought, used or commented on the first edition of the book and we are grateful for a number of useful suggestions that we have received. With a new Criminal Justice Act promised for the forthcoming Parliamentary session, we hope, but cannot guarantee, that these will be the last amendments to the 1991 Act requiring explanation and discussion. Given the public reaction to Parliament's efforts in 1991, this is perhaps not an inappropriate evening on which to be writing the preface.

Martin Wasik
Richard Taylor
Guy Fawkes' Night 1993

Preface to the First Edition

The first five Criminal Justice Acts of the century were spaced out over nearly 50 years, from 1925 to 1972, whereas the last five have come in less than 20 years since 1972 and the current Act is the third in only five years.

Increasing frequency has not led to any reduction in average size and although the current Act falls short of the 173 sections of the 1988 Act, at 102 sections and 13 schedules, it is no minnow. If the Act has a core theme, it is the treatment of offenders after conviction. In particular, part I of the Act, discussed in chapters 1–3, creates a new statutory framework for sentencing offenders. The centrality of this new framework means that the background to it is separately set out in an introductory chapter which also refers more briefly to the provisions of the other parts of the Act. Part II of the Act, which is fully introduced and discussed in chapter 5, continues the theme of the treatment of offenders and establishes a new regime for the early release of offenders sentenced to imprisonment. The theme can still be seen, at least partially, in part IV of the Act which is discussed in chapter 7. This part of the Act makes changes to the way various services affecting convicted offenders, but also affecting persons awaiting trial, can be carried out and controversially allows for the admission of the private sector into these areas. In between part III of the Act is rather more of a miscellany held-together by the theme of Children and Young Persons and is discussed in chapter 4 under the heading of Procedural Changes and in chapter 6 under the heading of Children's Evidence.

In discussing the complex provisions of the Act and the substitutions it makes in other enactments, we have endeavoured not only to describe the probable meaning of the Act but also to evaluate its likely effects and identify both the problems it might solve and the difficulties it might create. We are grateful to the friends and colleagues in discussion with whom we have honed our own appreciation of the aims of the legislation. In particular, we would like to express our gratitude to John Spencer who kindly read and commented on a draft of chapter 6 at short notice and Harry Rooney who similarly looked at that part of chapter 7 dealing with the Probation Service. We would also like to thank Ken Hargreaves MP for his help with the vagaries of Parliamentary procedure, particularly in July when the Bill seemed to be bouncing back and forth between the Lords and the Commons on almost a daily basis. That this Guide has appeared within weeks of the Royal Assent is a further tribute to the efficiency of all at Blackstone Press and could not have been achieved without the sensitivity of Heather Saward and Alistair MacQueen in knowing which were the times for patience and which were the times for encouragement. Patience is a virtue which is needed by any author's spouse and we both gratefully acknowledge its exercise by our respective wives, Pat and Karen, who once again have found their husbands spending a disproportionate part of what are supposed to be the summer months entwined with a word processor. As the sun finally asserts itself in September, we promise, like we did last year, that next Summer will be different, but of course the weather is beyond our control!

Martin Wasik
Richard Taylor
6th September 1991

List of Abbreviations

ACR	automatic conditional release
CJA	Criminal Justice Act
CLA	Criminal Law Act
CPO	chief probation officer
CSO	community service order
CYPA	Children and Young Persons Act
DPP	Director of Public Prosecutions
LRC	Local Review Committee
MCA	Magistrates' Courts Act
PACE	Police and Criminal Evidence Act
PCCA	Powers of Criminal Courts Act
PSA	Probation Service Act
PSR	pre-sentence report
RTA	Road Traffic Act
RTOA	Road Traffic Offenders Act
SOA	Sexual Offences Act

Introduction

Background to the Act

Mr David Waddington, then Home Secretary, introduced the provisions of the Criminal Justice Bill on 9 November, 1990 as 'a balanced package' of criminal justice reforms. The main emphasis was upon the strengthening of statutory sentencing guidelines, the reform of the parole system and the introduction of a wider range of community penalties. All these had been foreshadowed in the government's White Paper, *Crime, Justice and Protecting the Public*, Cm 965, London: HMSO, February 1990 and the Carlisle Committee Report, *The Parole System in England and Wales*, Cm 532, London: HMSO, November 1988. On the White Paper see Andrew Ashworth, 'The White Paper on Criminal Justice and Sentencing' [1990] *Criminal Law Review* 217–224 and Martin Wasik and Andrew von Hirsch, 'Statutory Sentencing Principles: the 1990 White Paper' (1990) 53 *Modern Law Review* 508–517.

The central proposal in the White Paper was for the creation of 'a coherent framework for the use of financial, community and custodial punishments' (para. 1.15). It has been clear for some years that English sentencing law lacks a consistent rationale, with a leading decision of the Court of Appeal, *Sergeant* (1974) 60 Cr App R 74, advocating retribution, deterrence, prevention and rehabilitation as being the four aims of sentencing, without providing any explanation as to how these aims are to be reconciled or which is to prevail where there is a conflict between them. The White Paper urged that proportionality should be the guiding criterion for deciding the severity of sentence (paras 1.6, 2.2 and 2.3), and was sceptical about relying on deterrence as the basis for determining sentence. It is seldom that the deterrent effects of particular penalty levels are ascertainable, and deterrence based sanctions can easily lead to disproportionate sanctions, including exemplary penalties. The White Paper was clear that the power to determine the appropriate severity of sanctions must remain with the judiciary, but that sentencers would be required to make decisions about form and length of sentence within the constraints of proportionality between the offence and the punishment. The government stated that the legislation would be 'in general terms', subject to detailed interpretation later from the Court of Appeal.

The White Paper explained that the use of custody must be confined to serious cases only. This is, of course, in line with declared government policy, which has been to stress 'bifurcation'; dealing with less serious offences within the community whenever possible while imposing custodial sentences on those convicted of more serious crimes. This policy, however, has to be seen in the context of statistics which show that the criminal courts in England and Wales now imprison more offenders, and a greater proportion of offenders per head of population than any other European country (Council of Europe figures show that the UK custodial population is 97.4 per 100,000, as compared with France (81.1), Sweden (50.6), Greece (44.0) and Holland (40.0). The White Paper proposed that the key section restricting the use of custody by the courts should be to the effect that 'a court, before it gives a custodial sentence [would have] to be satisfied that the offence for which the offender has been convicted by the court is so serious that only a custodial sentence is justified, or that a custodial sentence is necessary to protect the public from serious harm'. This language may be compared with the eventual form of s. 1 of the Act, discussed in Chapter 1. The language is similar to that formerly employed in the context of young offenders under the Criminal Justice Act 1988, s. 123, amending the Criminal Justice Act 1982, s. 1(4), though with less emphasis upon the offender's criminal record. These provisions, which have been heralded by the government as being directly responsible for the downturn in the use of custody for those under 21, are abolished by the Act and replaced by the new criteria which apply to young offenders and adults alike. The partly suspended sentence is abolished by the Act (s. 5), the use of the suspended sentence is severely restricted, and suspended sentences continue to be unavailable for those under 21.

In the White Paper the government seemed to accept that departure from the principle of proportionality or 'desert' should be exceptional. This is evidenced, for example, in its proposal to abolish the extended sentence, now achieved by s. 5 of the Act. It was nevertheless prepared to compromise desert requirements by permitting the use of predictive confinement by sentencers in cases where offenders had committed offences of a violent or sexual nature. This exception to the proportionality principle has been carried through, in rather different wording, into the legislation. Although critics have expressed serious misgivings over the provisions, the creation of special arrangements for those convicted of violent or sexual offences is a thread which is woven through the whole Act (see, for example, ss. 1 and 2 on form and length of custodial sentences, s. 34 on life sentence release arrangements, s. 44 on release arrangements for sexual offenders and s. 60 on remands of juveniles to secure accommodation). The matter remains controversial, and is discussed further below in this Introduction and in Chapter 1.10.

The government was at pains to stress that a reduction in the prison population was not a central objective of the Bill. Mr Waddington explained that 'If the end result is a fall in the prison population I will be very glad, but that is not the prime objective'. During the Bill's second reading in the House of Commons, however, Mr Waddington stated that the new sentencing framework should lead to a reduction of 1,500 prisoners, and that changes in the parole system should lead to a further reduction of 500. This is one of the central problems of the Criminal Justice Act 1991. Under the new early release arrangements, the effective sentence length for many offenders given custodial sentences will increase from about one third to one half of their sentence. The sentence imposed by the court will have more meaning than at present, since remission is abolished and replaced by a period on parole licence followed by the last quarter of the sentence under conditional release in the community. In order to avoid a sharp increase in the custodial population as a result of these parole changes, some compensating changes are clearly required at the sentencing stage. The Carlisle Report insisted that its proposals on parole reform must be accompanied by a reduction in the use of imprisonment. A 5 per cent reduction is mentioned in the Report, but 'a larger reduction in sentencing levels seems entirely possible given the enhancements which we are proposing to the meaning of a sentence' (Carlisle Report, para. 434, mentioning also the possibility of 10 per cent or 15 per cent reductions in sentence length). The balancing of these two effects is likely to prove critical for the government's whole criminal justice strategy. In order for it to work the statute must impinge significantly on sentencing practice, so as to reduce both the number of offenders receiving custodial sentences and the average duration of those sentences. Yet there is no clear word on the matter in the Act, the government merely expressing the 'hope' in the White Paper (para. 9.8) that as a result of parole changes sentencers will respond by making a 5 per cent decrease in the length of custodial sentences. It has long been a principle of sentencing policy that judges should have no regard to the likely impact of early release arrangements upon the sentences they pass, but the Lord Chief Justice, in a *Practice Statement (Crime: Sentencing)* [1992] 1 WLR 948, issued on 1 October 1992, to coincide with the bringing into force of the bulk of the Act's provisions, said that in the light of the Act a 'new approach' is essential. Henceforth judges in the Crown Court *should* have regard to the actual period likely to be served, so as to avoid the risk of an offender serving substantially longer under the new system of early release than would have been normal under the old.

The government sees non-custodial penalties, or 'community penalties', as they are now to be called, as sentences standing in their own right, rather than as 'alternatives' to custody. On these matters see Martin Wasik and Andrew von Hirsch, 'Non-Custodial Penalties and the Principles of Desert' [1988] *Criminal Law Review* pp. 555–572. In the White Paper the Government proposed the scaling of community sanctions in terms of the relative degree of restriction upon liberty which they each entail. This is reflected only very sketchily in the relevant provisions of the Act, and it remains to be seen how far the concept of proportionality will affect existing court practice in relation to community penalties. The Court of Appeal is less well placed to influence sentences in this area than in custodial sentencing, since it hears relatively few sentencing appeals where community sentences are involved. The probation service will have a key role to play and it, together with the courts, will have to give practical meaning to the provision in s. 6(2) of the Act, which provides that when a court passes a community sentence it must select that community order or combination of orders which is both the most suitable for the offender and commensurate with the seriousness of the offence. Some guidance may be derived from the various national standards issued under the auspices of the Act (see further, Chapter 2).

Another potential problem lies in the proliferation of community orders, and the greater opportunities which the courts now have for mixing them together. Many of the pre-existing restrictions on combining these orders are swept away by the Act (see Chapter 2) but the courts are left to work out for themselves when such combinations will constitute good sentencing practice. At one point in the White Paper the government stated that, in general, only one community order should be used at a time (para. 1.12), but this remark was submerged later in the enthusiasm for mixing probation with community service (in the form of a combination order, now introduced by s. 11) and either or both of these with a curfew order which could, otherwise or in addition, be mixed with a financial penalty. It may, perhaps, be doubted whether this 'cafeteria' style of sentencing can achieve very much, except further to confuse sentencing principles. It seems to owe more to the rather old-fashioned belief that a precise form of sentence can be selected to achieve a specific rehabilitative effect, than to the coherent grading of community orders. It seems to run contrary to the government's own stated preference for penalty scaling and tends to undermine recent official moves to standardise the operational and breach arrangements for community orders. Curfew orders, enforced by electronic monitoring, which are introduced by s. 13 of the Act, are also controversial. The early enthusiasm for introducing them to the English criminal justice system seems to outstrip the available data, both here and in the United States, and a number of schemes have run into considerable technical and managerial difficulty. These powers have not been brought into force, and there now seems little prospect of this happening in the near future.

The Opposition supported the emphasis which the Bill gave to greater use of community sentences but predicted that, in the absence of a Sentencing Council to ensure that the courts heeded the guidelines, the changes would have a minimal impact upon the custodial population. The idea of a Sentencing Council is discussed, below.

The White Paper also indicated that the government was at last prepared to implement a system of *unit fines*, whereby offenders are required to pay a certain proportion of their disposable income rather than a flat tariff sum. This ill-fated scheme was implemented by s. 18 of the Act. The idea was not novel: several European countries have been operating such a system successfully for years. Here, however, successive governments have been concerned about making the calculation of fines more complex for the courts and it had been thought that unit fines would require more intrusive investigation in the financial affairs of those convicted of offences. In 1988, four pilot schemes in magistrates' courts returned favourable reports on the operation of unit fines. These courts, and several others, anticipated the changes in the Criminal Justice Act 1991 and ran their own versions of unit fine schemes under the justices' inherent jurisdiction to control their own proceedings. Greater fairness in sentencing was the driving principle behind the move to unit fines. That might be thought to be sufficient reason in itself for making such a change, but the pilot courts discovered other benefits, too. The net amount of fine revenue recovered from offenders increased (by about 12 per cent), the rate of payment was better, the number of fine defaulters decreased and the number receiving prison sentences for default decreased sharply (by about 14 per cent). A further implication of more accurate calculation of offenders' ability to pay was the increased use of compensation orders in these cases.

A controversial issue which was resolved in different ways by the pilot courts, and which received statutory attention, was the setting of appropriate upper and lower limits for unit fines. While the pilot courts had identified a figure in the range of £25–£30 as the upper limit for the value of a unit, the government in the CJA 1991, fixed the upper limit at £100. Soon after the unit fine provisions came into force the press carried stories of very high fines being imposed for trivial offences (e.g., £1,200 on an offender convicted of throwing a crisp bag out of a window). These cases, together with anomalies which arose in motoring cases (because of the disparity between the unit fine and the equivalent fixed penalty), generated great criticism in the press about unit fines, and about the CJA 1991 in general. On 30 April 1993, Kenneth Clarke, then Home Secretary, was reported in *The Times* as saying that he supported the 'principle of linking fines to an offender's disposable income'. By 14 May, however, in the face of increasing government unpopularity, and the embarrassment of a by-election defeat at Newbury, the climate was such that the Home Secretary announced in a statement to Parliament the abolition of the unit fine system. This is achieved by CJA 1993, s. 65. See further Chapter 3. The principal limitation to unit fines was that they did not extend to the Crown Court. Even there, however, there was a move in the CJA 1991 towards greater equality of impact in setting fine levels by the adoption of a provision which allows the court to increase the level of the fine for a rich offender upon whom the tariff fine would have little impact. The CJA 1993 preserves the principle that the fine should be adjusted upwards or downwards to take account of means.

The Bill also contained many of the measures which had been recommended by Judge Pigot QC, in the *Report of the Advisory Group on Video Evidence*, issued by the Home Office in 1989. These are designed to make it easier to bring prosecutions in cases of child abuse and to reduce the stress on children giving evidence. For discussion of these proposals see Jenny McEwan, 'In the box or on the box? The Pigot Report and Child Witnesses' [1990] *Criminal Law Review* pp. 363–370. These provisions are discussed in Chapter 6 below.

A Summary of Controversial Matters in the Bill

Much press and public discussion centred on the following matters:

(1)   As had been indicated in the Working Paper, the government saw no role in their scheme for a *Sentencing Council*. This idea, which had been proposed by Professor Ashworth in his book *Sentencing and Penal Policy*, Weidenfeld and Nicholson, 1983, pp. 447–451, now has the support of the Labour Party, and (in various guises) has been urged upon the government by a range of different organisations. It has been endorsed by the Chairman of the Magistrates' Association's Sentencing of Offenders Committee, by JUSTICE and by 17 criminal justice organisations represented by the Penal Affairs Consortium. The idea is opposed, however, by Dr David Thomas, who argues that a Sentencing Council in England and Wales would 'be a direct competitor of the Court of Appeal' (*The Times*, 13 February, 1990) and that 'the ambitious claims for it owe everything to hope and nothing to experience'. Lord Justice Glidewell, Chairman of the Judicial Studies Board, is also reported to be against the idea of a Sentencing Council composed of judges and lay people, but to believe that there is a role for formalising the discussion of sentencing among judges. Sir Frederick

Lawton, a former Lord Justice of Appeal has said that 'Finding members of a sentencing council who would have had as much experience of dealing with crime as the senior judiciary would be difficult. Parliament, having decided what the sentencing policy should be, would be well advised to leave the Court of Appeal to implement the policy' (*The Times*, 8 January, 1991). In March 1991 an amendment to the Bill in the House of Lords to introduce a Sentencing Council was rejected by 152 votes to 91.

(2)   There was great disquiet in the press, and reported objection by judges and magistrates, over a change proposed in the Bill which was seen as requiring the courts to disregard an offender's *previous convictions* when passing sentence. The Law Society called for a clarification of this particular clause, commenting that if the provision is framed too loosely it will provide 'a way of getting round the new sentencing rules' (*The Times*, 21 August, 1990). In September 1990 it was reported that 'judges, magistrates and barristers' had forced the government to re-think the relevant provision, a deputy chairman of the Magistrates' Association commenting that it would make the courts 'look silly': 'Magistrates' courts deal with lots of people who commit offences many times and it is just not sensible that we should not be able to vary the punishment in line with how often the individual has appeared before the court' (*The Times*, 4 September, 1990). There is no doubt that the clause was poorly drafted, but much of the criticism was ill-directed, displaying a misunderstanding of the Court of Appeal's sentencing principles on 'progressive loss of mitigation' for persistent offenders. Confusingly, at a press conference on 9 November, Mr Waddington was reported as saying that, under the relevant clause, courts would be able to take previous convictions into account as much as they had previously done, and this was welcomed by the chairman of the Magistrates' Association, who claimed that 'One of the most frustrating things for both magistrates and the public is to see the same people constantly coming up before the courts, apparently undeterred by previous sentences'. The wording of the relevant clause was amended in the course of the Bill's progress through Parliament, but s. 29 continued to attract criticism once the CJA 1991 was implemented. It was one of the targets for criticism in a speech made by the Lord Chief Justice to the Law Society of Scotland in March 1993 in which he described the CJA 1991 as an 'ill-fitting straitjacket' for sentencers. Similar concern was expressed by the Magistrates' Association, and some lay magistrates resigned in protest. Section 29 of the CJA 1991 is now repealed by the CJA 1993, and a new, much more loosely worded provision, is substituted. For consideration of s. 29 see 1.14.

(3)   A *Times* leader on the Bill, published on 21 August, 1990, while welcoming most of the proposed sentencing changes in the Bill as 'enlightened', warned tht the proposals that offenders convicted of *violent or sexual offences* should be exempt from the general requirement of proportionality was an 'invitation to injustice' which would need to be 'most carefully defined in the Bill and even more carefully supervised by the Court of Appeal'. Paul Cavadino, senior information officer of the National Association for the Care and Resettlement of Offenders, has also criticised the provision, stating that 'The principles of justice require courts to seek proportionality between the severity of the punishment and the 'just deserts' of the offender. Once sentencers abandon this principle, they are no longer applying justice but a form of social

engineering devoid of moral content. Such sentencing decisions would be highly subjective, based not on what the offender has done but on the judge's guess as to what he might do in the future' (*The Times*, 28 August, 1990). The scope of the relevant clauses was reduced in the course of the Bill's progress through Parliament. They appear in their final form in part I of the Act, with the key terms of 'violent offence' and 'sexual offence' defined in s. 31. While originally envisaged in the White Paper as being exceptions to the general proportionality requirement in sentencing, it is possible that these provisions may be more generally applied by the courts. The main discussion of these sections of the Act may be found in Chapter 1.10.

(4) The government came under criticism with respect to their proposal to make it a criminal offence for parents to *fail to prevent their children from committing offences*. This new offence was to be in addition to existing powers to fine parents for their children's offences, unless it was unreasonable to do so. The Magistrates' Association, amongst others, criticised the new idea, commenting that many families needed help rather than punishment and that punishing parents could be counter-productive in some cases: 'The family of these youngsters is often such a fragile unit that we have to be very careful not to destroy what structure there is'. The idea was dropped by the government. Related changes to the courts' powers to require parents to pay fines and compensation, or bind over parents in respect of their children's wrongdoing, are considered at Chapter 4.5.

(5) Probation officers expressed disquiet in respect of the impending changes to the *rationale, structure and organisation of the probation service*. This echoed the service's opposition to many of the changes proposed in the Green Paper *Punishment and Supervision in the Community*, issued by the Home Office in February 1990. They commented that the proposals in the Bill would 'further reduce morale in a service already demoralised by government proposals to toughen community penalties by such means as introducing curfews' (*The Times*, 18 July, 1991). A particular concern has been whether the changes will be adequately funded. The extensive changes brought about by the Act to community penalties, and to the changes with respect to the provision of pre-sentence reports, are considered in Chapter 2. The role of the probation service in the supervision of offenders released on licence under the new arrangements are discussed in Chapter 5 and the structural changes to the organisation and funding of the probation service are discussed in Chapter 7.

(6) There was considerable pressure to introduce a clause into the Bill which would impose an *obligation on courts and other criminal justice agencies to treat all defendants fairly*, irrespective of nationality or race, and to create an inspectorate to enforce the provision. The proposal came about because of increasing awareness that although only 5 per cent of the population of England and Wales is non-white, ethnic minority prisoners account for 16 per cent of the sentenced custodial population. Among the remand population, the figure is 19 per cent. This information emerged from a report published by NACRO, which dealt with figures relating to the custodial population on 30 June, 1989. An amendment to this effect was withdrawn in the face of a government commitment to consider how best such a principle should be enshrined in the Bill. The resulting provision is greatly diluted from its original form and appears

in s. 95 in the shape of an obligation placed upon the Secretary of State to publish annually information to help enable those involved in the administration of criminal justice to avoid discrimination on the ground of race, sex or other improper ground. Mr John Patten explained that while allegations of racial bias by police officers and other decision makers in the criminal justice system required close investigation, the way forward was to commission further detailed surveys of the problem, since the data already collected did not uniformly support the claims of bias. He pointed out that courts were already bound to treat all defendants equally by the terms of the judicial oath and that defendants who felt that they had been treated unfairly could always appeal to a higher court. The first publications issued under the auspices of the CJA 1991, s. 95 were *Race and the Criminal Justice System* and *Gender and the Criminal Justice System*. They were published by the Home Office in September 1992. A further five volumes, collectively entitled *Costs in the Criminal Justice System* were published in October 1992. The first of these dealt with various matters of costs (including the relative costs of the imposition of different kinds of sentence) in the Crown Court and the other four gave similar information for magistrates' courts. It is envisaged that further such information will be published on an annual basis.

(7) The government's proposal to *deduct fines and compensation orders imposed upon an offender from that person's income support payments* came in for criticism. This idea was announced in November 1990. Penal reform groups and groups representing low income households were in agreement with the effort to keep defaulters out of prison, but there was concern about those offenders who already had their income support docked to pay rent or fuel arrears. The relevant provisions are discussed in Chapter 3.12.

(8) During the Bill's passage through Parliament there was a remarkable conflict between the Lords and the Commons over life sentences. On 18 April, 1991 the House of Lords moved, by 177 votes to 79, to abolish the *mandatory life sentence for murder*. The rebels included Lord Lane CJ, Lord Nathan and Lord Windlesham. The new Home Secretary, Kenneth Baker, told the House of Commons on 25 June that the abolition of the mandatory penalty would undermine public confidence and stated that 'The fairest system is the one we have now where the life sentence is fixed by law and the responsibility then passes to the Home Secretary to decide how the sentence should be spent. That is part of the Home Secretary's responsibility for the protection of the public, the preservation of the Queen's peace and the maintenance of confidence in the criminal justice system.' He added that 'One could imagine the outcry if a probation order was given for murder'.

The government's majority in the Commons ensured that the Lords' amendment abolishing the mandatory life penalty was rejected but one outcome of the raising of the issue was an improvement to the procedure for releasing prisoners serving *discretionary* life sentences. Release mechanisms for *mandatory* life sentences, however, were left unreformed in the Act, though some improvements have since been made by judicial decisions. These matters are discussed in more detail in Chapter 5 at paras 5.3 and 5.12.

(9) The clearest divergencies of view based on party political grounds were evident in relation to part IV of the Act which contains a number of provisions

enabling various services in the criminal justice system to be contracted out to the private sector. These include the provision of security in magistrates' courts and the escorting of prisoners to and from court but also, perhaps most controversially, the power to contract out the running of prisons. This started off being restricted to *new remand* prisons but, to the horror of the opposition, was broadened, following promptings from Conservative backbenchers, so as to countenance, in principle, the privatisation of *any* prison. These provisions are more fully discussed in Chapter 7.

Implementation

The Criminal Justice Act 1991 received the Royal Assent on 25 July 1991.

Initially the plan was to implement the Criminal Justice Act 1991 in the Spring of 1992. In the light of pressure from 'magistrates and other court officials' (*The Times*, 27 July, 1991), however, the Home Office subsequently settled on different implementation dates for different provisions of the Act, with the bulk of it brought into force in *October 1992*.

Training in respect of the Act was overseen by the Judicial Studies Board, and comprised a series of seminars for judges in various parts of the country. Justices' clerks acted as training officers for magistrates. Something in the order of 10 hours' training for each magistrate was thought to be appropriate.

Sections 12 and 13 of the CJA 1991 (curfew orders and electronic monitoring of offenders) have *not* been brought into effect.

The Criminal Justice Act 1993 received the Royal Assent on 27 July 1993. Sections 66 and 67 came into force on 16 August 1993 and s. 65 and sch. 3 came into force on 20 September 1993.

This Guide

The Criminal Justice Act 1991 has had an impact which has reached into many areas of criminal justice practice. It was the objective of the first edition of this *Blackstone's Guide* to the Act to help explain the changes brought about by this complex piece of legislation. Since the first edition was published a range of detailed guidance on the Act has been published. This material includes delegated legislation, national standards, Home Office guidance and judicial decisions of the Court of Appeal and the House of Lords. This second edition of the *Guide* includes reference to and, where appropriate, detailed extracts from, this new material. It is hoped that the second edition will be of help in offering insights to the Act's interpretation in the courts, especially in the light of amendments made to it by the CJA 1993.

In this *Guide*, extensive reference is made to official documents which preceded the publication of the original Criminal Justice Bill, particularly the Government's White Paper, *Crime, Justice and Protecting the Public*, Cm 965, London: HMSO, February 1990. This seems appropriate since the origins of so much of the Act may be found in that White Paper. We also refer, where appropriate, to Parliamentary debates on the Bills which became the CJA 1991 and the CJA 1993. In doing so we are mindful of the decisions of the House of Lords in *Attorney-General's Reference (No. 1 of 1988)* (1989) 89 Cr App R 60, in which their Lordships explained that when construing a penal statute, a criminal court may properly consult a government White Paper in order to ascertain the true purpose of a particular statutory provision, and in *Pepper* v *Hart* [1992] 3 WLR 1032, where their Lordships said that reference could be made to Hansard when construing ambiguous or obscure statutory provisions.

Chapter One
Custodial Sentences

Sections 1 to 5 of the CJA 1991 recast the arrangements for the passing of custodial sentences, both by the Crown Court and by magistrates' courts. The provisions apply to adult offenders (aged 21 and over) and to young offenders in respect of whom, prior to the Act, a different statutory regime applied. Sections 1 to 4 of the Act set out the grounds upon which a custodial sentence may now be imposed and the criteria for determining the length of a custodial sentence, these changes being described by the government as amounting to 'a new and more coherent statutory framework for sentencing' (White Paper, 1990, p. 1). Subject to certain important exceptions for those who commit violent offences or sexual offences, the guiding principle in these provisions is the proportionality of the custodial sentence to the seriousness of the offence 'so that convicted criminals get their just deserts' (White Paper, 1990, p. 2). Section 5 abolishes the partly suspended sentence and the extended sentence, and restricts the circumstances in which a suspended sentence may be imposed. There are also some changes to available maximum penalties, and these are considered first.

MAXIMUM PENALTIES

1.1 Custodial Sentences: Maximum Penalties: Theft and Burglary

By s. 26 of the CJA 1991, the maximum penalty for theft when tried on indictment is reduced from 10 years to seven years. This change is almost entirely symbolic, given that sentence levels for theft, for all practical purposes, never approach the former (or the revised) maximum. An exceptional case, perhaps, is *Higgs* (1986) 8 Cr App R (S) 440, where the offender, a management accountant, in breach of trust and over a period of five years, stole more than £3 million. The total sentence was reduced from 14 years (seven years on one group of counts sentenced consecutively to seven years on a second group) to eight years. In a case such as this consecutive sentencing will often be appropriate and other charges, such as obtaining property by deception, where the maximum penalty remains 10 years, might be brought. The maximum penalties for conspiracy to steal and attempted theft, which are tied to the maximum penalty for the full offence are also, accordingly, reduced. Anomalously, incitement to commit theft remains a common law offence, for which the penalty is at large.

Also by s. 26, the offence of burglary is, in effect, split into two for sentencing purposes. While for burglary in respect of dwellings (including an inhabited vehicle or vessel) the maximum penalty remains at 14 years when tried on indictment, other cases of burglary (e.g. of offices, shops or factories) will now attract the lower maximum penalty of 10 years. The higher maximum applies to all dwellings, whether the dwelling was occupied at the time of the burglary or not. Again, the reduction in the maximum penalty is of little practical importance since very few sentences for burglary approach these maxima, but it is an interesting example of the legislature endorsing what has become a well established 'two-tier' sentencing practice of the courts over recent years in respect of this offence. This approach has also surfaced in the *Practice Note (Mode of Trial: Guidelines)* [1990] 1 WLR 1439, where separate guidelines are given for burglary of a dwelling-house and burglary of non-dwellings. The government noted in the White Paper that 'the public makes a clear distinction between the burglaries of people's homes and other burglaries. Some burglaries of homes, especially when houses are ransacked and soiled, are regarded as more akin to assaults' (para. 3.14). The maximum penalties for conspiracy to commit burglary and attempted burglary, which are tied to the maximum penalty for the full offence, are also, accordingly, reduced. Anomalously, incitement to commit burglary remains a common law offence, for which the penalty is at large.

These changes took effect from 1 October 1992, and apply retrospectively to offences committed before that date: this conclusion follows from the exclusion of s. 26(1) and (2) from the ambit of the transitional provisions in sch. 12, para. 7, and from the fact that such penalty changes cannot be to the disadvantage of any offender.

1.2 Custodial Sentences: Maximum Penalties: Other Offences

For the mandatory penalty for murder which, ultimately, was not removed by the Act, see 1.24 below. The maximum custodial penalties in respect of two other criminal offences are, however, affected by the 1991 Act. These are:

(a)   Certain penalties under the Badgers Act 1973, s. 10(2), are increased from three months to six months summarily (CJA 1991, s. 26(3)). See now the Protection of Badgers Act 1992, s. 12 and sch.

(b)   Custodial penalties for bomb hoaxes under CLA 1977, s. 51(4), are increased from five years to seven years on indictment and from three months to six months, summarily (CJA 1991, s. 26(4)). This increase does not apply in relation to offences committed before 1 October 1992 (sch. 12, para. 7).

The maximum custodial penalties in respect of the following offences are increased by the CJA 1993:

(a)   The maximum penalty for causing death by dangerous driving under the RTA 1988, s. 1, is increased from five years to 10 years (CJA 1993, s. 67(1)).

(b)   The maximum penalty for causing death by careless driving while under the influence of drink or drugs, under the RTA 1988, s. 3A, is increased from five years to 10 years (CJA 1993, s. 67(1)).

1.3 Custodial Sentences: Young Offenders: Detention in a Young Offender Institution

Following the multitude of changes brought about to the sentencing of young offenders by CJA 1982 and CJA 1988, the CJA 1991 makes further alterations. The criteria for the imposition of custody are changed once again and there are now criteria for determining the duration of custody. Since these are identical to those which now apply in respect of adult offenders, they are dealt with together in 1.7 to 1.23 below. Other changes, which affect only the sentence of detention in a young offender institution, are dealt with now.

By the CJA 1988 the two sentences of detention centre order and youth custody were abolished and replaced by the single sentence of detention in a young offender institution, the sentence being available for males from the age of 14 and females from the age of 15. The following changes to these arrangements are effected by CJA 1991:

(a) The sentence of detention in a young offender institution can no longer be imposed on a 14-year-old (CJA 1991, s. 63(1) amending CJA 1982, s. 1A(1)).

(b) The minimum term of detention in a young offender institution is changed from a minimum which under the pre-1991 Act law varied both in accord with the age and sex of the offender, to a minimum of 21 days, in the case of an offender who is under 21 years of age but not less than 18, or of two months in the case of an offender who is under 18 (CJA 1991, s. 63(2), amending CJA 1982, s. 1A(2), (3) and (4) and inserting a new (4A)).

There is some confusion over the status of CJA 1982, s. 1A(4). Prior to the 1991 Act this created an exception to the minimum term provision, in the case of a young offender who committed an offence of breach of a supervision requirement after release from a term of detention in a young offender institution. The subsection refers to CJA 1982, s. 15(11), which creates the offence of breach. The problem is that CJA 1991 preserves the reference to CJA 1982, s. 15(11), in CJA 1982, s. 1A(4), but repeals s. 15 itself (CJA 1991, sch. 13). The offence of failing to comply with a supervision requirement is reinstated by CJA 1991, s. 65(6), but it is not clear whether CJA 1991 preserves the exception to the minimum sentence which may be imposed.

(c) The maximum term of detention in a young offender institution which may be imposed upon a 15 or 16-year-old remains the same as before CJA 1991, at 12 months or the maximum term of imprisonment which the court may impose for the offence, whichever is the lesser, but the provision is now extended to apply to 17-year-olds as well (CJA 1991, s. 63(3)(b), amending CJA 1982, s. 1B(2)). It may be noted that CJA 1982, s. 1B, now has no subsection (1) or (3).

(d) The total term (i.e. taking account of consecutive terms imposed on an offender on the same or different occasions) of a sentence of detention in a young offender institution which may be imposed on an offender aged 15 or 16 was previously governed by CJA 1982, s. 1B(4) and (5). These provisions are replaced by CJA 1991, s. 63(3). The effect is to ensure that in no case can a total term of more than 12 months be imposed (as before), but this provision is now also extended to 17-year-olds.

(e) The Secretary of State may, from time to time, direct that an offender sentenced to detention in a young offender institution shall be detained in a prison or remand centre instead, but only for a 'temporary purpose' (CJA 1982, s. 1C(2)). By CJA 1991, s. 63(4), this possibility is extended to apply to 17-year-olds as well as 15 and 16-year-olds.

One effect of these changes is that the powers available to impose a sentence of detention in a young offender institution are now the same in respect of male and female offenders. The government did consider abolition of the sentence in respect of the small number of female 15, 16 and 17-year-olds who receive it (see White Paper, para. 8.27) but, in the event, did not do so. The removal of 14-year-olds from the scope of the sentence will affect around 400 young males upon whom detention in a young offender institution was imposed annually.

1.4 Custodial Sentences: Young Offenders: Custody for Life

By CJA 1982, s. 8(2), an offender under the age of 21 may be sentenced to custody for life in respect of any offence for which a sentence of life imprisonment is available for an adult offender. The lower qualifying age for this sentence is raised from 17 to 18, by CJA 1991, s. 63(5) and see 1.6 below.

1.5 Custodial Sentences: Young Offenders: Default and Contempt

Under CJA 1982, s. 9, an offender under the age of 21 may be detained in respect of default of payment of a fine or other sum of money or in respect of committing a contempt of court or kindred offence. The lower qualifying age for this sentence is raised from 17 to 18, by CJA 1991, s. 63(5).

The CJA 1991 also amends CJA 1982, s. 1(5), which required a court detaining an offender under s. 9 only to do so where no other method of dealing with the offender is appropriate. This wording is amended by CJA 1991, sch. 11, para. 30, by the additional requirements that the court must have regard to the circumstances of the default or contempt (including any aggravating or mitigating features) and may take into account any information about the offender before making such an order. By a new s. 1(5A) inserted, a magistrates' court is further required in these circumstances to state in open court the reason for its opinion that no other method of dealing with the offender is appropriate and cause that reason to be specified in the warrant of commitment and entered in the register.

1.6 Custodial Sentences: Young Offenders: Grave Crimes

CJA 1991 amends CYPA 1933, s. 53(2), which provides for detention of young offenders for certain grave crimes. The effect of the change described in 1.4 above is to bring 17-year-olds within the scope of this section. One of the qualifying criteria for such a sentence is that the offender must have committed an offence punishable, in the case of an adult, with a prison term of 14 years or more. By CJA 1991, s. 64, in a case where the offender has reached the age of 16, the offence of indecent assault on a woman, under SOA 1956, s. 14(1), is to be regarded as a qualifying offence, notwithstanding the fact that this offence currently has a maximum sentence available of 10 years. Transitional provisions state that the above change shall not apply in any case where the offence in question was committed before the commencement of s. 64 and the offender is aged 16 at the date of his conviction. It may be noted that one effect of reducing the maximum penalty for burglaries not committed in a dwelling from 14 years to 10 years is to exclude those burglaries from the ambit of CYPA 1933, s. 53(2).

CJA 1993 further amends CYPA 1933, s. 53(2), by inserting a new para. (aa). This has the effect of extending the provisions of s. 53(2) to young persons convicted of causing death by dangerous driving, or causing death by careless driving while under the influence of drink or drugs, notwithstanding the fact that these offences carry maximum prison terms of 10 (rather than 14) years in the case of an adult. The maximum penalties for these offences have been increased from five years to 10 years by CJA 1993, s. 67(1).

CRITERIA FOR CUSTODY

1.7 Justifying the Imposition of Custody

CJA 1991, s. 1, creates a set of criteria to assist the courts in determining when the imposition of a custodial sentence is appropriate. Section 20 of PCCA 1973, which laid down certain limitations attendant upon the imposition of a first prison sentence on an offender, is repealed. The key provision is now s. 1(2) of the CJA 1991 as amended by CJA 1993, s. 66(1), which restricts the powers of the Crown Court and magistrates' courts to impose a custodial sentence to cases where the court is of the opinion either:

(a) that the offence, or the combination of the offence and one or more offences associated with it, was so serious that only such a sentence can be justified for the offence; or

(b) where the offence is a violent or sexual offence, that only such a sentence would be adequate to protect the public from serious harm from him.

These provisions have general application in the Crown Court and in magistrates' courts and they apply to all 'custodial sentences', which expression is defined in s. 31. For a person of or over 21 'custodial sentence' means 'a sentence of imprisonment', which includes life imprisonment and a suspended sentence, but it does not include a committal or attachment for contempt of court. For a person under 21 it means a sentence of detention in a young offender institution, detention under CYPA 1933, s. 53(2), or a sentence of custody for life, under CJA 1982, s. 8(2).

1.8 The Exceptions

Under earlier versions of the Bill offences triable only on indictment were largely excluded from the application of the criteria in s. 1(2), but that restriction was subsequently removed. Two exceptions to the application of these criteria are, however, retained in s. 1.

First, they naturally do not apply where the sentence for the offence is fixed by law (s. 1(1)). This, in practice, means the crime of murder (but not related offences, such as attempted murder or conspiracy to murder) where the penalty is fixed at imprisonment for life for an adult by Murder (Abolition of Death Penalty) Act 1965, s. 1(1). Custody for life (CJA 1982, s. 8(1)), or detention during Her Majesty's pleasure (CYPA 1933, s. 53(1)) are the equivalent sentences in the case of offenders under 21 convicted of murder. On the fixed penalty for murder see 1.24 below.

Second, the stated criteria shall not prevent a court from passing a custodial sentence on an offender who refuses to give his consent to a community sentence which is proposed by the court and requires that consent (CJA 1991, s. 1(3)). A custodial sentence imposed in these circumstances is a possible sanction for refusal to consent, but the court would not be bound to impose a custodial sentence, since a different community sentence (to which the offender was prepared to consent, or the imposition of which required no such consent) might be imposed instead. Where custody is imposed on these grounds the court does not, of course, have to justify it in terms of the custody criteria in s. 1, nor is it required to obtain a pre-sentence report, but it is required to explain to the offender in open court and in ordinary language why it is imposing custody on him (s. 1(4) and (5)). See further 1.11 below.

The community sentences in respect of which the offender's consent is required are a probation order (PCCA 1973, s. 2, as substituted by CJA 1991, s. 8(1)), a community service order (PCCA 1973, s. 14(2), as substituted by CJA 1991, s. 10(3)), a combination order (CJA 1991, s. 11 (although s. 11 does not specifically state that such consent is required, consent is a requirement for both constituent parts of a combination order)); and a curfew order (CJA 1991, s. 12(5)). Under CJA 1991, s. 13, a curfew order may include a requirement for securing the electronic monitoring of the offender. While s. 13 does not specify that the offender must consent to the monitoring requirement, it is clear from s. 12 that the curfew order itself cannot be made unless the offender 'expresses his willingness to comply with its requirements' including, where appropriate, the electronic monitoring. An attendance centre order does not require the offender's consent, nor does a supervision order, but the imposition of certain requirements within a supervision order does require consent. The CJA 1991 does not say whether the offender's refusal to consent to one part of a mixed order would amount to a refusal to consent to the whole order, but it is likely that the court would so construe such a refusal. Case law might in due course develop on the question of whether the offender's refusal to consent might in any circumstances be regarded as reasonable.

Pre-CJA 1991 case law on the consent requirement indicates that the offender must be given a fair opportunity to make a choice over whether to consent to the sentence. In *Marquis* [1974] 1 WLR 1087 the offender did not wish to be put on probation but consented because she thought that the only alternative was a custodial sentence. On the facts, according to Lord Parker CJ, custody was 'an exceedingly remote alternative', and the probation order was quashed. In *Barnett* (1986) 8 Cr App R (S) 200, however, it was explained by the Court of Appeal that where custody was a real possibility, the offender's consent to the probation order was not vitiated by his knowledge that, if he did not consent, a custodial sentence might well be passed. These two cases are of limited assistance in interpreting the 1991 Act, however, since they turned on the extent to which custody and probation could be seen as alternative disposals on the facts. The statutory framework for sentencing created by part I of the CJA 1991 makes these forms of sentence mutually exclusive and renders the concept of a community sentence as an 'alternative' to a custodial sentence meaningless.

In the post-CJA 1991 case of *Reynolds* [1993] Crim LR 468 the offender pleaded guilty to burglary. A co-defendant, who also pleaded guilty, received community service. At some stage of the proceedings (the report does not make this clear) Reynolds expressed a preference to receive probation rather than community service. In the event the sentencer imposed 12 months' detention in a young offender institution on Reynolds on the basis of the seriousness of the offence (distinguishing him from his co-defendant because of the latter's clean record). It would seem that s. 1(3) could have applied in this case only if the sentencer had been minded to impose community service, had proposed this to Reynolds, who had then declined. The sentencer should not use s. 1(3) on the basis of (say) an indication in a pre-sentence report that the offender would be unwilling to consent to the type of community order the court has in mind.

1.9   The 'Seriousness of the Offence' Criterion

We turn now to consider the criteria for imposing a custodial sentence in CJA 1991, s. 1(2), on the assumption that neither of the above exceptions apply. The first alternative ground is:

(a)   that the offence, or the combination of the offence and one or more offences associated with it, was so serious that only such a sentence can be justified for the offence.

It is suggested that this provision is best seen as a custody threshold requirement (see figure 1.1). It provides the key justification in the Act for a sentencer to select a custodial sentence rather than a community sentence. As we shall see, the Act also *requires* the sentencer to have regard to mitigating and aggravating factors which impinge upon offence seriousness and *permits* the sentencer to take account of any other mitigating (but not aggravating) factor. It follows from this that factors which are not associated with offence seriousness may operate to save the offender from custody, by pulling him back from the threshold, but can never provide the impetus for custody if the offence is not in itself serious enough to justify it. A clear example of a case where notwithstanding that the offence 'was so serious that only such a sentence can be justified', a custodial sentence was avoided in the light of personal mitigation is *Cox* [1993] 1 WLR 188. In that case Lord Taylor CJ said that 'Section 1(2) enjoins the court not to pass a custodial sentence unless it is of the opinion that the criteria of seriousness are met. The court is not required to pass such a sentence even when they are.' In *Cox* the 18-year-old offender had been riding a trials motor cycle on the road at night without lights and carrying a pillion passenger. He was seen by police officers in a patrol car. In an attempt to avoid them he mounted the pavement, drove along it for 50 metres and ignored a 'Give Way' sign. He then fell off the motor cycle. He was found to be in possession of various items of stolen property. The judge imposed sentences totalling four months detention in a young offender institution. The Court of Appeal agreed that only a custodial sentence was justified on the facts, but that such a sentence could be avoided in this case by having regard to the relevant personal mitigation, in particular the offender's youth, antecedent history and information in the pre-sentence report. A sentence of 12 months probation was substituted.

The offender must have been convicted of at least one offence, and this does of course cover both conviction after a trial and after a guilty plea (*Cole* [1965] 2 QB 388). Taking first the situation of an offender convicted of a single offence, the seriousness criterion appears to be quite clear. It is similar to, but supersedes, the provision in CJA 1982, s. 1(4A), para. (c) of which provided that, in respect of young adult offenders, a custodial sentence was appropriate where 'the offence of which he has been convicted or found guilty was so serious that a non-custodial sentence for it cannot be justified'. This provision is repealed by CJA 1991, which now provides a statutory scheme applicable to both adults and young offenders. The limited case law on para. (c) of s. 1(4A) may, however, be helpful by analogy.

In *Bradbourn* (1985) 7 Cr App R (S) 180 Lawton LJ said that the phrase 'so serious that a non-custodial sentence cannot be justified' means:

> the kind of offence which when committed by a young person would make right thinking members of the public, knowing all the facts, feel that justice had not been done by the passing of any sentence other than a custodial one. We think that is as good guidance as we can give to courts.

These words were expressly adopted in relation to the CJA 1991, s. 1(2)(a), by Lord Taylor of Gosforth CJ in *Cox* [1993] 1 WLR 188.

In *Hebron* (1989) 11 Cr App R (S) 226 it was pointed out by the Court of Appeal that in making that assessment the court has to consider not merely the legal category of the offence, but all the circumstances. It is clear that this advice holds good under the new law. There is, of course, a substantial body of case law which has built up over the years on whether and in what circumstances the commission of particular offences can properly be regarded as so serious that a custodial sentence has to be imposed. Some of this guidance has developed in respect of para. (c) of s. 1(4A) and, more generally, guideline judgments of the Court of Appeal address this issue (see further, *Blackstone's Criminal Practice 1993*, parts B and E).

The guideline decisions before the CJA 1991 tend to discuss the seriousness of a particular offence category in the context of a range of aggravating and mitigating factors which might apply, generating a series of 'starting-points' for different levels of seriousness of the offence. Thus, in *Billam* [1986] 1 WLR 349, the Court of Appeal explained that the offence of rape calls for a custodial sentence other than in wholly exceptional circumstances, and then proceeded to describe three broad categories of the offence with appropriate starting-points. A number of aggravating and mitigating considerations are then spelt out. In *Aramah* (1982) 4 Cr App R (S) 407, modified in certain respects by *Bilinski* (1987) 9 Cr App R (S) 360 and *Singh* (1988) 10 Cr App R (S) 402, the Court of Appeal , in dealing with sentencing for drug offences, indicated appropriate starting-points for importation, supply and possession of Class A, B and C

FIGURE 1.1

OUTLINE OF THE 1991 ACT SENTENCING SCHEME

CUSTODY
Imprisonment (21 and over)
Detention in a young offender institution (15–20)

Suspended sentence (21 and over)
Suspended sentence (21 and over)

CUSTODY THRESHOLD
offence seriousness (s. 1(2)(a))
or public protection following conviction for violent
or sexual offence (s. 1(2)(b))

COMMUNITY SENTENCES*
Pre-sentence report mandatory
Probation order (with additional requirements) (16 and over)
Community service order (16 and over)
Combination order (16 and over)
Supervision order (with additional requirements) (10–17)
Pre-sentence report not mandatory
Probation order (16 and over)
Curfew order (16 and over)
Attendance centre order (10–20)
Supervision order (10–17)

COMMUNITY SENTENCE THRESHOLD
offence seriousness (s. 6(1))

DISCHARGES	FINES
Conditional discharge (all age groups)	(all age groups)
Absolute discharge (all age groups)	

SERIOUSNESS OF OFFENCE

*Selection of particular community orders requires justification in terms of both 'suitability' and 'seriousness of offence' (s. 6(2)).

drugs. In *Barrick* (1985) 7 Cr App R (S) 142 Lord Lane CJ said that offenders who steal or obtain property by deception in the course of their employment should, notwithstanding their previous good characters, be given a custodial sentence unless the sum involved is small. The court then proceeded to indicate three starting-points, depending upon the amount of money involved, with variation in the light of aggravating and mitigating factors. It is likely that the CJA 1991, in making 'offence seriousness' the key factor in sentence selection, will in due course generate more detailed guidance of this kind from the Court of Appeal.

Following the implementation of the CJA 1991 there is now a batch of reported decisions of the Court of Appeal which, taken together, give some indication of the custodial threshold for particular offences. While these sentencing patterns certainly cannot yet be regarded as settled, and do not take account of the further changes to the law made by the CJA 1993, the early indications are that the Court of Appeal is placing the custodial sentence threshold, where the offence is to be regarded as 'so serious that only such a sentence can be justified', at a point somewhat lower than was applicable before the 1991 Act.

Consider first a group of cases concerning burglary. In *Kyle* (1993) 14 Cr App R (S) 613 the offender, aged 20, and another, broke into a house while the occupiers were away for the weekend. They were caught quickly and all property was recovered. Kyle had several previous convictions, including robbery. The Court of Appeal upheld a custodial sentence but reduced it from 12 months to 6 months, on the ground that the sentencer had paid too much regard to Kyle's previous convictions (this case was decided before the substitution of CJA s. 29, on the relevance of previous convictions, by CJA 1993: see 1.14). In *Lewis* (1993) 14 Cr App R (S) 744 the offender pleaded guilty to one count of burglary and eight counts of handling. Lewis and his co-accused were seen near a house where the occupier had died four days earlier. They had forced open the back door and stolen property worth between £5000 and £8000. Lewis's *modus operandi* was to burgle the homes of people whose deaths had been announced in the newspapers. Stolen property in excess of £5000, the produce from other burglaries committed in similar circumstances, was found at the offender's home. The sentencer imposed a sentence of 18 months for the burglary and two years consecutive for the handling. The Court of Appeal said that only custody could be justified and agreed that consecutive sentences were appropriate on the facts, but reduced the sentence for handling to 12 months, making a total of 30 months. See also *Husbands* (1993) 14 Cr App R (S) 709, where a custodial sentence of 12 months for three house burglaries was upheld. In his commentary on *Lewis* in the *Criminal Law Review* at [1993] Crim LR 469, Dr Thomas suggests that 'almost any burglary of a dwelling is likely to meet the criterion of seriousness in s. 1(2)(a)'. He draws a comparison with the earlier law under CJA 1982, s. 1(4A), Where the statutory custody threshold was applicable only to offenders under aged 21. He says that while 'the court was always dealing with a case with the built-in mitigation of youth and good record . . . under the CJA 1991 personal mitigation is taken into account after the criterion of seriousness has been considered . . . It follows that the threshold of seriousness required to satisfy s. 1(2)(a) of the 1991 Act will be rather lower.' In the subsequent case of

Bennett [1993] Crim LR 802, however, the offender, aged 20, at night broke into a house the occupier of which was known to the offender to be away on holiday. The offender was arrested at the scene and nothing was taken. The Court of Appeal said that the offence was 'unattractive', but *not* so serious that only a custodial sentence could be justified. The offender had several previous convictions for burglary, both residential and non-residential. The Court of Appeal stressed that the earlier offences were not relevant to the seriousness of the latest offence, and it is possible that a different view might be taken now that the original s. 29 (on the relevance of previous convictions) has been substituted by the CJA 1993. Cases decided after 1 October 1992, suggest that burglary of non-residential premises will often also be so serious that only custody can be justified. In *Dorries and Dorries* (1993) 14 Cr App R (S) 608 two offenders, aged 20 and 28, removed bricks from a wall to gain entry to a shop and stole £600 worth of property. A hammer, a crowbar and a radio scanner were found in the offenders' car. The elder offender received 21 months, and the younger received 10 months. The Court of Appeal said that defence counsel had been correct to concede that the burglary was too serious to justify anything other than custody, but reduced sentence on the younger offender to six months. A case which fell on the other side of the line, however, was *Tetteh* [1993] Crim LR 629. There the offender, aged 35, was seen coming out of the cellar at a YMCA club. The spirits store had been forced open and the drayman's entrance cover had been opened to give access to the street, but nothing had been stolen. The Court of Appeal considered that the offence of burglary was in this case *not* so serious that only a custodial sentence could be justified. The offender had many previous convictions and, of course, it is an open question whether the court would reach a different view now that the restrictions inherent in the original s. 29 have been removed. It may be noted that the current edition of the Magistrates' Association's *Sentencing Guidelines* (1993) indicate that where an offence of non-residential burglary is dealt with summarily, the entry point sentence is a community sentence.

The general comment about the lowering of the custody threshold seems to be borne out by recent decisions relating to other categories of offending, though the cases are too few for a consistent pattern to be discernible. It must be remembered that, following the ruling in *Cox* [1993] 1 WLR 188, even though the offence itself is so serious that only custody can be justified, the sentencer may avoid custody in the light of personal mitigation (see 1.9). As far as offences of violence are concerned, in *Corkhill* (1993) 14 Cr App R (S) 543, the offender pleaded guilty to unlawful wounding, after firing a high velocity rifle recklessly in the direction of a 14 year old boy and hitting him in the thigh. The pellet was later removed by surgery. A sentence of eight months' detention in a young offender institution was reduced to four months on appeal, having regard to personal mitigation. In *Morgan and Morgan* (1993) 14 Cr App R (S) 619 a sentence of 18 months for unlawful wounding was upheld where there was a premeditated attack on a man with a spanner and a truncheon, causing minor injuries. Custodial sentences were upheld in respect of assault occasioning actual bodily harm in *Audit* [1993] Crim LR 627 (offender, after consuming a large amount of alcohol, and unprovoked, punched a man in the face, and then punched him again as he lay on the ground, causing facial cuts (which required stitches) and bruising: offence so serious that only custody could be justified, though reduced from six months to three months on appeal), *Graham* [1993] Crim LR 628 (female offender punching female victim in the face after an argument in restaurant, causing fractured nose and black eye: offence so serious that only custody could be justified, though reduced from 6 months to 28 days on appeal) and in *Leather* (1993) 14 Cr App R (S) 736 (17-year-old woman seizing police officer by testicles to prevent the officer arresting her boyfriend: 8 months upheld). In *Barnes* (1993) 14 Cr App R (S) 547 a custodial sentence of 6 months was reduced to 28 days for an assault occasioning actual bodily harm where a man left in charge of the 10-month-old daughter of the woman with whom he was living slapped the child in the face causing bruises, and in *Actie* (1993) 14 Cr App R (S) 598 a custodial sentence for an attempt to assault occasioning actual bodily harm, where the offender had driven his car at police officer in an attempt to evade apprehension, was reduced on appeal from 18 months to 12 months.

Examples of the operation of the custody threshold in respect of property crimes are *Hill* (1993) 14 Cr App R (S) 556 (theft by 18-year-old warehouseman, committed over two to three months, totalling £1500: sentencer correct to conclude that offences so serious that only custody could be justified, but sentence varied to community service for 150 hours in the light of personal mitigation); *Flynn ynd Flynn* (1993) 14 Cr App R (S) 422 (custodial sentences of eight months and six months for theft of furniture worth £30 correct in principle, given that the offence involved intimidation of an elderly couple in their home, but sentences halved on appeal). In *Keogh* [1993] Crim LR 895 the offender pleaded guilty to obtaining goods worth £35 from a store by pretending that he had bought them earlier and was returning them. A sentence of one month's imprisonment was imposed for the deception, and was upheld on appeal. This case may be contrasted with *Crawford* (1993) 14 Cr App R (S) 782, where theft of £200 worth of goods from a supermarket was held *not* to be so serious that only custody could be justified. It is very hard to reconcile these last two cases; both were complicated by the fact that the offence placed the offender in breach of a suspended sentence. In *Allright* (1993) 14 Cr App R (S) 797, theft of a handbag from an office, together with theft of property worth £160 from a car which had already been broken into, was held *not* to be so serious that only custody could be justified.

When considering the gravity of a combination of two or more offences under CJA 1991, s. 1(2)(a), s. 31(2) provides that one offence is to be regarded as 'associated' with another offence if the offender is convicted of offences in the same proceedings, is sentenced for the offences at the same time, or if the offender is convicted of one offence and asks to have another offence or offences taken into consideration in sentencing for that offence. The implication is that a custodial sentence may be justified when looking at associated offences which could not be justified in respect of an offence standing alone. This provision tackles a problem in the pre CJA 1991 law. Section 31(2) may be compared with the restrictive interpretation given to para. (c) of CJA 1982, s. 1(4A), by Steyn J in *Roberts* (1987) 9 Cr App R (S) 152. In that case it was accepted that the criterion must be applied to each individual offence rather than to the totality of the offending conduct, so that where the offender pleaded guilty to three counts of burglary and asked for 12 similar offences to be taken into consideration, a custodial sentence could not be justified on this ground where no individual offence merited such a sentence. This law has since been changed twice. Under the original version of CJA 1991, s. 1(2)(a), the court was restricted to looking at only *two* associated offences when deciding whether custody was justified. This provision was a legislative compromise between the decision in *Roberts* and the position where the court could have regard to the totality of the offending. Following criticism from the judiciary, to the effect that looking at only *two* offences was an unnecessary fetter on the sentencer's discretion, this restriction was removed by CJA 1993, s. 66. Henceforth the court, when deciding on the custodial threshold, may have regard to the *full range* of the associated offences before the court. The risk inherent in this approach is that it may result in offenders receiving custody for repetition of rather minor offending.

In *Howard* (1990) 12 Cr App R (S) 426 it was held by the Court of Appeal that the wording of para. (c) of CJA 1982, s. 1(4A), did not permit the sentencer to have regard to offences taken into consideration when deciding whether to pass a custodial sentence. This was because taking an offence into consideration for the purposes of sentencing did not amount to a 'conviction' for that offence and hence fell outside the scope of para. (c). Under the CJA 1991 it is now clear that one or more of the associated offences being weighed for this purpose may be an offence (or offences) of which the accused has not been convicted but which is (or are) merely being taken into consideration.

While the 1993 Act has now removed the former restrictions, it must be remembered that an offence may still only be taken into account for these purposes where it is an 'associated offence'. It was held in *Crawford* (1993) 14 Cr App R (S) 782 that an offence in respect of which a suspended sentence is passed is *not* an associated offence of an offence committed during the operational period of that suspended sentence, but in *Godfrey* (1993) 14 Cr App R (S) 804 it was held that an offence in respect of which a conditional discharge is granted *is* an associated offence of an offence committed during the period of the conditional discharge, provided that the offender is sentenced for the earlier offence at the same time as being dealt with for the offence which placed him in breach of the discharge. In *Godfrey* itself, the sentencer had dealt with the earlier offence by imposing 'no separate penalty', so in those circumstances it could not be an associated offence of the new offence.

1.10 The 'Public Protection' Criterion

The second alternative ground justifying the imposition of a custodial sentence is provided by CJA 1991, s. 1(2)(b):

(b) where the offence is a violent or sexual offence, that only such a sentence would be adequate to protect the public from serious harm from him.

This provision is broadly comparable to CJA 1982, s. 1(4A)(b), which related only to young adult offenders. In relation to that provision it was held by the Court of Appeal in *Jacobs* (1989) 11 Cr App R (S) 171 that when relying on this ground the sentencer must consider that the public needs protecting from this particular offender, rather than from offenders of his type. The wording of CJA 1991, s. 1(2)(b), indicates that this still reflects the law. In other respects, para. (b) appears to be drafted quite broadly (though its scope has been cut down from earlier versions of the original Bill). Since paras (a) and (b) of s. 1(2) are alternative grounds for imposing custody there is, strictly, no requirement under (b) that the offence of which the offender stands convicted must, of itself, be sufficiently serious to merit a custodial sentence, though in practice that will often be the case. It seems that para. (b) must, in this way, be wider than para. (a). Otherwise, para. (a) would necessarily cover all cases which come within (b), and it would be superfluous to include para. (b) in the legislation. On the face of it, there would seem to be no requirement in (b) that the anticipated serious harm will be the commission of a further violent or sexual offence (rather than some other kind of offence). In fact, however, s. 31(3) clarifies this matter by explaining that when para. (b) is relied upon by the sentencer, the reference to public protection relates to the risk of the commission of 'further such offences' by the person being sentenced.

Section 1(2)(b) must be interpreted in the light of s. 31. There was concern, while the Bill was in passage through Parliament, that custody could be imposed by a court under (b) where only a minor assault or minor sexual offence had actually been committed. It is important to bear in mind that (b) can only be relied upon where a 'violent offence' or a 'sexual offence' has been committed and it is established that the case requires the protection of the public. Section 31(1) of the Act provides that 'violent offence' means an offence

> which leads, or is intended or likely to lead, to a person's death or to physical injury to a person, and includes an offence which is required to be charged as arson (whether or not it would otherwise fall within this definition).

This would appear to be a generous definition, covering cases which range from those where death or physical injury is actually caused, even where that was not intended or likely to occur, to cases where no harm at all was occasioned, but was risked by the offender. There is no requirement that the physical injury caused or risked need be 'serious'. So, it would include involuntary manslaughter, where death was caused but not intended, all the generally encountered non-fatal offences against the person and the more serious of the offences affecting public order. It would certainly be wide enough to include aggravated criminal damage under the Criminal Damage Act 1971, s. 1(2), and could also include a wide range of other offences, such as reckless (now dangerous) driving, under the Road Traffic Act 1991, some cases of contamination of goods under the Public Order Act 1986, s. 38, and some cases involving the supply of dangerous drugs. On the other hand, the commission of a robbery using an imitation firearm, and the carrying of an offensive weapon (Prevention of Crime Act 1953, s. 1), would probably fall outside the definition. Finally, the specific reference in the definition to 'an offence which is required to be charged as arson' is to the Criminal Damage Act 1971, s. 1(3), whereby any offence of criminal damage (simple or aggravated) committed by fire must be charged as an offence of arson.

The Court of Appeal in *Robinson* [1993] 1 WLR 168 confirmed that whether a particular offence falls within the definition of a 'violent offence' depends upon the individual facts of each case. On the particular facts of that case the court held that an attempted rape, as well as being a 'sexual offence' (see below) was *also* a violent offence within the meaning of s. 31(1).

Also, by s. 31(1) 'sexual offence' is compendiously defined as being an offence:

> under the Sexual Offences Act 1956, the Indecency with Children Act 1960, the Sexual Offences Act 1967, section 54 of the Criminal Law Act 1977 or the Protection of Children Act 1978, other than—
>
> (a)   an offence under section 12 or 13 of the Sexual Offences Act 1956 which would not be an offence but for section 2 of the Sexual Offences Act 1967;
>
> (b)   an offence under section 30, 31 or 33 to 36 of the said Act of 1956; and
>
> (c)   an offence under section 4 or 5 of the said Act of 1967.

The effect of this is to include all the serious sexual offences, including rape, incest, intercourse with under-age females, indecent assault, taking indecent photographs of children and the more serious cases of buggery. Offences excluded by paras (a) to (c) of the definition include the less serious cases of buggery, living on the earnings of prostitution and offences relating to brothel keeping. Burglary with intent to rape is not covered, nor is indecent exposure.

A difficulty brought about by merely listing the offence-creating sections to provide the definition of 'sexual offence', is that the definition does not thereby appear to include attempts, conspiracies or incitements to commit the relevant offences. The Court of Appeal in *Robinson* [1993] 1 WLR 168 considered whether the offence of attempted rape fell within the definition, and concluded that it did. Although attempted rape is charged as an offence under the Criminal Attempts Act 1981, rather than the Sexual Offences Act 1956, the latter statute provides for the prosecution and punishment of attempted rape as well as for other sexual offences, and so the Court of Appeal held that attempted rape could properly be regarded as an offence 'under' the SOA 1956. The key question, then, seems to be whether the relevant inchoate offence is listed in sch. 2 to the SOA 1956. For further comment on this point see Dr Thomas's discussion at [1993] Crim LR 145.

It should be emphasised that the essence of CJA 1991, s. 1(2)(b), is a judgment by the court, in the light of the offender's conviction of a violent or sexual offence, that the offender poses a risk of 'serious harm' to the public. Section 3(3)(b) allows the court to take into account 'any information' about the offender when making this prediction. It is possible that a court might be prepared to receive expert evidence on such an issue after conviction, but ultimately the assessment would have to be made by the sentencer. 'Serious harm' is defined for these purposes in CJA 1991, s. 31(3), as comprising 'death or serious personal injury, whether physical or psychological'. There is, however, no mention of the likelihood of risk which must be perceived by the court before reliance may be placed upon para. (b) of s. 1(2). It is clear that the court could not be justified in giving custody to an offender who was very likely to reoffend, but only in the commission of relatively minor offences (the 'social nuisance' offender). Less clear is whether custody could be justified under para. (b) where the court perceived a remote risk of serious harm. Little help can be derived from the pre-1991 Act law in resolving these problems, but the judgment of Mustill LJ in *Birch* (1989) 11 Cr App R (S) 202 is, by analogy, of some assistance.

Birch dealt with the Crown Court's power to add a restriction order to a hospital order under the Mental Health Act 1983, s. 37 and s. 41. Section 41 empowers the sentencer to impose a restriction order after having had regard 'to the nature of the offence, the antecedents of the offender and the risk of his committing further offences if set at large, that it is necessary for the protection of the public from serious harm so to do'. Mustill LJ said that the words 'from serious harm' in s. 41 meant that the court is required to assess, in that context, not the seriousness of the risk that the offender will reoffend, but the risk that if he does so the public will suffer serious harm. His Lordship said (at p. 213):

> The harm in question need not, in our view, be limited to personal injury. Nor need it relate to the public in general, for it would in our judgment suffice if a category of persons, or even a single person, were adjudged to be at risk: although the category of persons so protected would no doubt exclude the offender himself. Nevertheless the potential harm must be serious, and a high possibility of a recurrence of minor offences will no longer be sufficient.

It is suggested that the terms of this statement could equally apply to para. (b) of CJA 1991, s. 1(2).

1.11   Giving Reasons for Imposing Custody

Section 1(4) and (5) and s. 3 of CJA 1991 lay down certain procedural requirements which must be complied with before any custodial sentence may be imposed under s. 1(2) of the Act. Since a suspended sentence is a custodial sentence, all these procedural requirements must also be complied with before a suspended sentence is passed (see *Brewer* (1982) 4 Cr App R (S) 380).

Any court passing a custodial sentence is obliged by s. 1(4)(a) to explain in open court that either or both of paras (a) and (b) of s. 1(2) apply to the case and to explain why it has formed that view. This would not be appropriate and is therefore not required where custody is being imposed consequent upon the offender's failure to consent to a community penalty which the court was minded to impose. In all cases, however, the court is additionally obliged by s. 1(4)(b) to explain to the offender 'in open court and in ordinary language' why it is passing a custodial sentence. Section 1(5) requires that a magistrates' court must also record the reason relied upon in the warrant of commitment and in the court register. These provisions are parallel to those which existed in relation to the imposition of custodial sentences on young adult offenders under CJA 1982, s. 2(4), as amended by CJA 1988, s. 123. Despite the mandatory terms of the statutory language in the CJA 1991, s. 1(4) ('it shall be its duty . . .'), the Court of Appeal in *McQueen* (1989) 11 Cr App R (S) 305 decided in respect of identical wording under the earlier statutory regime that whilst the sentencer is 'obliged to identify the full basis for his decision by virtue of the amended s. 2(4) of the 1982 Act' the custodial sentence imposed in breach of those requirements was not invalid and could properly be upheld on appeal, though its duration was reduced for other reasons. Guidance on these provisions in the CJA 1991 has now been provided by the Court of Appeal in *Baverstock* [1993] 1 WLR 202. The court stated that s. 1(4) placed a statutory duty on the sentencer. In their Lordships' view a judge should state simply that, in his opinion, either or both paras (a) or (b) of (2) applied, using the words of the subsection. Having stated his opinion in that way the judge is then required to state why he has reached that opinion, and to explain his reasoning to the offender. In general their Lordships did not consider that this had to be a two-stage process. In most cases that should be unnecessary, and the judge should be able at one and the same time to explain in ordinary language the reasons for his conclusion and tell the offender why he was passing a custodial sentence. When complying with that second require-ment, however, the judge would be addressing the offender directly and if, in complying with s. 1(4)(a), he did not use ordinary language, it would be necessary for him to go on to do so in order to comply with s. 1(4)(b). The precise words used by a judge were *not* critical. The statutory provisions were not to be treated as a verbal tightrope for judges to walk. Given that the judge's approach accorded with the statutory provisions, the Court of Appeal would *not* be sympathetic to appeals based on fine linguistic analysis of the sentencing remarks.

As far as explaining the reasoning of the court to the offender under CJA 1991, s. 1(4)(b) is concerned, the statutory wording 'in open court and in ordinary language' implies that this explanation should be made to the offender personally. In *Wehner* [1977] 1 WLR 1143 it was held, in the context of a statutory requirement to explain the effect of a conditional discharge to an offender, that the task of explanation might be delegated to the offender's lawyer. The statutory language of CJA 1991, s. 1(4)(b), would seem to rule this out in the present context.

1.12 Pre-sentence Reports

Before giving the reasons for selecting a custodial sentence, CJA 1991, s. 3(1), requires that for the purpose of determining whether either of the grounds for the imposition of a custodial sentence under s. 1(2) is made out, the court shall 'obtain and consider a pre-sentence report'. Where, however, 'the offence or any other offence associated with it is triable only on indictment' a pre-sentence report need not be obtained or considered if the Crown Court considers that this would be 'unnecessary' (s. 3(2)). This avoids the need for the court to call for a report where, given the nature of the offence, custody is inevitable. The provision is broadly equivalent to the repealed CJA 1982, s. 2(3), applicable to young adults but, by making reference to the relevant offence being triable only on indictment it clearly ties the decision to dispense with a report to the issue of seriousness of offence. A reported case on the point prior to CJA 1991 is *Massheder* (1983) 5 Cr App R (S) 442, where a sentence of 18 months' detention under CYPA 1933, s. 53(2), was imposed on a 15-year-old for an offence of arson (lighting a fire in a lift shaft, causing damage to the value of £5,000). The sentencer proceeded without a social inquiry report. The reasons for doing so were (a) that no report had been prepared on the offender, because there was selective industrial action in the social services department of the local authority concerned, and (b) that, in the words of the sentencer, it was a very serious offence, 'quite beyond anything in the nature of probation'. The Court of Appeal ruled that on the facts of the case a report was necessary under CJA 1982, s. 2(3), and that the sentencer had implicitly made that clear by initially asking for a report and then commenting that 'in the absence of information about you the only thing for me to do is to make an order under s. 53'.

Section 3(4) of CJA 1991 provides that no sentence shall be invalidated by failure of the court to comply with s. 3(1), but on appeal against a custodial sentence passed without the court having obtained and considered a pre-sentence report, the appellate court must obtain and consider one. This provision replaces earlier comparable provisions in CJA 1982, s. 2(1), in respect of young adult offenders and PCCA 1973, s. 20A, in respect of the first prison sentence imposed on an adult.

No details of the preferred format of these reports is provided by the Act, s. 3(5) of which states merely that a pre-sentence report is a report in writing which:

> with a view to assisting the court in determining the most suitable method of dealing with an offender, is made or submitted by a probation officer or by a social worker of a local authority social services department.

The Secretary of State reserved the right, in s. 3(5)(b), to generate rules relating to the prescribed form and content of those reports. These rules have now been produced, in the form of national standards. These standards are reproduced at p. 293 of this *Guide*. The national standard on PSRs was issued following pilot trials run at five Crown Court centres (Birmingham, Bristol, Lincoln, Newcastle and Southwark) in the second half of 1991. For further information on the trials see *Pre-sentence Reports – Pilot Trials in the Crown Court*, joint circular issued on 11 May 1992 by the Home Office, Lord Chancellor's Department and CPS, and J. Bredar, *Justice Informed: The Pre-sentence Report Pilot Trials in the Crown Court* (Vera Institute of Justice, 1992).

The requirement that a PSR be in writing did not appear in the earlier legislation. In practice, social inquiry reports were almost always in that form, but it is now clear that whenever a PSR is required by law an oral 'stand down' report is unacceptable. It remains arguable (though perhaps contrary to the spirit of the legislation) that an oral report would suffice in cases where a PSR is thought by the court to be desirable but is not actually required by law (e.g. before a probation order without specified additional requirements is made by the court). The phrase 'made or submitted' allows continuation of the common pre 1991 Act practice whereby reports are presented by a liaison officer rather than personally by the report writer. In *Okinikan* [1993] 1 WLR 173, a case decided after the coming into force of the CJA 1991 but before the publication of the national standards, the Court of Appeal said that if the matter was disputed, it was for the 'trial judge to decide whether the report actually available to the court is adequate for sentencing purposes and constitutes proper compliance with the statute'.

A PSR *must* be considered before any custodial sentence is imposed (except in the case mentioned above, where the offence is triable only on indictment and the court considers that a PSR is unnecessary). A PSR *must* also be considered before any of what are perceived to be the more demanding community sentences is imposed: namely, community service order, combination order, probation order with specified additional requirements or supervision order with specified additional requirements. In many other cases, of course, notwith-standing the lack of a mandatory requirement to obtain a PSR, the obtaining of one would certainly be regarded as *good sentencing practice*. The national standard (ch. 2, para. 2) points out that a PSR 'may be of value in advising the court about suitability for community sentences for which a PSR is not required by law, and in seeking to ensure that supervision, if ordered, is able to start promptly and effectively'. On PSRs in the context of community sentences see further 2.5.

The national standard (ch. 2, para. 3) suggests that a PSR should address *the current offence(s)* (summarising the facts and assessing the seriousness of and the offender's attitude to the offence(s), *relevant information about the offender* setting the current offence in context, including his or her previous offending, and strengths and problems, and a *conclusion* and, where relevant, *a proposal for the most suitable community sentence*. This guidance ensures that the first task for the PSR writer is to address the seriousness of the offence. This approach is, of course, in line with the statutory framework of the CJA 1991. It represents a change of emphasis from the former position in relation to social inquiry reports, where information about the offence was often relegated to a subsidiary role in the report. Paragraphs 9 to 13 in ch. 2 of the national standard give very important and useful guidance on the evaluation of seriousness in individual cases. The national standards indicate that the probation officer should interview the offender, perhaps more than once, to obtain information about him or her:

Relevant information may include the offender's explanation for the offence, acceptance of responsibility and feelings of guilt or remorse, attitudes, motivation, criminal history, relationships (e.g. family, friends and associ-ates), strengths and skills, and personal problems, such as drug or alcohol misuse, or financial, housing, employment, medical or psychiatric problems. In the case of a violent or sexual offence, evidence of risk to the public of serious harm from the offender may also be relevant.

The report writer is thus required to make a provisional assessment of seriousness, in advance of the sentencer's determination of the matter. This provisional assessment is necessary to ensure that the PSR is 'properly focused and addresses only those outcomes that are broadly likely' (ch. 2, para. 10). It means that where a particular case seems likely to fall near the boundary between a custodial and a community sentence 'it will be appropriate for the report writer to recognise that more than one sentencing outcome may result, and to provide information relevant to both' (ch. 2, para. 10). For further discussion of PSRs and the framework of the CJA 1991 see N. Stone, 'Pre-sentence reports, culpability and the 1991 Act' [1992] Crim LR 558 and M. Wasik, 'Rethinking information and advice for sentencers' in C. Munro and M. Wasik (eds), *Sentencing, Judicial Discretion and Training* (London: Sweet and Maxwell, 1992), p. 173.

1.13   Other Information Required before Imposing Custody: Mitigation and Aggravation

CJA 1991, s. 3(3)(a), also provides that in addition to obtaining a pre-sentence report the court shall:

> take into account all such information about the circumstances of the offence or (as the case may be) of the offence and the offence or offences associated with it (including any aggravating or mitigating factors) as is available to it.

The meaning of s. 3(3)(a) has to be elucidated alongside s. 28(1), which states that nothing in the relevant part of the Act:

> shall prevent a court from mitigating an offender's sentence by taking into account any such matters as, in the opinion of the court, are relevant in mitigation of sentence.

These provisions would appear to be explicable in the following way. Since a key criterion in determining whether an offence merits custody or not is now to be the seriousness of that offence (CJA 1991, s. 1(2)(a)), regard must clearly be had to any aggravating or mitigating factors which impinge upon that offence seriousness (e.g., in relation to the extent of the harm caused to the victim or the degree of culpability of the offender). These factors form part of the weighting of seriousness which the sentencer must make in determining whether the offence is above the custody threshold or below it. Section 3(3)(a) clearly *requires* the court to have regard to all such matters. The sorts of consideration which, where relevant, a sentencer would be required to take into account under s. 3(3)(a) might well include, in mitigation of the sentence, the offender's diminished culpability for the offence, based upon provocation, temptation, acting on the spur of the moment rather than after careful planning, good motive, the offender's reduced or impaired mental capacity, his intoxication by drink or drugs, his genuine ignorance or error about the law, and circumstances of personal or social pressure akin to duress. Aggravating factors would include premeditation on the part of the offender, bad motive, abuse of position and abuse of trust, professionalism, selection of a particularly vulnerable victim such as an elderly person, a child or a public servant, and the use of excessive force, gratuitous violence or wanton destruction. For discussion of these and other factors relevant to offence seriousness see Martin Wasik, *Emmins on Sentencing*, 2nd ed. (London: Blackstone Press, 1993).

The phrase 'information about the circumstances of the offence' is not, however, so broad as to encompass other matters (unrelated to seriousness) which a court *might* take into account in deciding whether or not to impose a custodial sentence. Attention to these matters is permitted by reference to s. 28(1). Section 28(1) is couched in the broadest terms, and would appear to allow the sentencer to have regard, where appropriate, to all the wide range of matters of personal mitigation which traditionally have been urged upon the court and which the court *may, in its discretion*, wish to take into account. The decision in *Cox* [1993] 1 WLR 188 makes it clear that the sentencer may avoid custody in the light of personal mitigation even though the offence itself was so seriousness that only custody can be justified for it.

A number of mitigating factors are discussed here, in relation to the custody threshold question, and they are referred to again, in relation to length of custody, in para. 1.22 below. The court may have regard to exactly the same matters when determining the length of a custodial sentence, as it does when determining whether or not to impose it.

(1) Guilty Plea While there is considerable authority to the effect that a guilty plea will merit a proportionate reduction in the custodial sentence which an offender would have received if he had been found guilty after a trial (see 1.22 below), there is little authority on whether a guilty plea may make the difference between custody and a community penalty. One case on the point is *Hollyman* (1979) 1 Cr App R (S) 289, where two offenders were involved in stealing miniature bottles of gin from a plane which was being unloaded at Heathrow. One offender received three months' immediate imprisonment and the other two months' imprisonment suspended for two years. The Court of Appeal said that it was a sufficient justification for the different sentences that the latter pleaded guilty while the former contested the case. In *Tonks* [1980] Crim LR 59, on the other hand, the Court of Appeal said that such a course of action would leave the imprisoned offender with a legitimate sense of grievance.

(2) Age There are numerous Court of Appeal decisions to the effect that youthfulness or age can be an important mitigating factor though, again, these tend to be in the context of determining sentence length, rather than the avoidance of custody altogether. This factor was, however, an important strand in a line of cases (e.g., *Coleman* (1981) 3 Cr App R (S) 178 and *Seymour* (1983) 5 Cr App R (S) 85) in which the Court of Appeal commended the use of community service orders rather than custody in some cases of burglary committed by young offenders.

(3) Meritorious Conduct by the Offender In some cases this has been regarded as relevant personal mitigation, even where it was wholly unrelated to the offence. In *Reid* (1982) 4 Cr App R (S) 280, three months' custody for burglary and handling stolen goods was varied to a conditional discharge when it was discovered that the defendant, while on bail awaiting trial for these offences, had attempted to rescue three children trapped in a burning house.

(4) Serious and Unusually Adverse Impact of Custody While the Court of Appeal decisions are not consistent, on occasions the serious and unusually adverse impact upon the offender's family of the offender's receiving a custodial sentence has been taken into account on appeal. In *Franklyn* (1981) 3 Cr App R (S) 65 a 'perfectly proper' six-month sentence was varied to 21 days to allow the immediate release of a man who had been a single parent to four children since his wife's death six years earlier, and whose imprisonment had resulted in the children being taken into care. It is difficult to see this decision as a criticism of the sentencer; it seems rather to be a case where the appellate court effected a merciful early release from custody.

(5)   Serious Collateral Effects of Custody   Again, the decisions are inconsistent, but in *Rees* (1982) 4 Cr App R (S) 71 custodial sentences were varied to fines on offenders convicted of assaults, so as avoid their automatic discharge from the Army and to leave their possible retention in the service within the discretion of their commanding officer.

Leaving on one side the arguments on the merits of reducing sentence in these various cases, it is clear that none of the factors relied upon are related to the 'circumstances of the offence', and so they are not matters which the sentencer is required to consider under s. 3(3)(a), but it is within the court's discretion to bring them in under s. 28(1). It will be noticed that all the examples listed are mitigating rather than aggravating factors, and that s. 28(1) is limited to mitigating factors. It is in fact very hard to think of aggravating factors which are not linked to the seriousness of the offence. There is little discussion of aggravating factors in the sentencing texts, but a list is provided by Nigel Walker, *Sentencing Theory, Law and Practice* (Butterworths, London, 1985), pp. 44–47. That list comprises the existence of an offender's previous convictions, the prevalence of a particular type of offence, the youth or vulnerability of the victim, and the offender's professionalism, premeditation, abuse of trust or use of gratuitous violence against the victim. It had been thought that the relevance of previous convictions and of offence prevalence to sentence decision-making had been greatly curtailed by the CJA 1991, but the repeal and replacement of s. 29 of the CJA 1991 in the former case and the decision of the Court of Appeal in *Cunningham* [1993] 1 WLR 183 in the latter case means that this view must now be revised. Previous convictions and offence prevalence are considered in 1.14 and 1.18 below.

One other relevant aggravating factor is the commission of an offence while the offender is on *bail* in respect of other matters. A pre 1991 Act decision on the point in *Attorney-General's References (Nos. 3, 4 and 5* of 1992) (1993) 14 Cr App R (S) 191 was followed by the Court of Appeal in the post 1991 Act case of *Baverstock* [1993] 1 WLR 202, and has now received statutory reinforcement in the new CJA 1991, s. 29(2) (substituted by CJA 1993, s. 66), which provides that: 'In considering the seriousness of any offence committed while the offender was on bail, the court shall treat the fact that it was committed in these circumstances as an aggravating factor'. Note that the sentencer has no discretion in the matter: offending on bail *shall* be so regarded. Section 29(2) came into force on 16 August 1993.

Apart from the specific requirement under s. 3 to obtain a pre-sentence report in these cases, and the general question of mitigation and aggravation, s. 4 makes reference to the special problem of 'the offender [who] is or appears to be mentally disordered'. In such a case the court shall consider any information which relates to that condition (whether in a pre-sentence report, a medical report, or otherwise) and the likely effect of a custodial sentence on that mental condition and on any treatment which may be available for it. Such information may, no doubt, tempt the court to consider a medical disposal, such as a probation order with a condition of psychiatric treatment, or a hospital order. The Court of Appeal decision in *Hook* (1980) 2 Cr App R (S) 353, to the effect that a sentencer cannot recommend that an offender serve a custodial sentence at the psychiatric prison, Grendon Underwood, is, presumably, unaffected by this provision. The subsection, unlike the repealed CJA 1982, s. 2(1), makes no specific mention of the possibility of an offender's physical unfitness to undergo the rigours of a custodial regime though, where relevant, this could surely still be taken into account.

1.14 Previous Convictions

A key provision of the CJA 1991, which attracted considerable attention during the Bill's passage through Parliament, was s. 29, which relates to the relevance to sentence of an offender's previous convictions. It has long been accepted that the offender's record can often be of considerable importance in selecting the sentence, but there has been little appellate discussion of the point, and it has never been clear precisely what aspects of the offender's previous record should properly be regarded as relevant to sentence. The most settled point is that an offender who has a clean, or relatively clean, record is generally accorded a degree of mitigation in that respect. Section 28(1) of the CJA 1991, allows mitigation in such a case, in the complete discretion of the court. Credit might be given for a clean record, a relatively light record, a significant 'gap' in offending, and perhaps even a recent change in offending history from violent to non-violent offending. Section 28(1) was discussed in 1.13.

A more difficult issue is the extent to which a sentencer may sentence more severely an offender who does have a record of previous convictions. On one view (an approach which might be termed 'cumulative sentencing') each repetition of offending must attract a more severe sentence. This line would be consistent with a belief in the efficacy of deterrence. Each repetition should attract a more severe response until eventually the offender will (presumably) be deterred from offending or will be incapacitated for very lengthy terms of imprisonment. There are problems with that approach, however. One is that, as the government itself recognised in the White Paper, *Crime, Justice and Protecting the Public*, the efficacy of deterrent sentencing is very much open to doubt. A second problem is that, by cumulative sentencing, the persistent petty offender will end up serving custodial terms of a duration which should surely be reserved to mark out the most serious offences. A number of pre 1991 Act Court of Appeal decisions, such as *Galloway* (1979) 1 Cr App R (S) 311 and *Bailey* (1988) 10 Cr App R (S) 231, seemed to reject a simple model of cumulative sentencing, and held that it is wrong to impose a sentence longer than is justified by the seriousness of the offence, purely on the basis of previous record, that is to say that a poor record should not be regarded as an aggravating factor relevant to offence seriousness. One of the clearest statements of this principle can be found in *Queen* (1981) 3 Cr App R (S) 245. Queen had stolen a cheque which had arrived in a letter for another person who lived at the same address as Queen, signed the name of the payee on the back of the cheque, and then attempted to cash it. The offender, who had a long list of offences of dishonesty going back 25 years, was given a prison sentence of 18 months. In the Court of Appeal Kenneth Jones J said that it was clear that the offender had been sentenced 'not merely for the offences which he committed, but for his record'. Such an approach was 'wrong in principle':

Of course no prisoner is to be sentenced for the offences which he has committed in the past and for which he has already been punished. The proper way to look at the matter is to decide a sentence which is appropriate for the offence for which the prisoner is before the court. Then in deciding whether that sentence should be imposed or whether the court can extend properly some leniency to the prisoner, the court must have regard to those matters which tell in his favour, and equally to those matters which tell against him; in particular his record of previous convictions. Then matters have to be balanced up to decide whether the appropriate sentence to pass is one at the upper end of the bracket or somewhere lower down.

The sentence was varied so as to allow Queen, who at the time of the appeal had served a little over nine months of his sentence, immediate release from custody. The case can be seen as being in line with a different approach to previous convictions. This approach, often referred to as the 'theory of progressive loss of mitigation' holds that while a first offender often presents a good case for mitigation in light of his record, the accumulation of previous convictions results in the progressive loss of that mitigation so that by (say) the time of the fourth or fifth conviction, all mitigation for clean record is lost and the offender is sentenced purely in accordance with the seriousness of the offence. In contrast with cumulative sentencing, this approach entails that when all mitigation is lost an offender's sentence should *not* continue to increase with further repetitions to a level disproportionate to the seriousness of the current offence. Despite the Court of Appeal authorities cited, this principle has never been fully accepted by sentencers, many of whom undoubtedly do tend to regard a list of previous convictions as an aggravating factor, and sentence offenders to a significant extent 'on their records'. Walker's conclusion is that 'it would be more realistic to acknowledge that in practice a record with previous relevant convictions is an aggravating consideration' (Walker, *Sentencing Theory, Law and Practice* (1985), p. 44).

For a brief time the theory of progressive loss of mitigation seemed to have acquired statutory authority by virtue of s. 28 and s. 29(1) of the CJA 1991. Section 29(1) said that:

An offence shall not be regarded as more serious for the purposes of any provision of this part by reason of any previous convictions of the offender or any failure of his to respond to any previous sentences.

This provision had relevance whenever a court was deciding whether custody was justified under s. 1(2)(a), or was determining the length of that custody under s. 2(2)(a), or was deciding whether a community sentence was justified under s. 6(1), or was deciding which community sentence to impose under s. 6(2). It had no application when the court was considering whether to impose custody for a violent offence or a sexual offence under s. 1(2)(b) or the length of such a sentence under s. 2(2)(b), since in that context the guiding consideration is the protection of the public rather than the seriousness of the offence. Section 29(1) proved to be highly controversial, even though it did not seem to be inconsistent with the earlier law, as set out by the Court of Appeal. Because of the barrage of criticism directed at it, s. 29 has now been repealed and replaced by the CJA 1993, but in understanding the likely effect of the new s. 29 it is necessary to review briefly the problems which were encountered with the original version.

In *Bexley* [1993] 1 WLR 192 the Court of Appeal took the opportunity soon after the CJA 1991 came into force to comment upon the original s. 29. Lord Taylor CJ confirmed that s. 29(1) prohibited the sentencer from regarding an offence as more serious simply because the offender had previous convictions. He said that the prohibition applied whether the previous convictions were for different classes of offence or even for the same class of offence as that before the sentencing court. His Lordship explained that:

> The approach, commonly adopted before the Act, of regarding the instant offence as more serious and deserving of custody because it repeated previous offending which had been treated more leniently is now forbidden. . . . It follows that familiar sentencing remarks before the Act such as 'You have a long history of committing offences of this kind', or 'You have been given every chance, fines, probation, community service, and here you are again', will no longer be appropriate. They would be statutorily irrelevant as indicators of seriousness in the instant offence.

Despite this faithful representation of the effect of s. 29(1), it is clear that extrajudicially the Lord Chief Justice regarded the provision as founded on a 'misconceived notion' which unduly fettered the sentencer's discretion and forced judges into an ill-fitting strait-jacket' (*The Times*, 24 March 1993). His Lordship made these remarks in a speech to the Law Society of Scotland, and further commented that:

> However forward thinking the penologists, criminologists and bureaucrats in government departments may be, their views should not be allowed to prevail so as to impose a sentencing regime which is incomprehensible or unacceptable to right-thinking people. If that happens there could be a real risk of aggrieved parties taking the law into their own hands.

His Lordship apparently made no reference in his speech to the earlier decisions of the Court of Appeal cited above.

During the passage through Parliament of the Bill which became the Criminal Justice Act 1991 there had been much discussion about the circumstances in which an exception to s. 29(1), specifically provided for in s. 29(2), would operate, and the precise relation between the two subsections of s. 29. Section 29(2) provided that:

> Where any aggravating factors of an offence are disclosed by the circumstances of other offences committed by the offender, nothing in this part shall prevent the court from taking those factors into account for the purpose of forming an opinion as to the seriousness of the offence.

Since the whole of s. 29 has now been replaced by the CJA 1993 this debate can, thankfully, be kept to a minimum. In *Bexley*, Lord Taylor rejected the view that

s. 29(2) was in conflict with s. 29(1), explaining that while s. 29(1) referred to 'previous convictions', s. 29(2) referred to 'the circumstances of other offences', the effect being that a sentencer could not regard the mere existence of previous convictions as relevant to the seriousness of the instant offence, but he could take into account on that issue the circumstances of the previous offences or of other offences presently before the court. Such circumstances were only relevant when they disclosed some aggravating factor in the offences now being sentenced. An example would be where the court dealing with an offender convicted of assault committed on a black person could properly have regard to that offender's previous convictions (or offences being dealt with at the same time) for spraying racist graffiti on walls. The criminal damage offences would reveal an aggravating factor of the assault (that the offence was racially motivated). For other examples see the facts of *Lewis* [1993] Crim LR 469 and *Attorney-General's Reference (No. 37 of 1992)* [1993] Crim LR 632 (and the commentaries on both cases in the *Criminal Law Review* by Dr Thomas).

On 13 May 1993 the Home Secretary announced to Parliament that the provision in the CJA 1991 relating to previous convictions was to be repealed as soon as possible. He said that, '. . . we propose to restore to the courts their power to have full regard to the criminal record of an offender and his response to previous sentences' (Parliamentary Debates (Hansard), Commons, 6th ser., vol. 224, col. 939, 13 May 1993). This has now been done by way of s. 66(6) of the CJA 1993, which substitutes in the CJA 1991 a new s. 29 which begins:

(1)   In considering the seriousness of any offence, the court may take into account any previous convictions of the offender or any failure of his to respond to previous sentences.

The new s. 29(2) (which deals with the specific point of offending on bail) was discussed at 1.13 and is not considered further here. Subsections (3) and (4) of s. 29 have the effect of ensuring that when the court is assessing an offender's previous convictions or response to previous sentences it is not required to ignore previous probation orders or conditional discharges which have been imposed upon the offender. Subsections (3) and (4) are necessary since convictions followed by probation orders and conditional orders did not, before the coming into force of the CJA 1991 (and in the latter case, still do not), count fully as 'convictions' for a range of purposes: see 2.10.

On the face of it, the new s. 29(1) is very broadly drafted. Taken together with s. 28 it could be seen as giving the sentencer virtually complete discretion to take into account the offender's previous record whenever, and to whatever extent, the sentencer thinks appropriate. Thus Dr Thomas comments that the old s. 29(1) has now been 'replaced by a section with precisely the opposite effect' (*Sentencing News*, 27 July 1993). If this really is the width of the discretion, the likely impact on sentencing practice is far from clear. A provision which gives sentencers unfettered discretion on *when* to take account of previous convictions, what *aspects* of the offender's record may be regarded as relevant, and to what *extent* they should be taken to enhance the penalty to be imposed, provides a recipe for sentencing disparity. If s. 29(1) was so broadly construed it would fly in the face of the stated objectives of the CJA 1991 (as evidenced in the White

Paper, *Crime, Justice and Protecting the Public*), of creating 'a coherent framework for the use of financial, community and custodial punishments' (para. 1.15) based primarily on desert principles. There is evidence from the Parliamentary debates on the CJA 1993 of the opposition parties' concern that, in the government's haste to abandon the original s. 29(1), no principles at all would henceforth apply in this area. A private member's Bill (the Criminal Justice (Amendment) (No. 2) Bill) was tabled with the intention of substituting s. 29(1) but inserting a proviso that where the court passed a more severe sentence by reason of an offender's previous convictions that sentence should not be disproportionate to the seriousness of the offence. The Bill failed. At a late stage in the passage of the Bill which became the CJA 1993 an opposition amendment was tabled in identical terms. In moving the amendment Mr Michael said (Parliamentary Debates (Hansard), Commons, 6th ser., cols 906–7, 29 June 1993) that:

> The danger is that, if we do not write into the law a limiting principle of proportionality, we could return, not to the position before the 1991 Act, which is what the minister intends, but to a more punitive sentencing framework, under which some offenders could be given sentences out of all proportion to what they deserve as a result of their offence. . . .
>
> It could mean that a repeat burglar could eventually be sentenced more severely than a rapist. Surely that would not be right. It would offend against common sense. An offence does not become more serious than another simply because it has been repeated.

The amendment was, however, withdrawn after discussion.

How should the new s. 29(1) of the CJA 1991 be applied by the courts? Early guidance is certainly required from the Court of Appeal on the crucial issue of the relationship between mitigation for good record under s. 28 and aggravation under the new s. 29(1). The Lord Chief Justice responded quickly to concerns over the original s. 29(1) by issuing the advice in *Bexley* [1993] 1 WLR 192, and something similar is required for the new s. 29. In the meantime, we can only speculate on its likely effect. It may be that s. 29(1) will only come into play once the discretion to mitigate under s. 28 has been exhausted (by, say, the fourth or fifth conviction). Until that point arrives, s. 29(1) provides nothing for the sentencer which is not available simply by choosing to withhold the discretion to mitigate under s. 28. But once the 'ceiling' for the offence is reached (and all hope of mitigation under s. 28 is lost), s. 29 will allow the sentencer to exceed that ceiling in the light of further repetitions. It is submitted that the extent to which cumulative sentencing is permitted should be curtailed by the explicit reference in s. 29(1) to the 'seriousness of the offence', and by the general spirit of the 1991 Act which requires sentencers (violent and sexual cases apart) to justify any increase in the severity of sentence by focusing on the seriousness of the offending conduct itself (rather than on the offender's record). It is suggested, therefore, that the best way to make sense of the new s. 29(1) would be for the Court of Appeal quickly to reassert the importance of the theory of progressive loss of mitigation. A clear reassertion of this approach appears to be necessary, since the common law sentencing principles, as manifested in cases such as

Queen (1981) 3 Cr App R (S) 245, were superseded by the original s. 29(1) which has, in its turn, now been replaced.

The new s. 29 came into force on 16 August 1993.

CRITERIA FOR SENTENCE LENGTH

1.15 Fixing the Length of Custodial Sentences

Section 2 of the CJA 1991 lays down, for the first time in a UK statute, certain specific criteria for the proper determination of the length of custodial sentences imposed by the Crown Court or by magistrates' courts, whether passed on adults or young offenders. Originally these provisions did not extend to offences which were triable only on indictment, but they were so extended during the Bill's passage through Parliament. Section 2(1) excludes from the ambit of the section cases where the sentence for the offence is fixed by law (in practice, the offence of murder: see further 1.8 above). For all other offences, s. 2(2) of the 1991 Act, as amended by the CJA 1993, s. 66, sets out the following criteria:

> The custodial sentence shall be—
>
>   (a) for such term (not exceeding the permitted maximum) as in the opinion of the court is commensurate with the seriousness of the offence, or the combination of the offence and one or more offences associated with it; or
>
>   (b)   where the offence is a violent or sexual offence, for such longer term (not exceeding that maximum) as in the opinion of the court is necessary to protect the public from serious harm from the offender.

It is worth recalling that the permitted maximum duration of a sentence of detention in a young offender institution for a 15, 16 or 17-year-old is 12 months (see 1.3(c) above). The implications of s. 2(2) are explored in 1.16 to 1.20 below. Its structure is very similar to s. 1(2), which was considered in 1.9 to 1.12 above. Section 2(2)(a) is dealt with first.

1.16 Justifying Sentence Length under s. 2(2)(a)

The purpose of s. 2(2)(a) is to give priority to the principle that the length of a custodial sentence should be commensurate with the seriousness of the offence. This is in line with the resurgence of the concept of 'desert' in sentencing policy generally, and with the stated aims of the 1990 White Paper in which, at para. 2.2, the government explained that:

> Punishment in proportion to the seriousness of the crime has long been accepted as one of the many objectives in sentencing. It should be the principal focus for sentencing decisions.

The best known judicial statement of the traditional diversity of English sentencing aims is contained in the case of *Sargeant* (1974) 60 Cr App R 74, where Lawton LJ identified retribution, deterrence, prevention and rehabilitation as the 'classical principles of sentencing'. These aims are closely related to the perceived aims of imprisonment, as explained by Lord Lane CJ in cases such as *Hitchcock* (1982) 4 Cr App R (S) 160. In recent years, however, it has become more generally accepted that the weakness of such 'eclectic' sentencing, where sentencers are free to pick and choose among sentencing aims in accordance with the detailed facts of individual cases, and in accordance with their own personal preferences, is that it leads to unacceptable inconsistency and sentencing disparity. According to the 1990 White Paper, para. 2.9:

> The government's proposals therefore emphasise the objectives which sentencing is most likely to meet successfully in whole or in part. The first objectives for all sentences is denunciation of and retribution for the crime. Depending on the offence and the offender, the sentence may also aim to achieve public protection, reparation and reform of the offender, preferably in the community. This approach points to sentencing policies which are more firmly based on the seriousness of the offence, and just deserts for the offender.

While the thrust underlying CJA 1991, s. 2(2)(a), read in this light, is thus reasonably clear, the courts are likely to experience difficulty in applying its provisions against the complex background of pre 1991 Act sentencing practice. Guidance on the meaning of s. 2(2)(a) was given by the Court of Appeal in *Cunningham* [1993] 1 WLR 183. Lord Taylor CJ, in the context of sentencing a case of robbery of a small shop at knife-point said that:

> The purposes of a custodial sentence must primarily be to punish and to deter. Accordingly, the phrase 'commensurate with the seriousness of the offence' must mean commensurate with the punishment and deterrence which the seriousness of the offence requires. . . .
>
> What section 2(2)(a) does prohibit is adding any extra length to the sentence which by those criteria is commensurate with the seriousness of the offence, simply to make a special example of the defendant.

Section 2(2)(a) is strongly worded, declaring that the custodial sentence 'shall be' commensurate with the seriousness of the offence, rather than requiring that proportionality should provide the starting-point for the sentencer or provide a restraint or limit on the pursuit of other sentencing aims. This suggests, at first sight, that the custodial sentence must be neither longer nor shorter than is justified by the seriousness of the offence. This wording may be contrasted with s. 1(2)(a) which seems to be best understood as a threshold requirement (see 1.9 above).

The emphasis upon measuring sentence length by reference to offence seriousness clearly means that the court must take into account all aggravating and mitigating factors which impinge upon the seriousness of the offence. This is confirmed by CJA 1991, s. 3(3)(a), which requires the court to 'take into account all such information about the circumstances of the offence or (as the case may be) of the offence and the offence or offences associated with it (including any aggravating or mitigating factors) as is available to it'. While this provision provides no room for sentencers to take account of other matters which are *not* related to seriousness, including the offender's guilty plea, consideration of these matters is permitted by s. 28(1), which provides that: 'Nothing in this part shall prevent a court from mitigating an offender's sentence by taking into account any such matters as, in the opinion of the court, are relevant in mitigation of sentence'. It will be noticed that while *both* aggravating and mitigating factors *shall* be taken into account when determining the seriousness of the offence under s. 2(2)(a), mitigation (but *not* aggravation) which is unrelated to seriousness *may* be taken into account by the sentencer under s. 28(1).

It seems likely that custody length will be justified by the courts far more frequently under s. 2(2)(a) than under s. 2(2)(b) (see 1.19 below). Further, given the emphasis in s. 2(2)(a) upon proportionality, it is difficult to see how the imposition of a discretionary life sentence could ever be justified under s. 2(2)(a).

For examples of various custodial sentences upheld by the Court of Appeal after the implementation of CJA 1991 see **1.9**. In several of these cases the Court of Appeal has agreed with the sentencer's assessment that the offence was so serious that only custody could be justified under s. 1(2)(a), but has then adjusted the sentence length. These decisions are, however, unreliable in giving guidance on appropriate sentence length under s. 2(2)(a). It is often unclear whether the Court of Appeal is holding out the adjusted term as being the one which would have been appropriate in the first place. Sometimes the Court of Appeal's selection of the adjusted term takes account of the period already spent in custody by the offender, and is designed to have the effect of achieving the offender's immediate release from custody.

1.17   Combination with Other Offences

CJA 1991, s. 2(2)(a), states that the court may have regard to 'the combination of the offence and one or more offences associated with' the offence of conviction when determining the length of a custodial sentence. Section 31(2) (discussed in 1.9 above) applies to this provision, so that an offence is to be regarded as 'associated with' another where the offender is convicted of the offences in the same proceedings, is sentenced for the two offences on the same occasion, or where one offence is taken into consideration at the time of sentencing for the other.

Where several offences are involved, the danger of this approach is that it could lead to a total sentence which is disproportionate to the overall seriousness of the behaviour. Section 28(2)(b) of the Act, in an attempt to avoid this, apparently makes reference to the common law 'totality principle' developed by the Court of Appeal, by declaring that nothing in this part:

> shall prevent a court . . . in a case of an offender who is convicted of one or more other offences, from mitigating his sentence by applying any rule of law as to the totality of sentences.

An example of the application of the totality principle is *Holderness* (1974) CSP A5–3B01, where the offender had been convicted of a series of offences of driving while uninsured, driving with excess blood alcohol and possession of an offensive weapon. He was also in breach of a suspended sentence of 15 months. A total of 33 months' imprisonment was imposed, with the suspended sentence also activated consecutively. Lawton LJ said that while the sentences for each of the offences looked at in isolation could not be questioned, the sentencer had also to stand back and look at 'the overall effect of the sentences which had been passed'. The sentences were reduced to a total of 27 months, including the activated suspended sentence. There are several possible difficulties with s. 28(2)(b). First, it would have been much better if the principle had been spelt out in the legislation, rather than being incorporated by reference. Second, it may be questioned whether the totality principle is a 'rule of law' rather than a sentencing principle. Third, the subsection does not *require* the sentencer to have regard to that principle; it merely *permits* the sentencer to do so. No indication is given of the circumstances, if any, where that principle might be overridden.

1.18   Exemplary Sentencing, Offence Prevalence and Local Conditions

A custodial sentence which is more severe than is commensurate with the seriousness of the offence is only authorised under CJA 1991, s. 2(2)(b), for violent or sexual offences in order to protect the public from serious harm (see 1.19), and cannot be justified by the court on grounds of individual or general deterrence. The 1990 White Paper (para. 2.8) clearly intended this effect:

It is unrealistic to construct sentencing arrangements on the assumption that most offenders will weigh up the possibilities in advance and base their conduct on rational calculation. Often they do not.

It is clear that deterrence may be pursued as a sentencing aim under the Act, as interpreted and applied in *Cunningham* [1993] 1 WLR 183 (see 1.16), only so far as a deterrent effect may be achieved by passing a custodial sentence which is commensurate with the seriousness of the offence. There will always be some flexibility in the tariff, but exemplary sentences are now impermissible. While deterrent reasoning has often been invoked by the Court of Appeal in the past, in recent years the Court of Appeal has become more cautious in upholding disproportionate sentences on these grounds. In *Masagh* (1990) 12 Cr App R (S) 568, for example, the Court of Appeal disapproved an 18-month custodial sentence imposed upon an offender who had been active as a pickpocket in Oxford Street. In substituting a sentence of four months, Lloyd LJ commented that it was very difficult to determine the prevalence of an offence in a particular area and that nobody knew how effective deterrent sentences actually were.

On one view, offence prevalence is irrelevant to offence seriousness and should be disregarded when selecting sentence under the CJA 1991. To take the example of theft from shops, it would seem that if an individual example of shoplifting is not in itself sufficiently serious to justify a severe sentence, this assessment cannot be affected by the acknowledged prevalence of shoplifting. The offender is being sentenced for *his* offence, not for the prevalence of that form of offending generally. When in the past sentencers have had regard to perceived offence prevalence, this has generally been for deterrent reasons: to 'stamp out' this form of offending. Sentencers have chosen to make an example of a particular offender because the offence committed by him is regarded as a symptom of a local or national offending problem. The result has been that some offenders have been given sentences disproportionate to the seriousness of their offences in an attempt to achieve a general deterrent effect. We have seen that exemplary offending of this kind is impermissible under the CJA 1991. But does this mean that having regard to offence prevalence in sentencing is also impermissible? Lord Taylor CJ considered this question in *Cunningham* [1993] 1 WLR 183, where robbery from small shops was in issue. He said:

> Prevalence of this kind of offence was also mentioned by the judge. Is that a legitimate factor in determining the length of the custodial sentence to be passed? Again, our answer is 'Yes'. The seriousness of an offence is clearly affected by how many people it harms and to what extent. For example, a violent sexual attack on a woman in a public place gravely harms her. But if such attacks are prevalent in a neighbourhood, each offence affects not only the immediate victim but women generally in that area, putting them in fear and limiting their freedom of movement. Accordingly, in such circumstances, the sentence commensurate with the seriousness of the offence may need to be higher there than elsewhere. Again, and for similar reasons, a bomb hoax may at one time not have been so serious as it is when a campaign of actual bombings mixed with hoaxes is in progress.

Lord Taylor therefore approved the judge's reference to the need to bear in mind the prevalence generally of offences of robbery of small shops. This passage seems to raise more problems than it solves, and it cannot be regarded as the last word on what is a very difficult issue of sentencing principle. The passage has to be squared with his Lordship's acceptance, earlier in the speech, that s. 2(2)(a) 'does prohibit . . . adding any extra length to the sentence . . . simply to make a special example of the defendant'. Is not the grave seriousness of a sexual assault on a woman properly to be understood in terms of the harm caused to that victim and the culpability of that offender? Is anything added by noting that such crimes have become more (or less) frequent in recent years, or are perceived by the general public (or the judges) to have become so? Lord Taylor's point that when assessing the seriousness of an offence regard should be had to a climate of fear thereby generated among people who feel themselves, rightly or wrongly, to be at risk of becoming victims, is an interesting one. But when the individual offender falls to be sentenced, should not the severity of his sentence be determined by the seriousness of what *he* has done, rather than reflecting a general climate of fear to which he has made some unspecified contribution?

1.19   Justifying Sentence Length under s. 2(2)(b)

CJA 1991, s. 2(2)(b) deals with the extent to which the Crown Court or a magistrates' court is permitted to depart from the general principle of commen-surability set out in s. 2(2)(a). The court may impose a longer sentence, but not one which exceeds the statutory maximum for the offence (a possibility available to the Crown Court under pre-CJA 1991 extended sentence provisions), in the case of a custodial sentence passed for a violent or sexual offence, where it is the opinion of the court that the sentence is necessary to protect the public from serious harm from the offender. Definitions of 'violent offence' and 'sexual offence' are provided in CJA 1991, s. 31(1), and a definition of 'serious harm' is provided in CJA 1991, s. 31(3). These were discussed in 1.10 above. It would seem inappropriate for magistrates' courts to make anything other than exceptional use of this provision, since the normal maximum custodial term which magistrates can impose is six months. In a case where it is necessary to protect the public from serious harm the matter should either have been committed to the Crown Court for trial or be committed to Crown Court for sentence (see, on the latter, the important changes made by CJA 1991, s. 25 to MCA 1980,s. 38, discussed in 4.1 below).

In *Utip* (1993) 14 Cr App R (S) 746 the Court of Appeal held that s. 2(2)(b) was applicable in the case of an offender convicted of wounding with intent. He had attacked a stranger with a knife, causing serious facial lacerations. He had several previous convictions for offences of violence and possession of weapons but had served no custodial sentence longer than six months. The Court of Appeal upheld a sentence of six years' imprisonment. The commentary on this case in the *Criminal Law Review*, by Dr Thomas, raises several important issues on the appropriate use of the power under s. 2(2)(b). He suggests that the 'most sensible approach' would be:

> to confine it to cases where there is the clearest possible basis for inferring that the offender is dangerous, and in such cases allowing a sentence which is substantially longer than would be proportionate to the seriousness of the offence, on the analogy of life imprisonment. It would be regrettable if the power were to be used rather casually, on the basis of slender evidence for inferring dangerousness, to justify sentences which are only marginally more severe than could be justified as commensurate sentences under section 2(2)(a).

In *Bowler* [1993] Crim LR 799 the offender, who was described as a man of limited intelligence, possibly suffering from brain damage, and having little insight into his own behaviour, pleaded guilty to an indecent assault on a girl aged six. The offender had been helping out at a Sunday School class, and he put his hand up the girl's skirt and touched her private parts through her knickers. The offender had eight previous convictions for indecent assaults on adult women, usually involving touching or grabbing at their private parts. In the past he had undergone treatment to suppress his libido, but was now unwilling to undergo any further treatment. A sentence of six years' imprisonment was passed under CJA 1991, s. 2(2)(b), as a sentence intended to protect the public from serious harm. The Court of Appeal upheld the sentence, and said that it was not necessary for the operation of s. 2(2)(b) that serious harm had actually been caused in the past for a judge to form the opinion that there was a danger that serious harm might occur in the future. There was overwhelming evidence in the case that the offender was likely to continue to commit such offences and there was a danger that members of the public might suffer serious psychological injury as a result. An indecent assault might well lead to such injury in a young girl, and there were some adult women who might be seriously disturbed by it. The purpose of the section included the protection of those women, perhaps less robust than average, who might be vulnerable to the kind of conduct that the offender was likely to perpetrate. The Court further stated that in a case where the sentencer relied upon s. 2(2)(b) mitigating factors, such as the offender's guilty plea, were of less significance than they were when sentence length was determined under s. 2(2)(a).

Before imposing a longer than normal sentence under s. 2(2)(b), the sentencer should always warn counsel that this is a possibility, so that counsel may deal with that issue when addressing the court on sentence: *Baverstock* [1993] 1 WLR 202.

1.20 Giving Reasons for Sentence Length

Where the offence is one of a violent or sexual nature, procedural arrangements in CJA 1991, s. 2(3), require that the court must explain in open court that it is of the opinion that s. 2(2)(b) applies and why it is of that opinion, and it must explain to the offender in open court and in ordinary language why the sentence is for such a term (for comment upon the broadly parallel procedural arrangements in CJA 1991, s. 1(4) in respect of justifying the imposition of a custodial sentence, see 1.11 above). It should be noted, however, that while a magistrates' court is required to specify in the warrant of commitment and to enter in the register its reason for passing a custodial sentence (CJA 1991, s. 1(5)), it is not required so to specify in that manner its reasons for determining the length of the custodial sentence.

The effect of s. 2(4), taken together with s. 2(1), is to require the Crown Court to comply with the procedural requirements in s. 2(3) whenever it passes a discretionary life sentence. It must also justify the passing of that sentence, rather than a determinate custodial sentence, in accordance with s. 2(2)(a) or s. 2(2)(b). It is hard to envisage a case where the passing of a discretionary life sentence could be justified under s. 2(2)(a). See further 1.25 below.

1.21 Pre-sentence Reports

CJA 1991, s. 3(1), requires that before forming any opinion on the length of a custodial sentence under s. 2(2)(a) or s. 2(2)(b) the court shall 'obtain and consider a pre-sentence report'. Where 'the offence or any other offence associated with it is triable only on indictment', a pre-sentence report need not be obtained or considered if the Crown Court considers that this would be 'unnecessary' (s. 3(2)) (see further 1.12 above).

1.22 Other Information Required on Length of Custody: Mitigation and Aggravation

CJA 1991, s. 3(3)(a), provides that in addition to obtaining a pre-sentence report the court, when determining the length of a custodial sentence, shall:

take into account all such information about the circumstances of the offence or (as the case may be) of the offence and the offence or offences associated with it (including any aggravating or mitigating factors) as is available to it.

The meaning of s. 3(3)(a) has to be elucidated alongside s. 28(1) which states that nothing in the relevant part of the Act:

> shall prevent a court from mitigating an offender's sentence by taking into account any such matters as, in the opinion of the court, are relevant in mitigation of sentence.

These provisions would appear to be explicable in the following way. Since a key criterion in determining custodial sentence length is now to be the seriousness of the offence (CJA 1991, s. 2(2)(a)), regard must clearly be had to any aggravating or mitigating factors which impinge upon that seriousness (e.g., in relation to the extent of the harm caused to the victim or the degree of culpability of the offender). Section 3(3)(a) clearly *requires* this to be done. The sorts of consideration which, where relevant, a sentencer would be required to take into account under s. 2(2)(a) might well include, in mitigation of the sentence, the offender's diminished culpability for the offence, such as provocation, temptation, acting on the spur of the moment rather than after careful planning, good motive, the offender's reduced or impaired mental capacity, his intoxication by drink or drugs, his genuine ignorance or error about the law and circumstances of personal or social pressure akin to duress. Aggravating factors would include premeditation on the part of the offender, bad motive, abuse of position and abuse of trust, professionalism, selection of a particularly vulnerable victim such as an elderly person, a child or a public servant, and the use of excessive force, gratuitous violence or wanton destruction.

The phrase 'information about the circumstances of the offence' (in s. 3(3)(a)) is, however, not so broad as to encompass other matters (unrelated to seriousness) which a court might, *in its discretion*, take into account as mitigation. These would be catered for by reliance upon s. 28(1). Examples of mitigating factors which do not impinge upon offence seriousness are listed below.

(1)   Guilty Plea   Traditionally, the sentencing 'discount' applicable for a guilty plea has been an important factor in determining sentence length. The authorities suggest that it typically results in a sentence reduction in Crown Court of between one-quarter and one-third in the length of a custodial sentence. The discount appears to be of much less importance in magistrates' courts, however, probably because the percentage of defendants pleading guilty is very high and sentencing levels are appreciably lower. The guilty plea discount is effected for reasons of cost saving and administrative expedience, and has nothing to do with the seriousness of the offence. The only way in which the guilty plea discount may be preserved under the CJA 1991 is by placing reliance upon s. 28(1).

Current sentencing practice is to have regard to the strength of the case against the offender, so that where the offender has been caught red-handed any discount may be reduced or lost (*Morris* (1988) 10 Cr App R (S) 216). Occasionally the discount may be refused or reduced for other reasons, such as where the protection of the public requires it (*McLaughlin* (1979) 1 Cr App R (S) 298) or where the offender has delayed his plea in an attempt to secure a tactical advantage (*Hollington* (1985) 82 Cr App R 281).

(2)   Age   There are numerous Court of Appeal decisions to the effect that youthfulness or age is one of the most important of all mitigating factors. This is particularly so for offenders aged under 21, but there are cases where offenders in their thirties have benefited, especially where other mitigation has been present. Advanced age, again especially when combined with other mitigation such as a clean record, will also justify a sentence reduction.

(3)   Other Matters   There is a whole range of various matters which do not impinge upon offence seriousness but which have been taken into account by sentencers in mitigation of sentence. It would be pointless to review them in detail here. Nigel Walker, in *Sentencing Theory, Law and Practice* (1985) gives the examples of the offender's good character, including moral credit and unrelated meritorious conduct of his, indirect effect of the sentence upon the offender or upon his family, credit for providing assistance to the police and credit given because of the staleness of the offence. Perhaps the best flavour of the range and complexity of such matters may be found in Joanna Shapland's analysis of the contents of speeches in mitigation in her book, *Between Conviction and Sentence* (1981) .

Irrespective of the merits of reducing sentence in these various cases, it is clear that none of the factors relied upon are related to the 'circumstances of the offence'. The court is not, then, required to have regard to them under s. 3(3)(a), but may, in its discretion, take them into account under s. 28(1). It will be noticed that all the factors listed above are mitigating factors. It is hard to think of any aggravating factors which are not in fact tied to the seriousness of the offence. For discussion of this, see 1.13 above and for the relevance of a record of previous convictions see 1.14.

1.23   Custodial Sentence Length and Early Release

It was readily apparent that the early release arrangements put in place by the CJA 1991 would, without appropriate adjustment to sentencing levels, result in many offenders serving longer, sometimes substantially longer, in custody than those given similar sentences before 1 October 1992. The offenders who would be most affected by these changes are those given sentences in the range between 12 months and up to four years (the 'short-term' prisoners under the the new scheme), whose early release cannot now occur until half the term has been served. Formerly, a substantial number of these offenders were granted discretionary parole after they had completed one third of their sentence. In a *Practice Statement (Crime: Sentencing)* [1992] 1 WLR 948 issued to coincide with the coming into force of the CJA 1991, Lord Taylor CJ stated that:

It has been an axiomatic principle of sentencing policy until now that the court should decide the appropriate sentence in each case without reference to questions of remission or parole.

I have consulted the Lords Justices presiding in the Court of Appeal (Criminal Division) and we have decided that a new approach is essential.

Accordingly, from 1 October 1992, it will be necessary, when passing a custodial sentence in the Crown Court, to have regard to the actual period likely to be served, and as far as practicable, to the risk of offenders serving longer under the new regime than would have been normal under the old.

Existing guideline judgments should be applied with these considerations in mind.

In *Cunningham* [1993] 1 WLR 183 Lord Taylor emphasised that the *Practice Statement* did not require 'an arithmetically precise calculation to be made'. Its object was to alert sentencers to the changed regime of early release and to require them to have regard to the possible effects of passing sentences after October 1992 of the same length as those they would have passed before. The Court of Appeal, he said, would be concerned in an appropriate case with whether the custodial term imposed by a sentencer was correct under the 1991 Act criteria, but would be unmoved 'by nice arithmetical comparisons between periods under the old and new regimes'.

Apart from this general advice on sentence length, earlier decisions which permitted a sentencer to adjust sentence length to avoid an unusual and adverse effect upon an offender's release date would still appear to be valid (see *Waite* (1991) 13 Cr App R (S) 26 and *Burnley Magistrates' Court, ex parte Halstead* (1990) 12 Cr App R (S) 468). In the latter case the Divisional Court quashed a sentence of 14 days' detention for fine default which, when added to the sentence of 12 months which the offender was serving for burglary would have increased the actual time in custody by 74 days. On the other hand it seems that nothing in the *Practice Statement* should be taken to detract from the general principle that a sentencer should not increase sentence length merely to bring an offender within a different early release category (see *Kenway* (1985) 7 Cr App R (S) 45). Such a course would appear to be contrary to the general requirement of proportionality in CJA 1991, s. 2(2)(a).

SPECIAL CUSTODIAL SENTENCES

1.24 Mandatory Life Sentences

During the progress of the Criminal Justice Bill through Parliament there was a determined attempt by the House of Lords, led by Lord Lane CJ and Lord Nathan, to remove the fixed penalty for murder. In April 1991 there was a vote in that House of 177 to 79 in favour of abolishing the fixed penalty, but the Commons subsequently removed the Lords amendment which would have effected this change (by 236 votes to 158), returning matters to the status quo. The arguments against the fixed penalty for murder have been rehearsed on several occasions in recent years, notably in the House of Lords *Select Committee on Murder and Life Imprisonment* (Session 88-89, HL Paper 78, 3 vols) which reported in 1989 and most recently in the December 1993 Report of the Prison Reform Trust, Committee on the Penalty for Homicide (chaired by Lord Lane).

Despite the significant changes to the rationale for use of discretionary life sentences and to the procedures for review of those sentences (see 1.25 and chapter 5, respectively, for these), no procedural changes to mandatory life sentences were made in the 1991 Act. In particular, it may be noted that the trial judge's power to recommend a minimum term to be served, under the Murder (Abolition of Death Penalty) Act 1965, s. 1(2), is unaffected by the 1991 Act. There have however, been changes consequent on the House of Lords decision in *Secretary of State for the Home Department, ex parte Doody* [1993] 3 WLR 154 (see below pp. 106–107 and 123–124).

1.25 Discretionary Life Sentences

No mention was made in the White Paper of the relation between the new criteria for determining the imposition and length of determinate custodial sentences and the continuing existence of the discretionary life sentence. Such sentences are difficult to defend in a sentencing system based upon desert principles. Pre-1991 case law on the imposition of life sentences for offences other than murder (in particular *Hodgson* (1968) 52 Cr App R 113, *Wilkinson* (1983) 5 Cr App R (S) 105, *De Havilland* (1983) 5 Cr App R (S) 109, and *O'Dwyer* (1986) 86 Cr App R 313) indicates that such a sentence should be passed only in 'the most exceptional circumstances' (Lord Lane CJ in *Pither* (1979) 1 Cr App R (S) 209). The courts developed three now quite well established criteria. They were (a) that the offence or offences are in themselves grave enough to require a very long sentence, (b) that it appears that the offender is a person of mental instability who, if at liberty, would probably reoffend and present a grave danger to the public and (c) that the offender will remain unstable and a potential danger for a long and/or uncertain period of time.

These criteria will no longer apply in precisely the same way after the CJA 1991. As we have seen, when determining the length of any custodial sentence, including a discretionary life sentence, the court must comply with CJA 1991, s. 2(2), so that the term of the sentence must henceforth be justified either on the ground of offence seriousness, under s. 2(2)(a), or, where the offence is a violent or sexual offence, on the ground of public protection, under s. 2(2)(b), or, conceivably, both. The only circumstances in which a life sentence could be justified under s. 2(2)(a) would, presumably, be where the sentence was being imposed to reflect that the case was one of the worst conceivable examples of the given offence (say, manslaughter), and that no mitigation or redeeming features could be identified. Then, a life sentence would mean, literally, life. Such a possibility was referred to in the *Practice Direction (Crime: Life Sentences)* [1993] 1 WLR 223. In the vast majority of cases, surely, the relevant ground will be s. 2(2)(b). This might mean some slight narrowing of the range of cases in which a sentencer might now impose a life sentence as compared to pre-1991 Act law. In particular, without the commission of an offence of violence or a sexual offence, it could not now be justified. The definitions of these terms in CJA 1991, s. 31(1) is, therefore, crucial. These were discussed, with various examples, in 1.10 above.

In a case where the sentencer imposes a discretionary life sentence under s. 2(2)(b), he must now also have regard to the provisions in CJA 1991, s. 34, which introduce a new power whereby the sentencer may specify what part of the discretionary life sentence must expire before the offender is able to have his case referred to the Parole Board. The sentencer, when indicating the relevant period, must, by s. 34(2), have regard to both (a) the seriousness of the offence, or the combination of the offence and one or more offences associated with it (see, for a discussion of the meaning of these terms, 1.16 and 1.17 above) and (b) to the fact that, under ss. 33(2) and 35(1), a determinate long-term sentence prisoner will now be released at a point between one-half and two-thirds of his sentence (see chapter 5). This power of judicial recommendation was derived from the *Select Committee Report on Murder and Life Imprisonment* and was introduced into the Act to take account of the criticisms made by the European Court of Human Rights in *Thynne* v *UK* (1990) 13 EHRR 666. It is important to note, however, that the sentencer has no power to make this form of recommendation in respect of the mandatory life sentence for murder (though the sentencer's power under the Murder (Abolition of Death Penalty) Act 1965 remains intact), and is not *required* to make a recommendation when passing a discretionary life sentence. It is difficult to see why a sentencer would choose to refrain from influencing later events by not making a recommendation. The *Practice Direction (Crime: Life Sentences)* [1993] 1 WLR 223 says that a judge should make a recommendation, save in the 'very exceptional case' where the offence is so serious that detention for life is justified on that ground alone. In such a case the judge should state this in open court when passing sentence. When the judge is to specify the relevant part of the sentence under s. 34, he should permit counsel for the defendant to address the court on the matter. In specifying the relevant part, the *Practice Direction* requires the judge to have regard to the specific terms of s. 34 and to indicate reasons for his decision. Finally the *Practice Direction* states that whether or not the court orders that s. 34 shall apply, the judge shall no longer make a written report to the Secretary of State through the Lord Chief Justice (the pre-existing arrangements as described in *Secretary of State for the Home Department, ex parte Handscomb* (1987) 86 Cr App R 59). See further on this, Chapter 5.

1.26 Sexual Offences: Sentence Affecting Early Release Arrangements

There is a special sentencing provision relating to sexual offenders which is introduced by CJA 1991, s. 44, a matter which was not foreshadowed in the White Paper but which was introduced at report stage. This section states that where, in respect of an offender, the whole or part of his custodial sentence was imposed for a 'sexual offence' (for the definition of this see s. 31(1), and the discussion at 1.10 above), and the sentencing court so specifies, the offender will, after release on licence, be required to serve out the full term of his sentence under supervision in the community rather than, as will be the normal case, receiving unconditional release after three-quarters of the sentence. In making that decision, the sentencer must have regard to the need to protect the public from serious harm and the desirability of preventing the commission by the offender of further offences and of securing his rehabilitation.

The new arrangements for early release are dealt with in chapter 5, and the special provision relating to sexual offenders in 5.17. The purpose behind this particular power is to allow the sentencer to affect directly the arrangements for early release and to require a longer period of supervision in respect of this class of offender. To this extent it resembles the now abolished power which the sentencer had under PCCA 1973, s. 28, to add an extended sentence certificate.

1.27 Extended Sentences

By CJA 1991, s. 5(2)(a), the extended sentence provisions in PCCA 1973, ss. 28 and 29, simply cease to have effect. The complex and little-used procedure whereby the Crown Court could add an extended sentence certificate in respect of serious persistent offenders is thereby abolished. The government's view, expressed in para. 3.17 of the 1990 White Paper is that 'to the extent that this power may have been useful in dealing with persistent violent or sexual offenders and protecting the public, it will be replaced by the new Crown Court power' created by CJA 1991, s. 1(2)(b) (discussed in 1.10 above). The extended sentence would also have overlapped, to some extent, with the new sentencing power in respect of sexual offences, discussed in 1.26.

There are unlikely to be many tears shed for the demise of the extended sentence provisions. The extended sentence was the latest in a series of special sentences intended to cater for the serious persistent offender. It was designed to have the dual purpose of permitting a longer prison sentence to be passed than could be justified on grounds of proportionality, and also for providing for licence supervision for a longer period than would be available under the normal parole arrangements. The licence provisions were that an offender, if released on parole, would remain on licence until the expiry of the full term of the sentence, rather than until the two-thirds point, when a fixed-term prisoner was normally released with remission. In recent years, this latter justification had achieved greater prominence. Generally, however, the sentence was very little used by the courts. Two likely reasons for the lack of interest were (a) the complexity of the statutory provisions relating to its use and (b) the existence of sufficient flexibility within the normal sentencing tariff to allow a judge to impose a disproportionate sentence without explicit reliance upon the extended sentence.

1.28 Partly Suspended Sentences

CJA 1991, s. 5(2)(b), simply provides that CLA 1977, s. 47, shall cease to have effect. This abolishes the power of the courts to pass a sentence of imprisonment partly served and partly suspended which, although on the statute books since 1977, was only made available to the courts in 1982. The Carlisle Committee recommended the abolition of this sentence, pointing out that its continued existence would be difficult to reconcile with the new early release arrangements introduced by CJA 1991 (see chapter 5). These new arrangements put all released prisoners at risk of being returned to custody if they commit a further imprisonable offence before the end of their sentence. This effectively duplicates a major component of the now repealed partly suspended sentence.

It seems that, notwithstanding the abolition of the partly suspended sentence, a court may still act to restore the balance of such a sentence, imposed before 1 October 1992, following commission of a further offence. See *Tetteh* [1993] Crim LR 629 and commentary. The maximum duration of a partly suspended sentence was two years.

SUSPENDED SENTENCES

1.29   Suspended Sentences: General

According to the 1990 White Paper (para. 3.22):

> The suspended sentence does not fit easily into the proposed new sentencing arrangements. On the other hand, the courts clearly find the sentence useful. ... The government intends to retain the fully suspended sentence, for offenders over 21 years old for serious offences. It would be available to the courts only when an offence is so serious that it justifies a custodial sentence, but the court is satisfied that there are good reasons not to sentence the particular offender to immediate imprisonment and that community service or probation would not be suitable for that offender. Suspended sentences should normally be combined with compensation or fines, so that offenders do not seem to go unpunished.

CJA 1991, s. 5(1), is clearly designed to achieve an effect in line with the above-quoted passage, by replacing subsection (2) of s. 22 of the PCCA 1973 with new subsections (2) and (2A). The effect of the original subsection (2) was to state that a suspended sentence should not be used unless the case was such that a sentence of immediate imprisonment would have been appropriate in the absence of a power to suspend. The proviso is repeated, in slightly different terms, by the new subsection (2)(a). The new subsection (2)(b), however, additionally provides that the court shall not pass a suspended sentence unless it is of the opinion 'that the exercise of that power can be justified by the exceptional circumstances of the case'. The effect of this further requirement is to reinforce the approach which is endorsed in the pre-existing case law, that the sentencer's selection of a suspended sentence must properly be situated at the end of a long chain of reasoning. Perhaps the clearest statement of this is provided by Lord Parker CJ in *O'Keefe* [1969] 2 QB 29, at p. 32:

> It seems to this court that before one gets to a suspended sentence at all, a court must go through the process of eliminating other possible courses such as absolute discharge, conditional discharge, probation order, fine, and then say to itself: this is a case for imprisonment, and the final question, it being a case for imprisonment: is immediate imprisonment required, or can I give a suspended sentence?

Strict adherence to such a chain of reasoning will inevitably mean that the use of the suspended sentence is 'exceptional'. The problem, of course, has been that the courts have not always used the suspended sentence in the manner specified in *O'Keefe*, and the Court of Appeal has quashed suspended prison sentences on numerous occasions where the reasoning has not been complied with, a custodial sentence being inappropriate for the offence. One example is *Watts* (1984) 6 Cr App R (S) 61, where the offender, a person with a clean record, allowed her premises to be used for smoking cannabis in circumstances 'not by any means the gravest for this sort of offence'. On appeal, the suspended sentence was quashed and a conditional discharge was substituted. Another is *Jeffrey* (1985) 7 Cr App R (S) 11, where a suspended sentence was held to be 'wholly inappropriate' for a man with a clean record who stole an electric fire from his landlady.

In a series of cases decided subsequent to the implementation of the CJA 1991, the Court of Appeal has applied the new provisions very restrictively. In *Okinikan* [1993] 1 WLR 173 the offender, aged 21, pleaded guilty to various offences of dishonesty relating to motor vehicles and credit cards. A total of nine months' imprisonment was imposed. On appeal, Lord Taylor of Gosforth CJ dealt with the argument that the custodial term should have been suspended to take account of various matters in mitigation. His Lordship said, with reference to the amendments made by the CJA 1991 to s. 5(1) of the PCCA 1973, that:

> The significant amendment is the new emphasis on the exceptional nature of a suspended sentence. Parliament has given statutory force to the principle that a suspended sentence should not be regarded as a soft option, but should only be imposed in exceptional circumstances.
>
> This court cannot lay down a definition of 'exceptional circumstances'. They will inevitably depend on the facts of each individual case. However, taken on their own, or in combination, good character, youth and an early plea are not exceptional circumstances justifying a suspended sentence. They are common features of many cases. They may amount to mitigation sufficient to persuade the court that a custodial sentence should not be passed or to reduce its length. The statutory language is clear and unequivocal.

The sentence was upheld. See also, to similar effect, *Sanderson* (1993) 14 Cr App R (S) 361, *Lowery* (1993) 14 Cr App R (S) 485 and *Robinson* (1993) 14 Cr App R (S) 559. *Lowery* is a striking case. The offender was a police officer of 20 years service, who pleaded guilty to eleven counts of false accounting. His duties included the collection at the police station of fines paid in discharge of warrants issued by magistrates' courts. He had failed to pay the money to the court office and had kept it for himself. The total amount taken was £1,500. The mitigating circumstances were that the offender's wife had become severely disabled, and the offender had found himself in financial difficulties as a result of adapting their police house for her special use. His conviction had meant that the offender had now lost his employment and his house. His pension was frozen and would not be payable until he was aged 60. Since the offences he had been suffering from depression and had made two attempts at suicide. A medical report indicated that the offender was 'devastated' and was in need of continuing psychiatric care. A sentence of three months imprisonment had been imposed. The Court of Appeal held that the mitigating circumstances should not be allowed to obscure what was a very serious breach of trust, and that the admittedly 'catastrophic effect' which the dishonesty had had upon him was *not* 'exceptional' since offenders convicted of crimes involving breach of trust frequently found themselves 'visited with consequences which go far beyond the immediate impact of any sentence'. In mercy, however, the sentence was reduced to 42 days, so as to permit the offender's immediate release. The effect of these decisions is that the use made by the courts of the suspended sentence is bound to decline sharply. This will have important consequences. Take the example of theft in breach of trust, a form of offending which has often been dealt with in the past by way of suspended sentence. In 1991 it seems that the Crown Court sentenced 1,039 offenders for theft in breach of trust (the figure has been derived by adding together the categories of 'theft by employees' and 'theft or unauthorised taking from the mail' in Home Office, *Criminal Statistics England and Wales. Supplementary Tables*, vol. 2, 1991). Of these, 386 received immediate custody and 318 received suspended sentences. Other disposals included community service (168) and probation (64). If the use of suspended sentences generally does decline as sharply as the appellate decisions indicate, cases formerly dealt with by suspension of sentence will now have to receive either immediate custody (with a consequent impact on the custodial population) or a community sentence. Early indications are that the relative use of community service orders has increased by up to 60 per cent since the CJA 1991 came into force (survey of sentencing in 28 court areas between October 1992 and March 1993 by National Association of Probation Officers, *Criminal Justice Act 1991; The First Six Months* (London: NAPO, 1993)).

In two recent cases the Court of Appeal has displayed a greater readiness to find 'exceptional circumstances'. In *Cameron* [1993] Crim LR 721 the offender pleaded guilty to assault occasioning actual bodily harm. He had slapped one of his three children, a boy aged five, so hard as to leave extensive bruising on his face, arms and buttocks. The judge imposed an immediate custodial sentence of 12 months. The Court of Appeal's reason for suspending the sentence was to take account of the decision of the local authority that it was in the best interests of the family if the offender and three children could be reunited under supervision. In *Huntley* [1993] Crim LR 721 the offender had attacked the victim with a bottle, causing lacerations which needed stitches. A sentence of 18 months imprisonment was reduced to 12 months and suspended, in light of severe provocation. *Huntley* is difficult to reconcile with *Sanderson*, where the Court of Appeal regarded provocation as a common feature of offences of violence.

1.30 Suspended Sentences and Financial Orders

The new subsection (2A) of PCCA 1973, s. 22, requires a court which passes a suspended sentence to consider whether the circumstances of the case are such as to warrant in addition the imposition of a fine or the making of a compensation order. This is, no doubt, designed to achieve the effect that, whenever possible, the passing of a suspended sentence will not be perceived as a 'let-off', by the offender or by the public, since a financial order will have been added to it as a 'sting in the tail'. This approach is well documented in pre-existing case law, and subsection (2A) merely emphasises it to the courts as desirable sentencing practice. Care must be taken, however, when combining a suspended sentence with a fine. The Court of Appeal in *Genese* [1976] 1 WLR 958 explained the correct approach as follows (at p. 963):

> If the court decides that there is no other method appropriate of dealing with the offender than imprisonment, and imposes a prison sentence, the court can then, in the appropriate case, go on to consider that the sentence should be

suspended . . . the court can also consider whether an additional penalty by way of a fine is justified.

Thus a fine may be added to a suspended sentence, but it is clearly contrary to the reasoning in *O'Keefe* to combine them where a fine standing alone would have been the proper sentence. Where the proper reasoning is adhered to and a fine is to be added to a suspended sentence, the court must ensure that careful account is taken of the offender's means when fixing the level of the fine (*King* [1970] 1 WLR 1016; *Whybrew* (1979) 1 Cr App R (S) 121). The only possible problem here relates to CJA 1991 s. 28(2)(a), which states that nothing in the relevant part of the Act shall prevent a court 'from mitigating any penalty in an offender's sentence by taking into account any other penalty included in that sentence'. It is submitted that this provision cannot have the effect of undermining the well established principle explained in this paragraph. It could, however, properly result in the fixing of the fine at a lower level when in combination with a suspended sentence than when standing alone. It is likely that this would be in accord with pre-1991 Act sentencing practice, but there is no discussion in the appellate cases of the appropriate level of fine to add to a suspended sentence. Presumably, no reduction in the fine would be appropriate where it was being imposed as a means of removing the offender's profit from the offending.

As far as adding a compensation order to a suspended sentence is concerned, this is already a well recognised sentencing combination, and the new subsection (2A) of PCCA 1973, s. 22 seems merely to further emphasise it as desirable sentencing practice. The courts are, in fact, already empowered by PCCA 1973, s. 35(1), to make a compensation order instead of or in addition to dealing with the offender in any other way, and are now obliged by PCCA 1973, s. 35(1), as amended by CJA 1988, s. 104, to give reasons, on the passing of any sentence, why a compensation order was not made in a case where there was a power to do so. The possible problem with CJA 1991, s. 28(1)(b), does not recur here, since a compensation order is ancillary to sentence and cannot properly be regarded as a 'penalty'.

It does not seem that the new subsection (2A) of PCCA 1973, s. 22 will in any way affect the limitations upon the making of compensation orders which have developed through the case law, such as the requirement that any sum awarded in compensation should be agreed by the offender or established by evidence (*Horsham Justices, ex parte Richards* [1985] 1 WLR 986), that compensation orders should be confined to clear, straightforward cases (*Hyde* v *Emery* (1984) 6 Cr App R (S) 206) and that the sum payable and any period of payment by instalments takes proper account of the offender's ability to pay (*Beddow* (1987) 9 Cr App R (S) 235). With regard to the particular combination of a suspended sentence and a compensation order, the Court of Appeal has advised caution, in that if the offender is in breach of the suspended sentence, its activation may bring to an end any prospect of the payment of compensation (*McGee* [1978] Crim LR 370). It is, of course, clearly contrary to principle to suspend a prison sentence merely because of the offender's ability to pay a fine or meet an order for compensation.

The new subsection (2) of PCCA 1973, s. 22, leaves unaffected the pre-CJA 1991 position that a custodial sentence on an offender of or over the age of 21 can be suspended in accordance with PCCA 1973, s. 22, but a custodial sentence on a person under 21 cannot be suspended, in spite of criticism from some sentencers (see *Dobbs* (1983) 5 Cr App R (S) 378) that the courts should be given the power to suspend custodial sentences on those under 21. In *Horney* (1990) 12 Cr App R (S) 20 it was held that a custodial sentence could properly be imposed upon a person aged under 21 where a suspended prison sentence would have been appropriate in respect of an adult. The position becomes even more anomalous under the CJA 1991, since the criteria for imposing custody in respect of adults and young offenders are now the same.

1.31 Suspended Sentences: Justifying Custody

In respect of offenders over 21, since a suspended sentence is a custodial sentence (*Brewer* (1982) 4 Cr App R (S) 380), it is clear that before a suspended sentence can be passed the court must adhere to the relevant provisions in CJA 1991, ss. 1 to 3, which must be complied with before any custodial sentence is passed. The court must be satisfied that a custodial sentence is justified for the offence under s. 1(2)(a) or s. 1(2)(b). The suspended sentence should also comply with the new law on the duration of custodial sentences in s. 2(2). This may create some difficulty. Under s. 2(2)(a) the length of the custodial sentence must be determined in accordance with the seriousness of the offence. This seems appropriate on the face of it, since the length of the term of a suspended sentence must be determined prior to the decision whether to suspend it (*Mah-Wing* (1983) 5 Cr App R (S) 347). The decision to suspend the sentence must, logically, be made on the basis of mitigation admitted under s. 28(1), rather than s. 3(3)(a), since presumably all aggravating and mitigating factors relevant to the seriousness of the offence will have been taken into account when determining the suitability of custody and its appropriate length. The Act, however, provides no guidance on how the court is to fix the other dimension of the suspended sentence, the duration of the period of suspension. It would seem to be logically inconsistent to rely on s. 1(2)(b) to decide upon custody or on s. 2(2)(b) to determine the appropriate sentence length, and then to suspend the sentence, since that would defeat the requirement of public protection.

1.32 Suspended Sentences: Procedural Requirements

The same procedural requirements which apply to the decision whether to impose immediate custody and the decision over the appropriate length of custody apply equally to the suspended sentence. In particular, when imposing such a sentence the court must obtain and consider a pre-sentence report (CJA 1991, s. 3(1)) unless the offence is triable only on indictment and the court considers that obtaining a report is 'unnecessary' (s. 3(2)) and must justify its decision to impose custody by reference to the terms of s. 1(2)(a) or (b) and justify its decision on length of custody by reference to s. 2(2)(a) or (b).

Chapter Two
Community Sentences

Sections 6 to 16 of the Act make important changes to non-custodial penalties (now 'community sentences'). Sections 6 and 7 set out the appropriate grounds for the imposition of community sentences (where seriousness of the offence, as with custodial sentences, is again the key criterion) and the remaining sections make important changes to the legal status and operation of probation orders and community service orders. Additional requirements may now be written into probation orders by the courts, including new conditions relating to those convicted of sexual offences and for treatment for drug or alcohol dependency. Community service orders and probation orders may be combined together for the first time. There are changes made to supervision orders, attendance centre orders and discharges. A greater degree of harmonisation of the arrangements for breach of community sentences is attempted. Several of the community sentences are affected by the expansion of the legal category of 'young person' to include 17-year-olds.

CRITERIA FOR COMMUNITY SENTENCES

2.1 Community Sentences: General

Sections 6 and 7 of CJA 1991 explain the circumstances in which a community sentence may properly be imposed by the Crown Court or a magistrates' court. The language of 'non-custodial penalties' appears now to be obsolete. A 'community sentence' is composed of one or more 'community orders', the latter term encompassing each of the following orders (s. 6(1) and (4)):

(a) a probation order,
(b) a community service order,
(c) a combination order,
(d) a curfew order,
(e) a supervision order, and
(f) an attendance centre order.

The new arrangements affecting these various community orders are dealt with in turn in 2.5 to 2.15 below. After discussion of the new arrangements for enforcement of community orders, something is then said about changes made by the Act to discharges though they are not community orders.

2.2 Community Sentences: Consent

The question of the offender's consent to a community sentence is important under the new statutory scheme in two ways. First, consent is required before a number of the community orders may be imposed. These are listed below. If an offender refuses to give his consent to a community sentence which is proposed by the court and which requires that consent, the court may impose a custodial sentence (CJA 1991, s. 1(3)). Note that the court would not be bound to impose custody, since a different community sentence (to which the offender was prepared to consent, or the imposition of which requires no consent) might be imposed instead. See further on this, 1.8 above. Secondly, where an offender is found by a court to be in breach of a community sentence the court may, in certain circumstances, deem that the offender's 'wilful and persistent failure to comply' with the order amounts to a refusal on his part to consent to it. In these circumstances, again, the court may, but not must, impose a custodial sentence. See further 2.16 to 2.18.

The community sentences for which the offender's consent is required are a probation order (PCCA 1973, s. 2, as substituted by CJA 1991, s. 8(1)), a community service order (PCCA 1973, s. 14(2), as substituted by CJA 1991, s. 10(3)), a combination order (CJA 1991, s. 11 (although s. 11 does not specifically state that such consent is required, consent is a requirement for both constituent parts of a combination order); and a curfew order (CJA 1991, s. 12(5)). Under CJA 1991, s. 13, a curfew order may include a requirement for securing the electronic monitoring of the offender. While s. 13 does not specify that the offender must consent to the monitoring requirement, it is clear from s. 12 that the curfew order itself cannot be made unless the offender 'expresses his willingness to comply with its requirements' including, where appropriate, the electronic monitoring. An attendance centre order does not require the offender's consent, nor does a supervision order, but the imposition of certain requirements within a supervision order does require consent. The CJA 1991 does not say whether the offender's refusal to consent to one part of a mixed order would amount to a refusal to consent to the whole order, but it is likely that the court would so construe such a refusal. Case law might in due course develop on the question of whether the offender's refusal to consent might in any circumstances be regarded as reasonable.

2.3 Justifying Community Sentences

CJA 1991, s. 6, creates for community sentences a threshold provision similar to s. 1(2) in relation to custodial sentences. Under s. 6(1) as amended by CJA 1993, s. 66(4), a court shall not pass a community sentence:

> unless it is of the opinion that the offence, or the combination of the offence and one or more offences associated with it, was serious enough to warrant such a sentence.

Unlike the justification for imposing custody, however, offence seriousness is here the sole criterion. The effect is to regard all community orders as lying within a sentencing band located immediately below custody and immediately above fines and discharges, ranged in relation to an offence seriousness scale (see figure 1.1 at 1.9 above). The threshold below community sentences is determined entirely by offence seriousness, whilst the threshold between community sentences and custody is crucially determined by offence seriousness. It is helpful once again to refer to the White Paper, para. 4.6:

> Restrictions on liberty . . . become the connecting thread in a range of community penalties as well as custody. . . . The legislation will provide that, before making an order which places restrictions on liberty, a court would have to be satisfied that the offence for which the offender had been convicted by the court was so serious that restrictions on liberty were justified, but not serious enough to deserve a custodial sentence.

Given this model, it would seem appropriate for there to be some gradation of community orders within the sentencing band, to take account of the extent to which each order typically imposes restrictions upon the liberty of an offender who receives it, but this is not developed in the legislation. There is one other difference between the custodial and community sentence thresholds. Section 6(1) requires only that the offence be 'serious enough' to warrant a community sentence, rather than being so serious that only such a sentence can be justified. It seems to follow that there could thus be some cases where a fine can properly be regarded as a more severe penalty than a community sentence.

The requirement in s. 6(1) that the court must consider 'the offence, or the combination of the offence and one or more offences associated with it' mirrors the provision in CJA 1991, s. 1(2)(a), in relation to custodial sentences, discussed in 1.9 above. The offender must have been convicted of at least one offence, and this will, of course, cover both conviction after a trial and after a guilty plea (*Cole* [1965] 2 QB 388). In a case where only one offence is being sentenced, the court must reach a view on the seriousness of that offence. Unlike custodial sentencing, however, apart from a cluster of Court of Appeal decisions on community service orders in burglary cases, there is very little appellate or other guidance available to courts on the use of community sentences, and so this is an area where the courts will have to build up experience over time. Of course offence seriousness has always been an important dimension in imposing community sentences, but it achieves greater importance under the 1991 Act, together with the abandonment of the traditional representation of community sentences as 'alternatives' to custodial sentences. The Magistrates' Association's Guidelines offer some insights on the relative seriousness of offences as encountered in the lower courts, and the most recent edition (1993) is much more detailed in its approach.

When considering the gravity of a combination of two or more offences under CJA 1991 s. 6(1), s. 31(2) says that one offence is to be regarded as 'associated' with another offence if the offender is convicted of offences in the same proceedings, is sentenced for the offences at the same time, or if the offender is convicted of one offence and asks to have another offence or offences taken into consideration in sentencing for that offence. The implication is that a community sentence may be justified when looking at associated offences, though it could not be justified in respect of any of the offences standing alone. This raises issues parallel to those which have already been discussed in the context of custodial sentences at 1.9 above. It should be noted that under the original version of CJA 1991, s. 6(1), the court was restricted to looking at only *two* associated offences when deciding whether the offending was serious enough to justify such a sentence. This restriction has been removed by CJA 1993, s. 66. Henceforth the court may have regard to the *full range* of the associated offences before the court.

Section 6(2) requires that the court, when passing a community sentence, must achieve *two* objectives. By s. 6(2)(a) the community order or orders 'shall be such as in the opinion of the court is, or taken together are, the most suitable for the offender' and, by s. 6(2)(b), the 'restrictions on liberty imposed by the order or orders shall be such as in the opinion of the court are commensurate with the seriousness of the offence, or the combination of the offence and one or more offences associated with it'. The main difficulty with s. 6(2) is that the two objectives, (a) 'suitability' and (b) 'seriousness', will sometimes certainly conflict, and the statute gives no indication of which objective should prevail.

It is submitted that the most coherent way of tackling the conflict is to say that the most suitable community order or combination of orders should be selected for the offender but only imposed if this does not impose a more onerous burden upon the offender than is justified by the seriousness of the offence. This would be to treat (b) as a limiting factor, and would be in accord with the declared underlying principle of desert. It must be conceded, however, that sentencers are now faced with major problems in satisfying the requirements of s. 6(2), particularly where a mixture of different community orders is imposed. It seems that sentencers have been left very much on their own to resolve these problems and, as we have seen, there is no existing framework of Court of Appeal decisions on community sentencing to assist them. The national standard on pre-sentence reports offers a 'possible model' for tackling these problems. See annex 2.B, set out at p. 305 of this *Guide*.

2.4 Community Sentences: Procedural Requirements

In forming its opinion that a community sentence is justified under CJA 1991, s. 6(1) and in determining the appropriate restrictions on liberty under s. 6(2)(b), s. 7(1) requires that the court 'shall take into account all such information about the circumstances of the offence or (as the case may be) of the offence and the offence or offences associated with it (including any aggravating or mitigating factors) as is available to it'. This provision is parallel to s. 3(3) in relation to custodial sentences, which was considered in 1.13 above. The argument was made there that s. 3(3) requires the court to take into account all factors, whether aggravating or mitigating, which impinge upon the seriousness of the offence, such as the degree of harm caused to the victim or the culpability of the offender. Additionally the court, by s. 28 of the Act, may take into account any other matter in mitigation which does not impinge upon culpability (for discussion see 1.12 above), such as the tendering of a guilty plea. In determining the question of the most suitable community order or orders for the offender, the court may take into account any information about the offender which is before it (s. 7(2)).

2.5 Pre-sentence Reports

One of the main sources for the kind of information required before a community sentence is passed will be the pre-sentence report. Pre-sentence reports replace social inquiry reports, and were considered in 1.12, above. According to s. 7(3), such a report is mandatory whenever the court is considering imposing:

(a)   a probation order which includes additional requirements authorised by sch. 1A to the PCCA 1973,
(b)   a community service order,
(c)   a combination order, and
(d)   a supervision order which includes requirements imposed under s. 12, 12A, 12AA, 12B or 12C of the CYPA 1969.

It follows that a pre-sentence report is *not* mandatory whenever the court is considering imposing:

(a)   a probation order which does not include additional requirements,
(b)   a supervision order which does not include the specified requirements,
(c)   a curfew order, or
(d)   an attendance centre order,

though no doubt in many such cases it would be good sentencing practice to obtain one. Even in those cases where the obtaining of a pre-sentence report is mandatory, s. 7(4) states that no community sentence shall be invalidated by the failure of the court to comply with s. 7(3), but on appeal against a community sentence passed without the court having obtained and considered such a report, the appellate court must obtain and consider one. There is a parallel provision in respect of custodial sentences in s. 3(5), but it should be noted that in respect of community sentences there is no provision equivalent to s. 3(2) which applies to custodial sentences and which permits a Crown Court sentencer to proceed without a pre-sentence where such a report would, in the sentencer's view, be 'unnecessary'.

It may perhaps be inferred from the statutory requirement to obtain a pre-sentence report in respect of the first four community orders, but not the second four, that the first four can be regarded as imposing more onerous obligations upon an offender, and hence occupying the upper portion of the community sentence band, while the second four occupy the lower portion of that band. This inference has been incorporated into figure 1.1 (see 1.9 above). For further discussion of PSRs in the context of community sentences see the relevant national standards, set out at p. 295 of this *Guide*.

PROBATION ORDERS

2.6   Probation Orders: General

Before the CJA 1991 the main statutory provision relating to probation orders
was PCCA 1973, s. 2. This section is repealed by the 1991 Act and, by CJA 1991,
s. 8, a new PCCA 1973, s. 2, is substituted. The whole of the law relating to
probation orders is recast and a number of changes are effected, of which the
following seem to be the most important.

2.7   Reduction of Qualifying Age for Probation to 16

By the revised s. 2(1) of PCCA 1973, the minimum age of offender upon which a
probation order may be imposed is reduced from 17 to 16. This brings probation
into line with community service, where the minimum qualifying age was
reduced to 16 by CJA 1982, sch. 12. It does, however, entail an overlap between
those offenders who may be subjected to a probation order and those who may
receive a supervision order. A supervision order could always be imposed on a
16-year-old (CYPA 1969, s. 7(7)(b)), but may now also be imposed on a
17-year-old (CJA 1991, s. 68 and sch. 8, para. 4(2)) and the order may continue
in force until the person is 18 or older. For the changes to supervision orders see
2.24 below. The overlap between probation and supervision orders is government policy, as was explained in the White Paper, at para. 8.17:

> Since some 16 and 17-year-olds are more mature than others, the government
> believes that there should be some flexibility in the sentencing arrangements
> for this group. . . . At present supervision orders are available for those under
> 17. The corresponding disposal for older offenders is the probation order.
> They are broadly similar in their purpose but the practical effects of the two
> orders can differ. For example, most programmes of intermediate treatment,
> which has proved so successful in dealing with many juvenile offenders, are
> carried out under supervision orders. Attendance at day centres, which is a
> growing feature of work with older offenders, can be required as a condition
> of a probation order. In dealing with 16 and 17-year-olds, courts should be
> able to select either of these disposals according to the maturity of the offender
> and the arrangements available locally.

The complexity of existing provisions, however, particularly in relation to
supervision orders, may generate a degree of confusion such as to cancel out the
perceived advantages of overlap. The relevant national standards suggest that 'the
supervision order may often in practice be the more suitable form of supervision
for 16 and 17 year olds. Such supervision can assist the young person's
development into adulthood, whereas the probation order is more appropriate for
someone who is already an adult' (ch. 3, para. 9; and see further, p. 308 below).

2.8   Probation Now Sentence in Its Own Right

A probation order, under the revised s. 2(1) of PCCA 1973, is no longer imposed
'instead of sentencing' the offender, but becomes a sentence of the court in its

own right. The main implication of the former wording was that a probation order was not a 'punishment' (see *Parry* [1951] 1 KB 590) and, broadly, could not be combined with any other disposal which was punitive in nature. Thus a probation order could not be combined, in respect of sentencing for a single offence, with a suspended prison sentence (PCCA 1973, s. 22(3)), a fine or a community service order. A number of these limitations are now swept away. A table of the main permissible sentence combinations, following CJA 1991, is provided in table 2.1. Over the coming years, no doubt, the courts will develop principles over which of these combinations it is desirable for courts to employ. A secondary implication of making a probation order a sentence in its own right is that the amended legislation now speaks of an 'offender', rather than a 'probationer'.

It is confirmed by CJA 1991, sch. 11, para. 23, that a probation order may be combined with an order for exclusion from licensed premises under the Licensed Premises (Exclusion of Certain Persons) Act 1980, and by sch. 11, para. 38, it is confirmed that a probation order may be combined with an order for endorsement or disqualification under the Road Traffic Offenders Act 1988, s. 46(1). These combinations were already possible before the CJA 1991, but by way of reliance upon an exception to PCCA 1973, s. 13. Section 13 no longer applies to probation orders (see 2.10 below), and so these amendments simply achieve the same effect by a different statutory route.

2.9   Two Objectives of Probation

Also by the revised s. 2(1) of PCCA 1973, the purposes of a probation order are declared to be either 'securing the rehabilitation of the offender' or 'protecting the public from harm from him or preventing the commission by him of further offences'. The court must be of the opinion that the making of a probation order is desirable in the interests of securing one or other (or, conceivably, both) of these objectives.

Previously no rationale for the making of a probation order was stated in the legislation. Historically, a rehabilitative approach has been predominant, though in recent years greater emphasis has been given by some to the objectives of control and surveillance. It should be remembered, however, that the making of a probation order is also subject to the threshold requirement in CJA 1991, s. 6(1) and that the order and any requirements inserted within it require justification in terms of *both* the 'suitability' and 'seriousness' criteria in s. 6(2): see 2.2 above. The relevant national standards provide more detail on these matters and are set out at pp. 307–15 of this *Guide*. Paragraph 4 of the probation orders national standard states that:

> Effective probation order supervision requires high standards both from probation services and from individual probation staff and should generally entail establishing a professional relationship, in which to advise, assist and befriend the offender with the aim of:
> - securing the offender's cooperation and compliance with the probation order and enforcing its terms;
> - challenging the offender to accept responsibility for his or her crime and its consequences;

■ helping the offender to resolve personal difficulties linked with offending and to acquire new skills; and

■ motivating and assisting the offender to become a responsible and law-abiding member of the community.

2.10 Probation and 'Conviction'

Prior to the CJA 1991, PCCA 1973, s. 13, operated in respect of probation orders, such that a conviction which was followed by the making of a probation order was deemed not to count as a conviction for any purpose other than the purposes of the proceedings in which the order was made and of any subsequent proceedings which might be taken against the offender for breach of the order or commission of a further offence during the currency of that order. CJA 1991, s. 8(2) removes probation orders from the scope of PCCA 1973, s. 13, which is now limited to convictions which are followed by the grant of an absolute or conditional discharge. By CJA 1991, sch. 12, para. 2, this change shall not affect the operation of PCCA 1973, s. 13, in relation to persons placed on probation before the relevant commencement date.

In practice PCCA 1973, s. 13, had very limited impact, but one situation in which it did have an effect was where an offender who was under a suspended sentence was convicted of a further offence, which was then dealt with by way of a probation order. The conviction for the latter offence then did not count as a conviction for the purpose of taking any action with regard to the suspended sentence (*Tarry* [1970] 2 QB 560). This result is avoided in the 1991 Act.

2.11 Requirements in Probation Orders

A number of changes are made to the requirements which may be included in a probation order. CJA 1991, s. 9, brings about these changes. PCCA 1973, s. 2, s. 3, s. 4A and s. 4B, are all replaced by new provisions which now appear in PCCA 1973, sch. 1A, created by part II of sch. 1 to CJA 1991.

(1) General Requirements The so-called 'standard conditions', traditionally inserted into probation orders, are non-statutory in nature and are unaffected by CJA 1991. They are (a) that the offender shall be of good behaviour and lead an industrious life; (b) that the offender shall inform the probation officer immediately of any change of address or employment; and (c) that the offender shall comply with the instructions of the probation officer as to reporting to the officer and as to receiving visits from the probation officer at home. Section 2(6) additionally requires that the offender shall keep in touch with his probation officer in accordance with instructions given, and notify the officer of any change of address.

The new s. 3(1) of PCCA 1973 states that a probation order may require the offender to comply, during the whole or any part of the order, 'with such requirements as the court, having regard to the circumstances of the case, considers desirable'. For these purposes the court must have regard to the two stated objectives of probation orders, of securing the rehabilitation of the offender and protecting the public (see 2.9 above). Presumably such conditions,

Table 2.1 Permitted sentence combinations

(a) Before the Criminal Justice Act 1991

	Suspended sentence	Fine	Community service	Probation	Discharge	Compensation order
Custody	No / No	Yes (1) / Yes (1)	No / No	No / No	No / Yes	Yes (1) / Yes (1)
Suspended sentence		Yes (1) / Yes	No / No	No (2) / No	No / Yes	Yes (1) / Yes
Fine			No / Yes	No / Yes	No / Yes	Yes (3) / Yes
Community service				No (4) / Yes	No / Yes	Yes / Yes
Probation					No / Yes	Yes (5) / Yes
Discharge						Yes / Yes

In each square the comment at the top relates to combining the sentences when sentencing for a *single offence*; the lower comment relates to sentencing for *separate offences* on the same occasion.

(b) After the Criminal Justice Act 1991

	Suspended sentence	Fine	Community service	Probation	Combination order	Curfew order	Discharge	Compensation order
Custody	No No	Yes (1) Yes (1)	No No	No No	No No	No No	No Yes	Yes (1) Yes (1)
Suspended sentence		Yes (1, 6) Yes	Yes* Yes*	No No	Yes* Yes*	Yes* Yes*	No Yes	Yes (1, 6) Yes
Fine			Yes Yes	Yes Yes	Yes Yes	Yes Yes	No Yes	Yes (3) Yes
Community service				No (7) Yes* (8)	No No	Yes* Yes*	No Yes	Yes Yes
Probation					No No	Yes Yes	No Yes	Yes (5) Yes
Combination order						Yes Yes	No Yes	Yes Yes
Curfew order							No Yes	Yes Yes
Discharge								Yes Yes

Notes
(1) Though only where the financial order is added to the custodial sentence, which is itelf justified by the seriousness of the offence, and proper regard is had to the offender's means.
(2) This combintion may, in effect, be achieved by a suspended sentence supervision order.
(3) Where the offender is of limited means and cannot pay both, the compensation order takes priority.
(4) Community service not available as a condition of a probation order.
(5) Though compensation cannot be made a condition of a probation order.
(6) These combinations are encouraged by CJA 1991.
(7) Though, in a certain mix, they form a combination order.
(8) Such a mix might be regarded as circumventing the specific power in the Act to make a combination order.
* The combinations so marked appear not to be prohibited by the Act, but may not be regarded as attractive mixes. Regard should also be had to CJA 1991, s. 28(2)(a) which permits the court to mitigate any penalty 'included in an offender's sentence by taking into account any other penalty included in that sentence'.

insofar as they fall outside the specific conditions provided for in sch. 1A, would still be required to avoid the criticism of 'vagueness', deprecated by Lord Goddard in a *Practice Note* (1952) 35 Cr App R 207. It is also very likely that overelaborate, fanciful or unenforceable requirements would be struck down on appeal.

(2) Residence Requirements   Paragraph 1 of the new sch. 1A to PCCA 1973 replaces a similarly worded provision which was in s. 2(5) of the 1973 Act. One difference is that the new provision speaks of residence in an 'approved hostel' (para. 1(3)), rather than an 'approved probation hostel' (the now repealed PCCA 1973, s. 2(5)(b)). This appears to make no practical difference to the import of the section, since the phrase is, in both cases, followed by 'or any other institution'. The definitions of 'approved probation hostel' and 'probation hostel' in PCCA 1973, s. 57(1) are retained, however, despite the new legislation making no specific reference to such hostels.

(3) Requirements as to Activities and as to Attendance at Probation Centre   These are dealt with in paras. 2 and 3 of sch. 1A to PCCA 1973, inserted by the CJA 1991, which replace PCCA 1973, s. 4A and s. 4B, which were introduced into PCCA 1973 by CJA 1982, s. 62 and sch. 11. They are almost exactly reproduced in the new provisions, with just one significant change. A 'day centre' is now called a 'probation centre', and a 'probation centre' is defined in para. 3(7) of the new sch. 1A as being premises:

(a)   at which non-residential facilities are provided for use in connection with the rehabilitation of offenders; and
(b)   which are for the time being approved by the Secretary of State as providing facilities suitable for persons subject to probation orders.

The only difference from the definition of a 'day centre', which was contained in PCCA 1973, s. 4B(6), is that formerly day centres had either to be provided by a probation committee or be approved by the probation committee for the area in which the premises are situated. The change suggests more central approval and an attempt to achieve a more uniform approach and standardisation of facilities. CJA 1991, sch. 12, para. 3, provides that on commencement of part II of the Act all existing day centres will become probation centres. On approval of probation centres see annex 3.A to the relevant national standard, below, at p. 314.

(4) Requirements for Sexual Offenders   Paragraph 4 of the new sch. 1A to PCCA 1973 is innovative, by requiring that where an offender has been convicted of a sexual offence (defined in CJA 1991, s. 31(1): see 1.10 above), the normal 60-day limit in relation to required activities under PCCA 1973, sch. 1A, para. 2, and in relation to attendance at a probation centre (under PCCA 1973, sch. 1A, para. 3) does not apply. No alternative upper limit is specified where such a course is taken. The court which imposes the probation order must specify the number of days but it is clear that this requirement may now extend for the full duration of the order. It seems clear that the objective of this change is to encourage the courts to deal with offenders convicted of sexual offences,

where appropriate, by closer supervision in the community, rather than by incarceration. If this proves popular, it would have important resource implications for the probation service.

(5) Treatment for Mental Condition Requirements The relevant provisions in PCCA 1973, s. 3, are replaced by new provisions in PCCA 1973, sch. 1A, para. 5, which are, to all intents and purposes, identical.

(6) Treatment for Drug or Alcohol Dependency Conditions These provisions are innovative. They appear in para. 6 of the new sch. 1A to PCCA 1973, and create, for the first time, a statutory framework for the insertion into probation orders of conditions requiring an offender to undergo treatment for drug or alcohol dependency, where the court is satisfied that the dependency caused or contributed to the offence in respect of which the order is to be made and where the dependency is such as requires and may be susceptible to treatment (para. 6(1)). 'Dependency' is widely construed in the Act and includes, for these purposes, cases where the offender has 'a propensity towards the misuse of drugs or alcohol' (para. 6(9)). Prior to the 1991 Act, arrangements for treatment for drug or alcohol dependency were made informally, with the probation service informing the court of the availability of local facilities and the court inserting a requirement where it felt that it was appropriate to do so. The amended PCCA 1973 now imposes a scheme which is very similar to that which has been operating in respect of the insertion of a requirement for the treatment of a mental condition, whereby the court must ensure that arrangements have been made for the treatment specified, and for the reception of the offender at the place where the treatment is to be carried out (PCCA 1973, sch. 1A, para. 6(4)). As with the mental treatment condition, treatment for dependency shall be carried out at a place specified in the order (para. 6(3)) and may continue for the whole period of the probation order, or for such specific part of it as is specified by the court (para. 6(2)). Again, as with the mental treatment condition, the probation officer's normal supervision duties are effective only so far as is necessary for the purpose of revocation or amendment of the order (para. 6(5)).

It is quite clear from these provisions that the court is not confined to their use in cases where the offender has been convicted of an offence which was directly alcohol or drug related, or committed under the influence of alcohol or drugs. They could be used where the offender had committed theft in order to obtain money to purchase alcohol, or had committed assault in order to obtain drugs or had committed burglary or robbery in a chemist's shop in order to obtain drugs. Of course, in any of these cases, the court might properly regard the offence as being so serious that only a custodial sentence could be justified, and so a probation order would not be available in any event.

COMMUNITY SERVICE, COMBINATION AND CURFEW ORDERS

2.12 Community Service Orders

CJA 1991 has some impact on the law relating to community service orders. CJA 1991, s. 10 makes a number of changes to PCCA 1973, s. 14 and s. 15.

These are, first, the removal of the words 'instead of dealing with him in any other way' from PCCA 1973, s. 14(1). This allows the sentencer now to combine a community service order with another form of sentence on the same count. Most importantly, then, a community service order and a fine may now be combined (see, on the previous law, *Carnwell* (1978) 68 Cr App R 58). A community service order may now be combined with a probation order, but only in the form now to be known as a 'combination order', which is discussed in 2.13 below. The new arrangements for mixing the various community orders together are set out in table 2.1.

Second, the maximum number of hours of community service which may be imposed on a 16-year-old is increased from 120 to 240, to bring it into line with the available maximum for all other offenders given community service. This removes an unnecessary sentencing complication.

Third, there are some minor changes to the wording of PCCA 1973, s. 14(2) and s. 14(2A) (reports on availability of work and the offender's suitability for community service) necessitated by the new general provision in CJA 1991, s. 7(3), that the court obtain and consider a pre-sentence report before passing a sentence of community service.

Fourth, there is a minor rewording of the obligation of the person given a community service order to keep in touch with the relevant officer as and when required and to notify any change of address.

Under CJA 1991, s. 15(1), the Secretary of State is empowered to make rules for regulating the arrangements under PCCA 1973, s. 48 and sch. 3, in respect of persons who are subject to community service orders, for the performance of work under those orders and the responsibilities of the relevant probation officer. These rules may now be found in the relevant national standard, set out at pp. 324–31 of this *Guide*. According to the national standard:

> *The main purpose of a CSO is to reintegrate the offender into the community through:*
> ■ *positive and demanding unpaid work*, keeping to disciplined requirements; and
> ■ *reparation to the community* by undertaking socially useful work which, if possible, makes good damage done by offending.

2.13 Combination Orders

CJA 1991, s. 11, makes available to the courts for the first time the power to make a 'combination order' which is, in effect, a mixture of a probation order and a community service order. It should be noted that before making such an order the court must obtain and consider a pre-sentence report as to the offender's suitability for it (CJA 1991, s. 7(3)).

When found in this combination, the 'probation' part of the mix must be for not less than 12 months (as compared to six months in respect of a probation order standing alone) or more than three years, and the 'community service' part must be for not less than 40 hours and not more than 100 hours (as compared to 240 hours in respect of community service standing alone). The community service must be completed within 12 months of the making of the order (PCCA

1973, s. 15(2)). The offender must be of or over the age of 16 (this is now the equivalent age for the imposition of a probation order (see 2.7 above) and for the imposition of a community service order standing alone) and the offender must be convicted of an offence punishable with imprisonment, except murder (this is true of community service standing alone, but not true of a probation order standing alone, which is available in respect of any offence except murder). The court, before making such an order, must be satisfied that it is desirable in the interests of '(a) securing the rehabilitation of the offender; or (b) protecting the public from harm from him or preventing the commission by him of further offences'. These are the same criteria as now operate to justify the imposition of a probation order standing alone (see 2.8, above).

Insofar as a combination order is a mix of a probation order and a community service order, it may be questioned to what extent the various statutory provisions which apply to each of the constituent parts apply to the new order. CJA 1991, s. 11(3), states that part I of the 1973 Act shall apply to the probation element in a combination order as if it were a probation order and to the community service element as if it were a community service order. This must mean that the court is empowered to insert any of the additional requirements into the probation part of a combination order which it could have inserted into a probation order, provided only that their inclusion is not logically incompatible with the performance of the community service part of the combination order. This was certainly the intention, for in its White Paper (para. 4.16) the government explained that:

> It will be possible to combine community service either with basic probation supervision or with probation with specified activities. This new order should be particularly suitable for some persistent property offenders.

When imposing a combination order the court must comply with all the procedural requirements essential for both probation orders and community service orders.

The relevant provisions are further complicated by CJA 1991, s. 6(3), which, having regard to the possibility of the court making a combination order under s. 11, states that 'a community sentence shall not consist of or include both a probation order and a community service order'. The effect of this is to ensure that probation and community service can only be mixed together in the form of a combination order, and not otherwise. Neither s. 6(3) nor s. 11, however, would seem to prevent a court from sentencing an offender to community service on one count and placing him on probation in respect of the other. This was, of course, always possible under the pre-1991 law as confirmed in *Harkess* (1990) 12 Cr App R (S) 366, but now seems a little odd in the light of the new statutory arrangements.

The relevant national standard (see p. 331 for these) provides greater detail on the practical operation of combination orders. Paragraph 8 of the combination orders national standard suggests that:

> In practice, a combination order is likely to be most appropriate for an offender who has:

- committed an offence which is amongst the most serious for which a community sentence may be imposed;
- clearly identified areas of need that have contributed to the offending and which can be dealt with by probation supervision; and
- a realistic prospect of completing such an order, including both the probation and CS elements.

2.14 Curfew Orders (Not in Force)

New powers of the criminal courts to impose curfew orders on offenders of or over 16 years of age are introduced by CJA 1991, s. 12. Night restriction orders, as a condition of a supervision order, have been available since CJA 1982, and are contained in CYPA 1969, s. 12A(3)(b). It is arguable that a curfew order could have been imposed on an adult offender, prior to the 1991 Act, as a condition of a probation order, under PCCA 1973, s. 2(3). The so-called 'tracking' scheme, which has been operating in Leeds, and which attracted the favourable attention of the government in its White Paper, was based on this and had no separate authority. The White Paper comments, at para. 4.14, that 'no changes are needed to enable the courts to place requirements on an offender to inform the probation service in advance of his movements and activities during the day and not to depart from an agreed schedule of activities without informing the service'. The observations of the House of Lords in *Rogers* v *Cullen* [1982] 1 WLR 729, however, that no requirement should be made under s. 2(3) which would 'introduce a custodial or other element' into probation, meant that statutory authority was probably required for the imposition of a curfew upon an offender. CJA 1991, s. 12, makes a curfew order a community order in its own right, rather than a condition of a probation order. A court must obtain and consider a pre-sentence report before making a curfew order.

The curfew order may specify different places or different periods of curfew in respect of different days, but the curfew order cannot last for longer than six months from the date of the making of the order, and must not involve curfew periods of less than two hours' duration or more than 12 hours' duration in any one day during that period (s. 12(2)). The court must explain to the offender in ordinary language the effect of the order, the consequences of failure to comply with the requirements of the order, and the offender must consent to the making of the order (s. 12(5)). The order must name a person who is to be responsible for monitoring the offender's whereabouts during the curfew periods (s. 12(4)). It is as yet unclear whether this is a task to be performed by the probation service, which has grave misgivings about curfew orders in general, and the Act merely says that the Secretary of State will issue an order in due course to clarify the matter. The court must also have information about the place (or places) to be specified in the order, including information about the attitude of persons likely to be affected by the enforced presence there of the offender under curfew (s. 12(6)). No doubt this is one of the key issues to be addressed in the mandatory pre-sentence report. It will be possible to combine a curfew order with a range of other community orders and financial penalties. See further, table 2.1.

The government explained in the White Paper (para. 4.20) that it was *not* the purpose of curfew orders:

... to keep people at home for most of the day. The aim is to enable them to go to work, to attend training courses or probation centres, to carry out community service or to receive treatment for drug abuse. Curfews could be helpful in reducing some forms of crime, thefts of and from cars, pub brawls and other types of disorder. A curfew order could be used to keep people away from particular places, such as shopping centres or pubs, or to keep them at home in the evenings or at weekends.

It should be noted in this context that the courts have other powers to prevent offenders from frequenting specified places, under the Licensed Premises (Exclusion of Certain Persons) Act 1980, the Public Order Act 1986 (exclusion orders relating to designated football matches) and the Football Spectators Act 1989.

2.15 Electronic Monitoring (Not in Force)

A curfew order imposed under CJA 1991, s. 12 (see 2.14) may, in addition, include requirements for securing the electronic monitoring of the offender's whereabouts during the curfew periods specified in the order, under CJA 1991, s. 13. Electronic monitoring is clearly not a sentence or order in its own right, but solely a means of effective enforcement of a curfew order. The Act itself contains very few details of how the monitoring scheme is to operate. Section 13(2) states that the court can only impose such a requirement where it has been notified that a scheme for electronic monitoring exists in the relevant area and is otherwise satisfied that provision can be made. Again, it is as yet unclear whether the probation service is to be in operational control of electronic monitoring, and the Act merely provides that arrangements to be made in due course by the Secretary of State may include entering into contracts with other persons for the electronic monitoring by them of offenders' whereabouts.

Electronic monitoring of offenders is a totally new departure for the English criminal justice system and, of course, has attracted much interest and comment. Various schemes of electronic monitoring have been operational in the United States for some years, and the Home Office has been running three experimental schemes here, at Nottingham, North Tyneside and Tower Bridge, though in the context of reinforcing bail conditions rather than as part of the sentencing framework: see *Electronic Monitoring: The Trials and Their Results*, Home Office Research Study 120 (London: HMSO, 1990). The schemes all employed the 'active' system of monitoring, whereby a receiver-dialler attached to the telephone line to the offender's home relays signals from a transmitter which is worn on the offender's wrist or leg to a central computer which receives and stores the signals. The computer warns the operator if the signals stop, indicating that the person being monitored has exceeded the restricted area. The pilot schemes were not conspicuously successful, being characterised by a rather low take-up rate from the three courts and a high rate of equipment malfunction and violation. According to the researchers (at p. 64):

Most of those involved in the trials were not convinced of the success of monitoring as a condition of bail when used as an alternative to a custodial remand. They considered that if electronic monitoring had any future it was as just another condition of bail and not as an alternative to custody; or as part of a sentence where it might be used to monitor a curfew.

Although no final decision has yet been taken on electronic monitoring, in a Parliamentary answer given by Home Office Minister Michael Jack on 11 December 1992, it was explained that 'current spending priorities do not permit the early introduction of the arrangements under the CJA 1991, for monitoring curfew orders'.

BREACH, REVOCATION AND AMENDMENT

2.16   Enforcement of Community Orders: General

Section 14 and sch. 2 to the CJA 1991 reform the arrangements for enforcement (breach, revocation and amendment) of various community orders. Sections 5, 6, 16 and 17 of and sch. 2 to the PCCA 1973 are, in consequence, repealed. CJA 1991, sch. 2, applies to probation orders, community service orders, curfew orders and combination orders. It does not apply to supervision orders or attendance centre orders, as to which other changes are made (see 2.25 and 2.27 below). Nor does it apply to conditional discharges, which are not community orders, and as to which see 2.28. The national standards provide guidelines on the circumstances in which action for breach will be appropriate. The standard for probation orders, for example, says that 'breach action should normally be taken after no more than three instances of failure to comply with the order' (para. 26).

2.17   Breach of Community Orders: Magistrates' Courts

Breach of an order, in the sense of a failure to comply with any of the requirements of an order (rather than commission of a further offence during the currency of the order), means that a justice of the peace may issue a summons requiring the offender to appear or issue a warrant for the offender's arrest. The offender shall appear or be brought before a magistrates' court acting for the petty sessions area concerned.

If it is proved to the magistrates' court before which the offender is brought that he has failed without reasonable excuse to comply with the requirement or requirements of the probation order, community service order, curfew order or combination order, the court may take any one of four courses with him under CJA 1991, sch. 2, para. 3(1):

(a)   Impose a fine not exceeding £1,000 (this is an increase from a maximum of £400 under the previous law).

(b)   Make a community service order of not more than 60 hours (PCCA 1973, s. 6(10), had allowed for this possibility but was never brought into force). Where the offender is in breach of a community service order, the total number of hours under both orders must not exceed 240 hours (CJA 1991, sch. 2, para. 6(3)(b)).

(c)   Where the offender is in breach of a probation order, and it is a case where CJA 1982, s. 17, applies, make an attendance centre order.

(d)   Where the original order was made by a magistrates' court, the court may revoke the order and deal with him, for the offence in respect of which the order was made, in any manner in which it could deal with him if he had just been convicted by the magistrates' court of the offence.

Clearly the exercise of any of the options (a) to (c) is without prejudice to the continuation of the original order, but is in the form of a penalty for the failure to comply with the order's requirements. There would appear, in principle, to be no limit to the number of occasions upon which the court might exercise options (a) to (c) in respect of subsequent breaches of the same order by an offender, but, if the offender can be said to have 'wilfully and persistently failed to comply' with the order, para. 3(2)(b), discussed below, may be invoked. It may be noted that, as under the pre-1991 Act law, the court dealing with the breach has no power to extend the operational period of the original order (*Mullervy* (1986) 8 Cr App R (S) 41).

In dealing with an offender under para. 3(1)(d) the court, according to para. 3(2):

(a)   must take into account the extent to which the offender has complied with the requirements of the relevant order; and

(b)   may assume, in the case of an offender who has wilfully and persistently failed to comply with those requirements, that he has refused to give his consent to a community sentence which has been proposed by the court and requires that consent.

In exercising its powers under para. 3(1)(d) the original order will cease to have effect. There is perhaps an assumption that, once the court turns to para. 3(1)(d), the offender will now be facing a custodial sentence, but this is certainly not inevitable, particularly where, having regard to para. 3(2)(a), the offender has completed a substantial proportion of the order. Pre-1991 Act case law on breach of community service orders illustrates this point, and seems likely to remain valid after the Act. In *Paisley* (1979) 1 Cr App R (S) 196, six months' custody was varied to allow an offender's immediate release, where he had completed 61 of his 100 hours community service, although he had on three occasions failed to comply with the requirements of the order. Even if this cannot dissuade the court from using custody, it should properly serve to reduce the length of the term imposed. While the desirability of giving credit is most compelling where the offender has completed a large proportion of the hours, in *Whittingham* (1986) 8 Cr App R (S) 116 the Court of Appeal said that credit should have been given when one-third of the hours had been successfully completed. Hours of community service completed subsequently to the initiation of breach proceedings may still provide some mitigation (*Tebbutt* (1988) 10 Cr App R (S) 88).

Paragraph 3(2)(b) relates back to CJA 1991, s. 1(3), which empowers a court to pass a custodial sentence on an offender if he refuses to give his consent to a community sentence which is proposed and which requires that consent.

Paragraph 3(2)(b) deems the offender to have refused, in the light of his non-cooperation with the order. Again, there may be an assumption that the offender is then facing a custodial sentence, but that is not inevitable, given that the court 'may' make that assumption but is not bound so to do. While the CJA 1991 clearly reserves custody as the ultimate sanction for 'wilful and persistent' failure to comply with a community order, this should surely be seen as an exceptional course to take in the context of legislation which determines the key custody threshold to be the seriousness of the offence committed. According to the White Paper (para. 4.18):

> There is a careful balance to be drawn here. If the procedures are too lax, confidence in the effectiveness of these community penalties will be under- mined. On the other hand, if the procedures are too strict, for example, if they allow minor disciplinary infractions to be punished with custody, there is a danger that offenders who are otherwise not at risk of custody will find themselves in prison.

Where a custodial sentence is imposed consequent upon breach of a community sentence the court must, of course, have regard to the normal limitations upon the imposition of such sentences (e.g. the restriction on the maximum sentence which may be imposed by magistrates). But where custody is given for breach the sentencer is *not* required by the CJA 1991 to justify its imposition in accordance with s. 1(2)(a) or s. 1(2)(b) of the Act. The key issue is how far the offender can be said to have 'wilfully and persistently failed to comply' with the requirements of the community order.

It is suggested that the court, when dealing with breach, should always have regard to the seriousness of the original offence. See, for example, the pre 1991 Act case of *Simpson* [1983] Crim LR 820, where a custodial sentence imposed following a breach of a community service order was criticised by the Court of Appeal where it felt that custody had been passed in order to punish the offender, rather than to sentence him for the original offence. It is likely that case law will soon develop on the meaning to be ascribed to the term 'wilful and persistent' under the 1991 Act.

Where custody is imposed, allowance may be made for any period spent by the offender in custody before the community order was passed, though the extent of the allowance is a matter for judicial discretion (*Mackenzie* (1988) 10 Cr App R (S) 299).

2.18   Breach of Community Orders: Crown Court

Where the original probation order, community service order, curfew order or combination order was made by the Crown Court, a magistrates' court may commit the offender to the Crown Court to be dealt with there. The Crown Court has no jurisdiction to deal with breach of a community order unless the matter has first come before the magistrates' court and the offender is then sent to the Crown Court under CJA 1991, sch. 2, para. 3(3). The Crown Court's powers are identical to those of the magistrates' court, except, of course, under the equivalent power to para. 3(1)(d), which for the Crown Court is para.

4(1)(d), it is empowered to deal with the offender in any manner in which it could deal with him if he had just been convicted by or before the Crown Court of that offence. This means that there is little point in a magistrates' court committing an offender to the Crown Court to deal with breach of a Crown Court sentence unless the magistrates expect the Crown Court to revoke the order. The Crown Court, in dealing with an offender under para. 4(1)(d), must (by para. 4(2)) have regard to matters equivalent to those in para. 3(2). A person sentenced by the magistrates under para. 3(1)(d) may appeal to the Crown Court against sentence (para. 3(5)).

2.19 Revocation of Community Orders: General

A probation order, community service order, curfew order or combination order may be revoked for one of a number of reasons, to do with the offender's change of circumstances since the order was imposed, the most significant of which is the commission of a further offence during the currency of the order. A probation order may be revoked in the light of the probationer's good progress (CJA 1991, sch. 2, para. 7(3)). It should be noted that commission of a further offence forms the factual basis for revocation but does not constitute a breach of the order.

2.20 Revocation of Community Orders: Magistrates' Court

A magistrates' court acting for the petty sessions area concerned may revoke a probation order, community service order, curfew order or combination order or deal with the offender in some other way for the offence where, on the application of the offender or the responsible officer, it appears to be in the interests of justice to do so. Unless the offender is making the application, the court must summon the offender to appear or, if he does not appear, issue a warrant for his arrest. By CJA 1991, sch. 2, para. 7(2), the magistrates, if the order was made in a magistrates' court, may either under para. 7(2)(a)(i) simply revoke the order or under para. 7(2)(a)(ii) revoke it and deal with the offender for the offence in respect of which the order was made in any manner in which it could have dealt with him if he had just been convicted by the court. In the case of (ii), the magistrates must take into account the extent to which the offender has complied with the original order (this principle reflects pre-1991 law in *Anderson* (1982) 4 Cr App R (S) 252, and is parallel to that discussed in respect of breach at 2.38 above). If the original order was made in the Crown Court, the magistrates may commit him to Crown Court under para. 7(2)(b): see 2.21 below.

By sch. 2, para. 9, a magistrates' court, other than one acting for the petty sessions area concerned, which imposes a custodial sentence on an offender already under a community order may, if the community order was made by a magistrates' court, revoke it. Although the word 'may' is used in the statute, there would seem to be little option for the court here, since any community order will be incompatible with the custodial sentence. If the community order was made by a Crown Court, the magistrates' court should commit the offender to the Crown Court, together with relevant particulars of the case.

2.21 Revocation of Community Orders: Crown Court

Revocation of a probation order, community service order, curfew order or combination order will be an issue before the Crown Court where an offender under such an order is convicted of an offence by the Crown Court, or is committed by a magistrates' court to the Crown Court for sentence, or where the original order was made by the Crown Court and a magistrates' court commits the offender to the Crown Court under CJA 1991, sch. 2, para. 7(2)(b) or para. 9(2)(b). The powers of the Crown Court to revoke the order are identical to those of the magistrates' court, except, of course, under the equivalent power to para. 7(2)(a)(ii), which for the Crown Court is para. 8(2)(b), it is empowered to deal with the offender in any way in which it could deal with him if he had just been convicted by or before the Crown Court of that offence. In dealing with an offender under para. 8(2)(b) the Crown Court must take into account the extent to which the offender has complied with the requirements of the order (see further 2.20 above). A person sentenced by magistrates under para. 7(2)(a)(ii) may appeal to the Crown Court against sentence.

2.22 Amendment of Community Orders

In respect of any of the following powers, unless the offender is making application to the court himself, the court must normally summon the offender and, if he does not appear, may issue a warrant for his arrest (CJA 1991, sch. 2, para. 17(1); for the exceptions see para. 17(2)). The offender's consent to any amendments is also normally required (para. 17(1)). Paragraph 12 of sch. 2 allows for amendment of a probation order, community service order, curfew order or combination order to take account of a change in the offender's area of residence (this replaces, with some changes, PCCA 1973, s. 17(5) and (5A)). Paragraph 13 deals with the possibility of making amendment to the conditions or duration of a probation order or curfew order. Paragraph 14 relates to probation orders which contain a requirement of mental treatment or a condition of treatment for alcohol or drug dependence, for variation or cancellation of that requirement. Paragraph 15 allows for the extension of the period of a community service order beyond 12 months, for reasons such as ill-health or changed work commitments (this replaces PCCA 1973, s. 17, and see *Goscombe* (1981) 3 Cr App R (S) 61).

2.23 Reciprocal Enforcement of Community Orders

CJA 1991, sch. 3, deals with certain detailed matters relating to the transfer of community orders to Scotland or to Northern Ireland. Paragraphs 1 and 2 deal with probation orders made in England and Wales which are to be carried out in Scotland and Northern Ireland respectively. There are minor changes in terminology only. Since the new community order provisions in the Act do not apply to Scotland or Northern Ireland, the requirements relating to attendance at a 'probation centre' (see 2.11 above) are ineffective in Scotland, and in Northern Ireland should be taken to refer to a 'day centre' within the meaning of the Probation Act (Northern Ireland) 1950, s. 2B. Paragraphs 3 and 4 deal with community service orders made in England and Wales which are to be carried out in Scotland and Northern Ireland respectively. Paragraph 5 deals with the treatment of combination orders where they are to be carried out in Scotland. It has been possible to combine probation orders and community service orders in Scotland for some years now and so presumably the service arrangements for combination orders can fairly easily be put in place. Combination orders cannot, however, be carried out in Northern Ireland. Paragraphs 7 to 9 and paras 10 and 11 deal with community orders which are made by courts in Scotland and Northern Ireland respectively, which are to be carried out in England.

SUPERVISION ORDERS, ATTENDANCE CENTRE ORDERS AND DISCHARGES

2.24   Supervision Orders: General

The upper age limit for supervision orders is raised by CJA 1991, s. 68 and sch. 8, to include 17-year-olds, so that probation orders and supervision orders may now be imposed on 16 and 17-year-olds (see further 2.7 above). The Act makes no change to the already very complex statutory arrangements for the insertion of requirements into supervision orders (see *Blackstone's Criminal Practice 1993*, E8), but it does, by s. 66 and sch. 7, alter the law relating to variation, discharge and breach of supervision orders. These are now extremely complex. In each case a distinction must now be drawn between cases where the person being supervised is, at the time of variation, discharge or breach, under 18 years of age, in which case the relevant court is a youth court (see chapter 4), and cases where the person is 18, where the relevant court is an adult magistrates' court.

2.25   Supervision Orders: Discharge, Variation and Breach

As far as discharge and variation are concerned, the relevant court may, if it thinks it appropriate, on application of the supervisor or the person being supervised, make an order discharging the supervision order or varying it by cancelling any requirement included in it made under CYPA 1969, s. 12 (the basic order, which may contain a residence requirement and/or 'discretionary intermediate treatment'), s. 12A ('stipulated intermediate treatment'), s. 12AA (residence requirement in local authority accommodation, inserted by Children Act 1989 and brought into force from 14 October 1991), s. 12B (requirement of medical treatment), s. 12C (compulsory education) or s. 18(2)(b), or by inserting into it any provision which could have been included by the court when it made the order. After a period of three months has elapsed since the making of the order, however, no variation can be made to insert a fresh (as opposed to replacement) s. 12B medical treatment requirement or to insert a s. 12A(3)(b) 'night restriction' requirement. In relation to a s. 12B requirement, the relevant medical practitioner may also make a report to the supervisor recommending cancellation or variation of that requirement.

    In respect of breach of the order, if the person being supervised has not yet reached the age of 18 and it appears to the youth court that the person has failed to comply with the requirements of s. 12, s. 12A, s. 12AA, s. 12C or s. 18(2)(b) of the CYPA 1969, then, whether or not the youth court also varies or discharges the order, it may either order payment of a fine not exceeding £1,000 or, subject to CYPA 1969, s. 16A(1), make an attendance centre order. If the person being supervised is 18, and it appears to the magistrates' court that he has failed to comply with any of the above-mentioned requirements, the court may, if it also discharges the supervision order, impose any punishment on him, apart from a sentence of detention in a young offender institution, which it could have imposed if it had then the power to try him for the offence for which he was given the supervision order and had convicted him (see further the new CYPA 1969, s. 15(5), inserted by CJA 1991, sch. 7, for the case where the court has no power to try that offence). If the breach is in respect of a failure to comply with a s. 12A(3)(a) requirement (directing the person to participate in specified activities), the relevant court may, if the court which made the supervision order made a statement under s. 12D(1) (to the effect that it was making the supervision order in lieu of a custodial sentence), if it also discharges the order, impose any punishment on him, including a sentence of detention in a young offender institution, which it could have imposed if it had then the power to try him for the offence for which he was given the supervision order and had convicted him (see further the new CYPA 1969, s. 15(5), for the case where the court has no power to try that offence).

When punishing in any case of breach of a supervision order, the relevant court must take into account the extent to which the person supervised has complied with the requirements of the supervision order (new CYPA 1969, s. 15(8)).

2.26   Attendance Centre Orders: General

CJA 1991, s. 67, makes two amendments to the existing arrangements for the making of attendance centre orders. First, by s. 67(1), CJA 1982, s. 17(3), which prevented the passing of an attendance centre on an offender with previous custodial experience, is abolished. This would seem to be in tune with the emphasis throughout the Act on sentencing on the basis of the seriousness of the current offence, rather than the offender's previous convictions. Second, also by s. 67(1), the maximum number of hours which may be ordered in respect of a 16-year-old is raised to 36, in line with the maximum for 17-year-olds.

2.27   Attendance Centre Orders: Discharge, Variation and Breach

CJA 1991, s. 67, also makes changes to CJA 1982, s. 18, which is the provision governing discharge, variation and breach of attendance centre orders. The only change to the arrangements for discharge of such an order is, by the insertion of a new subsection (4A) into CJA 1982, s. 18, that the power to discharge an attendance centre order includes power to deal with the offender, for the offence in respect of which the order was made, in any other way in which he could have been dealt with for that offence by the court which made the attendance centre order. By CJA 1991, sch. 12, para. 21, this new power shall not apply in relation to an attendance centre order made before the commencement of s. 67. The only change to the rules relating to variation of an order is to widen the court's power to substitute a different attendance centre for the one originally specified in the order, under CJA 1982, s. 18(6)(b). Previously this could only be done if the offender was changing his residence, but now it may be done in any circumstances upon application by the offender or the officer in charge of the attendance centre specified in the order. Section 19 of CJA 1982 deals with breach of attendance centre orders and attendance centre rules. The first change introduced by CJA 1991, s. 67 is to provide the court with an additional power in respect of breach, which is, without prejudice to the continuation of the order, to impose a fine not exceeding level 3 on the standard scale (CJA 1991, s. 67(4) and (5)). Two further changes are made by CJA 1991, s. 67(6), by insertion of a new subsection (5A) into CJA 1982, s. 19. The first is that the court, when dealing with the breach under powers given in CJA 1982, s. 19(3)(a) or s. 19(5), and acting to revoke the order and deal with the offender for the offence in respect of which the order was made in any other manner in which he could have been dealt with for that offence, must take into account the extent to which the offender has complied with the requirements of the attendance centre order. The second is that, again in respect of s. 19(3)(a) or s. 19(5), the court may assume, in the case of an offender who has 'wilfully and persistently failed to comply' with the attendance centre order, that he has refused to give his consent to the order. This entails that the court may then deal with the offender by way of a custodial sentence: see CJA 1991, s. 1(3), and the discussion in 1.8 and 2.17 above.

2.28 Absolute and Conditional Discharge

Although discharges are not community orders, CJA 1991 makes some changes with respect to them, and it is appropriate to deal with them here. The changes are occasioned by the overhaul of the law relating to probation and by the fact that, under PCCA 1973 probation orders and discharges were the subject of a number of common statutory provisions. The effect of CJA 1991, s. 8(3), is to replace the pre-existing provisions on absolute and conditional discharge in PCCA 1973. Sections 7 and 9 of that Act are repealed and ss. 8 and 13, insofar as they refer to discharges, also cease to have effect. The new arrangements for discharges may be found in CJA 1991, sch. 1, part I, and they will take their new place in PCCA 1973 as s. 1A to s. 1C. In fact the changes to the law are relatively minor.

Subsections (1) to (4) of the new s. 1A of PCCA 1973 duplicate the wording of PCCA 1973, s. 7(1) to (4), with the sole change being the removal of the words 'and that a probation order is not appropriate' from s. 7(1). This change reflects the new status of the probation order as a sentence in its own right (see 2.8 above). The new s. 1B deals with breach of a conditional discharge, by commission of a further offence. It largely re-enacts the wording of PCCA 1973, s. 8, although with removal of all reference to probation orders. (For breach of probation orders see 2.16 and 2.17 above.) In line with provisions elsewhere in CJA 1991, under the new s. 1B(9) of PCCA 1973 (conditional discharge imposed on a young person for an offence triable only on indictment in the case of an adult) the relevant offenders now include 17-year-olds.

The new s. 1C of PCCA 1973 re-enacts, with some amendments, the repealed PCCA 1973, s. 13, which limits the circumstances in which a discharge qualifies as a 'conviction'. Probation orders, in line with their new status, are excluded from the ambit of the new s. 1C (see 2.8 above). In line with provisions elsewhere in CJA 1991, the new s. 1C(2) of PCCA 1973 (exception where an offender aged 17 or over is conditionally discharged but subsequently sentenced for the offence) now does not apply to 17-year-olds.

Chapter Three
Financial Orders

Sections 17 to 24 of CJA 1991 (as amended) make changes in the system of imposition of fines. Originally this included a 'unit fine' system for calculating fine levels in magistrates' courts. Unit fines were, however, abolished by the CJA 1993, s. 65 and sch. 3. Section 24 provides for sums owed by offenders in fines and compensation to be recovered by deduction at source from their income support payments. The standard scale of fines is increased and the maximum amount of compensation which may be ordered by a magistrates' court is also increased.

FINES

3.1 Fines: the Standard Scale

Section 17 of CJA 1991 amends the standard scale of fines which is contained in CJA 1982, s. 37(2), and in the Criminal Procedure (Scotland) Act 1975, s. 289G(2).

The relevant maxima increase as follows:

Level 1	from	£50	to	£200
Level 2	from	£100	to	£500
Level 3	from	£400	to	£1,000
Level 4	from	£1,000	to	£2,500
Level 5	from	£2,000	to	£5,000

None of these changes applies in relation to offences committed before the commencement of s. 17. The Home Secretary has power under MCA 1980, s. 143, as amended by CJA 1982, s. 48, to alter by order the amount of each level on the standard scale to take account of changes in the value of money since the making of a previous order. The present levels were set by the Criminal Penalties etc. (Increase) Order 1984, which came into operation on 1 May 1984. The latest increases have been introduced via s. 17 of CJA 1991 rather than in accordance with the Home Secretary's power because they represent more than a simple inflationary increase.

Other important changes are:

(a) Where an offender has been summarily convicted of an offence triable either way, the maximum fine increases, by s. 17(2)(c), from £2,000 to £5,000.

(b)   Where an offender under the age of 18 is fined in a magistrates' court, the maximum fine available, whether the offence is triable on indictment or only summarily, is increased by s. 17(2)(a), from £400 to £1,000.

(c)   Where an offender under the age of 14 is fined in a magistrates' court, the maximum fine available, whether the offence is triable on indictment or only summarily, is increased by s. 17(2)(b), from £100 to £250.

None of these changes (a) to (c) applies in relation to offences committed before the commencement of s. 17. Note that in respect of (b) and (c) above, there continues to be no limit on the fine which may be imposed by the Crown Court upon a juvenile. For changes to the provisions in CYPA 1933, s. 55, whereby a parent or guardian may be ordered to pay fines and compensation orders imposed upon a juvenile, see chapter 4.

(d)   There are increases in two general provisions relating to fines in magistrates' courts:

(i)   The fine available under MCA 1980, s. 33(1)(a) (criminal damage offences triable either way, but to be tried summarily in pursuance of MCA 1980, s. 22, if the value involved is small), is increased from £1,000 to £2,500.

(ii)   The maximum fine available on summary conviction where a statute provides no express power to fine, under MCA 1980, s. 34(3)(b), is increased from £400 to £1,000.

(e)   There are increases in respect of a range of offences relating to contempt of court, refusal to give evidence and neglect of a witness summons. The details may be found in sch. 4, part I.

(f)   The fines available in respect of a range of offences relating to whaling and fisheries conservation are increased on summary conviction to the statutory maximum: for details see sch. 4, part III.

No transitional provisions appear to be provided in respect of changes (d) to (f) above. In *Penwith Justices, ex parte Hay, Pender and Perkes* (1979) 1 Cr App R (S) 265, however, it was held that legislation which increases maximum penalties is not to be applied to offences committed before the legislation takes effect, unless the contrary intention is clear.

(g)   There is clarification that the maximum penalty available under CJA 1982, s. 70(1)(b)(i) (sleeping rough etc. under Vagrancy Act 1824, s. 4) is a fine not exceeding level 1 on the standard scale (CJA 1991, s. 26(5)).

3.2   Historical Note: Unit Fines

In terms of practical effect upon the criminal courts, the move to unit fines, ushered in by the CJA 1991, was very significant. Prior to the Act, two main sentencing principles governed the use of the fine. The first was that the level of the fine should reflect the seriousness of the offence (the so-called 'tariff'). The second principle was that, where the offender did not have the means to meet that sum, the fine could be reduced accordingly, to take account of ability to pay. On the other hand, it was said by the Court of Appeal to be wrong for a sentencer to increase the fine levied upon a relatively better off offender, who might be able to pay the tariff fine quite easily. The authorities usually cited in support of the last point were *Messana* (1981) 3 Cr App R (S) 88 and *Fairbairn* (1980) 2 Cr App R (S) 315, though in neither case was the principle very clearly stated.

Section 18 of CJA 1991 introduced a 'unit fine' system, which operated in magistrates' courts (but not the Crown Court). The basic idea was that, rather than offenders being fined a particular sum which was seen as being appropriate for the seriousness of that offence, offence seriousness was graded in terms of a number of penalty units. The value of the unit varied according to the individual offender's ability to pay. The unit fine system tried to achieve 'equality of impact' amongst offenders by fining offenders a certain proportion of their disposable or 'spare' income. So, under this system, for a given offence, a poor person paid proportionately less but a rich person paid proportionately more.

Schemes similar to this have been operational in other countries for several years, the best known being the Scandinavian 'day-fine' system (in place in Sweden since 1931). Currently Austria, Denmark, Finland, France, Greece, Germany, Portugal and Sweden have fully operational schemes (for further information see B. Gibson, *Unit Fines*, Waterside Press, 1990). Similar fine arrangements are in place in some areas of the United States. There had been debate over the introduction of such a scheme in this country at least since 1970, when the Advisory Council on the Penal System supported its introduction (ACPS, *Non-Custodial and Semi-Custodial Penalties*, HMSO, 1970), but the UK government was cautious in adopting the idea. In 1988 the Home Office initiated a 'unit fines' experiment in four magistrates' courts (Basingstoke, Bradford, Swansea and Teesside) and, in the light of favourable results from those, the government committed itself, in the White Paper, to the introduction of the scheme. Evaluation by the Home Office (D. Moxon, M. Sutton and C. Hedderman, *Unit Fines: Experiments in Four Courts*, Home Office Research and Planning Unit Paper 59, 1990) showed that, by using a simple means form which was completed by defendants before sentence, courts were able to obtain sufficient information about the means of offenders without undue difficulty or delay. The unit fine system seemed to produce fines that were pitched at a more realistic level than before. On average, fines were paid off more quickly than before, and there was a significant drop in the proportion of offenders who were ultimately imprisoned for default. All the pilot schemes adopted minimum and maximum figures which could be ascribed to a unit in any case, typically ranging between £5 and £25 per unit. The minimum figure was meant to ensure that in no case could the actual level of a fine appear derisory, and the maximum figure was meant to ensure that well-off offenders were not subject to enormous fines for rather minor offences.

Under the statutory scheme introduced in the CJA 1991 the lower and upper limits were fixed at £4 and £100, representing a considerable increase in the upper limit which had been agreed by the pilot courts. The move to a higher upper limit of course coincided with substantial increases in the values of standard fine levels 1 to 5. Level 5, for instance, was increased by the CJA 1991 from £2,000 to £5,000 (see 3.1). The combined effect of these two changes, not surprisingly in retrospect, was to result in very high unit fines for offenders in a middle income bracket, who had £100 or more disposable income available per week.

For the purposes of assessment of means the offender's disposable income was regarded as being his net weekly income, from which various standard allowances, fixed locally and reviewed annually, were deducted. The unit value was then taken to be one third of the resulting figure. The aim was to achieve a reasonably accurate overall assessment of the offender's ability to pay. Detailed arrangements were set out in the Magistrates' Courts (Unit Fines) Rules 1992 (SI 1991/1856). These required that the clerk to the justices for each petty sessions provided 'means inquiry forms' for completion by all defendants. Rule 4(2) relieved the court of the obligation to make inquiry into the offender's means if the offender consented to be fined at the maximum unit value without further inquiry being made. In effect, the offender would agree at the outset that his spare income amounted to at least £100 per week. If the offender failed to respond to a summons, or was being sentenced in his absence under MCA 1980, s. 11, or had pleaded guilty by post under MCA 1980, s. 12, or, even if present in court, the offender had refused to answer questions relating to his means, the magistrates were entitled to fine on the basis of the maximum unit value of £100.

When passing sentence, the court, as well as announcing the total value of the fine imposed, was required to state in open court the number of units which it had imposed upon the offender, and their value in his or her case. The relevant figures had to be entered in the court register, so that the court's reasoning was clear in the event of a subsequent means inquiry or appeal against the sentence.

There were certain exceptions to the unit fine system in magistrates' courts. Unit fines were restricted to 'individuals' dealt with in that court (thereby excluding corporations). Two special cases were anticipated where it seemed likely that the unit fine computation would result in a very low fine. The first was in respect of fixed penalty offences (within the meaning of the RTOA 1988, part III, including such offences as speeding). If the fixed penalty was *higher* than the calculated unit fine, the CJA 1991 allowed the court to increase the fine to the level of the fixed penalty. No special provision was made for cases in which the fixed penalty was *lower* than the calculated unit fine, so in that case it was clear that it was the unit fine which must be paid. In 1991, before the unit fine system came generally into operation, 5.6 million £40 fixed penalty notices were issued. Fines for equivalent offences imposed in the magistrates' courts averaged £60. Following the implementation of the CJA 1991, the Automobile Association reported that the average speeding fine had increased to £400. Another exception to the unit fine scheme was in cases of offenders installing or using a television set without a licence, an offence under the Wireless Telegraphy Act 1949, s. 1. Here the unit fine could be increased 'by an amount not exceeding the sum which would have been payable on the issue of such a licence'. Obviously this was to avoid the imposition of a unit fine which was less than the cost of the licence.

The unit fine system received much publicised criticism soon after it came into effect, mainly because apparently very high fines were being imposed for rather trivial offences. These attracted great press interest. In one case an unemployed man, who had failed to complete the means assessment form, was fined £1,200 for dropping litter (throwing a crisp bag out of the window). In another case a man of middle income who was marginally over the drink-drive limit was fined £1,500 while another who was more than twice the limit, but was in receipt of State benefits, was fined £104. In a third case a motorist, who exceeded his parking permit by 20 minutes and then ignored the means assessment form which he was sent, was fined £700. Another person was fined £500 after leaving his car on double yellow lines for 30 minutes because his radiator had overheated.

There seem to have been two main problems with the way the unit fine system was implemented in England and Wales. The first, as indicated above, is that at a time of economic recession the government made a serious error in at the same time increasing the maximum fine levels in magistrates' courts and fixing the maximum value of a unit at £100 (rather than at a figure much nearer the £25 arrived at by the pilot courts). The second problem was a failure to think through the proper relation between unit fines and fixed penalties. For an offence like speeding the driver, unless substantially in excess of the limit, will generally be offered at the roadside the opportunity to pay a fixed penalty of £40. This penalty is not a conviction, and no court appearance is involved, but the driver's licence is endorsed with penalty points. The driver simply writes a cheque for the amount and sends it to the clerk at the relevant magistrates' court. If a driver was well in excess of the speed limit and a prosecution was brought, or a driver decided to contest the case, and was convicted, the operation of the unit fine system meant that he faced a much higher fine. In April 1993 the Automobile Association issued advice to its members stating that they would be ill-advised to contest speeding and other similar cases.

In the face of criticism over how the unit fine scheme was working, the Home Secretary's initial response was to consider varying the unit values in the Act. On 30 April 1993, *The Times* reported that Mr Clarke 'supports the principle of linking fines to an offender's disposable income, and has told colleagues that the system can be made to work'. Then, after a meeting with the Magistrates' Association, a second approach was adopted. Advice was issued to magistrates on 4 May 1993 that if, after computation of the unit fine in accordance with the CJA 1991 'the value of the unit appears to be inappropriately high, taking into account all the circumstances [the magistrates] should look again at the value'. This advice was condemned by the Justices' Clerks' Society three days later as 'unsound, misleading, and in consequence perhaps illegal' (*The Times*, 8 May 1993). Then, on 4 May, in the face of increasing government unpopularity, and the embarrassment of a by-election defeat at Newbury, the political climate was such that the Home Secretary announced in a statement to Parliament the complete abolition of the unit fine system. The statutory scheme had been fully operational for only seven months.

3.3 Fines after the CJA 1993

The system of unit fines has been completely abolished by CJA 1993, s. 65(1) and sch. 3, and has been replaced by a pair of broad general principles, in a substituted s. 18 of the CJA 1991, relating to the use of the fine. These are very similar (though not identical) to the principles which existed in the law prior to the unit fine changes. The new s. 18 applies to magistrates' courts and to the

Crown Court, and has the effect of bringing back into line the relevant sentencing principles applicable to both. Unit fines did not apply to Crown Court sentencing though the Crown Court was required to use them in a number of circumstances, such as when dealing with an appeal against sentence imposed in a magistrates' court. The detail of the changes made to the system of fines by CJA 1993 is as follows:

(a) By CJA 1993, s. 65(1), a new CJA 1991, s. 18, is substituted and, by s. 65(2) of the 1993 Act, s. 19 of the 1991 Act is repealed.

(b) Further amendments to the 1991 Act are brought about by sch. 3 to the 1993 Act. Section 20(1) is substituted (and replaced by four subsections numbered (1) to (1C)), s. 20(2) and (3) are amended and s. 20(5) is repealed. Section 21 (remission of fines) is substituted and s. 22 (unit fine default) is repealed.

(c) Various consequential amendments are required to remove references to unit fines made in other legislation, namely, the CYPA 1969, the PCCA 1973, the MCA 1980, the Contempt of Court Act 1981 and the CJA 1991. These amendments are achieved by the CJA 1993, sch. 3, para. 6.

The general fining principles contained in the substituted s. 18 are:

(a) Before fixing the amount of any fine, the court *shall inquire* into the financial circumstances of the offender (s. 18(1)), and *shall take into account* those financial circumstances (s. 18(3)), so far as they are known, or appear to the court. Prior to the CJA 1991 magistrates' courts were required by MCA 1980, s. 35, to have regard to means when fixing fine levels but fresh statutory authority is now required since s. 35 was repealed by the CJA 1991. In taking account of an offender's means, the courts will have power, under a new s. 20(1) of the CJA 1991 (substituted by CJA 1993, sch. 3, para. 2) to make a 'financial circumstances order' against the offender. According to the new s. 20(1C), such an order is 'an order requiring him to give to the court, within such period as may be specified in the order, such a statement of his financial circumstances as the court may require'. The financial circumstances order looks rather similar to, but supersedes, the 'means inquiry form' introduced by the original s. 20(1) but which was applicable only to unit fines and, hence, magistrates' courts. The old s. 20(2) and (3) are amended accordingly, so that references to means inquiry forms now become references to financial circumstances orders. Two points arise from this. First, it remains to be seen how much difference this change of name will actually make to magistrates' courts' practice. Presumably new delegated legislation will have to be produced, giving details of how financial circumstances orders are to be made, and what information should be provided by the defendant, since the delegated legislation issued under the original provisions related, of course, to unit fines (Magistrates' Courts (Unit Fines) Rules 1992). Will the same sort of detailed information still be required? Second, it must be remembered that the new orders are applicable to the Crown Court as well as to magistrates' courts. Various Court of Appeal decisions in the past have stressed the importance of Crown Court judges having regard to an offender's means before imposing a fine, but the onus was always on the offender to furnish this evidence, with little obligation on the sentencer to make his own inquiries (*Higgins* (1988) 10 Cr App R (S) 144). If the making of financial circumstances orders is to become the norm in the Crown Court (and the language of the new s. 18(1) is mandatory) then this will involve some shift in Crown Court practice, requiring that Crown Court sentencers seek out more information on this issue than hitherto.

(b) The amount of the fine *shall be such* as, in the opinion of the court, 'reflects the seriousness of the offence' (s. 18(2)) and 'take[s] into account the circumstances of the case' (s. 18(3)). The original s. 18 contained specific reference, in s. 18(3), to the requirement that the court take account of all the circumstances of the offence, including any aggravating or mitigating factors relevant to the offence. No such specific direction is given in the new s. 18, but it may perhaps be inferred that the court, in assessing seriousness, should have regard to any mitigating or aggravating factors which relate to the seriousness of the offence (as s. 3(3) requires in relation to custodial sentences and s. 7(1) requires in relation to community sentences) and should have regard to the existence of previous convictions and/or the offender's response to previous sentences (by virtue of the new s. 29(1)). The court then may, in its discretion, also have regard to any relevant matter in personal mitigation (s. 28).

The effect of these changes is to replace a methodical (critics would say, mechanical) scheme of fine determination in magistrates' courts with a more flexible one. It may be objected that the two principles now set out in s. 18(1), applicable to magistrates' courts and to the Crown Court, are in conflict with each other. Dr Thomas has commented on 'the internal contradiction in the section; either the fine is to reflect the seriousness of the offence, or it is to reflect the financial circumstances of the offender; it can hardly do both' (*Sentencing News*, 27 July 1993). Certainly there will be many cases where both objectives cannot be fully achieved. This fact makes a mockery of the use of the word 'shall' in all the first three subsections of s. 18, language redolent of the requirement in s. 6(2) of the 1991 Act (sentence to reflect *both* 'suitability' and 'seriousness' in community sentences). It is submitted, however, that s. 18 can be understood in a common-sense way. The courts should apply the criteria sequentially, *first* by gauging the seriousness of the offence (including all relevant aggravating and mitigating factors) and then *second* by adjusting the level of the fine to take account of the offender's means. This is, in fact, the same series of steps which was required by the discipline of the unit fines system. If this suggested approach is the correct one, then it would have been better if the order of the subsections in s. 18 had reflected it clearly. 'Seriousness' should *always* be considered first. The danger of taking the offender's means into account before the seriousness of the offence (which is certainly one possible reading of s. 18) is that it leads to the kind of error which was made in *Markwick* (1953) 37 Cr App R 125 (where a well-off offender escaped a deserved custodial sentence because he had the means to pay a substantial fine) and in *Reeves* (1972) 56 Cr App R 366 (where an impecunious offender was sent to prison because he did not have the means to pay a fine). The principle of addressing offence seriousness before taking account of means was well understood in the pre 1991 Act cases. In *Fairbairn* (1980) 2 Cr App R (S) 315 Glidewell J said that 'in principle the amount of the fine should be determined in relation to the gravity of the offence, and then, and only then, should the offender's means be considered to determine whether he has the capacity to pay such an amount'. See also *Jamieson* (1975) 60 Cr App R 318. A case which, on the face of it, seems to state a contrary proposition is *Rizvi* (1979) 1 Cr App R (S) 307 but, it is suggested, that case is properly understood as saying merely that information about an offender's means should be taken into account at the time when the level of the fine is being considered, rather than later, when the size and duration of instalments are determined.

One of the driving forces behind the eventual move to unit fines in magistrates' courts was the consistent failure of sentencers to adjust fine levels to take proper account of means. There is, of course, a real danger that with the move back to a more flexible fine system there will be a return to old ways, and a consequent rise in fine default and commitment to prison. In the Parliamentary debates on the 1993 Act reforms Mr Robert Maclennan predicted yet more amending legislation to the fining provisions 'when the prisons are filled, as, predictably, they will be, with those who have defaulted because fines of unsuitable severity in comparison with their income were imposed and could not be paid' (Parliamentary Debates (Hansard), 6th ser., vol. 227, col. 917, 29 June 1993). An intriguing possibility, which might help to guard against this, is that magistrates' courts might choose to continue with their own informal unit fine arrangements. Several courts chose to introduce their own unit fine schemes following the success of the pilot studies and prior to the implementation of the CJA 1991. This was done under the inherent jurisdiction of the magistrates' courts to manage their own affairs, rather than under any statutory authority (see Gibson, *Unit Fines*, p. 90). There seems to be nothing in the CJA 1993 which would prohibit courts from continuing with this, and individual benches or groups of benches might see value in doing so. In the Parliamentary debates on the CJA 1993 Home Office Minister Mr David Maclean said that he had 'no objection to magistrates adopting an informal unit model if they find it helpful in setting a fine' (Parliamentary Debates (Hansard), Commons, 6th ser., vol. 227, col. 915, 29 June 1993).

The new s. 18(4) of the CJA 1991 empowers a court in three different situations, where it finds that 'it has insufficient information to make a proper determination of the financial circumstances of the offender' to 'make such determination as it thinks fit'. The three situations are:

(a)   where the offender has been convicted in his absence in a magistrates' court in pursuance of MCA 1980, s. 11 or s. 12,

(b)   where an offender has failed to comply with a financial circumstances order made by a magistrates' court or the Crown Court, or has otherwise failed to cooperate with the court in its inquiry into his means, and

(c)   where, in the magistrates' court or Crown Court, the parent or guardian of an offender (who is a child or young person) has similarly failed to comply.

These provisions bear similarity to the various exceptional cases covered in the original s. 18(7) and (8). However, in the new provision, there is no reference to the particular problem of the correlation between fines and fixed penalties for motoring offences which, as we have seen, was a defect which emerged starkly when unit fines were operational. The 1993 Act provides no solution to this problem. Magistrates will, it seems, simply be required to exercise their discretion appropriately to avoid the more stark disparities between fines and fixed penalties for the same conduct.

The new s. 18(5) explicitly retains the principle which was integral to unit fines and which was introduced to the Crown Court by CJA 1991, s. 19(2), that the level of a fine may be decreased *or increased* to take proper account of the offender's means. Prior to the CJA 1991 there was some authority, in *Messana* (1981) 3 Cr App R (S) 88 and in *Fairbairn* (1980) 2 Cr App R (S) 315, that it was inappropriate to increase fines on the better-off. It is now clear that those cases are wrong on the point, and that to this extent 'equality of impact', a principle central to unit fines, has been retained in the new law. Since s. 19 has been repealed by the CJA 1993, the relevant statutory authority for this rule, in magistrates' courts and in the Crown Court, is now CJA 1991, s. 18(5).

3.4 Imprisonment in Default

Under the original fining provisions in the CJA 1991, cases of default in payment of unit fines were specifically covered by s. 22 of the Act. That section had the effect of tying the terms to be served in default to the number of units comprised in the fine (rather than the total sum represented by the fine). Default in other cases (Crown Court fines, and fines imposed in magistrates' courts which were not unit fines, such as fines on corporations) continued to be governed by the relevant tables in PCCA 1973, s. 31(3A) and MCA 1980, sch. 4 (though these tables were slightly amended by CJA 1991, s. 23). Section 22 of the CJA 1991 is now, of course, repealed by CJA 1993 as part of the process of abolition of unit fines. Henceforth *all* periods of custody to be served in consequence of fine default are now to be found in the two relevant tables as amended by s. 23 of the CJA 1991. This is despite the fact that s. 23 still bears the now rather misleading marginal note 'Default in other cases' in the 1991 Act.

Section 23 amends the maximum periods to be served in default, but only those where the amount of the fine imposed does not exceed £5,000. This means that in the table in PCCA 1973, s. 31(3A), the lower six bands are compressed into five bands. The purpose of the change is to bring the table into line with the new maximum amounts of fines on the standard scale. These changes, by s. 23(2), also have effect in the equivalent legislation in Scotland, amending the Criminal Procedure (Scotland) Act 1975, s. 407(1A). It should be remembered that in England the actual terms to be served in default are subject to the new arrangements for early release. For prisoners serving a default term of less than one year, for example, there will be unconditional release after one half of the sentence has been served (CJA 1991, s. 37(2)). For details of these new arrangements see chapter 5.

The curious provision in s. 23(3) seems to have the effect of saving from repeal the Administration of Justice Act 1970, s. 41(8), which allows the Crown Court to specify an extended period of imprisonment in default of payment of a compensation order. This subsection was reformulated by CJA 1988, s. 106 and then, apparently, repealed by mistake by sch. 16 to that Act.

3.5 Compensation Orders

By CJA 1991, s. 17(3)(a) and sch. 4, part I, the maximum compensation order which may be ordered by a magistrates' court in respect of each offence is increased from £2,000 to £5,000, by amendment of MCA 1980, s. 40(1). This increase does not apply in relation to offences committed before the commencement of s. 17. Prior to 1991 there was a well known 'rule of thumb' that, where the loss occasioned to the victim was clearly in excess of £2,000, the magistrates should refuse jurisdiction. This change, then, together with the increase in the standard scale for fines, will have some impact in retaining criminal cases within the jurisdiction of magistrates' courts which otherwise might have resulted in committal to the Crown Court for trial. The amendment to s. 40(1) also has the effect of increasing the total amount of compensation which may be ordered by a magistrates' court in respect of offences taken into consideration. The total amount ordered must not exceed the maximum which could be ordered for the offences in respect of which the offender has been formally charged and convicted.

For changes to the provisions in CYPA 1933, s. 55, whereby a parent, guardian or local authority may be ordered to pay fines and compensation imposed upon a juvenile, see chapter 4. For the new power to recover orders for compensation from an offender's income support, see 3.6 below. The sentencing combination of suspended sentence plus compensation order, which was always permissible, is now positively encouraged by the Act: see 1.30 above for discussion.

3.6   Recovery of Fines and Compensation from Income Support

The controversial provision in CJA 1991, s. 24, now augmented by the Fines (Deductions from Income Support) Regulations 1992 (SI 1992/2182), provides for the deduction from an offender's income support payments of certain sums in respect of a fine or compensation order. The orders are widely defined for these purposes (s. 24(3) and (4)). Enforcement of fines and compensation orders, including those made in the Crown Court, is a task already undertaken by magistrates' courts: see MCA 1980, s. 75 to s. 91, and the Attachment of Earnings Act 1971.

The law already allows for deductions from income support for a whole range of reasons, such as:

(a)   housing-related charges, including mortgage payments, rent, fuel costs and water charges (Social Security (Claims and Payments Regulations) 1987 (SI 1987/1968), sch. 9),

(b)   community charge arrears (Community Charges (Deductions from Income Support) (No. 2) Regulations 1990 (SI 1990/545)),

(c)   recovery of overpayments made by the DSS, whether through claimant's fraud or otherwise (Social Security (Payments on Account, Overpayments and Recovery) Regulations 1988 (SI 1988/664), regs 15 to 17), and

(d)   social fund loans.

Some claimants are paid a reduced rate of income support, notably those who are considered to be voluntarily unemployed. Deductions may still be made from reduced-rate benefit. The thinking behind the scheme may be seen from the news release on 29 October 1990 issued by John Patten, then Minister of State at the Home Office:

Of course the level of the fine should reflect a person's disposable income and their ability to pay. But recent research has shown that of those people imprisoned for non-payment of fines about 90 per cent were largely dependent on State benefit. That is why, as part of our review of the court fine system, we have decided that magistrates should have another option apart from imprisonment for fine default, and have given them the power to order an attachment of income support to pay outstanding fines.

For further discussion see D. Moxon, M. Sutton and C. Hedderman, *Deductions from Benefit for Fine Default*, Home Office Research and Planning Unit Paper 60, 1990.

Detailed arrangments are set out in the Fines (Deductions for Income Support) Regulations 1992 (SI 1992/2182) and in Home Office Circular 74 of 1992. Courts have been able to use the new power since 1 October 1992. It is clear that the scheme is intended to provide an alternative to imprisonment for failure to pay a fine. In outline the system is that the justices' clerk of the maigstrates' court responsible for enforcement of the fine or compensation order, once the court has held an inquiry into an offender's means, may apply to the head of the appropriate district office of the Department of Social Security to make deductions at source from income support paid to the offender. The DSS must determine whether there is sufficient income support to allow the deduction to be made and, where other deductions are being made from income support, the priority of deductions. Deductions should not be made unless the offender is aged 18 or over when the application is made. If the DSS accepts the application the court will be informed that deductions at a standard rate have been started. The DSS will provide an account and make payments quarterly. Application may only be made by the magistrates' court which imposed the fine or compensation order but, by CJA 1991, s. 24(3), a magistrates' court may make such an application in respect of an order remitted to it from the Crown Court. The regulations also provide for setting aside decisions, correcting decisions, the withdrawal of applications, and time-limits for making appeals. Appeal by the offender from the decision of the DSS officer is to the social security appeals tribunal and further appeal (by either party) lies to the Social Security Commissioners, and ultimately to the Court of Appeal.

Chapter Four
Procedural Changes

The Criminal Justice Act 1991 makes a number of important changes to aspects of criminal procedure. The majority of these are contained in part III of the Act, relating to the responsibilities of parents with regard to offences committed by their children, a group of matters relating to the obligation of local authorities to provide secure accommodation for children and young persons charged with or convicted of criminal offences, changes in the jurisdiction of criminal courts over young offenders of different age groups, and the reconstituting of juvenile courts as youth courts. Some other matters are contained elsewhere in the Act, such as the important alteration to the criteria for committals for sentence. This question is considered first.

COMMITTALS FOR SENTENCE

4.1 Committals for Sentence: General

CJA 1991, s. 25, recasts MCA 1980, s. 38, which was formerly the main provision in respect of committal for sentence from magistrates' courts to the Crown Court. Other powers to commit for sentence are unaffected by this change but, quite independently, MCA 1980, s. 37, is amended by CJA 1991, s. 60 (see 4.13 below).

Under MCA 1980, s. 38, a magistrates' court, having dealt summarily with an offender in respect of an offence triable either way, could, in the light of information about the offender's 'character and antecedents', commit the offender to the Crown Court for sentence. That court would then be empowered to deal with the offender as if he had just been convicted on indictment. When a magistrates' court determines the question of mode of trial, it is kept in ignorance of the defendant's character and record, and so the main reason for committing to the Crown Court has been that, in the light of the offender's character and antecedents (a term which includes any matter relating to the offender's background but, in particular, previous convictions: *Vallett* (1950) 34 Cr App R 251), a more severe sentence is required than was apparent from the bare facts of the offence. Another reason for doing so has been that when he comes to be sentenced the offender has asked to have offences taken into consideration.

CJA 1991, s. 25, makes two important changes to these arrangements. The first is to amend the qualifying age for offenders under the section. The offender must now, subject to s. 38(2)(b), be not less than 18-years-old, whereas under MCA 1980, s. 38, he had to be not less than 17-years-old. See further on changes to jurisdiction in respect of offender age groups, 4.14 below. The second change relates to a magistrates' court's reason for committing for sentence. A magistrates' court may now only commit for sentence under the new MCA 1980, s. 38(2), if it is of the opinion:

(a)   that the offence or the combination of the offence and one or more offences associated with it was so serious that greater punishment should be inflicted for the offence than the court has power to impose; or

(b)   in the case of a violent or sexual offence committed by a person who is not less than 21 years old, that a sentence of imprisonment for a term longer than the court has power to impose is necessary to protect the public from serious harm from him.

This is a striking change, shifting the criteria from 'character and antecedents' to 'offence seriousness'. The rationale for the change may be found in the White Paper, para. 3.15, where the government explains that the purpose of the amendment is to 'reinforce the seriousness of the offence as the focus for sentencing decisions'. The emphasis in the Act upon offence seriousness was discussed in chapter 1. Seen in that context, the change to the committal criteria is entirely consistent. An offender the seriousness of whose offence brings him within the magistrates' jurisdiction should not be exposed to the far greater sentencing powers of the Crown Court purely because of the existence of his previous convictions. Paragraphs (a) and (b) mirror criteria (a) and (b) in CJA 1991, s. 2(2), in respect of determination of length of custodial sentences, which were discussed in 1.16 and 1.19. The meaning to be given to the terms 'violent offence' and 'sexual offence' was considered in 1.10.

It should be noted that s. 38(2)(a) has been further amended by CJA 1993, s. 66(8). 'One or more' has been substituted for 'other' offences, thereby bringing the wording into line with that used in CJA 1991, s. 1(2)(a) and s. 2(2)(a), as amended.

4.2   Committing for Sentence under MCA 1980, s. 38(2)(a)

Cases where the offence turns out to be more serious than was envisaged by the court when it took the decision on mode of trial should arise only very rarely. This is because it is the duty of the prosecutor, under MCA 1980, s. 19(3), to make clear to the court the relative seriousness of the offence when the decision over mode of trial is about to be taken. Both the magistrates and the prosecution must consider that the offence is such that summary trial is appropriate before the defendant is asked to consent to it (MCA 1980, s. 20(2)). It will still be appropriate to commit for sentence where, after conviction, the offender asks for offences to be taken into consideration, since the phrase 'one or more offences associated with it' in s. 38(2)(a) specifically includes that possibility (CJA 1991, s. 31(2), discussed at 1.9 above). It will not be appropriate, however, where the prosecutor indicates to the magistrates that the counts brought against the defendant are sample counts and the defendant is then convicted of those sample counts. Committal for sentence can only be justified in the light of information which was not available to the magistrates at the time of the decision to move for summary trial (*Derby and South Derbyshire Magistrates, ex parte McCarthy* (1980) 2 Cr App R (S) 140).

Prior to the CJA 1991, there were, however, occasionally cases where a committal for sentence under MCA 1980, s. 38, was upheld on appeal where there were no previous convictions and no offences to be taken into consideration, so that the offender was of good character apart from the offence for which he was to be sentenced. This arose when facts emerged about the offence, of which the magistrates were unaware when they agreed to summary trial. An example is *King's Lynn Justices, ex parte Carter* [1969] 1 QB 488, where the defendants were charged with theft of various items of clothing. When the prosecution summarised the facts after the guilty plea it emerged that there had been carefully planned dishonesty over a prolonged period, and a breach of trust. In respect of one defendant there was also the factor of corruption of the more junior employees. A similar example is *Lymm Justices, ex parte Brown* [1973] 1 WLR 1039 where the defendants pleaded guilty to what appeared to be a simple theft but was then revealed to be an elaborate offence involving breach of trust. Exceptional cases of this type will come within the revised s. 38(2)(a). So also will cases where the defendant asks for offences to be taken into consideration, since the phrase 'other offences associated with it' in the revised s. 38(2)(a) covers offences taken into consideration (see CJA 1991, s. 31(2)(b), discussed in 1.9 above).

In both of the cases cited the defendants pleaded guilty. In the situation where the magistrates agree to summary trial and the defendant denies the charges, the court may, at any stage before the close of the prosecution evidence, discontinue the trial and hold committal proceedings instead (MCA 1980, s. 25(2)). This power is unaffected by the 1991 Act.

4.3   Committing for Sentence under MCA 1980, s. 38(2)(b)

'Violent offence', 'sexual offence' and 'protecting the public from serious harm' are defined in CJA 1991, s. 31(1) and (3), and were discussed in 1.10 above. The rationale for MCA 1980, s. 38(2)(b), is said in the White Paper to be that 'the trial may reveal circumstances which require a longer sentence to protect the public from serious harm' (para. 3.15). This provision is likely to be used only rarely. It is difficult to envisage in what circumstances a magistrates' court would be dealing with a case of this degree of seriousness, rather than having committed it in the first place to the Crown Court for trial.

Committal under s. 38(2)(b) is restricted to offenders who are aged not less than 21, rather than aged not less than 18, which is the case under s. 38(2)(a).

4.4   More Committals to Crown Court?

It is difficult to predict the likely outcome of these changes to the rules on committals for sentence. The White Paper observes, at para. 3.16, that: 'The government does not intend that magistrates' courts should commit more cases to the Crown Court for trial. The government believes that this can be avoided if clear guidance is issued to the magistrates' courts.' Magistrates' courts have been issued with important guidance on mode of trial in *Practice Note (Mode of Trial: Guidelines)* [1990] 1 WLR 1439. This made it clear that in general, apart from where otherwise stated and where the offence charged is alleged to involve one or more specified aggravating features, either-way offences should be tried summarily. The guidance emanated from a working party set up by Lord Lane CJ, following the publication of D. Riley and J. Vennard, *Triable Either Way Cases: Crown Court or Magistrates' Court?,* Home Office Research Study 98, HMSO, 1988. Of particular interest in that report was that, of the sample of cases studied, in more than half of the cases committed by magistrates to the Crown Court for trial, the sentence imposed by that court would have been within the powers of the magistrates.

Additional guidance would have to make it clear to the magistrates (a) that the new arrangements under CJA 1991 will make committals on sentence less rather than more frequent, but that (b) they should not allow this to influence their decision on mode of trial. The change to the committal rules also has to be seen in the context of the increase in the standard scale of fines, which will bring more offenders within magistrates' courts' sentencing powers (though there has been no increase made by the Act to the maximum custodial sentences which magistrates may impose).

PARENTAL RESPONSIBILITY

4.5 Parental Responsibility: General

Sections 56 to 58 of CJA 1991 deal with various aspects of parents' responsibility for criminal offences committed by their children. It should be noted that an earlier proposal, set out by Home Office Minister Mr John Patten in a Home Office press notice of 30 March 1989, that it would be made a criminal offence for parents to fail to make reasonable efforts to prevent their children from committing offences, was subsequently dropped in the face of considerable opposition. The White Paper, however, emphasised the importance of involvement of parents in court proceedings against their children, both in terms of their attendance at court and in the requirement that they take responsibility for financial penalties imposed upon their children.

4.6 Parental Responsibility: Attendance at Court

CJA 1991, s. 56, repeals CYPA 1933, s. 34, and inserts a new s. 34A to strengthen the requirement of attendance of a parent or guardian at court where a child or young person is charged with an offence or is for any other reason brought before a court. Unless in all the circumstances it would be unreasonable to do so, the court must require a parent to be present whenever the child or young person is under the age of 16 and may so require in any other case. For these purposes, where the child or young person is in care or is provided with accommodation by the local authority under the Children Act 1989, a representative of the local authority rather than the parent must, or may be required to, attend.

By CJA 1991, sch. 12, para. 14, this change applies only in relation to offences committed after the commencement of s. 56.

4.7 Parental Responsibility: Financial Penalties

Section 55 of the CYPA 1933 is amended by CJA 1991, s. 57 and further amended by CJA 1993, sch. 3, to have the following two effects:

(a)   In the case of a young person who has reached the age of 16, the duty imposed by CYPA 1933, s. 55, upon the parent or guardian to pay any fine, order for costs or order for compensation imposed by the criminal court upon that young person shall be amended to take the form of a power rather than a duty. This reflects the view in the White Paper that young people aged 16 or 17 should, in appropriate cases, be considered to be independent of their parents and responsible for their own actions. Where parents are required to pay, the parents' means are taken into account (CJA 1991, s. 57(3)), and where the young person is required to pay it is the young person's means, rather than his or her parents' means, which are relevant.

(b)   The reach of CYPA 1933, s. 55, is also extended by CJA 1991, s. 57, to encompass local authorities who have responsibility for offenders under the age of 18 in their care. A local authority in whose care a juvenile had been placed by virtue of a care order had been held not to be a parent or guardian for the purposes of CYPA 1933, s. 55, in *Leeds City Council* v *West Yorkshire Metropolitan Police* [1983] 1 AC 29. That decision placed at a disadvantage victims of crimes committed by young people in local authority care, since they were effectively denied the possibility of a compensation order being made in their favour. Its effect is now reversed. Schedule 3 to the CJA 1993 makes minor changes to s. 57(3) and (4), which are consequent upon the abolition of unit fines by the 1993 Act.

4.8 Parental Responsibility: Binding Over

The effect of CJA 1991, s. 58, is to place a magistrates' court or the Crown Court under a duty to bind over the parents of a young offender who is under the age of 16, if it is satisfied that to do so would be desirable in the interests of preventing the commission by the young offender of further offences. If the court is not so satisfied, it should state in open court that it is not, and give reasons for that view. A proposal that the parent or guardian of a young offender of 16 or over should also be bound over, if the child is in full-time education and is living at home with them, was abandoned at an earlier stage of the Bill. These new powers are very similar to powers to bind over the parent or guardian of a young offender in care proceedings, formerly contained in CYPA 1969, s. 1(3), and which were repealed by the Children Act 1989, and virtually identical to powers to bind over the parent or guardian of a young offender, formerly contained in CYPA 1969, s. 7(7)(c), and which are repealed by CJA 1991, sch. 13. In the White Paper (para. 8.10) the government expressed the wish to see the courts making much more use of these powers than the 'handful of cases each year' in which they were imposed prior to the 1991 Act. The purpose of re-enacting these provisions in the 1991 Act is to place them on the footing of a separate option available to the courts on sentence and to require the courts to give reasons for not exercising the power.

By CJA 1991, s. 58, the court is empowered to order the parent or guardian to enter into a recognisance, in a sum not exceeding £1,000, to take proper care of the offender and exercise proper control over him. The duration of the recognisance is until the offender reaches the age of 18, or for three years, whichever is the shorter. Entry into the recognisance requires the consent of the parent or guardian, but if that person refuses consent and the court considers their refusal to be unreasonable, the parent or guardian may be punished by a fine not exceeding level 3 on the standard scale (raised by CJA 1991, s. 17, to £1,000). In fixing the amount of the recognisance the court shall take into account, amongst other things, the means of the parent or guardian, whether this has the effect of reducing or increasing the level of the recognisance. As far as forfeiture of the recognisance is concerned, s. 58(3) states that MCA 1980, s. 120, shall apply in relation to a recognisance under s. 58 as it does to a recognisance to keep the peace. By MCA 1980, s. 120(2), a recognisance can only be declared to be forfeit by way of an order on complaint. Proceedings for forfeiture are civil in character and require only the civil standard of proof (*R* v *Marlow Justices, ex parte O'Sullivan* [1984] QB 381). The court may order forfeiture of the whole or part of the recognisance, together with costs. A right of appeal against an order that a parent or guardian enter into a recognisance under CJA 1991, s. 58, is created by s. 58(6), in respect of an order made by a magistrates' court, and s. 58(7), where the order is made by the Crown Court. Formerly, under CYPA 1969, s.7(7)(c), it seems that there was no right of appeal. The new right does not extend to appeal against forfeiture of a recognisance, and there would appear to be no such right (*Durham Justices, ex parte Laurent* [1945] KB 33). Finally, by CJA 1991, s. 58(8), a court may vary or revoke an order made under s. 58 on the application of the parent or guardian, having regard to any change in the circumstances since the order was made.

By CJA 1991, sch. 12, para. 14, these changes apply only in relation to offences committed after the commencement of s. 58.

PROVISION OF SECURE ACCOMMODATION

4.9   Detention at a Police Station

By s. 59 of CJA 1991, changes are made to PACE 1984, s. 38(6), which deals with the duties of the custody officer after an arrested juvenile has been charged with an offence and the officer, in accordance with s. 38(1) and (2), has authorised that juvenile to be kept in police detention rather than being released, with or without bail. Subsections (6) and (6A) of PACE 1984, s. 38, are replaced by new subsections (6) and (6A), whereby the custody officer must now ensure that the juvenile is moved to local authority accommodation, unless (a) it is impracticable for him to do so (the circumstances must be specified in the certificate) or (b), in the case of a juvenile who is aged 15 or older, no secure accommodation is available and keeping the juvenile in other local authority accommodation would not be adequate to protect the public from serious harm from him.

If an arrested juvenile is charged with a 'violent offence' or a 'sexual offence' (defined in CJA 1991, s. 31(1): see 1.10 above) the phrase 'protecting the public from serious harm from him' is defined in the new s. 38(6A) of PACE 1984 in terms identical to those in CJA 1991, s. 31(3), which was discussed in 1.10 above. Oddly, however, even if the juvenile is not charged with a violent offence or a sexual offence, it would still be possible for the custody officer to certify under the new s. 38(6)(b) that anything other than secure accommodation would not be adequate to protect the public. In such cases 'adequate to protect the public from serious harm' lacks statutory definition. The terms 'local authority' and 'accommodation' are defined in the Children Act 1989, s. 105(1) and s. 22(2) respectively, the latter meaning 'accommodation which is provided for a continuous period of more than 24 hours'. 'Secure accommodation', according to the new s. 38(6A) of PACE 1984, means 'accommodation provided for the purpose of restricting liberty', and is described in identical terms in the Children Act 1989, s. 25(1). See further 4.11 below and Home Office Circular No. 78 of 1992, *Criminal Justice Act 1991: Detention etc. of Juveniles.*

Provisions relating to the fingerprinting of suspected young persons, in CYPA 1969, s. 8, and provisions relating to the duties of a custody officer with respect to young persons, in PACE 1984, s. 37(11) to (14), none of which have been brought into force, are repealed by CJA 1991, s. 72. The latter provisions appear in slightly modified form in PACE 1984 Code of Practice C, paras 3.7 to 3.9.

4.10   Remands and Committals to Local Authority Accommodation

In the White Paper the government commented that 'it is widely recognised that the arrangements for the remand of juveniles charged with criminal offences are unsatisfactory in certain respects' (para. 8.20). CJA 1991, s. 60, represents the legislative attempt to improve those arrangements. Section 60 recasts CYPA 1969, s. 23. It provides that where a court remands a child or young person charged with or convicted of one or more offences or commits him for trial or sentence, and bail has been refused, the remand or committal shall be to local authority accommodation (new s. 23(1) of CYPA 1969). The court must designate the relevant local authority which must be, in the case of a person who is being 'looked after' by a local authority, that local authority (for the duties of local authorities in relation to children looked after by them see Children Act 1989, s. 22) and, in other cases, the local authority for the area in which the person resides or where one of the offences was committed (new s. 23(2) of CYPA 1969).

When making such an order the court may, whether following an application to the court by the local authority or not, but nevertheless after consultation with that local authority, require the person to comply with any conditions which could be imposed under the Bail Act 1976, s. 3(6), if that person had been given bail (new s. 23(7) of CYPA 1969). Where a court does impose conditions under the new s. 23(7), it must explain the reasons to the offender in open court and in ordinary language and, if the court is a magistrates' court, it must specify that reason in the warrant of commitment and enter it in the register (new s. 23(8)). Conditions which are frequently imposed under the Bail Act 1976, s. 3(6), are requirements of place of residence, of reporting to the local police station, curfew requirements, a condition that the person must not enter a certain building or area or go within a specified distance of a certain address, and a condition not to contact the alleged victim or probable prosecution witnesses. The local authority may then be charged by the court with securing compliance with such conditions. The court may stipulate that the child or young person 'shall not be placed with a named person' (new s. 23(9) of CYPA 1969). Subsequently, the court is empowered to vary or revoke any conditions or requirements on the application of the child or young person concerned or the local authority.

By CJA 1991, sch, 12, para. 15, the new s. 23 of CYPA 1969 shall not apply in relation to any remand or committal which is in force immediately before the commencement of CJA 1991, ss. 60 and 62. For transitional arrangements see sch. 12, paras 15 and 16.

4.11 Remands and Committals: Secure Accommodation

In addition to the above, a court remanding or committing a child or young person, may, after consultation with the local authority, require that authority to place and keep the person in 'secure accommodation' (new s. 23(4) and (5) of CYPA 1969). This is defined as 'accommodation which is provided in a community home for the purpose of restricting liberty, and is approved for that purpose by the Secretary of State' (new s. 23(12)). Secure accommodation has been held to include a behaviour modification unit at a hospital where the regime was intended to restrict liberty (*R* v *Northampton Juvenile Court, ex parte London Borough of Hammersmith* [1985] Fam Law 25. The Children Act 1989, s. 53(1), requires that all local authorities must provide community homes for the care and accommodation of children looked after by them and for purposes connected with the welfare of children and CJA 1991, s. 61, now requires that local authorities must also be able to provide 'secure accommodation' for the purposes of the new CYPA 1969, s. 23(4) and (5), and also for the purposes of the amended MCA 1980, s. 37 (see 4.13 below). See further the Children (Secure Accommodation) Regulations 1991 (SI 1991/1505) as amended by the Children (Secure Accommodation) Amendment Regulations 1992 (SI 1992/2117), and Local Authority Circular (92) 13 issued by the Department of Health on 18 September 1992.

The power to commit or remand to secure accommodation is restricted to cases where the child or young person is at least 15 years old, and either (a) he is charged with or has been convicted of a 'violent offence' or a 'sexual offence' (for definitions of these see CJA 1991, s. 31(1) and 1.10 above) or an offence punishable in the case of an adult with a term of 14 years or more, or (b) he has a recent history of absconding while remanded to local authority accommodation, and is charged with or has been convicted of an imprisonable offence alleged or found to have been committed while he was so remanded. In a case where either (a) or (b) applies, the court also must be of the opinion that only a requirement to keep the person in secure accommodation would be 'adequate to protect the public from serious harm from him'. If a child or young person is charged with or has been convicted of a 'violent offence' or a 'sexual offence' the phrase 'protecting the public from serious harm from him' is defined in the new s. 23(13) of CYPA 1969 in terms identical to those in CJA 1991, s. 31(3), which was discussed in 1.10 above. If the juvenile is not charged with or convicted of a violent offence or a sexual offence, however, it would still be possible for the court to impose a security requirement under the new s. 23(4) and (5) of CYPA 1969 if the court was of the view that this was necessary to protect the public from serious harm from him. In such cases 'adequate to protect the public from serious harm' would lack statutory definition. In any case where a court imposes a security requirement it must state its opinion in open court and explain the reasons for that opinion to the person in open court and in ordinary language. A magistrates' court must specify the reason in the warrant of commitment and enter it in the register (new s. 23(6)).

4.12 Secure Accommodation: Transitory Provisions

Section 62 of CJA 1991 provides transitory provisions pending the general availability of local authority secure accommodation. The gist of these arrangements is that, unless the child or young person qualifies under the modified s. 23(5) of CYPA 1969 provided for in CJA 1991, s. 62(3), the remand or committal shall be to local authority accommodation. If, however, the child or young person is male and 15 or older and the court is of the opinion, in the light of the criteria set out in the modified new s. 23(5), that only remanding him to a remand centre or prison would be adequate to protect the public from serious harm from him, he shall be remanded to a remand centre, if one is available or, if not, to prison. By CJA 1991, sch. 12, para. 15, the modified new s. 23 of CYPA 1969 shall not apply in relation to any remand or committal which is in force immediately before the commencement of CJA 1991, ss. 60 and 62. For further detail on transitional arrangements see sch. 12, paras 15 and 16.

4.13 Remands and Committals: Associated Provisions

The changes consequent upon the new s. 23 of CYPA 1969 explained in 4.10 and 4.11 are, by the new s. 23(14) of CYPA 1969, made subject to MCA 1980, s. 37. This section deals with committal for sentence, in custody or on bail to the Crown Court, of persons convicted in a magistrates' court of an offence punishable on conviction on indictment with a term of imprisonment exceeding six months, where the court is of the opinion that the offender should be sentenced to a greater term of detention in a young offender institution than the magistrates have power to impose. This section is now amended to apply to 15, 16 and 17-year-olds, where formerly it applied only to 15 and 16-year-olds. In addition (though this provision has not yet been brought into force), CJA 1991, s. 60(2) inserts a new subsection (3) into MCA 1980, s. 37. This relates to 15 and 16-year-olds dealt with under s. 37, and will require that such persons shall be committed to local authority secure accommodation (see 4.11 above). So, the effect of the changes made to MCA 1980, s. 37, is that 17-year-olds are brought within the section, and may now be committed in custody or on bail to the Crown Court, but that offenders aged 15 and 16 will, when the relevant provision is brought into force, be committed to secure accommodation. All local authorities are now under a legal duty to make such accommodation available, either themselves or by arrangement with another local authority (CJA 1991, s. 61), but the reality is that not all local authorities are currently able to provide it.

The changes consequent upon the new s. 23 of CYPA 1969 are also made subject to MCA 1980, s. 128(7). This provision allows a magistrates' court, instead of remanding in custody, to commit the defendant to police detention for a period not exceeding three clear days, where this is necessary for the purpose of inquiries into offences other than the one for which he appears before the court. Section 128(7) is amended by the new s. 23(14) of CYPA 1969 so as to reduce the relevant period from three days to 24 hours, in respect of a child or young person.

YOUNG OFFENDER AGE CLASSIFICATION

4.14 'Juvenile Courts' renamed 'Youth Courts'

The simple effect of CJA 1991, s. 70, is to rename juvenile courts and juvenile court panels as youth courts and youth court panels. Paragraphs 40 and 41 of sch. 11 to the Act list numerous statutory changes which result from this, and transitional matters may be found in para. 23 of sch. 12.

The rationale for the change, according to the White Paper, para. 8.30, is that the age balance of defendants appearing in juvenile courts has been changing, so that in 1988 nearly 90 per cent were aged 14 to 16. Those under 14 are being dealt with very frequently without bringing them to court. Juvenile courts no longer hear care cases, following the Children Act 1989. Now that persons aged 17 are to be treated as young persons for a range of criminal justice purposes (see 4.15), the government estimates that about three-quarters of the defendants appearing before the juvenile courts will be aged 16 or 17, and that the name change 'should reflect this considerable change in its responsibilities'.

Prior to the 1991 Act, 16-year-old offenders were generally dealt with in juvenile courts, while 17-year-old offenders were dealt with in the adult court system. The White Paper (para. 8.16) indicated the government's view 'that 16 and 17-year-olds should be dealt with as near adults. They should normally appear in what is now the juvenile court.' Statutory changes to CYPA 1933, CYPA 1969, the Prison Act 1952, the Army Act 1955, the Air Force Act 1955, the Naval Discipline Act 1957, the Rehabilitation of Offenders Act 1974 and MCA 1980, necessitated by the amendment of juvenile age groups, are made by CJA 1991, sch. 8, and, in respect of laws relating to the armed services, s. 71 and sch. 9. The extension of availability of probation orders to 16-year-olds means that youth courts have powers to make such orders.

4.15 Pleading Guilty by Post: Extension to 16-Year-Olds

Section 12 of MCA 1980 sets out a procedure allowing a defendant to plead guilty by post (for details see *Blackstone's Criminal Practice 1993*, section D17.13). Prior to the 1991 Act this option was limited to proceedings by way of summons in an adult magistrates' court. An amendment to s. 12, by CJA 1991, s. 69, allows 16-year-olds and (taken together with the treatment of a 17-year-old as a young person: see 4.14 above) 17-year-olds to plead guilty by post in a case where a summons is issued for them to appear before a youth court. The scheme under s. 12 is limited to summary offences carrying a penalty of no more than three months' imprisonment, and these restrictions continue to apply in all cases as before.

4.16 Rehabilitation of Offenders

The Rehabilitation of Offenders Act 1974 is affected by s. 68 of and sch. 8 to CJA 1991. In the provision in s. 5(2) of the 1974 Act, which allows for rehabilitation periods to be reduced by half for young offenders, the relevant age is increased to include 17-year-olds.

Chapter Five
Parole, Remission and Early Release

Part II of the Criminal Justice Act 1991 radically changes the former systems of parole and remission and effectively fuses them together. It cuts down the case load of the Parole Board by restricting its operation to long-term and life-sentence prisoners and establishes a new category of short-term prisoners (serving sentences of under four years) who are automatically entitled to release having served half of their sentence. It provides for a higher proportion of prisoners to be supervised on release and attempts to restore meaning to the term imposed by the court by putting all offenders at risk of being recalled, right up to the end of the sentence, on commission of a further imprisonable offence. It introduces a special procedure for discretionary life sentences and contains a number of other provisions designed to rationalise the mechanisms for early release and to make them more equitable, open and accessible.

THE PREVIOUS BACKGROUND

5.1 Historical Development

Although the Parole Board is a relatively recent phenomenon as far as the English criminal justice system is concerned, the advantages of releasing offenders in advance of the full term of custodial sentences have long been recognised and given practical effect through a variety of mechanisms. Transported convicts who behaved themselves were given a 'ticket of leave' after four, six, or eight years, depending on whether they were transported for seven, 14 years or life respectively, and thus were given both an incentive and an opportunity to reform themselves even though they were not totally free so as to be able to leave the colony to which they had been sent until the end of their sentence.

When penal servitude replaced transportation, the ticket of leave was replaced by release on licence for a maximum period which varied but which by 1891 had become one-quarter of the sentence (one-third for female convicts). Until 1898 this produced the anomaly that those sentenced for the more serious offences to penal servitude (i.e., convicts) had some prospect of early release on licence but those sentenced to ordinary imprisonment (prisoners) for lesser offences had to face up to serving their (admittedly shorter) sentences in full. However, one of the results of the Gladstone Committee of 1895 was that remission for ordinary prisoners was introduced in 1898 for a period that settled down in 1907 at one-sixth of sentence but which differed significantly from release on licence in that remission of sentence was unconditional with no liability to be recalled to prison. For the next 30 odd years there were thus three potential periods of early release for three different categories of offenders – one-sixth remission for prisoners, one-quarter (on licence) for male convicts and one-third (on licence) for female convicts. Wartime pressure on secure accommodation meant that the maximum periods of early release (if not the terms and conditions thereof) were harmonised at one-third in 1940, and with the abolition of penal servitude in 1948 virtually all adult prisoners became eligible for unconditional release at the two-thirds point of their sentence. The exceptions which remained were those relating to life imprisonment, corrective training or preventive detention (the latter two of which were replaced by the extended sentence in 1967 which has now in its turn been repealed by the new CJA 1991 – see 1.27).

It was against this background that 1967 saw the creation of the Parole Board which reintroduced on a large scale the concept of release on licence with supervision in the community following upon release and liability to recall to prison for misbehaviour during the licence period. What was really new, however, was the fact that release could be as early as after just one-third of the sentence, which period represented only one-half of the two-thirds of the sentence customarily served by most prisoners. Also new was the genuine discretion exercised by the Parole Board as to whether or when a prisoner should be released on licence, as opposed to the virtually automatic operation of the remission system given reasonably good behaviour. The motives behind the creation of the Parole Board in the Criminal Justice Act of 1967 were somewhat mixed. They included pragmatic concerns about the increasing size of the prison population and a desire in some to avoid imposing the suffering of imprisonment on those who did not really need to be in custody. For others, parole represented an opportunity to release prisoners at the optimum time that they would have benefited from any rehabilitative effects of their training in prison and when they could gain further advantage from the supervision they would receive whilst on release on licence. These mixed motives meant that there was a fair degree of consensus about the introduction of parole but no clear theoretical underpinning. The selection of the one-third period was fairly arbitrary and the relationship between parole and remission was not fully thought out. The rules for remission remained those in the Prison Rules 1964, whilst parole was governed by the CJA 1967, which meant that a prisoner who had lost part of his remission for misconduct might still be released well in advance of the two-thirds point of his sentence because of a favourable parole decision.

5.2   The Mechanics of Obtaining Parole

Parole under the CJA 1967 has been described as a tripartite system operated by the Home Secretary, the Parole Board and the Local Review Committees. Although Local Review Committees will cease to have a role once the new regime under the CJA 1991 is fully operational, the effect of the transitional provisions (see below 5.20) is that the old tripartite system will continue to apply for some time to determinate-sentence prisoners sentenced before 1 October 1992. At each prison there is a Local Review Committee whose membership includes prison governors and probation officers but also 'independent members' whose time is given voluntarily. Parole reviews generally start off a matter of weeks before the prisoner becomes eligible for parole by being considered by a panel of the Local Review Committee, which recommends for or against parole having considered the case on the papers, including any written representations by the prisoner and the record of an interview between one of the panel members and the prisoner.

About a third of the cases (the more problematical ones, around 8,000 a year) are then referred to the Parole Board itself for a second opinion. If parole is recommended, as it is in about 45 per cent of these cases, then the Home Secretary may, but does not have to, grant parole although in most cases he would follow the Parole Board's recommendation (only seven recommendations were rejected in 1992) . If the Parole Board does not recommend parole, then parole cannot be granted but the prisoner's case will be reviewed again between 10 and 14 months later (or earlier if the Parole Board so recommends).

The cases not actually considered by the Parole Board itself (over 16,000 a year) fall into two main groups: (a) those (shorter sentence) cases where the Home Secretary is empowered to, and does decide to, grant parole solely on the recommendation of the Local Review Committee and (b) those where the Local Review Committee has recommended against parole and the Home Office feels able to accept that decision without reference to the Board itself. Thus although the system is in one sense tripartite, it is perhaps more accurately represented by the 'dual key' metaphor with a positive recommendation by *either* the Local Review Committee or the Parole Board being necessary on the one hand and acceptance of that recommendation by the Home Secretary being required on the other.

5.3 Life Sentences

Special mention ought to be made of the previous arrangements for life-sentence prisoners because of the controversies that have centred around this particular group. Remission has never applied to life-sentence prisoners and release on a parole licence, which will last for the rest of his or her life, is thus the only way a lifer can be released. Whereas determinate-sentence prisoners became eligible for parole at the one-third point of the sentence, which can be readily calculated, the point at which there should be a first review of whether parole should be granted to a lifer is much more difficult to identify. Furthermore CJA 1967, s. 61 (see now CJA 1991, s. 35(2)), required the Home Secretary not only to have a recommendation from the Parole Board before releasing a lifer, but also to have consulted the Lord Chief Justice, together with the trial judge if available. These factors led to the following procedure being followed in the years immediately prior to the 1991 Act (the procedures were slightly different before the case of *Secretary of State for the Home Department, ex parte Handscomb* (1987) 86 Cr App R 59 relating to discretionary life sentences and they were different again before 1983):

... in all life sentence cases in England and Wales ... the trial judge now writes to the Home Secretary, through the Lord Chief Justice, immediately after the trial, to inform the Home Secretary of the conviction and to give his views on the necessary period of detention to meet the requirements of retribution and deterrence. The Lord Chief Justice adds his own view. Taking these views into account, a junior Minister, on behalf of the Home Secretary, decides upon the period of imprisonment necessary to meet the requirements of retribution and deterrence. This period of imprisonment is widely known as the 'tariff'. . . . in the case of a discretionary life sentence (but not a mandatory life sentence), the tariff is fixed strictly in accordance with the judicial recommendation. . . .

If and when the Parole Board recommend release, the trial judge and the Lord Chief Justice are again consulted before the papers are referred to the Minister.

In murder cases, which at present attract a mandatory life sentence, the Home Secretary is not bound by the views of the judiciary when setting the tariff. . . .

The 'tariff' date determines the date when the prisoner's suitability for release will first be reviewed by the Local Review Committee (LRC) at his prison (the LRC date). In the case of tariffs of up to and including 20 years, the LRC date will be three years before the expiry of the tariff period. In the case of prisoners with tariffs longer than 20 years, the LRC date will be fixed at 17 years into the sentence. The prisoner is told his LRC date, not the tariff which has been set. . . .

Following the consideration of the case by the LRC, [the Home Office] will refer the case to a 'lifer panel' of the Parole Board. The panel must include a judicial member, a psychiatrist, and preferably a probation member of the Board. . . .

The panel inform the Home Office of the results of their consideration of the case, and make a recommendation. . . .

If the Parole Board recommend that a prisoner should be released, the Home Secretary is not bound to accept their recommendation. However, if the Board do not recommend release, the Home Secretary may not release the prisoner.

(House of Lords Select Committee on Murder and Life Imprisonment, 1988–89, HL Paper 78, pp. 38–40)

In considering the above procedure, the distinction between discretionary life sentences and mandatory life sentences should be kept in mind. Neither category of prisoner was happy with the procedure.

For the mandatory lifer, the concern was about the Home Secretary's ability to increase the 'tariff' recommended by the judiciary (as happened in about a third of the mandatory life cases considered by the Home Secretary in 1990), something which it was thought could not be done in the case of a discretionary lifer as a result of the *Handscomb* case. Nevertheless, in a series of decisions and appeals in the case of *Secretary of State for the Home Department, ex parte Doody* [1993] 3 WLR 154, which commenced prior to the passing of the 1991 Act but which was finally decided in the House of Lords nearly a year after the Act was brought into force, the courts have confirmed that the Home Secretary is not obliged to accept the 'tariff' or 'penal element' recommended by the judiciary. However, as a result of the House of Lords decision, mandatory lifers will benefit from a more open procedure including having the right to know the trial judge's recommendation, the right to make representations to the Home Secretary, and the right to be given the reasons for any departure from the judicial recommendation by the Home Secretary (or the junior minister to whom the decision is lawfully delegated). (Parliamentary Debates (Hansard), Commons, 6th ser., vol. 229, written answers, cols 863–5, 27 July 1993.) The decision in *Doody* has also led to the courts recognising similar rights for Category A prisoners to be given the gist of reports, and reasons for decisions made about them in the annual reviews of their security status (see *R v Secretary of State for the Home Department, ex parte Duggan* (1993) *The Times*, 9 December 1993).

For the discretionary lifer, the concern was, following *Handscomb*, no longer with the setting of the tariff but with the clandestine procedures of the Parole Board in reviewing whether parole could be recommended once that tariff, which was itself not openly communicated to the prisoner, had expired. In this regard, the discretionary lifers had more success than the mandatory lifers, both in the European Court of Human Rights, which, in *Thynne v UK* (1990) 13 EHRR 666, declared the Parole Board procedures to be insufficiently judicial to satisfy art. 5(4) of the European Convention on Human Rights, and also in Parliament, which reacted to this decision by creating a new procedure in the CJA 1991 for review of discretionary life sentences. In the interim, between the passing of the Act and its coming into force, the courts held that existing discretionary lifers were entitled to more openness and to disclosure of the reports on them being considered by the Board (see *Parole Board, ex parte Wilson* [1992] QB 740; *Secretary of State, ex parte Prem Singh* (1993) *The Times*, 27 April 1993). These cases have now been overtaken by the new statutory procedure for discretionary life prisoners (see 5.12).

5.4   Other Developments in the Parole System

Parole was originally conceived as a privilege for a relatively small percentage of those eligible, granted to those who were considered able to benefit from early release on licence without undue risk to the public. A release rate of 20 per cent was the estimate of the Home Secretary when introducing the Bill in 1967, but the actual rate in the first year was 27 per cent and 10 years later this had risen to over 50 per cent, an increase facilitated by the introduction in CJA 1972, s. 35, of the power to release on parole certain categories of prisoners solely on the recommendation of the Local Review Committee without reference to the Parole Board itself. By the early 1980s around 5,000 prisoners a year were getting parole and there were around 3,000 individuals on parole licences at any given time. The system seemed to be working reasonably well in identifying those prisoners who could safely be released back into the community.

However, worries were beginning to emerge about the justification for and fairness of the system. One way of illuminating these concerns is to focus on the minimum qualifying period for parole which, as introduced in 1967, meant that a prisoner had to serve at least 12 months after sentence (i.e., ignoring any period on remand) before being eligible for parole. The rationale for this was that there had to be a minimum period during which the offender might have been observed to have been rehabilitated by the prison regime thereby justifying release earlier than the date envisaged by the sentence originally passed in open court. But scepticism about the rehabilitative effects of incarceration had grown immensely since 1967 to the point where imprisonment was thought, if anything, to be more likely to confirm a person in criminal behaviour rather than effect his or her reform. Because of the fact that of those eligible for parole, those serving longer sentences for more serious offences were less likely to get parole than those serving shorter sentences for less serious offences, parole decisions could be seen to exaggerate disparities in sentencing, effectively double counting aggravating or mitigating factors. Parole could therefore be criticised as a form of re-sentencing done behind closed doors with few procedural safeguards. The injustice of course was to those refused rather than granted parole, but there was also the problem at the lower end of the scale that the 12-month qualifying period meant that it was very rare for a person serving a sentence of less than two years to get parole and yet prisoners serving three or four-year sentences were being released on parole (in increasing numbers) at about the same time that the two-year prisoner was being released on remission.

The concerns already being voiced were given more fuel by two decisions announced in 1983 at the Conservative Party conference by the Home Secretary, Leon Brittan. The more notorious of these was the announcement of a new tougher policy (subsequently declared valid in *Re Findlay* [1985] AC 318) for those sentenced to more than five years for offences involving drug trafficking, sex, arson or violence, whereby the Home Secretary's discretion to refuse parole would be exercised so as to ensure that such people did not get parole save in exceptional circumstances or where release under supervision for a few months before the end of a sentence was likely to reduce the long-term risk to the public. The policy statement also indicated that the discretion would be exercised so that certain categories of murderer could normally expect to serve at least 20 years in custody.

Less controversially, but perhaps more significantly in the longer term, the Home Secretary announced his intention to use the powers conferred in s. 33 of the CJA 1982 to reduce the minimum qualifying period for parole from 12 months to six, a change which took effect from 1 June 1984. A major effect of this change was to remove, for most practical purposes, the difference between sentences of anything between nine and 18 months. The nine- month prisoner would be free after six months because of remission, but so would the person serving 18 months if given parole. Previously, at least 12 months had to be served after sentence before release on parole. Although this had created the same sort of lack of distinction, between sentences ranging from 18 months to three years, the anomaly was much more pronounced under the new rules because (a) a much higher proportion of offenders sentenced to terms between nine and 18 months would actually get parole, as compared with those sentenced to terms between 18 months and three years, since they would by definition be better risks and (b) there are substantially more people sentenced to terms of nine to 18 months than to terms of 18 months to three years. Although the decision in 1987 to increase remission to 50 per cent for those serving 12 months or less subsequently made parole irrelevant for those serving less than 12 months, the nature and scale of parole decision-making had been changed dramatically. From a position in 1983 when very few sentences under two years were considered by the parole system, around 10,000 cases a year in that category were now having to be considered. At the other end of the scale, the restrictive policy in relation to certain sentences of more than five years meant that some offenders were staying in prison longer and therefore required a larger number of (usually unsuccessful) applications for parole, and the overall result was that the case load had more than doubled from around 10,000 cases annually to around 24,000. Not surprisingly, given this case load, the selectivity of the system has become less apparent – those serving less than two years would normally get parole and those serving more than five normally would not. Furthermore, the average period of freedom on licence, which is one of the main features distinguishing parole from remission, had reduced from eight months in 1983 to five and a half months in 1987 as a result both of shorter sentences being made eligible and parole being delayed longer for those sentenced to longer terms.

5.5 Reform Proposals

In response to these changes and the increased pressures on, and criticisms of, the system, the government set up the Carlisle Committeee to review the parole system, and most of the recommendations in its report (*The Parole System in England and Wales,* Cm 532, 1988) were endorsed by the government in its White Paper, *Crime Justice and Protecting the Public* (Cm 965), in February 1990. The major changes recommended by Carlisle, now for the most part embodied in part II of the CJA 1991, can be summarised as follows:

(a)   The abolition of the distinction between remission and parole.

(b)   In its place, a single concept of early release (normally on licence) for all prisoners.

(c)   This early release to be automatic after 50 per cent of the sentence for short-term prisoners (i.e., those sentenced to four years or less) but discretionary for long-term prisoners (more than four years) up to the two-thirds point of sentence at which point it becomes automatic. (These thresholds were adjusted in the White Paper to less than four years, and four years or more, respectively.)

(d)   Supervison under licence for *all* offenders (except those serving less than 12 months) from the point of release up to the three-quarters point of the sentence.

(e)   Liability to serve the remaining part of the sentence if convicted of a further imprisonable offence at any point after early release and before expiry of the full sentence.

(f)   The abolition of the Local Review Committees given the much smaller number of cases of discretionary release.

(g)   The establishment of *statutory* criteria for parole and the introduction of more openness into the system.

(h)   The parole decision to be entirely a matter for the Parole Board rather than merely a recommendation to the Home Secretary. (The White Paper only accepted this for sentences of less than seven years.)

The essential shape of the new system as compared with the old system can be seen in figure 5.1 which is based on one in the White Paper (p. 31). It is perhaps worth commenting at this stage that the chart is slightly disingenuous in labelling the final third of the current system merely as 'at liberty, no supervision or sanction against reoffending'; since a further offence can be sanctioned by a further term of imprisonment *for that offence*, the lack of any power to reactivate the original sentence is not that much of a handicap.

Figure 5.1

Old parole system for adult offenders

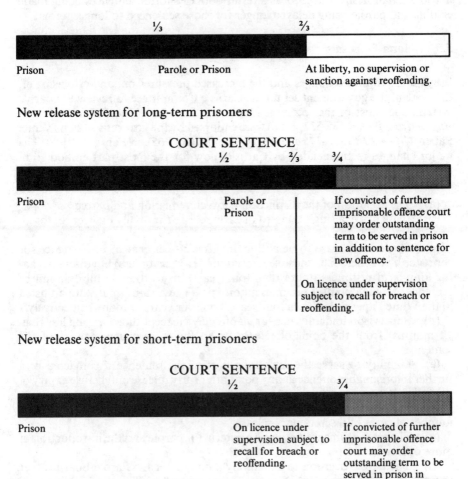

COURT SENTENCE

| ⅓   ⅔ |
| Prison | Parole or Prison | At liberty, no supervision or sanction against reoffending. |

New release system for long-term prisoners

COURT SENTENCE
        ½   ⅔   ¾

| Prison | Parole or Prison | If convicted of further imprisonable offence court may order outstanding term to be served in prison in addition to sentence for new offence.

On licence under supervision subject to recall for breach or reoffending. |

New release system for short-term prisoners

COURT SENTENCE
        ½   ¾

| Prison | On licence under supervision subject to recall for breach or reoffending. | If convicted of further imprisonable offence court may order outstanding term to be served in prison in addition to sentence for new offence. |

The main thrust of the above proposals was to restore the connection, which had been eroded, between the length of the sentence passed by the court and the actual period spent in custody and to focus the energies of a more open parole decision-making process on those cases where the length of time in prison and the nature of the offences mean that there is real judgment to be exercised. The proposals were also concerned to extend the benefits of release under supervision, 'the bridge between prison and total freedom', to all prisoners and to retain incentives to good behaviour during the period of the sentence whether served in custody or in the community. For those serving sentences of under four years, it should be noted that the new system means that they will spend a greater proportion of their sentences in custody than if they had been granted parole, although for the minority in this category who were formerly refused parole, automatic release after 50 per cent of the sentence means they will spend less time in custody than if they had only been released on remission after serving two-thirds. It is most important to appreciate, and it has been one of the concerns most frequently expressed about the 1991 Act, that, without a change in sentencing practice and a reduction in the tariff (recommended by the Carlisle Report, paras 296 and 297), the overall effect will be to increase the numbers in prison, especially given the new liability to be ordered to return to prison if convicted of further imprisonable offences during the period of the original sentence. (See the changed approach recommended by the Lord Chief Justice in the *Practice Statement (Crime: Sentencing)* [1992] 1 WLR 948.)

Bearing these general aims of the legislation in mind, we can now look at the detailed provisions contained in part II of the Act.

THE NEW REGIME

5.6 Machinery and Process

CJA 1991, s. 32, provides for the continuation of the Parole Board which was first established by the CJA 1967, s. 59. However, there is no longer (except under the transitional arrangements) any provision for Local Review Committees which were, as we have seen, the first filter through which all parole applications passed under the old system. These will no longer be required, given the estimated reduction from 24,000 to approximately 4,000 cases annually where there will remain a discretion as to release. The intention of the government, as stated in the White Paper, though not specifically enshrined in the legislation, is that the expertise of the members of the Local Review Committees should not be lost. Instead, they should be eligible (along with others) for appointment as parole assessors, formally appointed agents of the Board, who would assess the oral and written representations made by the prisoner and report to the Board and check the completion of the parole dossier being forwarded to the Board. The Parole Board was not entirely convinced about the latter aspect of the parole assessor's role and also had doubts about the term 'assessor'. 'What exactly the person will be required to assess and for what purpose is not entirely clear' (Report of the Parole Board for 1989, para. 9).

Whatever the precise role to be played by parole assessors, CJA 1991 does provide, in s. 32(3), for a member of the Parole Board itself to interview the prisoner 'if in any particular case the Board thinks it necessary', but the government resisted attempts to give the prisoner the *right* to have an interview with a Board member. Earl Ferrers stated for the government in the Lords (HL Deb, 21 May 1991, vol. 529, col. 115):

> We accept that it is important for an inmate to have an interview with someone involved in the decision-making process. We intend, by virtue of [s. 32(5)] to issue rules which would ensure that all inmates receive such an interview.
>
> The advantage of this approach is that it allows for flexibility and changes to the system in the light of experience. . . . The interview should be an administrative arrangement designed to assist the Board and not a legal right from which other rights could be inferred.

Again, the extent to which prisoners will have direct access to the Board will not be clear until the rules under s. 32(5) are issued, and it is of course possible that the interview with the parole assessor might be regarded as 'an interview with someone involved in the decision-making process'.

The question of oral interviews is part of the wider issue of the openness and accessibility of the system. One of the more frequent criticisms of the old system was the fact that prisoners were not given reasons for parole decisions (particularly refusals of parole), a practice formerly upheld as legitimate in the courts (*Payne* v *Lord Harris of Greenwich* [1981] 1 WLR 754, followed in *Parole Board, ex parte Bradley* [1991] 1 WLR 134 but contrast *Parole Board, ex parte Wilson* [1992] QB 740). The government acknowledged in its White Paper (para. 6.26) that the system could be improved by more openness and spoke of 'moving towards disclosing reports made to the Board and the Board giving reasons for its decisions'. Again, however, there is nothing specific in the Act to guarantee this, the government's preferred mechanism being to introduce the giving of reasons by administrative means, presumably by means of the rules to be made under s. 32(5). Paragraph 13 of the Parole Board's report for 1992 states that 'As the cases of those given determinate sentences after 1 October 1992 come up for review, their dossiers will be disclosed and we will be asked to give reasons for our decisions'. There has been, and will continue to be, no right of appeal against adverse decisions, but the rules will apparently provide for a right to complain to the Chairman of the Parole Board on procedural grounds whereas, at the moment, all the dissatisfied prisoner can do is to petition the Home Secretary. Judicial review of parole decisions will become much more feasible once reasons are given, particularly given the introduction of statutory criteria for parole. Judicial review will of course fall far short of an appeal procedure but would rather involve the questioning of decisions by alleging they were based on irrelevant reasons. Other than in exceptional cases where a court could be persuaded that the decision was completely irrational, judicial review would not normally extend to questioning the Board's judgment where it had asked itself the right questions.

The so-called statutory criteria for parole are themselves not spelled out in the statute. Instead s. 32(6) provides for the Secretary of State (the Home Secretary) to:

give to the Board directions as to the matters to be taken into account . . . and in giving any such directions the Secretary of State shall in particular have regard to—

(a) the need to protect the public from serious harm from offenders; and

(b) the desirability of preventing the commission by them of further offences and of securing their rehabilitation.

Apart from the reference to the harm being serious, these factors are very similar to the factors relevant in deciding to make a probation order under s. 2(1) of the PCCA 1973 as substituted by CJA 1991, s. 8(1) (see 2.9). The order in which the factors are mentioned is, however, different and this is significant in that it emphasises the priority to be given in the parole decision to the protection of the public from serious harm.

The directions given by the Home Secretary under s. 32(6) are set out at pp. 135–37. Their opening sentence (para. 1.1) stresses the protection of the public by stating that the 'decision whether or not to recommend parole should focus primarily on the risk to the public of a further offence being committed *at a time when the offender would otherwise be in prison*' (emphasis added). Although the directions go on to say that this 'should be balanced against the benefit, both to the public and the offender, of early release back into the community under a degree of supervision which might help rehabilitation and so lessen the risk of reoffending in the future', para. 1.3 directs that the Board should be satisfied before recommending parole, *inter alia*, that 'the longer period of supervision that parole would provide is likely to *reduce* the risk of further imprisonable offences being committed' (emphasis added). Paragraph 1.3 goes on to underline the need to protect the public *from serious harm* as required by s. 32(6) (see ss. 51(4) and 31(3) for the meaning of 'serious harm') by directing that, 'In assessing the risk to the community, a small risk of violent offending is to be treated as more serious than a larger risk of non-violent offending'.

These directions were intended to be more stringent than the previous criteria for parole which they replaced and the Home Secretary therefore felt able to abolish (on 29 June 1992) the former special restricted policy applicable to certain categories of offender sentenced to more than five years. The focus is now on the risk of reoffending when the offender would otherwise be in prison whereas the benefits of supervision can only logically reduce the risk of reoffending in the future, after the point at which the offender would have been released back into the community anyway. The benefits of early release on licence are probably going to carry less weight than before given that under the new regime, all offenders sentenced to 12 months or more, and certainly all those eligible for discretionary early release (whether or not they receive it), will receive some supervision on release (at least from the two-thirds to the three-quarters point of their sentence).

In the first edition of this book we commented (on p. 99) that 'obtaining parole may become somewhat more difficult for those left in the discretionary system (i.e., sentences of four years and over)' and this comment is echoed by para. 9 of the report of the Parole Board for 1992 which states:

We believe that paragraph 1.3 [of the Home Secretary's directions] represents a somewhat tougher line than hitherto and, taken with the introduction of an automatic period of supervision, may result in proportionately fewer recommendations for release, notwithstanding the abolition of the restricted policy.

5.7   Responsibility for Decisions

For some of the cases where there still is discretionary as opposed to automatic early release (i.e., for seven-year sentences and over), the 'dual key' system enshrined in the 1967 Act is still retained in CJA 1991, s. 35(1), whereby 'the Secretary of State may, if recommended to do so by the Board, release [the prisoner] on licence'. Thus the Home Secretary cannot release without a recommendation from the Parole Board but, on the other hand, he does not have to release even if given a positive recommendation from the Board. The numbers of cases each year where parole has been refused despite a positive recommendation from the Board have not been very large, sometimes in single figures, but as many as 30 in 1989. The Carlisle Committee recommended that the Parole Board's recommendations for individual cases should become binding. The government nevertheless took the view that the Home Secretary still should have the final say, at least in the most serious categories of case, and that the public interest and his own responsibility to Parliament demanded this, hence the dual key retained in s. 35(1). However, subsections (1) and (2) of s. 50 of CJA 1991 provide for the replacement by means of an order made by statutory instrument of the word 'may' in s. 35(1) by the word 'shall' in such classes of case as may be specified in the order. Such an order has been made (SI 1992/1829) in relation to sentences of less than seven years where, consequently, the recommendation of the Parole Board is now binding. This implements the government's intention (see the White Paper, para. 6.16) that the dual key should remain for sentences of seven years or more but that the decision should be solely that of the Board for determinate sentences of four years or more but less than seven years (see 5.12 below for the different regime applicable to discretionary life sentence prisoners).

5.8   Composition of Panels

The Board normally sits in panels of three or four at the moment but the White Paper envisaged it generally sitting in panels of three in future with a quorum of two. This, it was thought, alongside the overall reduction in the number of cases, should permit a reduction in the total number of members of the Board but in fact the 1992 report noted that membership had increased from 62 to 86, mainly to deal with extra work in relation to discretionary lifer panels, the composition of which is discussed separately below (5.12). CJA 1991, sch. 5, provides the criteria (unchanged) for appointment to and membership of the Board, for the remuneration and expenses of Board members and for the production of an annual report.

THE NEW CATEGORIES OF EARLY RELEASE

5.9 Terminology

The new arrangements replace the distinction between remission and parole with a new distinction between 'unconditional' release and release on licence, although it should be remembered that even 'unconditional' release is now subject to the possibility of recall for further offending during the term of the original sentence (see s. 40, discussed in 5.13 below). It was for this reason that the Carlisle Report recommended the use of the term 'conditional release' as the generic term for early release but the CJA 1991 uses the opposite term 'unconditional release' for one category of early release, to be distinguished from early release on licence which is itself now coming to be known as 'conditional release'. The legislation also creates a sharp distinction between the 'long-term prisoner' and the 'short-term prisoner', the former being 'a person serving a sentence of imprisonment for a term of four years or more' and the latter relating to a sentence of less than four years (s. 33(5)). It should be noted that a sentence of exactly four years, quite a common term, counts as a long-term sentence, contrary to the Carlisle proposals which would have made this term the upper limit of the short-term category. (The White Paper signalled this modification to the Carlisle proposal, seemingly influenced by the comment of the Parole Board, in its 1988 Report at para. 3, that judges tend to give sentences of four years and above for serious offences.) In calculating whether a prisoner is long term or short term, consecutive and concurrent terms 'shall be treated as a single term' (s. 51(2)) so that it is the total period to be served which counts, not the individual terms for particular offences. Section 49(1)(a) permits the Secretary of State to alter by order the four-year period, which distinguishes short-term and long-term prisoners, to 'such other period as may be specified in the order'. The draft order would have to be approved by each House of Parliament. In addition to short-term and long-term sentences, life sentences constitute a third, distinct category which will be looked at after further examining the distinctions between short-term and long-term prisoners.

5.10 Short-term Prisoners

Short-term prisoners are to be released automatically after half their sentence, 'unconditionally' if the sentence was for less than 12 months (the automatic unconditional release scheme), and on licence if it was for 12 months or more (the automatic conditional release scheme) (CJA 1991, s. 33(1)). The licence (and the supervision normally required by it) will expire (and the release will become unconditional) at the three-quarters point of the sentence (s. 37(1)). This is one reason why release from sentences of less than 12 months is unconditional, rather than being on licence, since licence periods of less than three months are not considered terribly meaningful or realistic, although about 13 per cent of licences under the old regime were for less than this period. However, there is a power for the Secretary of State to release any prisoner on licence 'if he is satisfied that exceptional circumstances exist which justify the prisoner's release on compassionate grounds' (s. 36(1)). This can apply to sentences of less than 12 months but, by s. 37(2), the licence will expire at the halfway point of the sentence, i.e., the point where the prisoner would have been released unconditionally irrespective of compassionate grounds. In some cases this could result in very short licence periods.

Failure by a short-term prisoner to comply with the conditions of a licence is now made a summary offence (s. 38(1)) punishable by a fine (not exceeding level 3 on the standard scale, raised by s. 17(1) to £1,000) but also sanctionable (under s. 38(2)) by suspension of the licence and recall to prison for a period not exceeding six months (but not, of course, exceeding the remaining period of the licence). (For further guidance on the breach procedure see Home Office Circular 104/1992 and Magistrates' Courts Division Circular 14/1992. See also national standards, 8.6 in the Appendix to this Guide at pp. 343–44.)

Illustration 1   D is sentenced to two years in total (e.g., two concurrent terms of 18 months and one consecutive term of six months). D would be released on licence after 12 months and the licence would expire after 18 months, at which point D would be totally free (subject to liability to serve the remainder of his sentence if he commits further offences before the full two years has expired, see s. 40 in 5.13). However, if after two months of freedom under the licence D is convicted by magistrates of failing to comply with the conditions of the licence, the magistrates could not only fine him but also, if they thought it appropriate, suspend his licence and order his recall to prison for anything up to the four-month period of his licence still then remaining. (Even if recalled to prison for the full four months remaining of his licence, he would then be entitled to be released unconditionally because he would have reached the three-quarters point in his sentence, see s. 33(3).)

Illustration 2   D is sentenced to 12 months exactly. He would be released on licence after six months and the licence would expire and the release become unconditional after a further three months.

Illustration 3   D is sentenced to less than 12 months, say 10 months. He would be released unconditionally after five months (although if he committed a further imprisonable offence during the next five months after release he could be ordered to serve the remainder of his sentence in addition to any sentence for the new offence – see s. 40 in 5.13 below; however, the summary offence procedure under s. 38 would not be applicable to him because he has not been released on licence).

Illustration 4   D is sentenced to 10 months. He is released on licence on compassionate grounds after three months. The licence will expire after a further two months, i.e., at the point where he would have been entitled to unconditional release irrespective of the compassionate grounds. (If he managed to be convicted by the magistrates of failing to comply with the conditions of his licence within the two-month life of that licence, the magistrates *could* order his recall to prison under s. 38(2) but he would still be entitled to unconditional release at the halfway point of his sentence – see s. 33(4).)

One general point to note about the first two of the above illustrations is that the licence imposed will not be as a result of a voluntary application for release on licence, as was the case under the old system, and there is concern amongst probation officers about the implications of this for the relationship between the supervising officer and the licensee. The same point can be made about long-term prisoners released automatically at the two-thirds point of their sentence, as explained below.

5.11 Long-term Prisoners

Automatic release only comes to long-term prisoners after two-thirds of the sentence (s. 33(2)). Release from the halfway point (automatic for short-term prisoners) is still possible, however, if the Parole Board recommends release on licence to the Home Secretary (s. 35(1)). This is coming to be known as 'discretionary conditional release'. The licence subsists beyond the two-thirds point (at which release on licence would have come automatically) up to the three-quarters point as with short-term prisoners. As already noted, the Parole Board's recommendations are binding as far as sentences of four years up to seven years, but the Home Secretary retains the final say for sentences of seven years and upwards although he still needs a recommendation from the Board before he can act (except under s. 36 on compassionate grounds, and even here he must consult the Board 'unless the circumstances are such as to render such consultation impracticable').

The focus of the Parole Board's decisions is therefore much more sharply defined under the new system, being limited (leaving aside lifers for the moment) to long-term prisoners and determining whether they serve one-half or two-thirds of the sentence rather than determining the wider range between one-third and two-thirds as previously.

The summary offence of failing to comply with the conditions of a licence is not applicable to long-term prisoners but the Home Secretary may, whether or not there is a technical breach of the licence conditions, revoke the licence and recall the prisoner if recommended to do so by the Board (s. 39(1)) or without such a recommendation (s. 39(2)) where it appears to him to be expedient in the public interest to do so. A long-term prisoner recalled under these provisons is entitled to make representations in writing about his recall and to be informed of the reasons for his recall and of his right to make representations. These provisions are not new and reflect similar provisions under s. 62 of the CJA 1967 which, of course, applied to all categories of parole licensees, not just long-term prisoners. It is the magistrates' court procedure for short-term prisoners which is new and part of the policy of restricting the Parole Board's sphere of operations to long-term (and life sentence) prisoners who are numerically fewer but where the decisions are more crucial and significant. Where a prisoner makes representations about his recall, or is recalled without a recommendation of the Board, then the case must be referred to the Board, and where the Board recommends the immediate release on licence of a prisoner so referred, the Home Secretary *shall*, not may, 'give effect to the . . . recommendation' (s. 39(5)).

Alongside the directions to the Parole Board about the criteria for release of determinate-sentence prisoners, the Home Secretary has also given directions concerning the recall of long-term prisoners released on licence (see pp. 136–37). These echo the criteria for release particularly in that they provide that 'a small risk of violent offending is to be treated as more serious than a larger risk of non-violent offending'. Further details about the mechanics of the recall scheme can be found in paras 71–5 of ch. 8 of the national standards set out at p. 344 of this *Guide*.

Illustration 5   D is sentenced to three years and one year consecutively. He is treated as a long-term prisoner. After two years, therefore, he is not entitled to be released on licence but shall be so released if the Parole Board recommends it. If the Parole Board does not recommend release on licence, D will be released on licence in any event six months later (32 months, the two-thirds point of the sentence) and the licence will expire after a further four months at 36 months, the three-quarters point of the sentence. If D's behaviour whilst on licence gives cause for concern or it seems expedient for any other reason to recall him to prison, this may be done provided he is given the chance and informed of his right to make written representations and his case is referred to the Board etc. Even if recalled, D will still be entitled to release unconditionally once he has reached the three-quarters point of his sentence (see s. 33(3)) although, curiously, this is not expressly stated to apply to a person recalled under s. 39(2) as opposed to s. 39(1), i.e., without a recommendation of the Board. This is probably an oversight as it could theoretically mean such a recalled prisoner serving the whole of the remainder of his sentence in custody, even though previously considered suitable for release on licence and not convicted of any further offence.

Illustration 6   D is sentenced to 12 years. He is eligible for release on licence after six years if the Board recommends it but the Home Secretary still has the final say in seven-year and over cases and will not be bound to accept the Board's recommendation, although in most cases it no doubt would be accepted. If the Board does not recommend release on licence (either after six years or on the subsequent review which would occur at about seven years), D will still be released on licence after eight years (the two-thirds point) and the licence will last for a year up to the three-quarters point of nine years at which point the release becomes unconditional (subject to recall for further offences before the 12 years expires). During the one-year licence period, D may be recalled, whether or not he reoffends, if he breaches licence conditions or his conduct otherwise gives cause for concern.

5.12   Life Prisoners

The mechanisms for determining the period to be served by life prisoners proved to be one of the most controversial issues during the passing of the Act. The background of the previous law and practice is set out earlier in this chapter at 5.3. The issue became further complicated by the ultimately unsuccessful attempt of the House of Lords to amend the Act so as to abolish the mandatory aspect of the life sentence for murder (see 1.24). In conjunction with that attempt, a House of Lords amendment provided that wherever a life sentence is passed (whether for murder or any other crime) the judge would have to state in open court the penal term that the court would have passed 'if it had not been open to it to pass a sentence of imprisonment for life and it had not taken into account the risk of serious harm to the public if the offender were to be released after a determinate number of years imprisonment'. A further amendment provided for the establishment of a Life Sentences Review Tribunal to review prisoners serving such life sentences, towards the end of the prescribed penal term, in order to determine whether to direct the release of the prisoner having 'regard to the risk of the life prisoner's committing further serious offences and the need to protect the public against that risk'. The tribunal, modelled on the Mental Health Review Tribunal, which since 1983 has had a similar function in relation to restricted patients, would have been chaired by a High Court judge and would have provided, for all lifers, the court-like procedure which the European Court of Human Rights had found lacking in the process for discretionary lifers in *Thynne* v *UK* (1990) 13 EHRR 666 (5.3 above).

These amendments were lost when the Bill returned to the Commons (25 June). The government was totally opposed to removing the mandatory element of the sentence for murder but was prepared to do something about the release procedure for discretionary (but not mandatory) lifers. It thus put forward its own amendments dealing with the length of time to be served by discretionary lifers which the House of Lords then substantially modified on 3 July, only for most of the modifications to be lost on 16 July when the Bill returned yet again to the Commons. The final act was played out in the Lords on 23 July when the House of Lords accepted the partial improvements which it had secured as the best that could be obtained without endangering the passage of the whole Bill.

The government amendment introduced at such a late stage (on 25 June) is now, subject to one main modification, s. 34 of the Act. It has no application to mandatory lifers (who are dealt with under s. 35(2) which continues the current procedure as explained above at 5.3). It applies only to discretionary lifers, and a life prisoner is a discretionary lifer for these purposes if (s. 34(1)):

    (a)   his sentence was imposed for a violent or sexual offence the sentence for which is not fixed by law; and

    (b)   the court by which he was sentenced for that offence ordered that this section would apply to him as soon as he had served a part of his sentence specified in the order.

Such a discretionary lifer is then given the right to have his case referred to the Parole Board once the part of his sentence specified by the court has expired (provided also that at least half of any concurrent determinate sentence has also expired). Although there is no special Life Sentence Review Tribunal as in the original Lords amendment, the government did undertake that rules would be made ensuring that in these cases the Parole Board will operate a special set of procedures.

These rules have now been made (the Parole Board Rules 1992) and came into force on 1 October 1992. A panel (generally known as a Discretionary Lifer Panel) will comprise three Parole Board members, the chairman of whom will hold or have held judicial office. In practice there will always by a psychiatrist member of the panel and in the more serious categories of case such as terrorist offences, attempted murder or wounding of police or prison officers, child sexual killings, serial rape and multiple life sentences, the chairman will be a High Court judge. The prisoner will normally see the reports that the panel sees, will be entitled to appear before the panel and (although the procedure is intended to be informal) may have legal representation or representation by some other person. The panel is convened at the prison where the prisoner is currently confined and seems normally be be able to hear two or three cases in a day. The prisoner is entitled to a decision (which may be by a majority) in writing giving reasons within seven days. Of 44 cases heard at 11 prisons during the last quarter of 1992, only six resulted in directions for release although in a further 17 cases there was a recommendation of transfer from closed to open prison (Parole Board Report 1992, para. 44).

The discretionary lifer panel only has jurisdiction once that part of the sentence specified by the order of the court which passed the discretionary life sentence has expired. (Time continues to run even if the prisoner has been transferred to a mental hospital — *ex parte Hickey, The Times*, 28 October 1993.) The part of the sentence specified by the court shall be (s. 34(2)):

such part as the court considers apppropriate taking into account—
(a) the seriousness of the offence, or the combination of the offence and other offences associated with it; and
(b) the provisions of this section as compared with those of section 33(2) above and section 35(1) below.

Paragraph (a) merely reflects s. 2(2)(a) (discussed at 1.16) but para. (b) is a little curious at first sight. In effect, it is directing the court to take account of the fact that a determinate long-term prisoner would be entitled to be released after serving two-thirds of his term and would have the possibility of being released after serving just one-half. The implication seems to be that the court should decide what the normal tariff sentence (under s. 2(2)(a)) should be (ignoring the factor of the unpredictability of the offender which justifies an indeterminate sentence) and then reduce it to somewhere between one-half and two-thirds of that period to take account of the fact that this is the actual term that would be served if a determinate sentence had been imposed. How the court is to decide on the precise point between one-half and two-thirds is not made clear. One would have thought that the halfway point would be the more appropriate because after that point, it is the element of risk to the public which primarily justifies continued custody for a long-term prisoner, and it is at that point that the issue is effectively put in the hands of the Parole Board. Thus, that would seem to be the appropriate time for the Parole Board to commence considering release of a discretionary lifer, but s. 34(2)(b) clearly envisages that it *may* be nearer to the two-thirds point of what would have been the normal determinate term. There may, indeed, be cases where the appropriate determinate sentence would have been less than four years, in which case the halfway point of that determinate term would certainly seem to be the correct point to specify since the prisoner would ordinarily have been short term rather than long term as s. 34(2)(b) seems to assume.

The court is not required in every case to specify a period under s. 34 when passing a discretionary life sentence for a violent or sexual offence. However, a *Practice Direction (Crime: Life Sentences)* [1993] 1 WLR 223 states that:

> the judge should do so, save in the very exceptional case where the judge considers that the offence is so serious that detention for life is justified by the seriousness of the offence alone, irrespective of the risk to the public. In such a case, the judge should state this in open court when passing sentence.

In the exceptional case where no order is made, the case would seem to fall, as with mandatory lifers, under s. 35(2) which effectively continues the present arangements applicable to mandatory lifers (see 5.3 above). There is a difficulty here, though, because the current procedure involves the judge notifying the Home Secretary of the appropriate period to be served on the grounds of retribution and deterrence (something which para. 6 of the above *Practice Direction*) says should no longer happen in the case of discretionary life sentences). If such a period can be identified, surely it would have been appropriate to specify it and make an order under the new procedure (no doubt a very long period of years in this type of case). The case is one by definition where *no* determinate period of years can be sufficient and therefore the sentence is life. If life really is supposed to mean life, then no possibility of early release should *logically* be provided for. Equally, if life is not really supposed to mean life, then there must be a determinate period, however long, which could have been specified in an order under s. 34. This reasoning does not apply to mandatory lifers because their life sentences have not been imposed in preference to an alternative determinate term but because it is the mandatory sentence imposed by Parliament to signify the (supposed) uniqueness of the offence of murder. Indeed in *Secretary of State for the Home Department, ex parte Doody* [1993] 3 WLR 154, the House of Lords took the view that a *mandatory* life sentence included a fixed period of years for the penal element rather than the proper penal element being invariably detention for life subject to mitigation by release on licence at the Secretary of State's discretion as a matter of leniency.

When the Parole Board, under the new procedure, comes to review the case of a discretionary lifer, it shall not direct his release unless 'satisfied that it is no longer necessary for the protection of the public that the prisoner should be confined' (s. 34(4)(b)).

In *Parole Board, ex parte Telling* (1993) *The Times*, 10 May 1993, the Divisional Court held that the Board was not confined to medical evidence in evaluating the risk to the public. It was entitled to take account of many kinds of experts and the final decision was for the Board which had a responsibility to ensure that a prisoner could be released without risk. The courts are clearly not going to be keen to interfere with the Parole Board's assessment of risk. In another unsuccessful challenge to a refusal to release a discretionary lifer under s. 34(4)b, *Parole Board, ex parte Gregory*, 29 July 1993 (LEXIS), Hutchinson J rejected the argument that there was a burden of proof on the Board to show that the risk to the public was 'substantial'. It was, the Divisional Court held, 'unrealistic to concentrate on burdens of proof'. Instead, the correct approach was 'to ask whether there was material on which the Board could conclude there was a more than perceptible or minimal risk of danger to the public, to life or limb, if the applicant were released'.

It the Board is 'satisfied' in relation to the matters required under s. 34(4)(b), and has directed the prisoner's release, under s. 34(3), it shall be the duty of the Secretary of State to release him on licence. Thus, there is no dual key here because the prisoner has already served that part of the sentence justified on punitive grounds. (This may be a factor for making the two-thirds, as opposed to halfway, point relevant in s. 34(2)(b) in that a determinate long-term prisoner is subject to the dual-key system up to the two-thirds point.) The section as originally introduced by the government did provide for the Home Secretary to defer the prisoner's release for six months in exceptional circumstances justifying such a deferment in the public interest but the removal of this power was the main permanent gain won by the House of Lords amendments of 3 July.

Where, under the special new procedure, the Board does not direct release, the prisoner has the right to have his case referred again two years later and at two-yearly intervals after that (s. 34(5)(b)). Section 34(5) also provides a right to a review, two years after a reference under s. 39(4), of a lifer who has been released on licence but who has been subsequently recalled. If a prisoner does not request a reference to the Board, there is no requirement on the Secretary of State to make a reference, although equally there is nothing to prevent the Secretary of State referring the prisoner's case though not specifically required to do so by the prisoner.

Section 48 makes provision for applying the s. 34 procedure to life prisoners transferred from abroad and empowers the Home Secretary, after consultation with the Lord Chief Justice, to certify the appropriate part of the sentence that would have been specified by a court if they had been sentenced in this country. In this case it appears not to be relevant whether or not the discretionary life sentence is in respect of a violent or sexual offence. This is presumably because discretionary life sentences might be imposed abroad for other sorts of offences. Under CJA 1991, discretionary life sentences based on the unpredictability of the offender rather than on the seriousness of the offence cannot be imposed other than for violent or sexual offences (see the discussion of s. 2(2)(b) in 1.25) and this is underlined by the fact that s. 34(1)(a) expressly limits itself to such offences in the first place. It is worth noting that if at some future date the mandatory element of the life sentence for murder should be abolished, it would automatically be open to a judge imposing a discretionary life sentence for murder (which is clearly within the definition of a violent offence no matter how quietly or peacefully death is caused) to make an order under s. 34. It is submitted that it would only be appropriate to so so where the life sentence was imposed in preference to a (long) determinate term because of the unpredictability of the offender. Furthermore, it can be argued that that is the only case where a life sentence, as opposed to a long, perhaps very long, determinate sentence, would be justified anyway.

As things stand at the moment, in the minds of many, including a majority of the House of Lords, there is a clear but unjustified distinction between the procedure applicable to mandatory life sentences and discretionary life sentences. For the discretionary lifers within the meaning of s. 34, the determination of the length of time to be served has been removed from the executive and placed back in the hands of the court and a special panel of the Parole Board. In the case of a mandatory lifer, the old procedures continue under s. 35(2) and the Home Secretary is still empowered to substitute his own view of the length of time to be served in preference to the tariff notified to him by the trial judge although, as a result of the decision in *Secretary of State for the Home Department, ex parte Doody* [1993] 3 WLR 154, the mandatory lifer will now be informed of the judicial recommendation, will be able to make representations to the Home Secretary and will be given reasons for the Home Secretary's decision (Michael Howard, Parliamentary Debates (Hansard), Commons, 6th ser., vol. 229, written answers, cols 863–5, 27 July 1993). It has also been announced that from April 1993 mandatory lifers whose tariffs have expired and who are thus being considered by the Parole Board (even though not by discretionary lifer panels) will be able to see their dossiers and will be given reasons for the decision of the Board. Even with these changes, it is difficult to believe that the system for mandatory sentences will survive for long alongside and in comparison with the more open and judicial system for discretionary lifers. Even Lord Waddington, for the government, in the final debate on the Bill in the House of Lords on 23 July (at col. 652), was prepared to concede that 'It may be that on maturer reflection, policy will move in the direction which some of your lordships wish to see'. Figures quoted in the Commons (16 July, col. 316) show that of the 274 mandatory life sentences considered in 1990, ministers set a longer period than that recommended by the trial judge in 90 cases and a shorter period in 43 cases.

Illustration 7   D is sentenced to life imprisonment for armed robbery, because he is clearly unstable and it is difficult to say when he could safely be released. The first question is whether this is a violent offence, i.e., one which leads, or is intended or likely to lead, to a person's death or serious personal injury (see the definition of violent offence in s. 31(1)). This answer might seem obvious with an offence such as armed robbery but suppose D was 'armed' with an unloaded gun (cf. *Ashdown* [1974] Crim LR 130 and see further 1.10). Assuming, though, that the gun is loaded, and that the offence is properly classified as violent (which is one of the preconditions under s. 2 of the Act to imposing a life sentence otherwise than on the basis of the seriousnes of the offence), the court would then have to consider what period to specify under s. 34. If the seriousness of the offence would normally justify a sentence of 12 years, then it would appear that the court should specify somewhere between six and eight years since that is the period that would actually be served before release on licence if a determinate sentence of 12 years was actually imposed. In the absence of any confidence about the true meaning of s. 34(2)(b), the court may well be tempted to specify the middle point between six and eight years, i.e., seven years. (Paragraph 5 of the *Practice Direction (Crime: Life Sentences)* requires the judge to give reasons for his decision as to the length of the relevant part.) After serving seven years, D would be entitled to have his case referred to the special panel of the Board who, if satisfied that it was no longer necessary for the protection of the public that he be confined, could (and presumably would) direct his release on licence. If the Board was not so satisfied, D would remain in custody until his case was referred to the Board again, and he could require it to be so referred after two years and, if still unsuccessful, every two years after that. Under each of these references to the Board, D would be entitled to attend and appear at the hearing and would be entitled to legal representation.

Compare this with the position of the mandatory lifer.

Illustration 8   D2 is sentenced to life imprisonment for the murder of a police officer committed in the course of resisting arrest. (Unlike D in the previous example who must have intended to kill, as is necessary for attempted murder, D2 did not intend to kill but was convicted on the basis of an intention to cause grievous bodily harm.) The s. 34 procedure is not applicable but the trial judge will write to the Home Secretary giving his view of how long D2 should serve to meet the requirements of retribution and deterrence (see 5.3). In this case the period is, in the view of the trial judge, 15 years and the Lord Chief Justice agrees with this. This information will at least now be disclosed to D2 and he will have the opportunity to make representations to the Home Office. A Home Office Minister then decides that the tariff should be 20 years (because the victim was a police officer) and that the first review of D2's case by the Parole Board should be three years earlier at 17 years (D2 will now at least be told the reasons for this). Whenever the review takes place, it will *not* be under the new special procedure and D2 will not be entitled to attend or to have legal representation although he will now be allowed to see his dossier and will be given reasons for the Board's eventual decision. Even if, at the first review, the Parole Board does recommend the release of D2 on licence in three years, the Home Secretary does not have to accept this recommendation (e.g., if public opinion seems particularly sensitive on the question of murder of police officers at the time). It is not clear how the new practice of giving reasons will operate where the Board recommends release but the Home Secretary does not accept the recommendation. How willing or able will the Home Secretary be to disclose his reasons? In his written answer of 27 July 1993 he was quite explicit that he would consider 'the public acceptability of early release. This means that I will exercise my discretion to release only if I am satisfied that to do so will not threaten the maintenance of public confidence in the system of criminal justice.'

For the position of existing prisoners currently serving discretionary life sentences, see the transitional provisions in sch. 12, para. 9, discussed below at 5.20.

Having considered the specific release procedures applicable to the three main categories of short-term, long-term and life-sentence prisoners, we can now turn to the other provisons of part II of the Act which are of more general application.

RESTORING MEANING TO THE SENTENCE OF THE COURT

This was an important policy underlying many of the recommendations of the Carlisle Committee and can be seen at work, *inter alia*, in some of the following provisions.

5.13   Return to Prison for Conviction during Currency of Original Sentence

CJA 1991, s. 40 is a new provision designed not only to help restore meaning to the sentence passed but also to increase the incentives not to reoffend after release from prison. It differs from recall for breach of licence conditions in that it applies even where the licence has expired and the release has become 'unconditional'. The section applies to a (released) long-term or short-term prisoner (but not to a life-sentence prisoner who remains on licence for life and who can be recalled to prison at any time, whether or not he reoffends). It operates where the offender commits an offence punishable with imprisonment 'before the date on which he would (but for his release) have served his sentence in full' (s. 40(1)(a)). Whether or not *the conviction* takes place before this date, the court convicting him 'may, whether or not it passes any other sentence on him, order him to be returned to prison for the whole or any part of the period ... equal in length to the period between the date on which the new offence was committed and [the date on which he would (but for his release) have served his sentence in full]' (s. 40(2)).

Illustration 9   D is released from a three-year sentence after 18 months but commits a further imprisonable offence six months later. He is liable to be returned to prison for any period up to the 12 months of his original sentence which remained unexpired at the date of the offence, and this is so even though he is *not convicted* of the further offence until after the expiry of the original sentence. Under s. 40(3), the maximum period that a magistrates' court can order for return to prison is six months but it may commit D to the Crown Court under s. 42 of the PCCA 1973.

The period ordered for return to prison is additional to any sentence imposed for the further offence and under s. 40(4):

> (a)   shall be taken to be a sentence of imprisonment for the purposes of this part;
> (b)   shall, as the court may direct, either be served before and be followed by, or be served concurrently with, the sentence imposed for the new offence; and
> (c)   in either case shall be disregarded in determining the appropriate length of that sentence.

Thus, in the above illustration, if the court considers that a three-year sentence is appropriate for the new offence, the court should first impose that sentence without regard to the fact that it may also be ordering a return to prison for the remainder of the original sentence. It then has to decide whether or not to order any period of return to prison to be served consecutively or concurrently with the new three-year sentence. If it decides that it should be served consecutively, because the return to prison is treated as a sentence of imprisonment in its own right, D is treated as being sentenced to a total of four years and thus will become a long-term prisoner and will be subject to discretionary rather than automatic release after serving two years of the new four-year term.

The real sting in s. 40 is that it applies even where, unlike in the above example, the new offence is not committed until after the expiry of the licence period, when the release has become 'unconditional', provided that the period of the original sentence has not expired. It thus differs significantly from the old power to revoke a licence for a further offence under CJA 1967, s. 62(7), not only in this sense, but also in the fact that the sanction under s. 62(7) was limited to the unexpired part of the licence rather than that of the original sentence, and also in the fact that s. 62(7) was only concerned with offences punishable *on indictment* with imprisonment.

Illustration 10   D is sentenced to three years and is released on licence after 18 months. After a further nine months (at 27 months) his release becomes 'unconditional' but if three months later (at 30 months) he commits a further offence (even a summary one) punishable with imprisonment, there is power for the court to order the remaining six months of the original sentence to be served in addition to any sentence imposed for the new offence.

The new offence must, however, be punishable with imprisonment which, it should be noted, is not true of the summary offence under s. 38 of failing to comply with licence conditions.

Illustration 11   D is sentenced to two years and released on licence after one year but two months after release is convicted under s. 38 for failure to comply with his licence conditions. Under s. 38, D may have all or part of the remaining four months of his licence suspended and be *recalled* to prison for the period of that suspension, but he is not liable under s. 40 to be *returned* to prison for the 10 months unexpired of his sentence because the offence under s. 38 is not *punishable* by imprisonment (even though it may trigger suspension of a licence and recall to prison under the original sentence). There is a further difference between recall under s. 38 and return under s. 40 in that D is only at risk of recall for the period of his licence still unexpired at the date of his appearance in court, whereas under s. 40 D may not appear in court until after his original sentence has expired but is still liable to be ordered to return to prison for the period of his original sentence which was unexpired at the date of the further imprisonable offence.

Illustration 12   D is sentenced to two years and is released on licence after 12 months. In the last few weeks of his licence (i.e., just before 18 months from the start of his sentence) he breaches the conditions and is summoned to appear before the magistrates under s. 38. He appears before the magistrates just a few days after the 18-month point of his original sentence and, therefore, just after the expiry of the licence. The magistrates have no power to order his recall to prison since the licence has already expired and cannot be suspended. The magistrates can of course fine him under s. 38. Just under three months later (i.e., 21 months after the start of the original sentence of two years), D commits an imprisonable offence but is not brought to court for it for a further six months (i.e., after the expiry of the original term of two years). Nevertheless, the court can order his return to prison under s. 40 for up to the three months of his original sentence which remained when he committed the further imprisonable offence.

The examples given so far have been of short-term prisoners but s. 40 applies equally to long-term prisoners. Indeed, the changes which it introduces are of more significance to long-term prisoners since they will tend to spend a greater proportion of their sentences (and, certainly, longer periods in absolute terms) on unconditional release rather than on release on licence.

Illustration 13   D is sentenced to six years. He is eligible for discretionary release on licence after three years but is not released until he becomes entitled to release on licence after four years. The licence expires after six months but D remains at risk of being returned to prison for further imprisonable offences for a further 18 months until the expiry of his original sentence of six years. For longer sentences the period at risk after the expiry of the licence will be longer still.

This is one of those aspects of the Act which has an unpredictable potential for increasing rather than reducing the prison population. Various estimates have been made of the likely resultant increase in the prison population based on return rates of 20 per cent giving net increases of anything between 1,100 and 2,000 in the prison population (HC Standing Committee A, 17 January 1991, col. 366). The government defended the changes introduced by s. 40 on the grounds of them being part of the overall strategy of restoring the true meaning of sentences imposed by the court and on the grounds that 'when those people in our society who choose to commit crime realise that they must avoid committing a crime for the entirety of the sentence imposed by the court, they will be less likely to offend' (ibid., col. 368). The more sceptical will wonder whether the deterrent effect of the threat of reactivation of the original sentence will really be significant to an offender contemplating the commission of an offence for which he knows in any event he can be sentenced to imprisonment and whether any putative gains in deterrent effect will be sufficient to outweigh the potential increases in the prison population.

5.14   Time Spent in Custody before Sentence

As has already been seen, the provisions for early release depend on the serving or expiry of various proportions of the original sentence, one-half, two-thirds and three-quarters being the significant periods. In many cases, the prisoner may already have been in custody on remand prior to being sentenced. Section 67 of the CJA 1967 already makes it clear that such periods should reduce the sentence to be served rather than the sentence to be pronounced and CJA 1991, s. 41, makes it equally clear that such remand time counts towards the calculation of the various proportions of the sentence served.

Illustration 14   D is remanded in custody for two months on a charge of burglary before being sentenced to 12 months for that burglary. Under CJA 1967, s. 67, he is only liable to serve a maximum of a further 10 months and after four months will be treated as having served half his sentence (four months post sentence plus two months on remand = six months) and will be entitled to release on licence. The licence will last for three months after which (i.e., from seven months after sentence) he will be entitled to unconditional release for the remaining three months subject to the possibility of being ordered to return to prison under s. 40 for committing a further imprisonable offence. Ten months after sentence he will be totally free of any liability under the original sentence since he would by then (but for his release) have served his sentence (treated under CJA 1967, s. 67, as reduced by two months) in full.

However, CJA 1991, s. 41(3), enigmatically provides that none of this shall have the effect of reducing a licence period below one-quarter of the sentence of a short-term prisoner or one-twelfth of the sentence of long-term prisoner.

Illustration 15 As in illustration 14 but D is in custody on remand for seven months before being sentenced to 12 months. He is entitled to immediate release on licence having already served more than half his sentence. The licence would normally expire after a further two months (when he is treated as having served three-quarters of the sentence) but s. 41(3) would appear to mean that the licence will continue in force for a further month so that it lasts for a total of three months (one-quarter of the sentence pronounced by the court).

Formerly, CJA 1967, s. 67, did not apply to time spent in custody abroad awaiting extradition to this country although normally the sentencer in such a case would reduce the sentence by an equivalent period (see *Scalise* (1985) 7 Cr App R (S) 333). This could result in a different sentence being pronounced for precisely the same offence in precisely the same circumstances save that one defendant had spent 12 months in custody on remand in this country whereas the other had spent 12 months in prison abroad awaiting extradition. If four years was the appropriate sentence for the offence, the first defendant would be sentenced to four years but would be treated as having already served one year under s. 67, whereas the second defendant should normally only be sentenced to three years in the first place. This anomaly could not be allowed to stand since it ran contrary to the principle of restoring meaning to the sentence actually passed by the court and also could make the difference between one prisoner being treated as long term and another as short term. The problem is now addressed by CJA 1991, s. 47, which empowers the sentencing court to order that all or part of the period of custody abroad awaiting extradition shall be treated as a relevant period for the purposes of CJA 1967, s. 67. This is still distinguishable from the position for remand time in this country which is automatically counted under s. 67, since CJA 1991, s. 47, gives a discretion to the judge as to whether, or what proportion of, the period abroad should be treated as a relevant period under CJA 1967, s. 67. Thus where, for example, the accused is considered to have deliberately spun out extradition proceedings, the full period may not be counted in his favour (cf. *Stone* (1988) 10 Cr App R (S) 322).

5.15 Additional Days for Disciplinary Offences

Under the old system, disciplinary offences in prison were sanctioned by loss of remission but did not, at least formally, affect eligibility for parole. Now that remission has been abolished and there is a single concept of early release, it is no longer possible or appropriate to speak of loss of remission but CJA 1991, s. 42, instead now provides for additional days (in custody) to be awarded under rules to be made under s. 47 of the Prison Act 1952 (see SI 1992/2080 and SI

1992/2081). Such additonal days, insofar as they are not themselves remitted under prison rules, e.g., for subsequent good behaviour, extend the periods which must be served before becoming entitled to or eligible for early release and also extend the period of any licence.

Illustration 16   D is sentenced to three years but is awarded an extra 28 days for disciplinary offences. Although he would normally be automatically released on licence after 18 months, he will not be released until a further 28 days have elapsed. Furthermore, when he is released the licence will not expire at the normal point of three-quarters through his sentence (i.e., at 27 months) but will extend for a further 28 days beyond that date. Although the wording of s. 42(2)(b) is not altogether felicitous in this respect, it seems clear that the intention is that the period of freedom on licence should remain the same in length but should start and finish at a later date (28 days in this example).

Illustration 17   D is sentenced to six years and in the first year is awarded 28 additional days but 14 of these have subsequently been remitted by the time D has served three years and would be eligible as a long-term prisoner for discretionary release on licence. The remaining 14 additional days mean that his eligibility for release is put back by those 14 days and also, if he is not recommended for early release by the Parole Board, his normal entitlement to early release at four years is also put back by 14 days (unless some or all of those remaining 14 days have not themselves been remitted during the ensuing year).

EARLY RELEASE PROCEDURES IN SPECIAL CATEGORIES OF CASE

CJA 1991 deals with four special categories: (a) young offenders, (b) sexual offenders, (c) fine defaulters and contemnors, and (d) deportees and other persons liable to removal from the UK.

5.16   Young Offenders (under the Age of 21)

CJA 1991, s. 43, specifically deals with these since they do not come within the definition of prisoners and cannot be sentenced to imprisonment.

Section 43(1) deals with determinate sentences. It treats sentences of detention in a young offender institution (the most common custodial sentence for young offenders, always imposed for a determinate period) and determinate sentences of detention under s. 53(2) of the CYPA 1933 (much rarer and reserved for serious cases) as sentences of imprisonment for the purposes of part II of the Act. Depending on the period of detention ordered, the young offender will therefore be treated as either a long-term or, more usually, as a short-term prisoner. This is, however, subject to subsections (4) and (5). Subsection (4) alters the application of s. 33(1) to short-term prisoners *under the age of 18* so that if the sentence is exactly 12 months (the maximum for such an offender for detention in a young offender institution), the offender is released unconditionally halfway through the sentence rather than on licence as would be the case for a prisoner aged over 18. If the sentence is for more than 12 months (as can only happen under CYPA 1933, s. 53(2)) or less than 12 months, then s. 33(1) applies in its normal way. The subsection is not specific about the precise date when the offender must be under 18 but it is presumably the date when he is halfway through his sentence and eligible for early release under s. 33(1). These provisions, however, have to be read in the light of CJA 1991, s. 65, which effectively provides for three months' supervision by a probation officer or social worker for all offenders released under the age of 22.

Illustration 18   D is aged 17 years and 4 months when sentenced to 12 months' detention in a young offender institution. He becomes entitled to release after six months and being still under 18 (17 years 10 months) is entitled to be released unconditionally as a result of CJA 1991, s. 43(4)(a). Nevertheless, although his release is not 'on licence' he will be subject to supervision for three months under s. 65. If D had been 17 years and seven months when sentenced to 12 months, he would have become aged 18 before he becomes entitled to release halfway through his sentence and so his release would be on licence under the normal rule in s. 33(1) for sentences of 12 months or more. The licence may, however, require supervision by a social worker rather than by a probation officer because s. 43(5) provides that for a person aged under 22 released on licence, the reference in s. 37(4) to supervision by a probation officer shall include a reference to supervision by a local authority social worker. The net effect may, therefore, not be very different. Section 43(4) seems merely to ensure that offenders under 18 serving sentences of exactly 12 months are released 'under supervision' rather than 'on licence'.

Section 43(2) deals with the indeterminate sentences which may exceptionally be passed on young offenders under CYPA 1933, s. 53(1), or CJA 1982, s. 8. Young offenders serving these sentences are treated for the purposes of the early release procedures as though they were life-sentence prisoners, the only difference being that if they are released on licence whilst still under 22, the supervision may include supervision by a social worker (CJA 1991, s. 43(5)).

5.17   Sexual Offenders

In the general run of cases, the period representing the final quarter of an offender's sentence will be a period when he is at liberty in the community and not under supervision. However, the Bill was amended at report stage in the Commons (20 February) by the addition of what is now CJA 1991, s. 44, to provide for a longer period of supervision right up to the end of the sentence in the case of certain sexual offenders where the sentencing court so directs. Section 44 is not primarily designed to increase the punitive or custodial aspect of the sentence but rather to extend the period of supervision with a view to protecting the public from serious harm and also further securing the rehabilitation of the offender. It is thus conceived as being desirable from the point of view of the offender as well as of the public. However, the reference in s. 44 to s. 33(3) also means that where the offender is recalled to prison for breach of his licence conditions, he may be liable to remain there until the end of his sentence rather than just up to the three-quarters point. This certainly appears to be the case for a long-term prisoner whose licence is revoked under s. 39 unless subsequently the

Parole Board reviews his case and he is released once more on what must be a fresh licence, the first one having been revoked.

Illustration 19   D is sentenced to six years for a sexual offence and a direction is made under s. 44. He will be released on licence at the latest after four years but the licence will last not just for six months (i.e., up to the three-quarters point of the sentence) but for two years (i.e., up to the point where the whole sentence would have been served). If D's licence is revoked under s. 39 and he is recalled to prison, whether it be during the first six months or the last 18 months of the licence, he will be liable to remain in prison until the end of the sentence (unless a further recommendation to release him on a fresh licence is subsequently made).

The situation seems slightly different for a short-term prisoner since breach of the licence conditions will result only in the suspension rather than the revocation of the licence under s. 38, and then only for a maximum of six months. There will thus be many cases where the period of suspension expires before the end of the original sentence and therefore before the end of the original (suspended) licence. In such a case, the offender is presumably entitled to be released again once the period of suspension expires, though not unconditionally but, rather, under the terms of the original extended licence.

Illustration 20   D is sentenced to three years for a sexual offence and a direction is made under s. 44. He will be released on licence after 18 months but that licence will last for a full 18 months up to the end of his sentence. If he breaches the conditions of his licence after, say, six months, the magistrates may suspend his licence for a maximum of six months under s. 38. He would then be entitled to be released again for the remaining six months (or more) of his sentence under the terms of the original, now revived, licence.

Although by s. 51(1) 'sexual offence' is given the same definition as in part I of the Act (see 1.10), the increased duration of the supervision on licence only applies if:

the court by which he was sentenced for that offence, having had regard to the matters mentioned in section 32(6)(a) and (b) above, directed that this section should apply.

The matters mentioned in s. 32(6) are:

(a)   the need to protect the public from serious harm from offenders; and

(b)   the desirability of preventing the commision by them of further offences and of securing their rehabilitation.

Whenever a court is sentencing a sexual offender it therefore needs to consider whether to make a direction under s. 44. The relationship of s. 44 with s. 2(2)(b) of the Act is interesting. Section 44 may on occasions enable a court to avoid passing a longer term under s. 2(2))b) than is commensurate with the seriousness of the offence since it may reason that the extended duration of the supervision under licence may be adequate to protect the public from serious harm and that it is not necessary to pass a longer sentence for this reason. Even if the court still thinks the protection of the public requires a longer term in custody, the power to make a direction under s. 44 may persuade it to increase the term by less than would otherwise be the case.

Illustration 21   D is being sentenced for indecent assault. Twelve months would be the sentence commensurate with the offence under s. 2(1)(a). The court feels that this will not be adequate to protect the public from serious harm since D will be released on licence after six months and will not even be under supervision after nine months. The court may consider increasing the sentence under s. 2(2)(b) to, say, 16 months in order to ensure that the offender is either in custody or at least under supervision for 12 months. The court can achieve the same result by not increasing the sentence but by making a direction under s. 44. D will be released from custody after six months but will be under supervision on licence for the remaining six months of the sentence. Alternatively, to protect the public, the court may have been considering increasing the sentence to two years which would normally entail custody or supervision for 18 months. It can achieve a similar result by increasing the sentence to only 18 months and making a direction under s. 44. In both cases, by selecting the lower sentence and making a direction under s. 44 the court keeps the custodial part of the sentence closer to that commensurate with the seriousness of the offence and maximises the period of supervision under licence which is the part of the sentence generally more likely to have rehabilitative effects rather than the reverse.

5.18   Fine Defaulters and Contemnors

The ordinary provisions on early release in CJA 1991 do not apply to persons committed to prison (or young adults ordered to be detained) for failure to pay a fine or for contempt of court or kindred offences because s. 51(1) specifically excludes such cases from the definition of a 'sentence of imprisonment'. Section 45(1), however, applies a modified scheme of early release to them. This modified scheme is implemented largely through s. 45(3) and (4) which substitute different provisions for s. 33(1) to (4) and s. 37(1) to (3). The essence of the substituted provisions is that there is normally no release on licence but instead unconditional release at the point where remission would have been earned under the old law. Thus under s. 33(1) as substituted, a person committed for under 12 months would be released after serving half his term and a person committed for 12 months or more would be released after two-thirds. Release on licence is only a possibility under s. 36 (on compassionate grounds) and such a licence will normally continue (subject to suspension or revocation for breach of the conditions) up to the point where unconditional release would have occurred under s. 33 (i.e., at the halfway or two-thirds point). Section 40 (return to prison on further conviction of an imprisonable offence during the currency of the original sentence) is not applicable to these cases.

5.19   Deportees and Other Persons Liable to Removal from the United Kingdom

The normal rules are slightly amended by s. 46 in two respects for this category of prisoners. First, for long-term prisoners, the Secretary of State is given power to release on licence from the halfway point of the sentence without any recommendation from the Parole Board being neccesary. The reason for this is that if the prisoner is going to be deported the question of protection of the public and prevention of reoffending does not really arise, at least as far as this country is concerned. The Home Secretary will, however, have to take care in the way he exercises his discretion to release deportees after serving half of a long-term sentence. The Carlisle Committee noted that there would be a great deal of resentment from other prisoners if deportees seemed to be getting more favourable treatment in terms of early release.

The second difference applicable to deportees is that the application of s. 37(4) is modified so that the conditions in any licence (whether for a long-term or short-term prisoner) need not include a condition as to supervision by a probation officer. Again, if the prisoner is to be deported, that would be inappropriate.

5.20   Transitional Provisions

Transitional provisions are contained in CJA 1991, sch. 12, paras 8 to 13, and are quite important given that they are the provisons applicable to 'existing prisoners' and therefore, in the case of prisoners currently serving long sentences, may be relevant for many years to come. Their general drift is to apply the new provisions to existing prisoners in such a way that they are treated, at worst, no less favourably than they would have been under the old system. An 'existing prisoner' under para. 8(1) is 'any person who (at the commencement of part II of the Act) is serving a custodial sentence' and the term 'custodial sentence' is itself defined in para. 8(8). Paragraph 8(1) also defines an 'existing licensee' as someone who at commencement has already been released on a licence under CJA 1967, s. 60, and whose licence is still in force at commencement (i.e., someone currently 'on parole' at commencement).

The new provisions in part II of the CJA 1991 do apply to both existing prisoners and to existing licensees but with important modifications and exceptions. In addition to their practical importance, these are interesting because they point up many of the changes made by the Act.

First of all, the new liability under s. 40 to be returned to prison because of further imprisonable offences during the currency of the original sentence does not apply either to existing licensees or to existing prisoners (para. 8(3)).

An existing prisoner whose sentence is for a term of 12 months is treated as though it were a term of less than 12 months (para. 8(4)). The effect of this is to allow unconditional release after six months. This avoids worsening the position of an existing prisoner sentenced to exactly 12 months who, under the old system, was entitled to release on remission after six months but who under the new provisions would only be entitled to release on licence.

An existing prisoner or licensee whose sentence is for a term of more than 12 months but less than four years (or such other period as may be substituted in

s. 33(5)) would ordinarily be treated as a short-term prisoner but by para. 8(5) he is to be treated as a long-term prisoner. This provision ensures that the discretionary system continues to apply to existing prisoners and para. 8(6) adjusts the normal points for eligibility for release on licence and unconditional release. These are changed, from one-half and three-quarters of the sentence, to one-third and two-thirds respectively so that they mirror the existing system of eligibility for release on licence at one-third and entitlement to remission at two-thirds.

Paragraph 8(7) provides for the continuation, in relation to existing prisoners or licensees, of the existing system whereby the Home Secretary is able to act solely on the recommendation of the Local Review Committees in certain categories of case. Thus the LRCs are not to disappear immediately for the very sound reason that the numbers of existing prisoners eligible for discretionary early release under the transitional provisions will be too great for the Parole Board to handle itself.

Paragraph 10 provides for forfeited remission to be treated as additional days and paras 11, 12 and 13 contain provisions dealing with young persons, extended sentence prisoners and fine defaulters and contemnors.

Finally, para. 9 deals with existing discretionary lifers in a manner similar to that applicable under s. 48 to discretionary lifers transferred from abroad. As with that provision there is no strict requirement that the sentence should have been imposed for a violent or sexual offence (although that will almost always be the case) since, prior to the Act, there was no restriction to such offences as being the only ones for which a sentence not based on the seriousness of the offence could be passed. The Home Secretary is empowered to certify that, had s. 34 been in force at the time of sentencing, the court would have made an order within s. 34 specifying a particular part of his sentence. All existing lifers have therefore been certified in the light of the tariff already notified to the Home Secretary under the old *Handscombe* procedure. (The Home Secretary is not bound by the existing tariff but equally he should give the prisoner the opportunity to comment before finalising it in the certificate issued — *ex parte McCartney* (1993) *The Times*, 28 October 1993.) This created an immediate backlog of 330 prisoners entitled to a hearing on 1 October 1992 which the Parole Board has committed itself to hearing by March 1994 via the new discretionary lifer panels. Thus existing discretionary lifers get the benefit of the new procedures authorised by s. 34. It was held in *Secretary of State for the Home Department, ex parte Hickey, The Times*, 28 October 1993 that this applies equally to lifers who have been transferred to a mental hospital so that for these purposes such a prisoner is still regarded as serving his sentence. Such a decision seems inevitable and correct in the light of the Home Office Policy (successfully defended in *ex parte S, The Times*, 19 August 1992) of considering the release of lifers transferred to mental hospital via the Parole Board rather than via the provisions of the Mental Health Act 1983.

5.21   Other Provisions for Early Release

A concluding point that perhaps ought to be made about the provisons of part II of the CJA 1991 is that they do not contain a comprehensive code relating to early release. Quite apart from the fact that a lot of important detail is still to be filled in by means of regulations, certain other provisions relating to early release do not appear to have been rescinded by the Act. These include provision under s. 28 of the Prison Act 1952 for temporary discharge on the grounds of ill health and under r. 6 of the Prison Rules 1964 for temporary release for special purposes. Furthermore, s. 32 of the CJA 1982 appears to be unaffected. This section allows the Home Secretary, by statutory instrument approved by Parliament, to release a class of prisoners no more than six months earlier than they would otherwise be released. Lifers and prisoners serving sentences for excluded offences, which include most sexual, violent or drug-related offences, are not eligible for release under this procedure which is designed for cases where there is exceptional pressure on the prison system. Section 32 is a reminder that government continues to need release mechanisms in order to regulate the numbers that public or judicial perceptions of appropriate sentence lengths put into prison in the first place. Given this essentially pragmatic background, one should not perhaps be too critical of the new system introduced by the CJA 1991, and in any event, it is impossible to evaluate it fairly until it has become fully operational in all its aspects.

SECRETARY OF STATE'S DIRECTIONS

5.22   Secretary of State's Directions for the Release and Recall of Determinate Sentenced Prisoners, 1992

1.   Release of Determinate Sentence Inmates
1.1   The decision whether or not to recommend parole should focus primarily on the risk to the public of a further offence being committed at a time when the offender would otherwise be in prison. This should be balanced against the benefit, both to the public and the offender, of early release back into the community under a degree of supervision which might help rehabilitation and so lessen the risk of reoffending in the future.

1.2   Each case should be considered on its individual merits, without discrimination on any grounds.

1.3   Before recommending parole, the Parole Board should be satisfied that:

(a)   the longer period of supervision that parole would provide is likely to reduce the risk of further imprisonable offences being committed. In assessing the risk to the community, a small risk of violent offending is to be treated as more serious than a larger risk of non-violent offending;

(b)   the offender has shown by his attitude and behaviour in custody that he is willing to address his offending and has made positive efforts and progress in doing so;

(c)   the resettlement plan will help secure the offender's rehabilitation.

1.4   Before deciding whether or not to recommend parole, the Parole Board must take into account the supervising officer's recommendation as to suitability for release, including cooperation with a programme of supervision and adherence to the conditions of the licence.

Training Guidance

The following factors should generally be taken into account when making a recommendation about parole. The weight and relevance attached to each factor differs and may vary according to the circumstances of the case.

(a)   the offender's background, including any previous convictions and their pattern, and responses to any previous periods of supervision;

(b)   the nature and circumstances of the original offence;

(c)   where available, the sentencing judge's comments and probation and medical reports prepared for the court;

(d)   any risk to the victim or possibility of retaliation by the victim, victim's family or local community;

(e)   any risk to other persons, including persons outside the jurisdiction;

(f)   any available statistical indicators as to the likelihood of reoffending;

(g)   attitude and behaviour in custody including offences against prison discipline;

(h)   attitude to other inmates and positive contributions made to prison life;

(i)   remorse, insight into offending behaviour, attitude to the victim and steps taken, within available resources, to achieve any treatment or training objectives set out in a sentence plan;

(j)   realism of the release plan and resettlement prospects, including home circumstances and the likelihood of cooperation with supervision, relationship with the home probation officer, attitude of the victim and local community, extent to which the release plan continues rehabilitative work started in the prison and the extent to which it lessens or removes the occurrence of circumstances which led to the original offence;

(k)   any medical or psychiatric considerations;

(l)   any other information, including representations by or on behalf of the offender, which may have a bearing on risk assessment.

2.   Recall of Determinate Sentenced Prisoners

2.1   In considering the recall of a long-term prisoner released on licence, or in confirming an emergency recall, the Parole Board should consider:

(a)   whether the offender's continued liberty would present a serious risk to the safety of other persons or the offender is likely to commit further imprisonable offences. In assessing the risk to the community, a small risk of violent offending is to be treated as more serious than a larger risk of non-violent offending;

(b)   the extent to which the offender has complied with the conditions of the licence, or failed to do so or otherwise to have cooperated with the supervising officer;

(c)   whether the offender would be unlikely to comply with the conditions of the licence and submit to supervision if allowed to remain in the community.

2.2   Before deciding to recall an offender released on licence, or confirm an emergency recall, the Parole Board must take into account the supervising officer's recommendation as to whether the offender should remain on licence and any representations made by the offender.

Training Guidance

The following factors should generally be taken into account when considering the recall of a long-term prisoner. The weight and relevance attached to each factor differs and may vary according to the circumstances of the case.

(a)   the offender's background, including any previous convictions and their pattern and, in particular, performance during any previous periods of supervision;

(b)   the nature and circumstances of the original offence and the offender's present attitude to it;

(c)   how far the causes of offending behaviour have been addressed on release, together with any new areas of concern that have arisen while on licence;

(d)   general behaviour on licence, including response to supervision, compliance with licence requirements, cooperation with the supervising officer and general attitude to authority;

(e)   the proportion of the licence already served and the seriousness of the breach in relation to the amount of licence period successfully completed;

(f)   the extent and seriousness of any further offences committed while on licence and/or charges which have been laid in connection with such offences;

(g)   the suitability of the offender's current accommodation;

(h)   the offender's relationships with his or her family and people outside the family circle;

(i)   any contact by the offender with or concerns expressed by the victim or victim's family, any adverse local reaction to the offender's release on licence;

(j)   work record – the extent to which jobs have been held down, relationships with colleagues and employer;

(k)   current medical or psychiatric views, if any;

(l)   any other information, including representations from other people or bodies (e.g. police, social services) which may have a bearing on whether the offender should be permitted to remain on licence.

Chapter Six
Children's Evidence

The provisions of sections 52 to 55 of the Criminal Justice Act 1991 are based on, although they do not fully implement, the recommendations of the Home Office Advisory Group on Video Evidence (the Pigot Committee) which reported in December 1989. They build upon reforms enacted under the Criminal Justice Act 1988 which provided for children's evidence to be given by a live televison link in certain cases and which abolished the requirement of corroboration for unsworn evidence of children. Indeed it was as a result of pressure for more far-reaching reform in the debates on that Act that the Advisory Group was set up. Section 52 of the 1991 Act provides for the evidence of all children under the age of 14 to be given unsworn and removes the special competency tests for such children. Section 53 provides for committal proceedings to be by-passed following a certificate from the Director of Public Prosecutions in certain cases involving child witnesses. Section 54 provides for the admissibility of video-recorded interviews of child witnesses to violent or sexual offences and s. 55 makes a number of further changes to existing legislation concerning the evidence of children in such cases, including removing the right of the accused in person to cross-examine a child witness.

BACKGROUND – THE CRIMINAL JUSTICE ACT 1988

6.1 Introduction

The engine behind both the 1988 reforms and those in CJA 1991 has been increasing public awareness of the issue of child abuse and concern about the difficulties (in the absence of a confession) of convicting those responsible in such cases. There has also been concern about the additional trauma and damage that the criminal justice system can inflict on the children whose evidence is crucial if a conviction is to be sought (see Spencer and Flin, *The Evidence of Children: The Law and the Psychology*, especially chapter 1, for a thorough and readable account). Enthusiasm for improving the position of child witnesses and dispensing with some of the rules which cause them most difficulties has, however, had to be tempered with caution in not putting defendants in such cases at an unfair disadvantage, particularly given the serious consequences for an accused convicted of a violent offence, and particularly a sexual offence, against a child. It is partly for this reason that the reforms do not, controversially, go as far either as the Pigot Committee recommended or as far as some would like, as will be seen when looking at the details of the new provisions, but it is first necessary to put them into context by outlining the reforms made in 1988.

6.2   Live Television Links

Section 32 of CJA 1988 enabled, *inter alia*, a child witness under the age of 14 in a trial on indictment (or in certain appeals) to give evidence through a live television link (with the leave of the court) if the offence is one of those listed in s. 32(2). The listed offences are essentially sexual offences, child cruelty and offences involving assault, injury or the threat of injury. The section has proved a useful way of reducing the stress placed on child witnesses when giving evidence in open court, and in particular of avoiding the necessity of having to do so in the physical presence of the accused. In advance of this provision coming into force, courts had started to permit the erection of screens to shield child witnesses from the dock for similar reasons and the Court of Appeal in *X* (1989) 91 Cr App R 36 approved the practice as being not unfair or prejudicial to the accused (see *Schaub* (1993) *The Times*, 3 December 1993 for different considerations applicable to adult witnesses). Although screens will continue to be important in magistrates' courts (see Home Office Circular 61/1990), they will gradually become less and less common in the Crown Court as live television equipment becomes available in more and more trial centres. A *Practice Direction (Crown Court: TV Links)* [1992] 1 WLR 838 lists 40 such centres.

6.3   Evidence of Children under 14 in Committal Proceedings for Assault, Sexual Offences etc.

Section 33 of CJA 1988 precluded the calling of a child as a witness for the prosecution in committal proceedings for the same range of offences as are listed in relation to s. 32 (above). In place of the oral testimony of the child, statements made by or taken from the child were made admissible instead. The purpose behind s. 33 (which substituted a new s. 103 in the Magistrates' Courts Act 1980) was to avoid the child witness having to go through the trauma of giving evidence in court of harrowing or disturbing experiences on two separate occasions, once in the committal proceedings and then again in the trial itself. The flaw, however, was that the defence could object (under the new s. 103(3)(a) of MCA 1980) to the statement being admitted. It could thus compel the child to give evidence orally if, as is normally the situation, a prima facie case could not be made out without that evidence. Defendants continued therefore to be able to try to 'crack' the child witness at the committal proceedings and then, if unsuccessful, to have another go at the trial itself. Indeed the introduction of television links at the Crown Court has increased the incentive for the defence to confront the child witness at the committal stage. As the Pigot Report noted at para. 6.11:

> . . . defendants accused of child abuse have sought to confront the principal prosecution witness [in the magistrates' court], apparently because they are conscious that this can be prevented at the trial by the use of the live television link.

6.4   Abolition of Corroboration Requirements for Children's Evidence

Prior to CJA 1988, there were a number of restrictive rules relating to the corroboration of the evidence of children under 14. These depended on whether the evidence was sworn or unsworn, which itself depended on whether the particular child was found to understand the nature of an oath which would normally be at about the age of eight to 10. Section 34(1) of the 1988 Act repealed the proviso to CYPA 1933, s. 38, which had required corroboration of a child's *unsworn* evidence as a matter of law. Section 34(2) abolished the common law rule of practice that in the case of sworn evidence of children, the judge should warn the jury of the danger of convicting on the uncorroborated evidence of a child and s. 34(3) abolished the rule that unsworn evidence of one child could not corroborate the unsworn evidence of another child.

Despite the reforms in CJA 1988, s. 34, a number of difficulties remained. In particular, the distinction between sworn and unsworn evidence was not totally removed and child witnesses still had to undergo what to them might seem an oppressive series of questions about whether they understood the nature of an oath and 'the added responsibility to tell the truth . . . over and above the duty to tell the truth which is an ordinary duty of normal social conduct' (*Hayes* [1977] 1 WLR 234 at p. 237). If the child was not able to understand the nature of the oath, then he might still give evidence unsworn 'if he is possessed of sufficient intelligence to justify the reception of the evidence, and understands the duty to speak the truth' (CYPA 1933, s. 38), which test itself would require questions to be asked of him by the judge that might make him feel the court suspected him from the outset of telling lies. As to the lowest age at which children should be allowed to testify, Lord Goddard CJ, in *Wallwork* (1958) 42 Cr App R 153, had expressed the view that it was most undesirable to call a child as young as five and, for over 30 years, this case had a profound and highly restrictive impact on the practice of admitting, or rather not admitting, the evidence of young children in England, particularly as compared with other jurisdictions, including Scotland. *Wallwork* was approved as recently as the case of *Wright* (1987) 90 Cr App R 91, but the Court of Appeal in *Z* [1990] 2 QB 355, influenced by the changes in the 1988 Act, has taken a more liberal approach. Lord Lane CJ took the view that it was a matter for the discretion of the trial judge and it was possible, though likely to be rare, that a five-year-old's (unsworn) evidence could be admitted. In contrast, the Pigot Committee commented on practice in Scotland:

> where it is not unusual for children of four, five and six to give evidence and where witnesses as young as three have testified.

However, further evidence of the more liberal approach now being taken by the English courts can be found in David James N (1992) 95 Cr App R 256. In that case (decided prior to the coming into force of the 1991 Act provisions) the Court of Appeal approved the admission by the trial judge of the unsworn evidence of a six-year-old victim of sexual abuse.

It should also be noted that, whilst s. 34 of the 1988 Act removed any requirement of corroboration of a child's evidence as such, if the child is the complainant in a sexual case, a corroboration warning still has to be given on that quite separate ground. (For proposals to reform this rule, see 6.8 below.)

THE NEW PROVISIONS

Having looked at what CJA 1988 did and did not do, we can now turn to CJA 1991 and examine to what extent it takes matters further.

6.5   Competence of Children as Witnesses

CJA 1991, s. 52, follows on quite naturally from the discussion just undertaken of the rules about sworn and unsworn evidence and their modification in s. 34 of CJA 1988. Subsection (1) of CJA 1991, s. 52 inserts a new s. 33A into the 1988 Act which removes any necessity to enquire into whether or not a child understands the nature of an oath by providing:

(1)   A child's evidence in criminal proceedings shall be given unsworn.
(2)   A deposition of a child's unsworn evidence may be taken for the purposes of criminal proceedings as if that evidence had been given on oath.
(3)   In this section 'child' means a person under fourteen years of age.

This, together with CJA 1991, s. 52(2), which provides that CYPA 1933, s. 38(1) (evidence of child of tender years to be given on oath or in certain circumstances unsworn) 'shall cease to have effect', makes it clear that all evidence of children under 14 will now be given unsworn and that evidence of children of 14 years and above will be given on oath. The flexible but slightly imprecise concept of 'a child of tender years' is thus abandoned and a fixed age limit of 14 established which now distinguishes those who give evidence on oath from those who give it unsworn. Aside from the fact of giving their evidence unsworn, children under 14 are thus seemingly treated as equally competent as adults, a conclusion also apparently drawn by the closing words of CJA 1991, s. 52(2), which read as follows:

. . . accordingly the power of the court in any criminal proceedings to determine that a particular person is not competent to give evidence shall apply to children of tender years as it applies to other persons.

These closing words have, however, been severely criticised by J. R. Spencer in (1990) 140 NLJ 1750 as letting the competency requirement in again through the back door. The first, more extreme, version of his argument is that since an adult would not be competent to testify if, for example, because of mental handicap, he did not understand the nature of the oath (see *Blackstone's Criminal Practice 1993*, F4.22), the concluding words of s. 52(2) mean that a child who does not understand the nature of the oath is similarly not competent. Spencer himself accepts that this argument, though plausible, would ultimately be rejected by the courts because it would be absurd to require children to understand the nature of an oath that they have specifically been exempted from taking. However, he then points out a second, less extreme, version which says that a court would not accept as a witness an adult who does not understand the ordinary everyday duty to tell the truth (as opposed to the special obligation to do so imposed by an oath) and that therefore, since the same rules apply to children as to other persons, a child who does not understand the ordinary duty to tell the truth is not a competent witness. The difficulty for this argument is that it appears to cause the repeal of s. 38(1) of the 1933 Act to be largely, if not completely, without effect, but Spencer fears that the argument may nevertheless be accepted by the courts.

These fears were in fact discussed in the committee stage of the Bill but dismissed by the Minister of State on the grounds that the first part of s. 52(2) provides that the words in s. 38 of the 1933 Act, referring to the understanding or the duty to speak the truth, should no longer be of effect and therefore 'that is the end of the matter'. It is to be hoped that the Minister is right but one cannot help but observe that s. 52(2) is not as helpfully worded as it might be. Quite apart from the concluding words criticised by Spencer, the first part of the subsection is peculiar in that the words in parentheses purporting to summarise the effect of s. 38(1) of the 1933 Act do not do so terribly accurately. The parenthesised words read '(evidence of child of tender years to be given on oath or in certain circumstances unsworn)'. In fact, s. 38 does not give any authority for children to give evidence on oath; that already existed at common law. Section 38 merely authorised the giving of unsworn evidence where the conditions for giving sworn evidence were not satisfied. Therefore a more accurate summary of s. 38(1) would read '(evidence of child of tender years, who does not understand nature of an oath, to be given unsworn in certain circumstances)'. Given the misleading summary actually contained in s. 52(2), it is hardly surprising that there should be dispute about its precise effect.

The Act therefore appears to leave it open as to whether the judge should question the child to see if he is competent or whether the child should be allowed to start to give evidence subject to the judge's power to stand him down should his evidence be incoherent. The latter would appear to be the better view, at least for the majority of instances even if in some individual cases of very young children the judge may feel it advisable to question the child first. The government made it clear in the debate in Standing Committee A that it felt that s. 52 as drafted implemented the Pigot recommendation in para. 5.13 of the report that:

> the competence requirement which is applied to potential child witnesses should be dispensed with and . . . should not be replaced. Once the witness has begun to testify he or she may appear to be of unsound mind, become incoherent or fail to communicate in a way that makes sense. The judge is already able to rule that such a witness is incompetent and to advise the jury to ignore any evidence that may have been given.

If this is right, then the concluding words of s. 52 will be interpreted as merely applying to the judge's power to stand down a witness who is incoherent or unable to communicate. The case of Z [1990] 2 QB 355 (6.4 above) was referred to by the Minister as having already effectively abolished at common law any lower age limit for child witnesses so that, subject to the judge's discretion to exclude any witness, of whatever age, incompetent to give coherent evidence, evidence of a child of five years, or even less, could be admitted. Although it was accepted in committee that the courts would not be able to admit the evidence of a child as young as six months, it seems, following the enactment of s. 52, that one cannot draw a fixed minimum age at two or three years since it depends on the nature of the evidence to be given and the ability of the particular child to communicate.

6.6   Notices of Transfer to the Crown Court

CJA 1991, s. 53, can be related back to the failure of CJA 1988, s. 33, effectively to protect child witnesses from being exposed to giving their evidence at committal proceedings (6.3 above and see the discussion of s. 55(1) below). It has wider aims than that, however, because by making it possible to dispense altogether with the committal proceedings, it is designed to bring on the actual trial at the Crown Court much more quickly. The main benefits of a speedy trial as far as child witnesses are concerned are twofold. First, child witnesses are much more likely to be able to give accurate and coherent evidence of an incident the shorter the period of time between the incident and the giving of the evidence. (This is likely to be true of all witnesses but is considered to be particularly true of children – see Flin and Spencer [1991] Crim LR 189.) Second (and this is the consideration most directly in point under s. 53(1)(c)), child witnesses are often in need of therapy to help them to recover from the incident of which they are victim and/or witness and it is difficult for that therapy or recovery to begin until after they have completed giving their evidence.

The procedure adopted by s. 53 is modelled on that first introduced in the CJA 1987 to enable committal proceedings to be by-passed in complex fraud cases by means of a 'notice of transfer' (see *Blackstone's Criminal Practice 1993*, D7.6 to D7.20). CJA 1991, s. 53(1), now authorises the Director of Public Prosecutions, in the case of certain offences, to serve a 'notice of transfer' on the magistrates' court in whose jurisdiction the offence has been charged, certifying that he is of the opinion:

(a)   that the evidence of the offence would be sufficient for the person charged to be committed for trial;
(b)   that a child who is alleged—
     (i)   to be a person against whom the offence was committed; or
     (ii)   to have witnessed the commission of the offence;
will be called as a witness at the trial; and
(c)   that, for the purpose of avoiding any prejudice to the welfare of the child, the case should be taken over and proceeded with without delay by the Crown Court.

Paragraph (b) initially only referred to child victims of the offence but was extended during the passage of the Bill to include, under subparagraph (ii), child witnesses who were not actual victims since the trauma involved in witnessing abuse may be as great as, or in some cases greater than, that of the victim.

The offences to which s. 53(1) applies are those to which s. 32(2) of the CJA 1988 (permitting evidence of children to be given through television links) applies, i.e.:

(a) to an offence which involves an assault on, or injury or a threat of injury to, a person;
(b) to an offence under section 1 of the Children and Young Persons Act 1933 (cruelty to persons under 16);
(c) to an offence under the Sexual Offences Act 1956, the Indecency with Children Act 1960, the Sexual Offences Act 1967, section 54 of the Criminal Law Act 1977 or the Protection of Children Act 1978; and
(d) to an offence which consists of attempting or conspiring to commit, or of aiding, abetting, counselling, procuring or inciting the commission of, an offence within paragraph (a), (b) or (c) above.

The list of sexual offences does not have the exclusions in relation to consensual and certain other offences that apply to the definition of a sexual offence in part I of CJA 1991 (see 1.10) since we are here dealing with children and therefore different considerations apply.

By CJA 1991, s. 53(6), the meaning of a 'child' for the purposes of s. 53(1) varies according to whether the offence charged falls (or consists of attempting or conspiring etc. to commit an offence) within para. (a), (b) or (c) of CJA 1988, s. 32(2). For an offence under paras (a) or (b), it means a person aged under 14, whereas for para. (c) (sexual offences) it means a person under 17. In the absence of any specific guidance in CJA 1991, s. 53, the relevant date for determining the child's age seems to be the date on which the notice of transfer is served. In each case, if a video recording under CJA 1988, s. 32A(2) (see below), was made of him when he was below the relevant age (14 or 17), then the relevant age is increased by one year to 15 years and 18 years respectively.

CJA 1991, s. 53(3) provides that once a notice of transfer has been served, 'the functions of the magistrates' court shall cease in relation to the case except as provided by paragraphs 2 and 3 of Schedule 6 to this Act or by section 20(4) of the Legal Aid Act 1988'. Schedule 6, para. 2, ensures that the magistrates still have appropriate powers to remand in custody or on bail. Paragraph 3 in effect preserves the power to make witness orders in relation to anyone indicated in the notice of transfer as a proposed witness and s. 20(4) of the Legal Aid Act 1988 is itself amended by CJA 1991, sch. 6, para. 9, to enable the magistrates' court to grant legal aid for the Crown Court proceedings where a notice of transfer has been issued. The procedure to be followed by magistrates where a notice of transfer is given is contained in the Magistrates' Courts (Notice of Transfer) (Children's Evidence) Rules 1992 (SI 1992/2070). Schedule 6, para. 7, of the Act requires both the Crown Court and the magistrates' court, in exercising any powers in relation to the case, to 'have regard to the desirability of avoiding prejudice to the welfare of any relevant child witness that may be occasioned by unnecessary delay in bringing the case to trial'.

Once a magistrates court' has started committal proceedings, it seems that it is too late for a notice of transfer to be issued because s. 53(2) provides that a notice 'shall be served before the magistrates' court begins to inquire into the case as examining justices'. The form of the notice of transfer and other provisions related to the serving of copies of the notice are contained in the Criminal Justice Act 1991 (Notice of Transfer) Regulations 1992 (SI 1992/1670). Under r. 5(1)(c) of the Indictments (Procedure) Rules 1971 (inserted by SI 1992/1670), a bill of indictment is to be preferred within 28 days of the notice of transfer being served on the magistrates' court. A *Practice Direction (Crown Courts: TV Links)* [1992] 1 WLR 838 provides that the place of trial specified in the notice of transfer shall be a Crown Court centre which is equipped with live television link facilities and lists the 40 centres already so equipped.

It is important to realise that a notice of transfer merely certifies that it is the DPP's *opinion* that the matters in paras (a), (b) and (c) of s. 53(1) are satisfied and, furthermore, s. 53(4) provides that:

> The decision to serve a notice of transfer shall not be subject to appeal or liable to be questioned in any court.

This provision is unlikely to make such notices completely unreviewable since an attack could be made on the validity of the notice itself rather than on the decision to serve it, e.g., if the notice did not specify the details required by sch. 6, para. 1, such as the charge or charges to which it relates. Furthermore, a notice issued in excess of jurisdiction, e.g., in relation to an offence not contained in CJA 1988, s. 32(2), or in relation to a child outside the relevant age limits, would presumably not be valid. More importantly, however, for an accused faced with a notice of transfer who feels there is not sufficient evidence justifying a trial, sch. 6, para. 5, provides for an application to be made to the Crown Court, at any time before arraignment, to have the charge dismissed. The application can be made in writing or orally but written notice must be given of an intention to make an oral application. Oral evidence may be given only by leave or order of the judge where it appears to him that the interests of justice so require. Paragraph 5(5) prohibits the judge from permitting or requiring oral evidence from a child who is alleged to be the victim or witness of the offence since that would go against the whole object of the exercise. If the charge is dismissed under para. 5, no further proceedings can be brought on that charge except by means of a voluntary bill of indictment (para. 5(7)). Further details of the procedure for applications for dismissal can be found in the Criminal Justice Act 1991 (Dismissal of Transferred Charges) Rules 1992 (SI 1992/1848) which, it should be noted, provide for the application to be made normally within 14 days of the notice of transfer being given.

6.7 Video Recordings of Testimony of Child Witnesses

Although this is in many ways the centre-piece of the reforms on children's evidence, CJA 1991, s. 54, is in the eyes of many people somewhat disappointing as it only goes part way to implementing the reforms recommended by the Pigot Committee. The essence of the committee's recommendations was that no child witness should be required to give evidence in open court unless it was by choice. The evidence of children in violent or sexual cases should be recorded on video at as early a stage as possible because that would be least damaging to the child and most likely to provide accurate and useful evidence. There should then be a video-recorded preliminary hearing in informal surroundings where the account in the first video could be confirmed or, where appropriate, expanded on by the child. The accused would not be present in the same room but would be able to hear and see the proceedings through closed-circuit television and would be able to communicate with his counsel through an audio link. Counsel for the accused could cross-examine the child and the whole video could subsequently be shown to the jury at the trial without the child having to attend at all. In this way, the child could give evidence at an earlier stage when the incidents were still relatively fresh in his mind and without the pressures inherent in giving evidence in open court. It might still be necessary to recall the child to be cross-examined again where further evidence emerging since the making of the video made that necessary, but even that further cross-examination would not be in open court but could be done by means of a further recorded video. In many cases no such further cross-examination would be necessary and the child's recovery from the trauma of the incident would not need to be disturbed at all.

Section 54 does not go nearly so far as this but in effect only allows the child's evidence in chief to be given by means of a video. It does not provide for a preliminary informal hearing or for the child to be cross-examined in advance of the trial. Indeed it insists that the child is called as a witness at the trial, largely in order to enable the child to be cross-examined, although, of course, this cross-examination may take place by live televsion link rather than in the actual court-room in the presence of the accused (see CJA 1988, s. 32; 6.2 above). Strong pressure was brought to bear in both Houses to try and persuade the government to accept amendments which would go further towards implementing the Pigot proposals. It was pointed out that separating the (videoed) evidence in chief from the cross-examination at the trial, which could be several months or more later, would be guaranteed to give the defence the opportunity to force an adult witness, let alone a child, into inconsistencies and confusion. It also ensured, it was argued, that the child's rehabilitation could not properly start until after the trial because the cross-examination was bound to reawaken, and perhaps intensify, the distress caused by the original incident. The government's response to these arguments included the following points:

(a)   the defence could not properly cross-examine a witness in advance of knowing all the other evidence to be called;

(b)   fairness to the accused would necessitate a further cross-examination or even a number of further examinations which would be worse for the child than just having the one cross-examination at the trial;

(c)   even the suggested amendments involved the *possibility* of the child having to be recalled for further cross-examination at the time of the trial and therefore effective therapy would be difficult up to that point anyway because of the risk of confusing the child's evidence or of opening it up to allegations that the witness had been coached;

(d)   the giving of the evidence in chief on video will often precipitate a guilty plea thereby avoiding the necessity at any time of a cross-examination which is never going to be a pleasant experience for a child witness whenever or however it is done.

Whatever the merits of the respective arguments, s. 54 emerged substantially in the form in which it was originally drafted, with the government being prepared to monitor closely its implementation and introduce further reforms later should that prove necessary.

6.8 The Operation of s. 54

CJA 1991, s. 54, operates by inserting a new s. 32A into CJA 1988, following on from the original s. 32 which introduced the live television link procedure. As with the notice of transfer procedure in CJA 1991, s. 53 (6.6 above) it applies only to offences to which CJA 1988, s. 32(2), applies and these (essentially violent and sexual) offences are listed in 6.6 above. Furthermore, apart from proceedings in the Criminal Division of the Court of Appeal (s. 32A(1)(b)), it only applies to trials on indictment and to proceedings in youth courts (s. 32A(1)(a)).

CJA 1988, s. 32A(2), permits a video recording of an interview with a child, which relates to any matter in issue in the proceedings, to be given in evidence with the leave of the court. A *Practice Direction (Crime: Child's Video Evidence)* [1992] 1 WLR 839 relating to the granting of such leave and the admission of such evidence has been issued and is set out below at p. 154. Under CJA 1988, s. 32A(3), the court shall (subject to its inherent discretion to exclude otherwise admissible evidence) give leave unless:

(a) it appears that the child witness will not be available for cross-examination;

(b) any rules of court requiring disclosure of the circumstances in which the recording was made have not been complied with to the satisfaction of the court; or

(c) the court is of the opinion, having regard to all the circumstances of the case, that in the interests of justice the recording ought not to be admitted; and where the court gives such leave it may, if it is of the opinion that in the interests of justice any part of the recording ought not to be admitted, direct that that part shall be excluded.

Paragraph (a) underlines the point that the video recording will not itself include the cross-examination and that the child will be required to attend court for this purpose. This is further underlined by s. 32A(5) which requires that where a video recording is admitted under the section, the child witness shall be called by the party who tendered it in evidence but the child shall not be examined in chief on any matter which in the opinion of the court has been dealt with in his recorded testimony. An amendment to s. 32A(5) which would have inserted the word 'adequately' in front of the words 'dealt with' was rejected on the grounds that it is already implicit. However, one wonders whether this is so and one can well envisage the situation where the prosecution wish to ask the child to expand on something dealt with in the video recording and it would be regrettable if the court took the view that they should be precluded from doing so because the matter has already been 'dealt with'. It should be noted that a video recording can be tendered under the section by either party although it will normally be by the prosecution. The defence would not have to rely on the section if they wanted to make use of a video as a previous inconsistent statement and indeed this is not uncommon under the pre-Act law. There may be cases, though, where the defence want to put in the evidence of their own child witness which contradicts the evidence of the victim or indeed any other prosecution evidence. The experience of testifying in court about an allegedly violent or sexual offence will be no less distressing just because it is given on behalf of the defence, and it is therefore right that the procedure should also be available to defence witnesses.

CJA 1988, s. 32A(3)(b), refers to rules of court requiring disclosure of the circumstances in which the recording was made and these are now included in the Crown Court (Amendment) Rules 1992 (SI 1992/1847) inserting a new r. 23C into the Crown Court Rules 1982. Rule 23C(4) requires information, *inter alia*, about timing, duration, location, persons present and equipment used in the interview. The Pigot Committee also recommended a *statutory* code of practice containing 'guidance relating to the location, style and structure of interviews' and 'directions relating to the timing of interviews . . ., the standard of equipment to be used, the persons permitted to be present during a recording, the use of interviewing aids, the circumstances under which a recording is to be shown to an accused and the custody, copying, storage and destruction of tapes'. In the event, a non-statutory *Memorandum of Good Practice on Child Evidence* was jointly issued by the Home Office and Department of Health in August 1992. It stresses that police forces and social services teams should not start to make video recordings for use in criminal proceedings until the trained staff and equipment required are available.

CJA 1988, s. 32A(3), makes it clear in its concluding words that leave to admit the recording may be given subject to the exclusion of just part of the recording. However, s. 32A(4) requires the court, before excluding just a part, to consider whether any prejudice to the accused which might result from admitting that part would be outweighed by the desirability of showing the whole or substantially the whole of the interview. This is intended to discourage judges from being overzealous in their editorial work on the video recording, particularly in relation to sections which are of relatively minor prejudicial effect, in a way which deprives the jury of the full flavour of the child's evidence.

Under s. 32A(6), any statement made by the child witness disclosed by a video recording given in evidence is treated as though it was direct oral testimony given by the child. This takes it formally outside the hearsay rule which is what prevents recorded statements being admissible in the first place. It also means, as is specifically pointed out by s. 32A(6)(b), that it cannot count as corroboration of other evidence given by the child. This may seem an unnecessary point to make, given the abolition of the corroboration requirements for children's evidence by CJA 1988, s. 34. However, as was pointed out in the discussion of that section (6.4 above), the evidence of a child witness who is the complainant in a sexual case still attracts a corroboration warning on the grounds of being that of a complainant rather than of a child. The Pigot Committee recommended the abolition of this rule and was of the view (para. 5.17) that 'unless the rule is altered our proposals for facilitating the testimony of children and other vulnerable witnesses may, at any rate insofar as sexual offences are concerned, have a much more limited effect than we intend'. The Law Commision, in Report No. 202, Cm 1620 (1991), has itself now recommended abolition of the rule, a recommendation more recently endorsed by the Royal Commission on Criminal Justice (CM 2263) 1993 and likely to be enacted in the 1994 Criminal Justice Act.

On a separate point, the word 'statement' is helpfully defined in CJA 1988, s. 32A(9), as including 'any representation of fact, whether made in words or otherwise'. This is particularly appropriate to young children who may find it difficult to give their evidence wholly in words but who can communicate very well non-verbally. This might include the use of drawings, diagrams, dolls or figures but the Pigot Committee warned (at para. 4.22) that 'unless these are approached with caution their use will be regarded by the courts as suggestive and prejudicial' and went on to propose that 'the code of practice should make clear that such aids should only be used to help a child establish details with which he or she may have verbal difficulties once the general substance of a complaint is clear'. The *Memorandum of Good Practice* follows this advice and also recommends against the use of anatomically detailed dolls.

As with CJA 1991, s. 53 (discussed in 6.6 above), the meaning of 'child' in CJA 1988, s. 32A, varies according to the offence to which the evidence relates (s. 32A(7)). It is normally a person under 14 years but for sexual offences under para. (c) of s. 32(2) of the 1988 Act, the relevant age is (under) 17 years. The date for assessing the child's age would normally appear to be the date of the trial and again the relevant maximum ages are increased by one year (to under 15 and under 18 respectively) provided that the witness was under 14 or under 17 at the date when the video recording was made. CJA 1988, s. 32A(7), it might be thought, is expressed in a very convoluted way. Its meaning can, perhaps, be more helpfully conveyed by saying that a child is a person who was under 14 (or 17 for para. (c) offences) at the time the video was made and who has still not attained 15 (or 18) years of age.

If leave is to be sought to introduce a video recording at the trial then the video may be considered by examining magistrates even though the child witness is not to be called at the committal proceedings (CJA 1988, s. 32A(10)). This is part of the range of measures designed to protect children from having to give evidence in committal proceedings and complements the amended s. 103 of MCA 1980 under which statements made by or taken from a child are admissible. For the purposes of CJA 1988, s. 32A(10), the witness obviously has to be under 15 (or 18) at the time of the committal (and have been under 14 (or 17) at the time the video was made) but presumably it must also be at least in prospect that he or she will still be under 15 (or 18) by the estimated date of the trial, which would not be satisfied if at the time of the committal the child was just a matter of days away from reaching 15 or 18.

6.9 Other Provisions Allowing for Admissibility of Video Recordings

It is made clear in CJA 1988, s. 32A(12), that the procedure introduced by s. 32A is without prejudice to any other grounds on which video-recorded evidence might be admitted (for a full discussion of the possibilities, see Spencer and Flin, *The Evidence of Children*, pp. 147–54). One example particularly worth discussing arises under s. 23 of the CJA 1988 dealing with first-hand documentary hearsay, for the purposes of which, a videotape is a document (via CJA 1988, sch. 2, para. 5. and the Civil Evidence Act 1968, s. 10).

CJA 1988, s. 23, does not require the (child) witness to appear or be available for cross-examination at the trial and indeed is based on the premise that the witness is unable to do so. Because of that very fact, however, there is a discretion to exclude the evidence, *inter alia,* on the grounds of unfairness to the accused. Moreover, if the video recording of the (child) witness's statement has been prepared for the purposes of the criminal proceedings or criminal investigation, as will normally be the case with most such videos, leave of the court is required under s. 26 before it can be given in evidence. Paradoxically, it may be that the more vital the video to the prosecution case, the less likely it is that leave will be given since the inability to cross-examine the only or crucial witness will tend to be regarded as unfair to the accused. (For further discussion of the potential problems, under the European Convention on Human Rights, raised by the admission of untested recorded evidence, see Spencer (1991) 141 NLJ 787.)

AMENDMENTS TO EXISTING PROVISIONS ON CHILDREN'S EVIDENCE

6.10   Committal Proceedings

CJA 1991, s. 55(1), effectively implements recommendation 24 of the Pigot Committee:

> that where a violent offence is alleged, no child witness under the age of 14, or, if the offence is of a sexual character, no child witness under the age of 17, shall be required to give evidence in person at a magistrates' court hearing unless the offence is to be tried summarily and the child's evidence is given during the summary trial.

(And even here, it might be added, consideration ought to be given to the use of screens.)

CJA 1991, s. 55(1), amends MCA 1980, s. 103 (as substituted by CJA 1988, s. 33, see 6.3 above) in two respects.

First, MCA 1980, s. 103(3)(a), is repealed so as to remove the defence's power to object to the admission in committal proceedings of a statement made by or taken from a child in place of the child's oral testimony. This addresses the major weakness of s. 103 as it stood and will prevent the defence from confronting, at committal proceedings, the child witness who is protected at the later trial in the Crown Court. One of the changes made by CJA 1988, s. 33, to MCA 1980, s. 103, was the deletion of the requirement that the statement be a written statement, and it has already been noted that CJA 1988, s. 32A(10) (6.8 above) now expressly provides that the statement may be in the form of a video recording proposed to be admitted at the trial.

Secondly, the definition of a child for the purposes of MCA 1980, s. 103, is amended from being simply a person under 14 to the same meaning as CJA 1991, s. 53 (notices of transfer, see 6.6 above). This change essentially means that for sexual offences, the age limit is raised to under 17 years and that, for either sexual or violent offences, where the child was under 17 or 14 respectively at the time a relevant video recording was made, the age limit is raised by one year (to under 18 or under 15). The following description of the legislative process involved renders any comment on it superfluous. CJA 1991, s. 55(1), replaces the definition of a child in MCA 1980, s. 103 (as that section is substituted by CJA 1988, s. 33) by the definition of a child which is to be found in CJA 1991, s. 53, which definition itself refers to offences falling within CJA 1988, s. 32(2), and refers also to video recordings possibly made under s. 32A(2) of the 1988 Act as inserted by CJA 1991, s. 54.

6.11   Child Witnesses Not to be Cross-examined by the Accused in Person

CJA 1991, s. 55(7), inserts a new s. 34A into CJA 1988 in line with para. 2.30 of the Pigot report which said:

> defendants should be specifically prohibited by statute from examining child witnesses in person or through a sound or video link. The limitation which this places upon the defence is, in our view, far less significant than the damage which can be inflicted upon the child and the interests of justice if, in certain circumstances, such an exercise is allowed to take place.

The new CJA 1988, s. 34A, applies to the usual list of violent and sexual offences listed in s. 32(2) of the 1988 Act and is applicable both to trials on indictment and to summary trial. The prohibition applies primarily to the cross-examination of a victim or witness who is 'a child' but also applies to a witness who narrowly falls outside the highly contrived definiton of a child which the new section contains.

'Child' is defined in CJA 1988, s. 34A(2), by reference to CJA 1988, s. 32A(7), 'but with the omission of the references to a person being, in the cases there mentioned, under the age of 15 years or under the age of 18 years'. This masterful piece of obfuscation simply seems to mean that a child is a person under 17 in the case of sexual offences under CJA 1988, s. 32(2)(c) (and attempts etc. to commit them under s. 32(2)(d)), but is a person under 14 in the case of other offfences to which s. 32(2) applies. In other words, there is no increase of one year for cases where the child was under 14 (or 17) when a relevant video recording was made. At least this is the case in summary trials. However, in trials on indictment, the extra year is potentially available again because the prohibition on cross-examination in person by the accused applies not only to 'a child' but to a person who 'is to be cross-examined following the admission under section 32A above of a video recording of testimony from him' (CJA 1988, s. 34A(1)(b)). Such a person only has to be child within the full (and more generous) original definition in s. 32A(7). Thus, what is taken away by the restricted definition in s. 34A(2) has already been given back again by s. 34A(1)(b) as far as trials on indictment are concerned. It does not help with summary trials because the video recording of testimony is not admissible in the first place in summary trial. The thinking behind not giving the benefit of the extra year on the age limit in summary trial is presumably that there should not be the same delay before summary trial and therefore the extension of the age limit is not as necessary. The wording of the section is made extraordinarily complex merely to deny a one-year increase in the age limit to a child who, after all, must have been under 14 or 17 at the time the alleged offence was committed.

An illustration might be helpful at this point.

Illustration 1   D is accused of the rape of a 16-year-old girl. The girl's statement about the offence is video-recorded and leave is obtained under CJA 1988, s. 32A, to admit the recording in evidence at the trial in the Crown Court, and this is permissible as a result of s. 32A(7) even though the girl is 17 by the time the trial takes place (provided she was still under 17 when the video recording was made). As a result of s. 34A, the accused personally is not permitted to cross-examine the girl but must do so through counsel. The girl is no longer within the definition of a child within s. 34A (as opposed to s. 32A) but she is 'to be cross-examined following the admission under section 32A' of a video recording of her testimony.

If she was very close to 17 at the time of the alleged offence and had reached 17 by the time the video recording was made, it would not be admissible under s. 32A in the first place, and neither would she be protected from cross-examination in person by the accused (and neither would she be eligible to give evidence by live televsion link under CJA 1988, s. 32). Equally, none of these protections would apply to her if, even though she was under 17 at the time the video recording was made, there was a delay in bringing the case to trial and she had reached 18 by the time of the trial. Hopefully, any such potential delay would have been obviated by the DPP issuing a notice of transfer under CJA 1991, s. 53, but the point remains that there will be vulnerable, often relatively young, witnesses who do not fall within the definition of a child. In this connection it is worth quoting para. 3.15 of the Pigot Committee report where it was said:

> Once our recommendations in relation to child witnesses are implemented and working successfully, we believe a high priority must then attach to extending the new measures to vulnerable adults. If changes of the sort which we have suggested cannot be introduced reasonably soon in respect of all vulnerable witnesses we would propose that the earliest provision should be made for victims of serious sexual offences, who face special and generally recognised difficulties.

Illustration 2   D commits an act of gross indecency knowing that he is being watched by A and B, two girls aged 13 and 16 respectively. Both girls make video-recorded statements which, had the case been committed for trial on indictment, would have been admissible both at the committal proceedings and at the actual trial. However, the offence (under the Indecency with Children Act 1960) is to be tried summarily and the video recordings will not be admissible. D cannot personally cross-examine A (the victim of the offence, which can only be committed in respect of children under 14), even if she has become 14 by the time of the summary trial, since the offence is one listed in CJA 1988, s. 32(2)(c), and therefore she is under the relevant age limit of 17. Neither will he be able personally to cross-examine B if she is still under 17 since, although she is not 'a person against whom the offence was committed' (s. 34A(1)(a)(i)), she is alleged 'to have witnessed the commission of the offence' (s. 34A(1)(a)(ii)). However, if B has become 17, he will be able to personally cross-examine her since she is not a child (as defined in s. 34A(2)) nor is she to be cross-examined following the *admission* of a video recording. If the trial had been on indictment she would have been protected if the cross-examination was to follow the admission of the recording.

6.12   Amendments to CJA 1988, s. 32 (Evidence through Television Links)

There are two main aspects to the amendments which subsections (2) to (6) of CJA 1991, s. 55, make to CJA 1988, s. 32. First, by a new subsection (1A) inserted into CJA 1988, s. 32, the availability of the live television link procedure is extended to youth courts (consistently with the new provision for video-recorded evidence to be available in youth courts as well as in the Crown Court and Court of Appeal). If suitable facilities for receiving such evidence are not available in the petty-sessional court-house where the youth court would normally sit, provision is made in new subsections (3A) and (3B) of CJA 1988, s. 32, for the youth court to sit in an appointed court-house that is so equipped and which does not necessarily have to be within the petty sessions area.

Secondly, CJA 1988, s. 32, is amended so that it applies to children under 17, rather than just those under 14, as far as offences to which s. 32(2)(c) applies (sexual offences). A new s. 32(6) is inserted which defines 'child' in the same convoluted way as s. 34A(2), i.e., by incorporating part of the definition of 'child' in s. 32A(7) but not the part extending the age limits where the video recording was made before the expiry of those age limits. Again, however, the extension to the age limit is largely retained by the fact that, under s. 32(1)(b), the live video link is now available not only to a child but also to a witness who 'is to be cross-examined following the admission under section 32A below of a video recording of testimony from him'. Such a recording will only be admissible if the child was under 14 (or 17) at the time the recording was made and is still under 15 (or 18) at the time of the trial (s. 32A(7)). As with s. 34A, this labyrinthine method of definition does have some practical effects (whether intended or not). In particular, it would seem that if a video recording is admitted of a witness who has become 14 or 17 since the making of the recording but the defence choose not to cross-examine on the recording, then s. 32 will not apply. This will be a rare case and it might be thought not to matter since if there is to be no cross-examination, there is no need for a live television link. However, the video recording may not cover all the matters on which evidence is needed from the child and any further evidence in chief will have to be given in court and not over a television link. As against that, if there had been *no* video recording, the one-year extension to the age limits would not have been applicable in the first place, but this merely underlines further some of the arbitrary (and complex) distinctions that are being drawn. The whole scheme would have been simpler (and arguably fairer) if all the definitions had related to the age of the child at the time of the alleged offence. The fact that the trial comes when the child is a little older and over a certain age limit does not lessen the distress, which may indeed be worse, and is certainly suffered over a longer period, the longer after the incident the trial comes.

It would be churlish, though, to end on a sour note since CJA 1991 undeniably improves the position for child witnesses, albeit at a cost of some complexity. Just as the 1991 Act has built upon the reforms initiated in CJA 1988, a subsequent Act may build upon and improve the current changes and perhaps extend some of the benefits to a wider group of vulnerable witnesses.

PRACTICE DIRECTION

6.13   Text of *Practice Direction (Crime: Child's Video Evidence)*

1   The procedure for making application for leave to adduce a video recording of testimony from a child witness under section 32A of the Criminal Justice Act 1988, as inserted by section 54 of the Criminal Justice Act 1991, is laid down in rule 23C of the Crown Court Rules 1982, as inserted by the Crown Court (Amendment) Rules 1992.

2   Where a court grants leave to admit a video recording in evidence under section 32A(2) of the Act of 1988 it may direct that any part of the recording be excluded: section 32A(3). When such a direction is given, the party who made the application to admit the video recording must edit the recording in accordance with the judge's directions and send a copy of the edited recording to the appropriate officer of the Crown Court and to every other party to the proceedings.

3   Where a video recording is to be adduced during proceedings before a Crown Court, it should be produced and proved by the interviewer, or any other person who was present at the interview with the child at which the recording was made. The applicant should ensure that such a person will be available for this purpose, unless the parties have agreed to accept a written statement in lieu of attendance by that person.

4   It is for the party adducing the video recording to make arrangements for the operation of the video playing equipment in court during the trial.

5   Once a trial has begun, if by reason of faulty or inadequate preparation or for some other cause, the procedures set out above have not been properly complied with, and an application is made to edit the video recording, thereby making necessary an adjournment for the work to be carried out, the court may make at its discretion an appropriate award of costs.

6   This practice direction shall take effect on 1 October 1992.

Taylor of Gosforth CJ
31 July 1992

Chapter Seven
The Provision of Services

Part IV of the Criminal Justice Act 1991 contains a range of provisions which reflect the government's belief that many of the functions traditionally performed by State agencies can be more efficiently undertaken if they are opened up to the private sector, and that those which remain in the public sector can benefit from closer scrutiny of their effectiveness and efficiency. It has thus been aptly described as the 'ideological sharp end' of the Act, particularly insofar as it provides not only for the privatisation of prisoner escort services and new remand prisons but also a framework for the possible future privatisation of existing prisons, whether for those on remand or for sentenced prisoners. It also provides for the contracting out of court security services in the magistrates' courts and for certain structural changes in the organisation of the probation service which is, however, left in the public sector.

THE PROBATION SERVICE

7.1 Background

The probation service has been essentially a local service with a traditionally pastoral role towards offenders, inherited from its origins in the Police Court missionaries of 100 years ago. Probation officers are officers of the court and are employed neither by central nor local government but by the area probation committtee which is drawn primarily from justices of the peace in the area. The probation committee is funded by the local authority who are reimbursed as to 80 per cent of the expenditure (100 per cent in the case of certain expenditure) from the Home Office. This system has not in the past imposed the degree of financial discipline which the government considers desirable or the consistency of approach from one area to another which the government would like to see. The nature of the service has also changed over recent years with the introduction of more non-custodial sentences, such as community service orders. These have fallen to the probation service to administer and have imposed on it an increased emphasis on controlling as well as caring for its clients. This trend is further accelerated by CJA 1991 with its increase in the range of community sentences and its greater encouragement to courts to make use of them. The White Paper on which much of the Act is based (*Crime Justice and Protecting the Public*, Cm 965) was accompanied by a Green Paper (Cm 966), the title of which, *Supervision and Punishment in the Community,* neatly encapsulates the twin roles that the probation service now has to accommodate. This Green Paper set out a number of options for the development of the probation service to enable it to fulfil the enhanced role which the implementation of CJA 1991 demands. Paragraph 1.5 of the Green Paper conveys the essence of the government's approach:

> The probation service has already responded to pressure for change. Over a short period of time there have been rapid improvements in consistency of standards, objectives and of management approach. These have been partly on the service's own initiative and partly in response to the Statement of National Objectives and Priorities published in 1984, the National Standards for Community Service Orders and further guidance from the Home Office. But the question must be asked whether further improvements of any substance can be achieved without also changing the organisational structure of the service. It cannot be taken for granted that the demands of the White Paper and the needs of the criminal justice system into the next century can be met by a collection of independent probation areas, loosely coordinated, with varying management structures and a professional base established in a working environment bearing little relationship to today's. It must also be asked what enhanced role can be played by the voluntary and private sectors.

Some of the options which the government outlined in the Green Paper were capable of implementation without recourse to legislation but the Act does specifically provide for changes in four principal respects:

(a)   it places Her Majesty's inspectors of probation on a statutory footing (s. 73);

(b)   it gives the Secretary of State a default power where a probation committee is operating unsatisfactorily (s. 74);

(c)   it provides for a single Inner London probation area (s. 75);

(d)   in part V of the Act, it imposes cash limits on the 80 per cent of funding provided by the Home Office. (Note: all of these provisions have been re-enacted with minor modifications and re-drafting in the Probations Services Act 1993, a consolidating statute in the process of receiving Royal Assent at the time of writing.)

7.2   Inspectors of Probation

There were formerly 12 inspectors of probation (including the chief inspector and his deputy) but they had no statutory basis. Their inital advisory role was expanded, following an efficiency scrutiny in 1987, to include the inspection of the effectiveness and efficiency of probation services. The Green Paper envisaged the probation service increasingly as a facilitator, making use of voluntary agencies and private sector organisations in the delivery of community-based penalties and other work with offenders, and it saw the inspectors having a role in monitoring the work of these agencies and organisations. The increased role and importance of the inspectorate suggested placing it on a statutory footing, on a par with the inspectorates of constabulary and of prisons, which would underline its status and independence and clarify its role and powers.

Consequently CJA 1991, s. 73 (PSA 1993, ss. 23–24), provides for the appointment of inspectors of probation whose duty it shall be under s. 73(3):

> (a)   to inspect and report to the Secretary of State on the probation service for each probation area, and the activities carried out by or on behalf of that service; and
> (b)   to discharge such other functions in connection with the provision of probation or related services (whether or not provided by or on behalf of the probation service for any area) as the Secretary of State may from time to time direct.

The words 'on behalf of' in para. (a) are apt to include the inspection of agencies utilised by the probation service, e.g., to provide programmes of work or training. In this connection, it should be noted that CJA 1991, s. 97, inserted a new para. 12A into sch. 3 to the PCCA 1973 so as to provide for a probation committee to make grants in prescribed cases. This would cover the provision of funding to voluntary and charitable organisations utilised by the probation service. The Green Paper also clearly envisaged the use of private sector organisations with which the probation service would contract.

CJA 1991, s. 73(3)(a), is essentially concerned with inspections of a particular area, whereas s. 73(3)(b) can apply to issues that go beyond individual areas. An example might be the possible role, suggested in para. 6.6 of the Green Paper, for the inspectorate:

> in developing professional practice in work with the courts and with offenders. Given the resources it could, for example, mount a systematic programme of seminars and other events with the aim of stimulating exchanges of ideas about good professional practice and disseminating the lessons of inspections.

The inspectorate produced an early report on the Probation Service's response to the implementation of the CJA 1991 and the introduction of National Standards: *The Criminal Justice Act 1991 Inspection* (May 1993). Another example of a thematic inspection is that which resulted in the *Report on Approved Probation and Bail Hostels* in August 1993.

Although para. 6.5 of the Green Paper stated that the inspectorate would be given statutory powers of access to documents, staff and premises, no specific provisions seem to have been included in CJA 1991. However, the Probation Rules 1984 (SI 1984/647) have been amended in a number of respects by SI 1992/349 and 2077 and in particular r. 23 dealing with inspection of premises and facilities has been amplified and strengthened.

7.3   Default Powers

The strengthening of the role of the Inspectorate of Probation is just part of the movement to increase the accountability of the probation service to central government. The inspectorate can provide information to the Home Office but the Green Paper floated proposals to give the Secretary of State actual power to intervene where a probation committee was seriously failing to carry out its duties. This power is now contained in CJA 1991, s. 74 (PSA 1993, s. 11), which enables the Secretary of State to make an order where he:

> is of the opinion that, without reasonable excuse, a probation committee—
>   (a)   is failing properly to discharge any duty imposed on it by or under any enactment; or
>   (b)   has so failed and is likely to do so again.

Such an order shall make 'such provision as he considers requisite for the purpose of securing that the duty is properly discharged by the committee' (s. 74(2)(b)).

This power, which is based on similar default powers in the National Health Service Act 1977 applicable to regional and district health authorities, is intended to be a power of last resort. If it were to be exercised, the committee members would be required to vacate office and the Secretary of State would appoint new members and send in commissioners to run the area in the meantime. Before this could happen, the committee would have been given notice of the complaints against it and an opportunity to respond, as the power only applies where the committee is failing in its duty 'without reasonable excuse'.

More important in practice may be developments since the 1991 Act whereby probation committees are to become more streamlined, focusing on policy issues rather than day-to-day executive functions with a smaller membership of 16–19 including the chief probation officer. The committees are to become known as probation boards, and shadow boards have been established in a number of areas although further legislation will be required to implement these changes fully.

7.4   The Inner London Probation Area

Chapter 5 of the Green Paper canvassed the increased effectiveness, efficiency, and responsiveness to government policy which could be achieved through the amalgamation of probation areas which might, as a result, relate more closely to the boundaries of other agencies, such as police force areas, or which might be of a size amenable to more appropriate management structures. Paragraph 5.11 noted that, with the exception of the City of London probation area, 'amalgamations of all probation services could be effected without primary legislation'. Paragraph 2 of annexe A also noted that areas vary in size 'from the Inner London Probation Service, with over 1,000 staff, to the City of London, with just five'. CJA 1991, s. 75 (PSA 1993, s. 2(3)), therefore amended PCCA 1973, sch. 3, so as to allow probation areas outside of the Inner London area to be included in 'the Inner London probation area'. This will, *inter alia*, permit the City of London probation area, (which was specifically excluded from the Inner London area by the original sch. 3, para. 1(4)) to be included in the Inner London probation area. Other amalgamations, as already noted, do not need primary legislation and decisions on these have not yet been announced.

7.5   Cash Limits

Paragraph 7.3 of the Green Paper pointed out that:

> on the vast majority of probation service spending, the government has an
> open-ended commitment to pay 80 per cent of any expenditure incurred
> locally. This undermines financial planning and does not provide incentives
> for efficient use of resources locally. A system of cash limits will impose greater
> financial discipline on the service.

CJA 1991, s. 94 (see now PSA 1993, s. 17(4) and s. 4), implemented the
government decision, already announced in November 1989 in advance of the
Green Paper, to cash-limit the specific grant paid to local authorities towards
probation expenditure. It does so by inserting a new subsection (3A) into s. 53 of
the PCCA 1973, which, as well as enabling a quantitative limit to be put on the
expenditure to be funded centrally, also provides flexibility as to the percentage
of approved probation expenditure to be so funded. (There does not seem to be
any intention to decrease the percentage contributed by central government but,
rather, one of the options discussed in the White Paper was 100 per cent funding
from the Home Office, a possibility which has perhaps become more likely in the
light of recent reviews of the community charge and of local government finance.
Overall funding for the probation service is planned to increase by 25 per cent in
real terms from 1990 to 1994 in recognition of the increased work load that is to
fall on it.) More detailed discussion of the possible methods of distributing the
cash-limited grant as between different authorities can be found in annexe B of
the Green Paper.

Because any expenditure over the cash-limited 80 per cent contribution of
central government will fall on the local authority, the local authority needs to
be able to object to particular items of expenditure which would take total
expenditure over the 100 per cent implied by the cash limit. Existing arrangements give it that right to object over most items of expenditure but s. 94(2) now
gives it the power to object in the crucial and expensive area of staffing numbers.
The probation committee will determine what it considers to be a sufficient
number of officers which it will be entitled to appoint in the absence of objection
from the local authority. If the authority does object, then the numbers shall be
as agreed between the probation committee and the local authority to be
sufficient and, in default of agreement, shall be determined by the Secretary of
State. Section 94(2) operated by making substitutions in para. 3 of sch. 3 to the
PCCA 1973, but para. 3(1)(a) still retains the requirement of the approval of the
Secretary of State for the individual appointment of certain grades of officer,
currently chief and deputy chief probation officers. Paragraph 5.26 of the Green
Paper commented that:

> In practice, he exercises this by approving a short list of candidates
> leaving the final decision to the probation committee. There may in
> future be occasions when the Secretary of State himself will want to
> decide which particular candidate should have a particular post. This
> would be done in full consultation with the probation committee. Such

a situation might particularly arise where the Secretary of State considered that one candidate in a short list was of outstanding ability or was particularly suitable for a specific appointment.

In its decision document of April 1991, the Home Office stepped back from this idea, noting at para. 29 that the responses to the Green Paper were 'generally opposed to this suggestion' and stating that 'the government has decided not to pursue it further as a matter of general practice but to rely, save in the most exceptional circumstances, on its existing power to approve short lists'.

This comment has to be read alongside others in ch. 5 of the Green Paper which refer to fixed-term contracts and performance-related pay and the fact that 'As the demands on the probation service increase, there may be a case for broadening the service's management base by appointing people with management experience in other fields' (para. 5.23). The decision document noted that performance pay has been introduced for chief and deputy chief probation officers 'which should increase the attractiveness of top posts in the probation service'.

Overall, it would seem that whilst there are only a limited number of provisions in CJA 1991 which directly relate to the organisation and management of the probation service, these are in many ways just the tip of the iceberg and the government intends to utilise its existing powers or if necessary to take new ones in future legislation, to exercise much greater influence over the direction and policies of the service.

MAGISTRATES' COURT SECURITY OFFICERS

7.6 Court Security Officers

Prior to the establishment of the Crown Prosecution Service, the maintenance of order in the public areas of magistrates' courts did not appear to be a problem since there was always a police presence due to the fact that the police were conducting prosecutions. The withdrawal of the police from the prosecuting role means that they can no longer be regarded as providing routine security even though they can be called on in the case of a serious disturbance. The Le Vay Report (*Magistrates' Courts: Report of a Scrutiny* (London: HMSO, 1989)) at para. 3.7 was 'struck by the potential for disorder at some courts where large numbers of defendants and their supporters are waiting for court appearances' and recommended that courts should employ staff to maintain order, perhaps provided by outside contractors. It was announced, in the discussion paper published by the Home Office in July 1990 (*Court Escorts, Custody and Security*), that this recommendation had been acccepted by the government and that the Home Secretary had issued appropriate guidelines to magistrates' courts committees. Thus court security staff are already being provided in many magistrates' courts, but the 1990 discussion paper went on to say (at p. 2) that:

[a]lthough the present powers available to deal with disorder in the face of the court appear sufficient to enable civilian staff to deal with problems in the courtroom itself, the government intends to introduce further measures to

ensure that civilian court security officers have sufficient authority to deal with problems that may arise in the course of their duties as such.

Those further measures are now contained in CJA 1991, ss. 76 to 79. Section 76(1) requires magistrates' courts committees to determine from time to time whether court security officers should be provided and, if so, how many, and whether they should be provided by the committee or by the authority (as defined in s. 76(6), essentially the local authority). The local authority can appeal to the Secretary of State if it is aggrieved at the determination of the committee, e.g., as to the numbers to be employed (s. 76(4)) but the local authority will ultimately be liable to pay for them whether they are provided by the committee or by the authority (see s. 79). (Although the authority receives 80 per cent of the net cost of expenditure of this type in grant from the Home Office, this is itself now to be subject to cash limits as a result of s. 93.) Whether it is the committee or the local authority that provides the court security officers, it can do so by employing them itself (s. 76(2)(a)) or by contracting out to the private sector (s. 76(2)(b)). The opposition attempted to remove the power under para. (b) to contract out and were unhappy about the prospect of the unregulated private security industry being involved, but the government was clearly not inclined to give way on this issue, which pervades many of the provisions in this part of the Act. At least in this area, it could be pointed out that the private sector was already involved in that some magistrates' courts are already contracting out court security services. It was stressed that it is very much a local decision whether or not to have court security officers and, if so, on what basis. Guidance to magistrates' courts committees and a code of practice on recruitment is contained in a Home Office Circular 29/1992.

7.7 Powers and Duties of Court Security Officers

What is undeniably new is the conferral by CJA 1991, ss. 77 and 78, of a special status on court security officers. Section 77 defines the powers and duties of court security officers acting in the execution of their duties. These powers include the power to search anyone who is in, or seeking to enter, the court-house, or to search any article (such as a bag) in their possession (s. 77(1)(a)) and to exclude or remove anyone who refuses to permit such a search (s. 77(1)(b)). Furthermore, s. 77(1)(c) contains a power to exclude, remove or restrain any person:

where . . . it is reasonably necessary to do so in order—
    (i)   to maintain order in the court-house;
    (ii) to enable court business to be carried on without interference or delay; or
    (iii) to secure his or any other person's safety.

Section 77(2) limits the power of search so that it does not extend to authorising a court security officer to require the removal of any clothing other than an outer coat, jacket or gloves and there is no power to use reasonable force in pursuance of the power to search. Someone who refuses to be searched is to be excluded or removed instead, but s. 77(3) does confer a power to use reasonable force in excluding or removing such a person under s. 77(1)(b) or in excluding, removing or restraining someone under s. 77(1)(c). Under s. 77(6), a court security officer 'shall not be regarded as acting in the execution of his duty at any time when he is not readily identifiable as such an officer (whether by means of a uniform or badge which he is wearing or otherwise').

Section 78 creates two special offences designed to protect court security officers: (a) assaulting one in the execution of his duty and (b) resisting or wilfully obstructing one in the execution of his duty. Both offences are triable only summarily, the former carrying a maximum penalty of a level 5 fine and/or six months in prison and the latter a maximum penalty of a level 3 fine. These offences are obviously modelled on the offences relating to constables in s. 51 of the Police Act 1964 (although the lesser of the Police Act offences is also punishable by one month's imprisonment in addition to, or as well as, a level 3 fine). This was another ground on which the possibility of contracting out court security work was (unsuccessfully) attacked in that it potentially seemed to put members of the private security industry on a par with police officers.

PRIVATISING PRISON SERVICES

7.8 Prisoner Escort Arrangements

Transporting prisoners to and from court appearances and guarding them whilst at court are duties traditionally carried out by the prison service and the police, and it was estimated that it occupied about 1,000 prison officers and about 1,400 police officers. Quite apart from the sheer volume of the drain on trained manpower, which is in short supply for other duties, the demands of prisoner escorting fluctuate and are difficult to predict with accuracy and thus created further problems for the prison service. For this reason, the idea of separate provision for prisoner escorting had been floated several times, most recently in the Woolf Report (*Prison Disturbances April 1990: Report of an Enquiry,* Cm 1456, February 1991).

One way of doing this would have been to set up a separate government service but the government had for some time been investigating the possibility of contracting out this activity to the private sector, where it believes there is the expertise in transport and distribution arrangements to provide a more cost-effective service. The development of the government's thinking can be traced through the Green Paper, *Private Sector Involvement in the Remand System,* July 1988, Cm 434, and a report commissioned from management consultants, Deloitte, Haskins & Sells, *The Practicality of Private Sector Involvement in the Remand System,* published in March 1989. The government's intention to legislate was signalled in July 1990 with the issue by the Home Office of a paper entitled *Court Escorts, Custody and Security.*

Sections 80 to 83 of CJA 1991 now give substance to these proposals. Section 80 empowers the Home Secretary to make 'prisoner escort arrangements', i.e., he make may make arrangements:

> for any of the following functions, namely—
>   (a)   the delivery of prisoners to court premises;

    (b)   the custody of prisoners held on such premises (whether or not they would otherwise be in the custody of the court) and their production before the court;

    (c)   the delivery of prisoners so held to a prison or police station;

    (d)   the delivery of prisoners from one prison to another; and

    (e)   the custody of prisoners while they are outside a prison for temporary puposes,

to be performed . . . by prisoner custody officers who are authorised to perform such functions.

(By virtue of CJA 1991, s. 92(3), the meanings of 'prison' and 'prisoners' in s. 80 include local authority secure accommodation and persons kept in it under CYPA 1969, s. 23(4).)

Under s. 80(2), prisoner escort arrangements 'may include entering into contracts with other persons for the provision by them of prisoner custody officers'. Thus contracting out to the private sector is expressly authorised and commenced on 5 April 1993 for a term of five years in the East Midlands and Humberside areas with the Metropolitan Police District being put out to tender during 1993 with a view to a 1994 start.

Turning over such functions to the private sector is clearly a sensitive issue and s. 81 provides for the monitoring of prisoner escort arrangements by a prisoner escort monitor, a Crown servant, whose duty it will be to monitor and report on the arrangements to the Home Secretary and to investigate and report on any allegations against prisoner custody officers acting under the arrangements or on any alleged breaches of discipline by prisoners under their charge. Section 81 also provides for a panel of lay observers whose duty it will be to inspect the conditions in which prisoners are transported or held and to make recommendations to the Home Secretary. In addition s. 89 and sch. 10 make it necessary for prisoner custody officers to have certificates of approval from the Secretary of State which shall not be issued unless he is satisfied that the applicant is a fit and proper person to perform the relevant functions and has received an approved standard of training. These certificates can be suspended by the escort monitor under certain circumstances (see SI 1992/727) or revoked by the Secretary of State. Furthermore, although it is not specifically provided for in the legislation, each contract entered into will have a liaison group of prison, police and court representatives to ensure that the required standard of service is delivered. The size of the areas to be contracted out (the country has been divided into ten areas for these purposes) means that only the larger private firms are likely to have the capacity to meet the standards specified in the contracts. Category A high-security-risk prisoners are not at this stage being included in the contracting-out arrangements.

7.9 Powers and Duties of Prisoner Custody Officers

Section 82 of CJA 1991 provides for the powers and duties of prisoner custody officers when acting in pursuance of prisoner escort arrangements. Under s. 82(1) they have two separate powers of search. First, they can search any prisoner for whom they are responsible 'in accordance with rules made by the

Secretary of State' (s. 82(1)(a)). These rules, the Prisoner Escorts Rules 1993 (SI 1993/515), authorise searches 'when it appears necessary to do so in the interests of security, good order or discipline' and in appropriate circumstances include the authority to conduct a strip search. In contrast, the second power to search given by s. 82(1)(b), which relates to other persons who are in, or who are seeking to enter, any place where a prisoner is or is to be held, is limited so as not to extend to authorising requiring a person to remove any of his clothing other than an outer coat, jacket or gloves. This second power is therefore more in line with the limited power of search given to court security officers (7.7 above) but it differs in that a prison custody officer is given (by s. 82(5)) the power to use reasonable force in relation to all his powers and duties under s. 82. Section 82(4) also imposes a duty to carry out a search where the Crown Court orders a search of a person before it under PCCA 1973, s. 34A.

In addition to performing the main functions of delivery and/or custody of prisoners under the prisoner escort arangements, the main duties of a prisoner custody officer are listed under the five paragraphs of s. 82(3). These include a duty to prevent the escape of prisoners but also, under para. (d), a duty to attend to their well being, and the Secretary of State is specifically authorised to make rules with respect to the performance of the duty under para. (d). This rule-making power was specifically added in response to a proposed amendment based on the European Prison Rules, model rules recommended by the Council of Europe. These relate to the protection of prisoners in transit from insult, curiosity and publicity and they prohibit the transportation of prisoners in conveyances with inadequate ventilation or light or in a manner which would subject them to unnecessary physical hardship or indignity. The government indicated that it agreed that the duty to attend to the welfare of prisoners should include these points and that the rules would ensure that prison custody officers are under no less an obligation than prison officers under the Prison Rules. It is not, however, clear that the current Prison Rule, r. 38, is fully consistent with the European model rules, but perhaps this point will be addressed in making the rules under s. 82(3).

7.10   Breaches of Discipline and Protection of Prisoner Custody Officers

Section 83 of CJA 1991 provides for prisoners who commit disciplinary offences whilst under prisoner escort arrangements. On delivery to a prison they are deemed to have been in the custody of the prison governor (or its director in the case of a contracted-out prison) at all times when they were the responsibility of a prisoner custody officer. This ensures that they can be disciplined by the prison governor by means of loss of remission, or rather the award of additional days as it is now to become (see CJA 1991, s. 42, discussed in 5.15 above). None of this applies if the act or omission has already been punished by a court (s. 83(2)).

Similar summary offences, of assault and resistance or wilful obstruction, apply under s. 90 in respect of prisoner custody officers 'acting in pursuance of prisoner escort arrangements' as apply under s. 78 (see 7.7 above) in relation to court security officers acting in pursuance of their duty. The maximum penalties are the same but under s. 90(2), the more serious of the two offences (assault) in respect of prisoner custody officers is made subject to s. 17(2) of the Firearms Act

1968 where the accused is in possession of a firearm or imitation firearm either at the time of the offence or when being arrested for it. An offence under s. 17(2) is triable only on indictment and the maximum penalty is life imprisonment (see *Blackstone's Criminal Practice, 1993*, B12.3 and B12.55).

As with court security officers, a prisoner custody officer 'shall not be regarded as acting in pursuance of prisoner escort arrangements at any time when he is not readily identifiable as such an officer' (s. 90(4)).

7.11   Contracted-out Prisons

A small proportion of prisons in the United States are run by the private sector and the idea of importing that practice in the United Kingdom was canvassed in 1984 by a report of the Adam Smith Institute, *Justice Policy*, whilst a further report in 1987, *The Prison Cell*, looked in more detail at the American system. At the same time, the Select Committee on Home Affairs was examining the possibilities of involving the private sector and the majority of the committee were in favour of the government experimenting with the idea (Fourth Report, Session 1986/87, HC 291, *Contract Provision of Prisons*). It recommended that 'tenders should be invited in particular for the construction and management of new remand centres because it is there that the worst overcrowding in the prison system is concentrated'.

In July 1987, the then Home Secretary, Douglas Hurd, said:

> I do not think that there is a case, and I do not believe that the House would accept that there is a case, for auctioning or privatising the prisons, or handing over the business of keeping prisoners safe to anyone other than government servants. (Hansard HC, 16 July 1987, vol. 119, col. 1299).

However, the more limited idea of private sector involvement in the remand system was discussed in a Green Paper (Cm. 434) published in July 1988, which was followed in March 1989 by the management consultants' report, *The Practicality of Private Sector Involvement in the Remand System*. In July 1990, the government announced its intention to experiment with private sector involvement in a proposed new remand prison (Wolds remand centre) near Hull (Hansard HC, 11 July 1990, vol. 176, col. 205–6) and the Criminal Justice Bill as originally introduced into the House of Commons provided for this in cl. 65. This clause has now effectively become, with some rearrangement of the wording, subsections (1) and (2) of CJA 1991, s. 84, which only authorise the contracting out of future remand prisons. The remainder of s. 84 was subsequently, and somewhat controversially, added at report stage in the Commons. In particular, s. 84(3) enables the Secretary of State, by statutory instrument, to extend the operation of s. 84(1) in various ways which would have the effect of authorising the contracting out of any of the following alternatives:

(a)   *all remand* prisons (whether existing or future),
(b)   *all future* prisons (whether for remand or sentenced prisoners),
(c)   *all* prisons (whether existing or future and whether for remand or sentenced prisoners).

(Section 92(1) defines prison quite widely to include a young offender institution or remand centre.)

The language in which s. 84(3) creates these possibilities has been described as 'remarkable in its almost Proustian complexity' (Lord Richard, HL Deb, 23 April, vol. 528, col. 205) and it means that, in principle, the whole prison service could be turned over to the private sector purely through the affirmative resolution procedure (see s. 84(5)). The government was at pains to stress that none of the options in s. 84(3) would be used until after seeing how the experiment with the Wolds remand centre had gone and until there had been full consultation, but critics regard it as unacceptable to have such a potentially wide power added to what was initially quite a narrow clause. In the event, the government has relatively quickly expanded the scope of s. 84 first to all future prisons (option b) in SI 1992/1656 and then to all prisons (option c) by virtue of SI 1993/368 which superseded the 1992 Order. Blakenhurst became the second contracted-out prison in May 1993 and tendering is underway for Doncaster Prison. Manchester (Strangeways) Prison is to continue to be run by the Prison Service but under a service level agreement which mirrors the contracts with the Private Sector following 'market testing', the, in this case, successful participation of the Prison Service as a competitor in the tender process. Plans have been announced by the Home Office to contract-out more prisons and to involve the private sector in the building of new prisons. Meanwhile, a report by the Chief Inspector of Prisons into the Wolds Remand Prison (August 1993) mixed praise for the staff with criticism of the contract between the Home Office and the contractor which made assessment of value for money impossible and did not do enough to discourage the lethargic lifestyle of the majority of inmates.

7.12   Staffing of contracted-out prisons

Section 85 of CJA 1991 divides the functions normally performed by a prison governor between the director of the prison (appointed by the contractor) and the controller, a Crown servant appointed by the Secretary of State. Most of the functions of the prison governor, and especially those relating to the general management of the prison, are vested in the director (see also s. 87(4)) but s. 85(3) provides that the director shall not:

(a)   inquire into a disciplinary charge laid against a prisoner, conduct the hearing of such a charge or make, remit or mitigate an award in respect of such a charge; or

(b)   except in cases of urgency, order the removal of a prisoner from association with other prisoners, the temporary confinement of a prisoner in a special cell or the application to a prisoner of any other special control or restraint.

These will no doubt be amongst the functions conferred on the controller under prison rules under s. 85(4), according to which subsection the controller is additionally under a duty:

(a)   to keep under review, and report to the Secretary of State on, the running of the prison by or on behalf of the director; and

(b) to investigate, and report to the Secretary of State on, any allegations made against prisoner custody officers performing custodial duties at the prison.

The creation of the office of controller is thus intended to deal with criticisms about the State relinquishing its control over those it has ordered to be incarcerated. The controller has not dissimilar duties in some respects to those which the prisoner escort monitor has in relation to prisoner escort arrangements (7.8 above). Contracted-out prisons will continue to have a Board of Visitors and to be subject to inspection by H.M. Chief Inspector of Prisons (as has already occurred at the Wolds). The Secretary of State has the power to intervene under s. 88 where it appears that the director has lost or is likely to lose control, and in this event, the controller is the most likely person to be appointed (temporarily) as governor for the purposes of that section.

Section 85 also provides that every officer of the prison who performs custodial duties shall be a prison custody officer authorised to perform such duties. Therefore each officer will need a certificate of approval under s. 89 (as with officers performing prisoner escort functions, 7.8 above). However, there is a distinction between approval for the purpose of performing prisoner escort functions, on the one hand, and custodial duties on the other. Different types of training will no doubt be required for the two different types of function, although of course it will be possible, and not unusual, for an individual to be trained for both functions and to be approved for both.

The duties of prisoner custody officers performing custodial duties are set out in s. 86(3) and are, formally at least, the same as those of officers performing escort functions in s. 82(3) save that para. (e) of s. 82(3) is omitted from s. 86(3), as is any reference to rules to be made in relation to para. (d), the duty to attend to prisoners' wellbeing. It appears that this reference is omitted because prisoner custody officers performing custodial duties will be subject to the existing prison rules. Section 86(1) confers very similar powers of search on prisoner custody officers perfoming custodial duties as are available to those performing escort functions. These powers are to be exercised in accordance with prison rules and carry the same limitation as far as non-prisoners are concerned so as only to authorise requiring outer clothing to be removed (s. 86(2)). Again, reasonable force can be used where necessary in pursuance of any of their powers and duties (s. 86(4)).

The offences in s. 90 (see 7.9 above) apply to assaults etc. on prisoner custody officers performing custodial duties as they do to such officers acting in pursuance of prisoner escort arrangements. On the other side of the coin, s. 91 makes it an offence, triable either way, to disclose information relating to a particular prisoner acquired in the course of employment at a contracted-out prison or in pursuance of prisoner escort arrangements. This offence is not limited to prisoner custody officers but could apply equally to ancillary staff.

7.13 Concluding Comments on Privatising Prison Services

The above powers to bring the private sector into the provision of prison services have raised sensitive issues over and above the political arguments that always accompany privatisation proposals in any field. Opponents see the proposals as 'obscene' and a dereliction of the State's responsibility to maintain the conditions in which prisoners are held. Supporters argue that the private sector will be able to provide better conditions in a more cost-effective way. For example, the specification and operating requirements for Doncaster Prison provides for a weekly minimum of six hours supervised physical education and for prisoners to spend at least 12 hours a day out of the cell, and all cells have integral sanitation. How far the privatisation programme will go will no doubt depend on the extent to which the specified standards are maintained and at what cost. Similarly, as the prisoner escort arrangements are brought in area by area, the cost and efficiency of the service provided will be the important factors in deciding whether to continue or extend the privatisation proposals. We remarked in the first edition that the specification of standards for the private sector is likely to be used as a bench-mark to assess the state of the public sector. The service level agreement entered into by the Prison Service as a result of the 'market testing' of Manchester (Strangeways) Prison is concrete evidence of this process in operation.

Criminal Justice Act 1991

(as amended by the Criminal Justice Act 1993)

CHAPTER 53

ARRANGEMENT OF SECTIONS

PART I POWERS OF COURTS TO DEAL WITH OFFENDERS

Custodial sentences

PART II   EARLY RELEASE OF PRISONERS

Preliminary

New arrangements for early release

Misbehaviour after release

Remand time and additional days

Special cases

SCHEDULES

Criminal Justice Act 1991

1991 CHAPTER 53.   An Act to make further provision with respect to the treatment of offenders and the position of children and young persons and persons having responsibility for them; to make provision with respect to certain services provided or proposed to be provided for purposes connected with the administration of justice or the treatment of offenders; to make financial and other provision with respect to that administration; and for connected purposes.

[25th July 1991]

BE IT ENACTED by the Queen's most Excellent Majesty, by and with the advice and consent of the Lords Spiritual and Temporal, and Commons, in this present Parliament assembled, and by the authority of the same, as follows:—

PART I   POWERS OF COURTS TO DEAL WITH OFFENDERS

Custodial sentences

Restrictions on imposing custodial sentences.
1.—(1)   This section applies where a person is convicted of an offence punishable with a custodial sentence other than one fixed by law.

(2)   Subject to subsection (3) below, the court shall not pass a custodial sentence on the offender unless it is of the opinion—

(a)   that the offence, or the combination of the offence and one or more offences associated with it, was so serious that only such a sentence can be justified for the offence; or

(b)   where the offence is a violent or sexual offence, that only such a sentence would be adequate to protect the public from serious harm from him.

(3)   Nothing in subsection (2) above shall prevent the court from passing a custodial sentence on the offender if he refuses to give his consent to a community sentence which is proposed by the court and requires that consent.

(4)   Where a court passes a custodial sentence, it shall be its duty—

(a)   in a case not falling within subsection (3) above, to state in open court that it is of the opinion that either or both of paragraphs (a) and (b) of subsection (2) above apply and why it is of that opinion; and

(b)   in any case, to explain to the offender in open court and in ordinary language why it is passing a custodial sentence on him.

(5)   A magistrates' court shall cause a reason stated by it under subsection (4) above to be specified in the warrant of commitment and to be entered in the register.

Note. Section 1 is printed as amended by the CJA 1993, s. 66(1).

Length of custodial sentences.
2.—(1)   This section applies where a court passes a custodial sentence other than one fixed by law.
(2)   The custodial sentence shall be—
(a)   for such term (not exceeding the permitted maximum) as in the opinion of the court is commensurate with the seriousness of the offence, or the combination of the offence and one or more offences associated with it; or
(b)   where the offence is a violent or sexual offence, for such longer term (not exceeding that maximum) as in the opinion of the court is necessary to protect the public from serious harm from the offender.
(3)   Where the court passes a custodial sentence for a term longer than is commensurate with the seriousness of the offence, or the combination of the offence and one or more offences associated with it, the court shall—
(a)   state in open court that it is of the opinion that subsection (2)(b) above applies and why it is of that opinion; and
(b)   explain to the offender in open court and in ordinary language why the sentence is for such a term.
(4)   A custodial sentence for an indeterminate period shall be regarded for the purposes of subsections (2) and (3) above as a custodial sentence for a term longer than any actual term.

Note. Section 2 is printed as amended by the CJA 1993, s. 66(2).

Procedural requirements for custodial sentences.
3.—(1)   Subject to subsection (2) below, a court shall obtain and consider a pre-sentence report before forming any such opinion as is mentioned in subsection (2) of section 1 or 2 above.
(2)   Where the offence or any other offence associated with it is triable only on indictment, subsection (1) above does not apply if, in the circumstances of the case, the court is of the opinion that it is unnecessary to obtain a pre-sentence report.
(3)   In forming any such opinion as is mentioned in subsection (2) of section 1 or 2 above a court—
(a)   shall take into account all such information about the circumstances of the offence or (as the case may be) of the offence and the offence or offences associated with it (including any aggravating or mitigating factors) as is available to it; and
(b)   in the case of any such opinion as is mentioned in paragraph (b) of that subsection, may take into account any information about the offender which is before it.
(4)   No custodial sentence which is passed in a case to which subsection (1) above applies shall be invalidated by the failure of a court to comply with that subsection but any court on an appeal against such a sentence—

(a)   shall obtain a pre-sentence report if none was obtained by the court below; and

(b)   shall consider any such report obtained by it or by that court.

(5)   In this Part "pre-sentence report" means a report in writing which—

(a)   with a view to assisting the court in determining the most suitable method of dealing with an offender, is made or submitted by a probation officer or by a social worker of a local authority social services department; and

(b)   contains information as to such matters, presented in such manner, as may be prescribed by rules made by the Secretary of State.

Note. Section 3 is printed as amended by the CJA 1993, s. 66(3).

Additional requirements in the case of mentally disordered offenders.

4.—(1)   Subject to subsection (2) below, in any case where section 3(1) above applies and the offender is or appears to be mentally disordered, the court shall obtain and consider a medical report before passing a custodial sentence other than one fixed by law.

(2)   Subsection (1) above does not apply if, in the circumstances of the case, the court is of the opinion that it is unnecessary to obtain a medical report.

(3)   Before passing a custodial sentence other than one fixed by law on an offender who is or appears to be mentally disordered, a court shall consider—

(a)   any information before it which relates to his mental condition (whether given in a medical report, a pre-sentence report or otherwise); and

(b)   the likely effect of such a sentence on that condition and on any treatment which may be available for it.

(4)   No custodial sentence which is passed in a case to which subsection (1) above applies shall be invalidated by the failure of a court to comply with that subsection, but any court on an appeal against such a sentence—

(a)   shall obtain a medical report if none was obtained by the court below; and

(b)   shall consider any such report obtained by it or by that court.

(5)   In this section—

"duly approved", in relation to a registered medical practitioner, means approved for the purposes of section 12 of the Mental Health Act 1983 ("the 1983 Act") by the Secretary of State as having special experience in the diagnosis or treatment of mental disorder;

"medical report" means a report as to an offender's mental condition made or submitted orally or in writing by a registered medical practitioner who is duly approved.

(6)   Nothing in this section shall be taken as prejudicing the generality of section 3 above.

Suspended and extended sentences of imprisonment.

5.—(1)   For subsection (2) of section 22 (suspended sentences of imprisonment) of the Powers of Criminal Courts Act 1973 ("the 1973 Act") there shall be substituted the following subsections—

"(2)   A court shall not deal with an offender by means of a suspended sentence unless it is of the opinion—

(a)   that the case is one in which a sentence of imprisonment would have been appropriate even without the power to suspend the sentence; and

(b)   that the exercise of that power can be justified by the exceptional circumstances of the case.

(2A)   A court which passes a suspended sentence on any person for an offence shall consider whether the circumstances of the case are such as to warrant in addition the imposition of a fine or the making of a compensation order."

(2)   The following shall cease to have effect, namely—

(a)   sections 28 and 29 of the 1973 Act (extended sentences of imprisonment for persistent offenders); and

(b)   section 47 of the Criminal Law Act 1977 (sentence of imprisonment partly served and partly suspended).

Community sentences

Restrictions on imposing community sentences.

6.—(1)   A court shall not pass on an offender a community sentence, that is to say, a sentence which consists of or includes one or more community orders, unless it is of the opinion that the offence, or the combination of the offence and one or more offences associated with it, was serious enough to warrant such a sentence.

(2)   Subject to subsection (3) below, where a court passes a community sentence—

(a)   the particular order or orders comprising or forming part of the sentence shall be such as in the opinion of the court is, or taken together are, the most suitable for the offender; and

(b)   the restrictions on liberty imposed by the order or orders shall be such as in the opinion of the court are commensurate with the seriousness of the offence, or the combination of the offence and one or more offences associated with it.

(3)   In consequence of the provision made by section 11 below with respect to combination orders, a community sentence shall not consist of or include both a probation order and a community service order.

(4)   In this Part "community order" means any of the following orders, namely—

(a)   a probation order;
(b)   a community service order;
(c)   a combination order;
(d)   a curfew order;
(e)   a supervision order; and
(f)   an attendance centre order.

Note. Section 6 is printed as amended by the CJA 1993, s. 66(4).

Procedural requirements for community sentences.

7.—(1)   In forming any such opinion as is mentioned in subsection (1) or (2)(b) of section 6 above, a court shall take into account all such information about the circumstances of the offence or (as the case may be) of the offence and the offence or offences associated with it (including any aggravating or mitigating factors) as is available to it.

(2)   In forming any such opinion as is mentioned in subsection (2)(a) of that section, a court may take into account any information about the offender which is before it.

(3)   A court shall obtain and consider a pre-sentence report before forming an opinion as to the suitability for the offender of one or more of the following orders, namely—

(a)   a probation order which includes additional requirements authorised by Schedule 1A to the 1973 Act;

(b)   a community service order;

(c)   a combination order; and

(d)   a supervision order which includes requirements imposed under section 12, 12A, 12AA, 12B or 12C of the Children and Young Persons Act 1969 ("the 1969 Act").

(4)   No community sentence which consists of or includes such an order as is mentioned in subsection (3) above shall be invalidated by the failure of a court to comply with that subsection, but any court on an appeal against such a sentence—

(a)   shall obtain a pre-sentence report if none was obtained by the court below; and

(b)   shall consider any such report obtained by it or by that court.

Note. Section 7 is printed as amended by the CJA 1993, s. 66(5).

Probation and community service orders

Probation orders.

8.—(1)   For section 2 of the 1973 Act there shall be substituted the following section—

"Probation

Probation Orders.

2.—(1)   Where a court by or before which a person of or over the age of sixteen years is convicted of an offence (not being an offence for which the sentence is fixed by law) is of the opinion that the supervision of the offender by a probation officer is desirable in the interests of—

(a)   securing the rehabilitation of the offender; or

(b)   protecting the public from harm from him or preventing the commission by him of further offences,

the court may make a probation order, that is to say, an order requiring him to be under the supervision of a probation officer for a period specified in the order of not less than six months nor more than three years.

For the purposes of this subsection the age of a person shall be deemed to be that which it appears to the court to be after considering any available evidence.

(2)   A probation order shall specify the petty sessions area in which the offender resides or will reside; and the offender shall, subject to paragraph 12 of Schedule 2 to the Criminal Justice Act 1991 (offenders who change their residence), be required to be under the supervision of a probation officer appointed for or assigned to that area.

(3)   Before making a probation order, the court shall explain to the offender in ordinary language—

(a)   the effect of the order (including any additional requirements proposed to be included in the order in accordance with section 3 below);

(b)   the consequences which may follow under Schedule 2 to the Criminal Justice Act 1991 if he fails to comply with any of the requirements of the order; and

(c)   that the court has under that Schedule power to review the order on the application either of the offender or of the supervising officer, and the court shall not make the order unless he expresses his willingness to comply with its requirements.

(4)   The court by which a probation order is made shall forthwith give copies of the order to a probation officer assigned to the court, and he shall give a copy—

(a)   to the offender;

(b)   to the probation officer responsible for the offender's supervision; and

(c)   to the person in charge of any institution in which the offender is required by the order to reside.

(5)   The court by which such an order is made shall also, except where it itself acts for the petty sessions area specified in the order, send to the clerk to the justices for that area—

(a)   a copy of the order; and

(b)   such documents and information relating to the case as it considers likely to be of assistance to a court acting for that area in the exercise of its functions in relation to the order.

(6)   An offender in respect of whom a probation order is made shall keep in touch with the probation officer responsible for his supervision in accordance with such instructions as he may from time to time be given by that officer and shall notify him of any change of address.

(7)   The Secretary of State may by order direct that subsection (1) above shall be amended by substituting, for the minimum or maximum period specified in that subsection as originally enacted or as previously amended under this subsection, such period as may be specified in the order.

(8)   An order under subsection (7) above may make in paragraph 13(2)(a)(i) of Schedule 2 to the Criminal Justice Act 1991 any amendment which the Secretary of State thinks necessary in consequence of any substitution made by the order."

(2)   Section 13 of that Act (effect of probation and discharge) shall cease to have effect so far as relating to offenders placed on probation.

(3)   For the purpose of rearranging Part I of that Act in consequence of the amendments made by subsections (1) and (2) above, that Part shall have effect subject to the following amendments, namely—

(a)   after section 1 there shall be inserted as sections 1A to 1C the provisions set out in Part I of Schedule 1 to this Act;

(b)   sections 7 and 9 (which are re-enacted with minor modifications by sections 1A and 1B) shall cease to have effect;

(c)   sections 8 and 13 (which, so far as relating to discharged offenders, are re-enacted with minor modifications by sections 1B and 1C) shall cease to have effect so far as so relating; and

(d) immediately before section 11 there shall be inserted the following cross heading—

"Probation and discharge".

Additional requirements which may be included in such orders.
9.—(1)   For sections 3 to 4B of the 1973 Act there shall be substituted the following section—

"Additional requirements which may be included in such orders.

3.—(1)   Subject to subsection (2) below, a probation order may in addition require the offender to comply during the whole or any part of the probation period with such requirements as the court, having regard to the circumstances of the case, considers desirable in the interests of—

(a)   securing the rehabilitation of the offender; or

(b)   protecting the public from harm from him or preventing the commission by him of further offences.

(2)   Without prejudice to the power of the court under section 35 of this Act to make a compensation order, the payment of sums by way of damages for injury or compensation for loss shall not be included among the additional requirements of a probation order.

(3)   Without prejudice to the generality of subsection (1) above, the additional requirements which may be included in a probation order shall include the requirements which are authorised by Schedule 1A to this Act."

(2)   After Schedule 1 to that Act there shall be inserted as Schedule 1A the provisions set out in Part II of Schedule 1 to this Act.

Community service orders.
10.—(1)   In subsection (1) of section 14 of the 1973 Act (community service orders in respect of offenders), the words "instead of dealing with him in any other way" shall cease to have effect.

(2)   In subsection (1A) of that section, for paragraph (b) there shall be substituted the following paragraph—

"(b)   not more than 240."

(3)   For subsections (2) and (2A) of that section there shall be substituted the following subsections—

"(2)   A court shall not make a community service order in respect of any offender unless the offender consents and the court, after hearing (if the court thinks it necessary) a probation officer or social worker of a local authority social services department, is satisfied that the offender is a suitable person to perform work under such an order.

(2A)   Subject to paragraphs 3 and 4 of Schedule 3 to the Criminal Justice Act 1991 (reciprocal enforcement of certain orders) a court shall not make a community service order in respect of an offender unless it is satisfied that provision for him to perform work under such an order can be made under the arrangements for persons to perform work under such orders which exist in the petty sessions area in which he resides or will reside."

(4)   In section 15(1) of that Act (obligations of persons subject to community service orders), for paragraph (a) there shall be substituted the following paragraph—

"(a)   keep in touch with the relevant officer in accordance with such instructions as he may from time to time be given by that officer and notify him of any change of address;".

Orders combining probation and community service.

11.—(1)   Where a court by or before which a person of or over the age of sixteen years is convicted of an offence punishable with imprisonment (not being an offence for which the sentence is fixed by law) is of the opinion mentioned in subsection (2) below, the court may make a combination order, that is to say, an order requiring him both—

(a)   to be under the supervision of a probation officer for a period specified in the order, being not less than twelve months nor more than three years; and

(b)   to perform unpaid work for a number of hours so specified, being in the aggregate not less than 40 nor more than 100.

(2)   The opinion referred to in subsection (1) above is that the making of a combination order is desirable in the interests of—

(a)   securing the rehabilitation of the offender; or

(b)   protecting the public from harm from him or preventing the commission by him of further offences.

(3)   Subject to subsection (1) above, Part I of the 1973 Act shall apply in relation to combination orders—

(a)   in so far as they impose such a requirement as is mentioned in paragraph (a) of that subsection, as if they were probation orders; and

(b)   in so far as they impose such a requirement as is mentioned in paragraph (b) of that subsection, as if they were community service orders.

Curfew orders

Curfew orders.

12.—(1)   Where a person of or over the age of sixteen years is convicted of an offence (not being an offence for which the sentence is fixed by law), the court by or before which he is convicted may make a curfew order, that is to say, an order requiring him to remain, for periods specified in the order, at a place so specified.

(2)   A curfew order may specify different places or different periods for different days, but shall not specify—

(a)   periods which fall outside the period of six months beginning with the day on which it is made; or

(b)   periods which amount to less than 2 hours or more than 12 hours in any one day.

(3)   The requirements in a curfew order shall, as far as practicable, be such as to avoid—

(a)   any conflict with the offender's religious beliefs or with the requirements of any other community order to which he may be subject; and

(b)   any interference with the times, if any, at which he normally works or attends school or other educational establishment.

(4)   A curfew order shall include provision for making a person responsible for monitoring the offender's whereabouts during the curfew periods specified in the order; and a person who is made so responsible shall be of a description specified in an order made by the Secretary of State.

(5)   Before making a curfew order, the court shall explain to the offender in ordinary language—

(a)   the effect of the order (including any additional requirements proposed to be included in the order in accordance with section 13 below);

(b)   the consequences which may follow under Schedule 2 to this Act if he fails to comply with any of the requirements of the order; and

(c)   that the court has under that Schedule power to review the order on the application either of the offender or of the supervising officer,

and the court shall not make the order unless he expresses his willingness to comply with its requirements.

(6)   Before making a curfew order, the court shall obtain and consider information about the place proposed to be specified in the order (including information as to the attitude of persons likely to be affected by the enforced presence there of the offender).

(7)   The Secretary of State may by order direct—

(a)   that subsection (2) above shall have effect with the substitution, for any period there specified, of such period as may be specified in the order; or

(b)   that subsection (3) above shall have effect with such additional restrictions as may be so specified.

Electronic monitoring of curfew orders.

13.—(1)   Subject to subsection (2) below, a curfew order may in addition include requirements for securing the electronic monitoring of the offender's whereabouts during the curfew periods specified in the order.

(2)   A court shall not make a curfew order which includes such requirements unless the court—

(a)   has been notified by the Secretary of State that electronic monitoring arrangements are available in the area in which the place proposed to be specified in the order is situated; and

(b)   is satisfied that the necessary provision can be made under those arrangements.

(3)   Electronic monitoring arrangements made by the Secretary of State under this section may include entering into contracts with other persons for the electronic monitoring by them of offenders' whereabouts.

Orders: supplemental

Enforcement etc. of community orders.

14.—(1)   Schedule 2 to this Act (which makes provision for dealing with failures to comply with the requirements of certain community orders, for amending such orders and for revoking them with or without the substitution of other sentences) shall have effect.

(2)   Sections 5, 6, 16 and 17 of, and Schedule 1 to, the 1973 Act (which are superseded by Schedule 2 to this Act) shall cease to have effect.

Regulation of community orders.
15.—(1)   The Secretary of State may make rules for regulating—
    (a)   the supervision of persons who are subject to probation orders;
    (b)   the arrangements to be made under Schedule 3 to the 1973 Act for persons who are subject to community service orders to perform work under those orders and the performance by such persons of such work;
    (c)   the monitoring of the whereabouts of persons who are subject to curfew orders (including electronic monitoring in cases where arrangements for such monitoring are available); and
    (d)   without prejudice to the generality of paragraphs (a) to (c) above, the functions of the responsible officers of such persons as are mentioned in those paragraphs.
  (2)   Rules under subsection (1)(b) above may in particular—
    (a)   limit the number of hours of work to be done by a person on any one day;
    (b)   make provision as to the reckoning of hours worked and the keeping of work records; and
    (c)   make provision for the payment of travelling and other expenses in connection with the performance of work.
  (3)   In this Part "responsible officer" means—
    (a)   in relation to an offender who is subject to a probation order, the probation officer responsible for his supervision;
    (b)   in relation to an offender who is subject to a community service order, the relevant officer within the meaning of section 14(4) of the 1973 Act; and
    (c)   in relation to an offender who is subject to a curfew order, the person responsible for monitoring his whereabouts during the curfew periods specified in the order.
  (4)   This section shall apply in relation to combination orders—
    (a)   in so far as they impose such a requirement as is mentioned in paragraph (a) of subsection (1) of section 11 above, as if they were probation orders; and
    (b)   in so far as they impose such a requirement as is mentioned in paragraph (b) of that subsection, as if they were community service orders.

Reciprocal enforcement of certain orders.
16.   Schedule 3 to this Act shall have effect for making provision for and in connection with—
    (a)   the making and amendment in England and Wales of community orders relating to persons residing in Scotland or Northern Ireland; and
    (b)   the making and amendment in Scotland or Northern Ireland of corresponding orders relating to persons residing in England and Wales.

Financial penalties

Increase of certain maxima.
17.—(1)   In section 37 (standard scale of fines) of the Criminal Justice Act 1982 ("the 1982 Act") and section 289G of the Criminal Procedure (Scotland) Act 1975 (corresponding Scottish provision), for subsection (2) there shall be substituted the following subsection—

"(2)   The standard scale is shown below—

Level on the scale	Amount of fine
1	£200
2	£500
3	£1,000
4	£2,500
5	£5,000".

(2)   Part I of the Magistrates' Courts Act 1980 ("the 1980 Act") shall be amended as follows—

(a)   in section 24(3) and (4) (maximum fine on summary conviction of young person for indictable offence) and section 36(1) and (2) (maximum fine on conviction of young person by magistrates' court), for "£400" there shall be substituted "£1,000";

(b)   in section 24(4) (maximum fine on summary conviction of child for indictable offence) and section 36(2) (maximum fine on conviction of child by magistrates' court), for "£100" there shall be substituted "£250"; and

(c)   in section 32(9) (maximum fine on summary conviction of offence triable either way), for "£2,000" there shall be substituted "£5,000";

and in section 289B(6) of the Criminal Procedure (Scotland) Act 1975 (interpretation), in the definition of "prescribed sum", for "£2,000" there shall be substituted "£5,000".

(3)   Schedule 4 to this Act shall have effect as follows—

(a)   in each of the provisions mentioned in column 1 of Part I (the general description of which is given in column 2), for the amount specified in column 3 there shall be substituted the amount specified in column 4;

(b)   in each of the provisions mentioned in column 1 of Part II (the general description of which is given in column 2), for the amount specified in column 3 there shall be substituted the level on the standard scale specified in column 4;

(c)   in each of the provisions mentioned in column 1 of Part III (the general description of which is given in column 2), for the amount specified in column 3 there shall be substituted a reference to the statutory maximum;

(d)   the provisions set out in Part IV shall be substituted for Schedule 6A to the 1980 Act (fines that may be altered under section 143); and

(e)   [repealed by the CJA 1993, sch. 3, para. 1(1), and sch. 6, part I]

Fixing of fines.
18.—(1)   Before fixing the amount of any fine, a court shall inquire into the financial circumstances of the offender.

(2)   The amount of any fine fixed by a court shall be such as, in the opinion of the court, reflects the seriousness of the offence.

(3)   In fixing the amount of any fine, a court shall take into account the circumstances of the case including, among other things, the financial circumstances of the offender so far as they are known, or appear, to the court.

(4)   Where—

(a)   an offender has been convicted in his absence in pursuance of section 11 or 12 of the Magistrates' Courts Act 1980 (non-appearance of accused),

(b)   an offender—

(i)   has failed to comply with an order under section 20(1) below; or

       (ii)   has otherwise failed to cooperate with the court in its inquiry into his financial circumstances, or

    (c)   the parent or guardian of an offender who is a child or young person—

       (i)   has failed to comply with an order under section 20(1B) below; or

       (ii)   has otherwise failed to cooperate with the court in its inquiry into his financial circumstances,

and the court considers that it has insufficient information to make a proper determination of the financial circumstances of the offender, it may make such determination as it thinks fit.

    (5)   Subsection (3) above applies whether taking into account the financial circumstances of the offender has the effect of increasing or reducing the amount of the fine.

Note. Section 18 is printed here as substituted by the CJA 1993, s. 65(1).

19.   [Repealed by the CJA 1993, s. 65(2) and sch. 6, part I.]

Statements as to offenders' means.

20.—(1)   Where a person has been convicted of an offence, the court may, before sentencing him, make a financial circumstances order with respect to him.

    (1A)   Where a magistrates' court has been notified in accordance with section 12(2) of the Magistrates' Courts Act 1980 that a person desires to plead guilty without appearing before the court, the court may make a financial circumstances order with respect to him.

    (1B)   Before exercising its powers under section 55 of the Children and Young Persons Act 1933 against the parent or guardian of any person who has been convicted of an offence, the court may make a financial circumstances order with respect to the parent or (as the case may be) guardian.

    (1C)   In this section 'a financial circumstances order' means, in relation to any person, an order requiring him to give to the court, within such period as may be specified in the order, such a statement of his financial circumstances as the court may require.

    (2)   A person who without reasonable excuse fails to comply with a financial circumstances order shall be liable on summary conviction to a fine not exceeding level 3 on the standard scale.

    (3)   If a person in furnishing any statement in pursuance of a financial circumstances order—

    (a)   makes a statement which he knows to be false in a material particular;

    (b)   recklessly furnishes a statement which is false in a material particular; or

    (c)   knowingly fails to disclose any material fact,

he shall be liable on summary conviction to imprisonment for a term not exceeding three months or a fine not exceeding level 4 on the standard scale or both.

    (4)   Proceedings in respect of an offence under subsection (3) above may, notwithstanding anything in section 127(1) of the 1980 Act (limitation of time), be commenced at any time within two years from the date of the commission of the offence or within six months from its first discovery by the prosecutor, whichever period expires the earlier.

Note. Section 20 is printed as amended by the CJA 1993, sch. 3, para. 2 and sch. 6, part I.

Financial penalties: supplemental

Remission of fines.

21.—(1) This section applies where a court has, in fixing the amount of a fine, determined the offender's financial circumstances under section 18(4) above.

(2) If, on subsequently inquiring into the offender's financial circumstances, the court is satisfied that had it had the results of that inquiry when sentencing the offender it would—

(a) have fixed a smaller amount; or

(b) not have fined him,

it may remit the whole or any part of the fine.

(3) Where under this section the court remits the whole or part of a fine after a term of imprisonment has been fixed under section 82(5) of the Magistrates' Courts Act 1980 (issue of warrant of commitment for default) or section 31 of the Powers of Criminal Courts Act 1973 (powers of Crown Court in relation to fines), it shall reduce the term by the corresponding proportion.

(4) In calculating any reduction required by subsection (3) above, any fraction of a day shall be ignored.

Note. Section 21 is printed as substituted by the CJA 1993, sch. 3, para. 3.

22. [Repealed by the CJA 1993, sch. 3, para. 4, and sch. 6, part I.]

Default in other cases.

23.—(1) In the Tables in section 31(3A) of the 1973 Act and paragraph 1 of Schedule 4 to the 1980 Act (maximum periods of imprisonment for default in paying fines etc.), for the entries relating to amounts not exceeding £5,000 there shall be substituted the following entries—

"An amount not exceeding £200	7 days
An amount exceeding £200 but not exceeding £500	14 days
An amount exceeding £500 but not exceeding £1,000	28 days
An amount exceeding £1,000 but not exceeding £2,500	45 days
An amount exceeding £2,500 but not exceeding £5,000	3 months".

(2) For the Table in section 407(1A) of the Criminal Procedure (Scotland) Act 1975 (maximum period of imprisonment for failure to pay fine or find caution) there shall be substituted the following Table—

"Amount of fine or caution	*Maximum period of imprisonment*
An amount not exceeding £200	7 days
An amount exceeding £200 but not exceeding £500	14 days
An amount exceeding £500 but not exceeding £1,000	28 days
An amount exceeding £1,000 but not exceeding £2,500	45 days
An amount exceeding £2,500 but not exceeding £5,000	3 months
An amount exceeding £5,000 but not exceeding £10,000	6 months
An amount exceeding £10,000 but not exceeding £20,000	12 months

"Amount of fine or caution	*Maximum period of imprisonment*
An amount exceeding £20,000 but not exceeding £50,000	18 months
An amount exceeding £50,000 but not exceeding £100,000	2 years
An amount exceeding £100,000 but not exceeding £250,000	3 years
An amount exceeding £250,000 but not exceeding £1 million	5 years
An amount exceeding £1 million	10 years."

(3) In Schedule 16 (repeals) to the 1988 Act, the entry relating to subsection (8) of section 41 of the Administration of Justice Act 1970 shall cease to have effect; and that subsection (discretion of Crown Court to specify extended period of imprisonment in default of payment of compensation) shall have effect as if that entry had not been enacted.

Recovery of fines etc. by deductions from income support.
24.—(1) The Secretary of State may by regulations provide that where a fine has been imposed on an offender by a magistrates' court, or a sum is required to be paid by a compensation order which has been made against an offender by such a court, and (in either case) the offender is entitled to income support—

(a) the court may apply to the Secretary of State asking him to deduct sums from any amounts payable to the offender by way of income support, in order to secure the payment of any sum which is or forms part of the fine or compensation; and

(b) the Secretary of State may deduct sums from any such amounts and pay them to the court towards satisfaction of any such sum.

(2) The regulations may include—

(a) provision that, before making an application, the court shall make an enquiry as to the offender's means;

(b) provision allowing or requiring adjudication as regards an application, and provision as to appeals and reviews;

(c) provision as to the circumstances and manner in which and the times at which sums are to be deducted and paid;

(d) provision as to the calculation of such sums (which may include provision to secure that amounts payable to the offender by way of income support do not fall below prescribed figures);

(e) provision as to the circumstances in which the Secretary of State is to cease making deductions;

(f) provision requiring the Secretary of State to notify the offender, in a prescribed manner and at any prescribed time, of the total amount of sums deducted up to the time of notification; and

(g) provision that, where the whole amount to which the application relates has been paid, the court shall give notice of that fact to the Secretary of State.

(3) In subsection (1) above—

(a) the reference to a fine having been imposed by a magistrates' court includes a reference to a fine being treated, by virtue of section 32 of the 1973 Act, as having been so imposed; and

(b)   the reference to a sum being required to be paid by a compensation order which has been made by a magistrates' court includes a reference to a sum which is required to be paid by such an order being treated, by virtue of section 41 of the Administration of Justice Act 1970, as having been adjudged to be paid on conviction by such a court.

(4)   In this section—

"fine" includes—

(a)   a penalty imposed under section 8(1) or 18(4) of the Vehicles (Excise) Act 1971 or section 102(3)(aa) of the Customs and Excise Management Act 1979 (penalties imposed for certain offences in relation to vehicle excise licences);

(b)   an amount ordered to be paid, in addition to any penalty so imposed, under section 9, 18A or 26A of the said Act of 1971 (liability to additional duty);

(c)   an amount ordered to be paid by way of costs which is, by virtue of section 41 of the Administration of Justice Act 1970, treated as having been adjudged to be paid on a conviction by a magistrates' court;

"income support" means income support within the meaning of the Social Security Act 1986, either alone or together with any unemployment, sickness or invalidity benefit, retirement pension or severe disablement allowance which is paid by means of the same instrument of payment;

"prescribed" means prescribed by regulations made by the Secretary of State.

(5)   In the application of this section to Scotland—

(a)   references in subsections (1) and (2) above to a magistrates' court shall be construed as references to a court; and

(b)   in subsection (3) above, for paragraphs (a) and (b) there shall be substituted the following paragraphs—

"(a)   the reference to a fine having been imposed by a court includes a reference to a fine being treated, by virtue of section 196(2) of the Criminal Procedure (Scotland) Act 1975, as having been so imposed; and

(b)   the reference to a compensation order having been made by a court includes a reference to such an order being treated, by virtue of section 66 of the Criminal Justice (Scotland) Act 1980, as having been so made."

Miscellaneous

Committals for sentence.

25.—(1)   For section 38 of the 1980 Act there shall be substituted the following section—

"Committal for sentence on summary trial of offence triable either way.
38.—(1)   This section applies where on the summary trial of an offence triable either way (not being an offence as regards which this section is excluded by section 33 above) a person who is not less than 18 years old is convicted of the offence.

(2)   If the court is of opinion—

(a)   that the offence or the combination of the offence and other offences associated with it was so serious that greater punishment should be inflicted for the offence than the court has power to impose; or

(b)   in the case of a violent or sexual offence committed by a person who is not less than 21 years old, that a sentence of imprisonment for a term longer than the court has power to impose is necessary to protect the public from serious harm from him,

the court may, in accordance with section 56 of the Criminal Justice Act 1967, commit the offender in custody or on bail to the Crown Court for sentence in accordance with the provisions of section 42 of the Powers of Criminal Courts Act 1973.

(3)   Paragraphs (a) and (b) of subsection (2) above shall be construed as if they were contained in Part I of the Criminal Justice Act 1991.

(4)   The preceding provisions of this section shall apply in relation to a corporation as if—

(a)   the corporation were an individual who is not less than 18 years old; and

(b)   in subsection (2) above, paragraph (b) and the words 'in custody or on bail' were omitted."

(2)   In Schedule 3 to the 1980 Act, paragraph 5 (provisions relating to committal to Crown Court for sentence not to apply to a corporation) shall cease to have effect.

Note. The CJA 1993, s. 66(8), provides as follows:

In section 38 of the Magistrates' Court Act 1980 (committal for sentence on summary trial of offence triable either way), in subsection (2)(a), for the word "other" there shall be substituted "one or more".

Alteration of certain penalties.
26.—(1)   In section 7 of the Theft Act 1968 (theft), for the words "ten years" there shall be substituted the words "seven years".

(2)   For subsections (3) and (4) of section 9 of that Act (burglary) there shall be substituted the following subsections—

"(3)   A person guilty of burglary shall on conviction on indictment be liable to imprisonment for a term not exceeding—

(a)   where the offence was committed in respect of a building or part of a building which is a dwelling, fourteen years;

(b)   in any other case, ten years.

(4)   References in subsections (1) and (2) above to a building, and the reference in subsection (3) above to a building which is a dwelling, shall apply also to an inhabited vehicle or vessel, and shall apply to any such vehicle or vessel at times when the person having a habitation in it is not there as well as at times when he is."

(3)   [Repealed by Protection of Badgers Act 1992, sch.]

(4)   In section 51(4) of the Criminal Law Act 1977 (penalties for bomb hoaxes)—

(a)   in paragraph (a), for the words "three months" there shall be substituted the words "six months"; and

(b)   in paragraph (b), for the words "five years" there shall be substituted the words "seven years".

(5)   The power saved by subsection (1) of section 70 of the 1982 Act (vagrancy offences) shall not include, in the case of an offence mentioned in paragraph (b)(i) of that subsection (sleeping rough), power to impose a fine which exceeds level 1 on the standard scale.

Treatment of offenders under 1983 Act.
27.—(1)   After section 39 of the 1983 Act there shall be inserted the following section—

> *"Information to facilitate guardianship orders.*
> 39A.   Where a court is minded to make a guardianship order in respect of any offender, it may request the local social services authority for the area in which the offender resides or last resided, or any other local social services authority that appears to the court to be appropriate—
>   (a)   to inform the court whether it or any other person approved by it is willing to receive the offender into guardianship; and
>   (b)   if so, to give such information as it reasonably can about how it or the other person could be expected to exercise in relation to the offender the powers conferred by section 40(2) below;
> and that authority shall comply with any such request."

(2)   After section 54 of that Act there shall be inserted the following section—

> *"Reduction of period for making hospital orders.*
> 54A.—(1)   The Secretary of State may by order reduce the length of the periods mentioned in sections 37(4) and (5) and 38(4) above.
>   (2)   An order under subsection (1) above may make such consequential amendments of sections 40(1) and 44(3) above as appear to the Secretary of State to be necessary or expedient."

(3)   In section 143(2) of that Act (general provisions as to regulations, orders and rules), after the words "this Act" there shall be inserted the words "or any order made under section 54A above".

Supplemental

Savings for mitigation and mentally disordered offenders.
28.—(1)   Nothing in this Part shall prevent a court from mitigating an offender's sentence by taking into account any such matters as, in the opinion of the court, are relevant in mitigation of sentence.

(2)   Without prejudice to the generality of subsection (1) above, nothing in this Part shall prevent a court—
   (a)   from mitigating any penalty included in an offender's sentence by taking into account any other penalty included in that sentence; or
   (b)   in a case of an offender who is convicted of one or more other offences, from mitigating his sentence by applying any rule of law as to the totality of sentences.

(3)   [Repealed by the CJA 1993, sch. 6, part I.]

(4)   Nothing in this Part shall be taken—

(a)   as requiring a court to pass a custodial sentence, or any particular custodial sentence, on a mentally disordered offender; or

(b)   as restricting any power (whether under the 1983 Act or otherwise) which enables a court to deal with such an offender in the manner it considers to be most appropriate in all the circumstances.

Effect of previous convictions and of offending while on bail.
29.—(1)   In considering the seriousness of any offence, the court may take into account any previous convictions of the offender or any failure of his to respond to previous sentences.

(2)   In considering the seriousness of any offence committed while the offender was on bail, the court shall treat the fact that it was committed in those circumstances as an aggravating factor.

(3)   A probation order or conditional discharge order made before 1st October 1992 (which, by virtue of section 2 or 7 of the Powers of Criminal Courts Act 1973, would otherwise not be a sentence for the purposes of this section) is to be treated as a sentence for those purposes.

(4)   A conviction in respect of which a probation order or conditional discharge order was made before that date (which, by virtue of section 13 of that Act, would otherwise not be a conviction for those purposes) is to be treated as a conviction for those purposes.

Note. Section 29 is printed as substituted by the CJA 1993, s. 66(6).

Rules, regulations and orders.
30.—(1)   Any power of the Secretary of State to make rules, regulations or orders under this Part—

(a)   shall be exercisable by statutory instrument; and

(b)   shall include power to make different provision for different cases or classes of case.

(2)   A statutory instrument containing any rules, regulations or order under this Part (other than an order under section 12(4) above) shall be subject to annulment in pursuance of a resolution of either House of Parliament.

Note. Section 30 is printed as amended by the CJA 1993, sch. 6, part I.

Interpretation of Part I.
31.—(1)   In this Part—

"attendance centre order" means an order under section 17 of the 1982 Act;

"combination order" means an order under section 11 above;

"community order" has the meaning given by section 6(4) above;

"community sentence" has the meaning given by section 6(1) above;

"curfew order" means an order under section 12 above;

"custodial sentence" means—

(a)   in relation to an offender of or over the age of twenty-one years, a sentence of imprisonment; and

(b)   in relation to an offender under that age, a sentence of detention in a young offender institution or under section 53 of the Children and Young Persons Act 1933 ("the 1933 Act"), or a sentence of custody for life under section 8(2) of the 1982 Act;

"mentally disordered", in relation to any person, means suffering from a mental disorder within the meaning of the 1983 Act;

"pre-sentence report" has the meaning given by section 3(5) above;

"responsible officer" has the meaning given by section 15(3) above;

"sentence of imprisonment" does not include a committal or attachment for contempt of court;

"sexual offence" means an offence under the Sexual Offences Act 1956, the Indecency with Children Act 1960, the Sexual Offences Act 1967, section 54 of the Criminal Law Act 1977 or the Protection of Children Act 1978, other than—

> (a)   an offence under section 12 or 13 of the Sexual Offences Act 1956 which would not be an offence but for section 2 of the Sexual Offences Act 1967;

> (b)   an offence under section 30, 31 or 33 to 36 of the said Act of 1956; and

> (c)   an offence under section 4 or 5 of the said Act of 1967;

"supervision order" means a supervision order under the 1969 Act;

"violent offence" means an offence which leads, or is intended or likely to lead, to a person's death or to physical injury to a person, and includes an offence which is required to be charged as arson (whether or not it would otherwise fall within this definition).

(2)   For the purposes of this Part, an offence is associated with another if—

(a)   the offender is convicted of it in the proceedings in which he is convicted of the other offence, or (although convicted of it in earlier proceedings) is sentenced for it at the same time as he is sentenced for that offence; or

(b)   the offender admits the commission of it in the proceedings in which he is sentenced for the other offence and requests the court to take it into consideration in sentencing him for that offence.

(3)   In this Part any reference, in relation to an offender convicted of a violent or sexual offence, to protecting the public from serious harm from him shall be construed as a reference to protecting members of the public from death or serious personal injury, whether physical or psychological, occasioned by further such offences committed by him.

PART II   EARLY RELEASE OF PRISONERS

Preliminary

The Parole Board.

32.—(1)   There shall continue to be a body to be known as the Parole Board ("the Board") which shall discharge the functions conferred on it by this Part.

(2)   It shall be the duty of the Board to advise the Secretary of State with respect to any matter referred to it by him which is connected with the early release or recall of prisoners.

(3)   The Board shall deal with cases as respects which it makes recommendations under this Part on consideration of—

(a)   any documents given to it by the Secretary of State; and

(b)   any other oral or written information obtained by it,
and if in any particular case the Board thinks it necessary to interview the person
to whom the case relates before reaching a decision, the Board may authorise
one of its members to interview him and shall consider the report of the interview
made by that member.

(4)   The Board shall deal with cases as respects which it gives directions
under this Part on consideration of all such evidence as may be adduced before
it.

(5)   Without prejudice to subsections (3) and (4) above, the Secretary of State
may make rules with respect to the proceedings of the Board, including
provision authorising cases to be dealt with by a prescribed number of its
members or requiring cases to be dealt with at prescribed times.

(6)   The Secretary of State may also give to the Board directions as to the
matters to be taken into account by it in discharging any functions under this
Part; and in giving any such directions the Secretary of State shall in particular
have regard to—

(a)   the need to protect the public from serious harm from offenders; and

(b)   the desirability of preventing the commission by them of further
offences and of securing their rehabilitation.

(7)   Schedule 5 to this Act shall have effect with respect to the Board.

New arrangements for early release

Duty to release short-term and long-term prisoners.
33.—(1)   As soon as a short-term prisoner has served one-half of his sentence, it
shall be the duty of the Secretary of State—

(a)   to release him unconditionally if that sentence is for a term of less than
twelve months; and

(b)   to release him on licence if that sentence is for a term of twelve months
or more.

(2)   As soon as a long-term prisoner has served two-thirds of his sentence, it
shall be the duty of the Secretary of State to release him on licence.

(3)   As soon as a short-term or long-term prisoner who—

(a)   has been released on licence under subsection (1)(b) or (2) above or
section 35 or 36(1) below; and

(b)   has been recalled to prison under section 38(2) or 39(1) below,
would (but for his release) have served three-quarters of his sentence, it shall be
the duty of the Secretary of State to release him unconditionally.

(4)   Where a prisoner whose sentence is for a term of less than twelve months
has been released on licence under section 36(1) below and recalled to prison
under section 38(2) below, subsection (3) above shall have effect as if for the
reference to three-quarters of his sentence there were substituted a reference to
one-half of that sentence.

(5)   In this Part—

"long-term prisoner" means a person serving a sentence of imprisonment
for a term of four years or more;

"short-term prisoner" means a person serving a sentence of imprisonment
for a term of less than four years.

Duty to release discretionary life prisoners.

34.—(1) A life prisoner is a discretionary life prisoner for the purposes of this Part if—

(a) his sentence was imposed for a violent or sexual offence the sentence for which is not fixed by law; and

(b) the court by which he was sentenced for that offence ordered that this section should apply to him as soon as he had served a part of his sentence specified in the order.

(2) A part of a sentence so specified shall be such part as the court considers appropriate taking into account—

(a) the seriousness of the offence, or the combination of the offence and other offences associated with it; and

(b) the provisions of this section as compared with those of section 33(2) above and section 35(1) below.

(3) As soon as, in the case of a discretionary life prisoner—

(a) he has served the part of his sentence specified in the order ("the relevant part"); and

(b) the Board has directed his release under this section, it shall be the duty of the Secretary of State to release him on licence.

(4) The Board shall not give a direction under subsection (3) above with respect to a discretionary life prisoner unless—

(a) the Secretary of State has referred the prisoner's case to the Board; and

(b) the Board is satisfied that it is no longer necessary for the protection of the public that the prisoner shoud be confined.

(5) A discretionary life prisoner may require the Secretary of State to refer his case to the Board at any time—

(a) after he has served the relevant part of his sentence; and

(b) where there has been a previous reference of his case to the Board, after the end of the period of two years beginning with the disposal of that reference; and

(c) where he is also serving a sentence of imprisonment for a term, after he has served one-half of that sentence;

and in this subsection "previous reference" means a reference under subsection (4) above or section 39(4) below made after the prisoner had served the relevant part of his sentence.

(6) In determining for the purpose of subsection (3) or (5) above whether a discretionary life prisoner has served the relevant part of his sentence, no account shall be taken of any time during which he was unlawfully at large within the meaning of section 49 of the Prison Act 1952 ("the 1952 Act").

(7) In this Part "life prisoner" means a person serving one or more sentences of life imprisonment; but—

(a) a person serving two or more such sentences shall not be treated as a discretionary life prisoner for the purposes of this Part unless the requirements of subsection (1) above are satisfied as respects each of those sentences; and

(b) subsections (3) and (5) above shall not apply in relation to such a person until after he has served the relevant part of each of those sentences.

Power to release long-term and life prisoners.

35.—(1)   After a long-term prisoner has served one-half of his sentence, the Secretary of State may, if recommended to do so by the Board, release him on licence.

(2)   If recommended to do so by the Board, the Secretary of State may, after consultation with the Lord Chief Justice together with the trial judge if available, release on licence a life prisoner who is not a discretionary life prisoner.

(3)   The Board shall not make a recommendation under subsection (2) above unless the Secretary of State has referred the particular case, or the class of case to which that case belongs, to the Board for its advice.

Power to release prisoners on compassionate grounds.

36.—(1)   The Secretary of State may at any time release a prisoner on licence if he is satisfied that exceptional circumstances exist which justify the prisoner's release on compassionate grounds.

(2)   Before releasing a long-term or life prisoner under subsection (1) above, the Secretary of State shall consult the Board, unless the circumstances are such as to render such consultation impracticable.

Duration and conditions of licences.

37.—(1)   Subject to subsection (2) below, where a short-term or long-term prisoner is released on licence, the licence shall, subject to any suspension under section 38(2) below or, as the case may be, any revocation under section 39(1) or (2) below, remain in force until the date on which he would (but for his release) have served three-quarters of his sentence.

(2)   Where a prisoner whose sentence is for a term of less than twelve months is released on licence under section 36(1) above, subsection (1) above shall have effect as if for the reference to three-quarters of his sentence there were substituted a reference to one-half of that sentence.

(3)   Where a life prisoner is released on licence, the licence shall, unless previously revoked under section 39(1) or (2) below, remain in force until his death.

(4)   A person subject to a licence shall comply with such conditions (which shall include on his release conditions as to his supervision by a probation officer) as may for the time being be specified in the licence; and the Secretary of State may make rules for regulating the supervision of any description of such persons.

(5)   The Secretary of State shall not include on release, or subsequently insert, a condition in the licence of a long-term or life prisoner, or vary or cancel any such condition, except—

(a)   in the case of the inclusion of a condition in the licence of a discretionary life prisoner, in accordance with recommendations of the Board; and

(b)   in any other case, after consultation with the Board.

(6)   For the purposes of subsection (5) above, the Secretary of State shall be treated as having consulted the Board about a proposal to include, insert, vary or cancel a condition in any case if he has consulted the Board about the implementation of proposals of that description generally or in that class of case.

(7)   The power to make rules under this section shall be exercisable by statutory instrument which shall be subject to annulment in pursuance of a resolution of either House of Parliament.

Misbehaviour after release

Breach of licence conditions by short-term prisoners.
38.—(1)   A short-term prisoner—
   (a)   who is released on licence under this Part; and
   (b)   who fails to comply with such conditions as may for the time being be
specified in the licence,
shall be liable on summary conviction to a fine not exceeding level 3 on the
standard scale.
   (2)   The magistrates' court by which a person is convicted of an offence under
subsection (1) above may, whether or not it passes any other sentence on him—
   (a)   suspend the licence for a period not exceeding six months; and
   (b)   order him to be recalled to prison for the period during which the
licence is so suspended.
   (3)   On the suspension of the licence of any person under this section, he shall
be liable to be detained in pursuance of his sentence and, if at large, shall be
deemed to be unlawfully at large.

Recall of long-term and life prisoners while on licence.
39.—(1)   If recommended to do so by the Board in the case of a long-term or
life prisoner who has been released on licence under this Part, the Secretary of
State may revoke his licence and recall him to prison.
   (2)   The Secretary of State may revoke the licence of any such person and
recall him to prison without a recommendation by the Board, where it appears
to him that it is expedient in the public interest to recall that person before such a
recommendation is practicable.
   (3)   A person recalled to prison under subsection (1) or (2) above—
   (a)   may make representations in writing with respect to his recall; and
   (b)   on his return to prison, shall be informed of the reasons for his recall
and of his right to make representations.
   (4)   The Secretary of State shall refer to the Board—
   (a)   the case of a person recalled under subsection (1) above who makes
representations under subsection (3) above; and
   (b)   the case of a person recalled under subsection (2) above.
   (5)   Where on a reference under subsection (4) above the Board—
   (a)   directs in the case of a discretionary life prisoner; or
   (b)   recommends in the case of any other person,
his immediate release on licence under this section, the Secretary of State shall
give effect to the direction or recommendation.
   (6)   On the revocation of the licence of any person under this section, he shall
be liable to be detained in pursuance of his sentence and, if at large, shall be
deemed to be unlawfully at large.

Convictions during currency of original sentences.
40.—(1)   This section applies to a short-term or long-term prisoner who is
released under this Part if—
   (a)   before the date on which he would (but for his release) have served his
sentence in full, he commits an offence punishable with imprisonment; and

(b)   whether before or after that date, he is convicted of that offence ("the new offence").

(2)   Subject to subsection (3) below, the court by or before which a person to whom ths section applies is convicted of the new offence may, whether or not it passes any other sentence on him, order him to be returned to prison for the whole or any part of the period which—

(a)   begins with the date of the order; and

(b)   is equal in length to the period between the date on which the new offence was committed and the date mentioned in subsection (1) above.

(3)   A magistrates' court—

(a)   shall not have power to order a person to whom this section applies to be returned to prison for a period of more than six months; but

(b)   may commit him in custody or on bail to the Crown Court for sentence in accordance with section 42 of the 1973 Act (power of Crown Court to sentence persons convicted by magistrates' courts of indictable offences).

(4)   The period for which a person to whom this section applies is ordered under subsection (2) above to be returned to prison—

(a)   shall be taken to be a sentence of imprisonment for the purposes of this Part;

(b)   shall, as the court may direct, either be served before and be followed by, or be served concurrently with, the sentence imposed for the new offence; and

(c)   in either case, shall be disregarded in determining the appropriate length of that sentence.

Remand time and additional days

Remand time to count towards time served.

41.—(1)   This section applies to any person whose sentence falls to be reduced under section 67 of the Criminal Justice Act 1967 ("the 1967 Act") by any relevant period within the meaning of that section ("the relevant period").

(2)   For the purpose of determining for the purposes of this Part—

(a)   whether a person to whom this section applies has served one-half or two-thirds of his sentence; or

(b)   whether such a person would (but for his release) have served three-quarters of that sentence,

the relevant period shall, subject to subsection (3) below, be treated as having been served by him as part of that sentence.

(3)   Nothing in subsection (2) above shall have the effect of reducing the period for which a licence granted under this Part to a short-term or long-term prisoner remains in force to a period which is less than—

(a)   one-quarter of his sentence in the case of a short-term prisoner; or

(b)   one-twelfth of his sentence in the case of a long-term prisoner.

Additional days for disciplinary offences.

42.—(1)   Prison rules, that is to say, rules made under section 47 of the 1952 Act, may include provision for the award of additional days—

(a)   to short-term or long-term prisoners; or

(b)   conditionally on their subsequently becoming such prisoners, to persons on remand, who (in either case) are guilty of disciplinary offences.

(2)   Where additional days are awarded to a short-term or long-term prisoner, or to a person on remand who subsequently becomes such a prisoner, and are not remitted in accordance with prison rules—

(a)   any period which he must serve before becoming entitled to or eligible for release under this Part; and

(b)   any period for which a licence granted to him under this Part remains in force,

shall be extended by the aggregate of those additional days.

Special cases

Young offenders.

43.—(1)   Subject to subsections (4) and (5) below, this Part applies to persons serving sentences of detention in a young offender institution, or determinate sentences of detention under section 53 of the 1933 Act, as it applies to persons serving equivalent sentences of imprisonment.

(2)   Subject to subsection (5) below, this Part applies to persons serving—

(a)   sentences of detention during Her Majesty's pleasure or for life under section 53 of the 1933 Act; or

(b)   sentences of custody for life under section 8 of the 1982 Act,

as it applies to persons serving sentences of imprisonment for life.

(3)   References in this Part to prisoners (whether short-term, long-term or life prisoners), or to prison or imprisonment, shall be construed in accordance with subsections (1) and (2) above.

(4)   In relation to a short-term prisoner under the age of 18 years to whom subsection (1) of section 33 above applies, that subsection shall have effect as if it required the Secretary of State—

(a)   to release him unconditionally if his sentence is for a term of twelve months or less; and

(b)   to release him on licence if that sentence is for a term of more than twelve months.

(5)   In relation to a person under the age of 22 years who is released on licence under this Part, section 37(4) above shall have effect as if the reference to supervision by a probation officer included a reference to supervision by a social worker of a local authority social services department.

Sexual offenders.

44.   Where, in the case of a long-term or short-term prisoner—

(a)   the whole or any part of his sentence was imposed for a sexual offence; and

(b)   the court by which he was sentenced for that offence, having had regard to the matters mentioned in section 32(6)(a) and (b) above, ordered that this section should apply,

sections 33(3) and 37(1) above shall each have effect as if for the reference to three-quarters of his sentence there were substituted a reference to the whole of that sentence.

Fine defaulters and contemnors.

45.—(1)   Subject to subsection (2) below, this Part (except sections 35 and 40 above) applies to persons committed to prison or to be detained under section 9 of the 1982 Act—

    (a)   in default of payment of a sum adjudged to be paid by a conviction; or

    (b)   for contempt of court or any kindred offence,

as it applies to persons serving equivalent sentences of imprisonment; and references in this Part to short-term or long-term prisoners, or to prison or imprisonment, shall be construed accordingly.

    (2)   In relation to persons committed as mentioned in subsection (1) above, the provisions specified in subsections (3) and (4) below shall have effect subject to the modifications so specified.

    (3)   In section 33 above, for subsections (1) to (4) there shall be substituted the following subsections—

       "(1)   As soon as a person committed as mentioned in section 45(1) below has served the appropriate proportion of his term, that is to say—

        (a)   one-half, in the case of a person committed for a term of less than twelve months;

        (b)   two-thirds, in the case of a person committed for a term of twelve months or more,

it shall be the duty of the Secretary of State to release him unconditionally.

       (2)   As soon as a person so committed who—

        (a)   has been released on licence under section 36(1) below; and

        (b)   has been recalled under section 38(2) or 39(1) below,

would (but for his release) have served the appropriate proportion of his term, it shall be the duty of the Secretary of State to release him unconditionally."

    (4)   In section 37 above, for subsections (1) to (3) there shall be substituted the following subsection—

       "(1)   Where a person committed as mentioned in section 45(1) below is released on licence under section 36(1) above, the licence shall, subject to—

        (a)   any suspension under section 38(2) below; or

        (b)   any revocation under section 39(1) below,

continue in force until the date on which he would (but for his release) have served the appropriate proportion of his term; and in this subsection 'appropriate proportion' has the meaning given by section 33(1) above."

Persons liable to removal from the United Kingdom.

46.—(1)   In relation to a long-term prisoner who is liable to removal from the United Kingdom, section 35 above shall have effect as if the words "if recommended to do so by the Board" were omitted.

    (2)   In relation to a person who is liable to removal from the United Kingdom, section 37(4) above shall have effect as if the words in parentheses were omitted.

    (3)   A person is liable to removal from the United Kingdom for the purposes of this section if—

    (a)   he is liable to deportation under section 3(5) of the Immigration Act 1971 and has been notified of a decision to make a deportation order against him;

    (b)   he is liable to deportation under section 3(6) of that Act;

(c)   he has been notified of a decision to refuse him leave to enter the United Kingdom; or

(d)   he is an illegal entrant within the meaning of section 33(1) of that Act.

Persons extradited to the United Kingdom.

47.—(1)   A short-term or long-term prisoner is an extradited prisoner for the purposes of this section if—

(a)   he was tried for the offence in respect of which his sentence was imposed—

(i)   after having been extradited to the United Kingdom; and

(ii)   without having first been restored or had an opportunity of leaving the United Kingdom; and

(b)   he was for any period kept in custody while awaiting his extradition to the United Kingdom as mentioned in paragraph (a) above.

(2)   If, in the case of an extradited prisoner, the court by which he was sentenced so ordered, section 67 of the 1967 Act (computation of sentences of imprisonment) shall have effect in relation to him as if a period specified in the order were a relevant period for the purposes of that section.

(3)   The period that may be so specified is such period as in the opinion of the court is just in all the circumstances and does not exceed the period of custody mentioned in subsection (1)(b) above.

(4)   In this section—

"extradited to the United Kingdom" means returned to the United Kingdom—

(i)   in pursuance of extradition arrangements;

(ii)   under any law of a designated Commonwealth country corresponding to the Extradition Act 1989;

(iii)   under that Act as extended to a colony or under any corresponding law of a colony; or

(iv)   in pursuance of a warrant of arrest endorsed in the Republic of Ireland under the law of that country corresponding to the Backing of Warrants (Republic of Ireland) Act 1965;

"extradition arrangements" has the meaning given by section 3 of the Extradition Act 1989;

"designated Commonwealth country" has the meaning given by section 5(1) of that Act.

Life prisoners transferred to England and Wales.

48.—(1)   This section applies where, in the case of a transferred life prisoner, the Secretary of State, after consultation with the Lord Chief Justice, certifies his opinion that, if—

(a)   he had been sentenced for his offence in England and Wales after the commencement of section 34 above; and

(b)   the reference in subsection (1)(a) of that section to a violent or sexual offence the sentence for which is not fixed by law were a reference to any offence the sentence for which is not so fixed,

the court by which he was so sentenced would have ordered that that section should apply to him as soon as he had served a part of his sentence specified in the certificate.

(2) In a case to which this section applies, this Part except section 35(2) above shall apply as if—

(a) the transferred life prisoner were a discretionary life prisoner for the purposes of this Part; and

(b) the relevant part of his sentence within the meaning of section 34 of this Act were the part specified in the certificate.

(3) In this section "transferred life prisoner" means a person—

(a) on whom a court in a country or territory outside England and Wales has imposed one or more sentences of imprisonment or detention for an indeterminate period; and

(b) who has been transferred to England and Wales, in pursuance of—

(i) an order made by the Secretary of State under section 26 of the Criminal Justice Act 1961 or section 2 of the Colonial Prisoners Removal Act 1884; or

(ii) a warrant issued by the Secretary of State under the Repatriation of Prisoners Act 1984,

there to serve his sentence or sentences or the remainder of his sentence or sentences.

(4) A person who is required so to serve the whole or part of two or more such sentences shall not be treated as a discretionary life prisoner for the purposes of this Part unless the requirements of subsection (1) above are satisfied as respects each of those sentences; and subsections (3) and (5) of section 34 above shall not apply in relation to such a person until after he has served the relevant part of each of those sentences.

Supplemental

Alteration by order of relevant proportions of sentences.

49.—(1) The Secretary of State may by order made by statutory instrument provide—

(a) that the references in section 33(5) above to four years shall be construed as references to such other period as may be specified in the order;

(b) that any reference in this Part to a particular proportion of a prisoner's sentence shall be construed as a reference to such other proportion of a prisoner's sentence as may be so specified.

(2) An order under this section may make such transitional provisions as appear to the Secretary of State necessary or expedient in connection with any provision made by the order.

(3) No order shall be made under this section unless a draft of the order has been laid before and approved by resolution of each House of Parliament.

Transfer by order of certain functions to Board.

50.—(1) The Secretary of State, after consultation with the Board, may by order made by statutory instrument provide that, in relation to such class of case as may be specified in the order, the provisions of this Part specified in subsections (2) to (4) below shall have effect subject to the modifications so specified.

(2) In section 35 above, in subsection (1) for the word "may" there shall be substituted the word "shall"; but nothing in this subsection shall affect the

operation of that subsection as it has effect in relation to a long-term prisoner who is liable to removal from the United Kingdom (within the meaning of section 46 above).

(3)   In section 37 above, in subsection (5)(a) after the words "in the case of" there shall be inserted the words "the licence of a long-term prisoner or", and subsection (6) shall be omitted.

(4)   In section 39 above, in subsection (1) for the word "may" there shall be substituted the word "shall", and subsection (2) shall be omitted.

(5)   No order shall be made under this section unless a draft of the order has been laid before and approved by resolution of each House of Parliament.

Interpretation of Part II.
51.—(1)   In this Part—
"the Board" means the Parole Board;
"discretionary life prisoner" has the meaning given by section 34 above (as extended by section 43(2) above);
"life prisoner" has the meaning given by section 34(7) above (as extended by section 43(2) above);
"long-term prisoner" and "short-term prisoner" have the meanings given by section 33(5) above (as extended by sections 43(1) and 45(1) above);
"sentence of imprisonment" does not include a committal in default of payment of any sum of money, or for want of sufficient distress to satisfy any sum of money, or for failure to do or abstain from doing anything required to be done or left undone.
"sexual offence" and "violent offence" have the same meanings as in Part I of this Act.

(2)   For the purposes of any reference in this Part, however expressed, to the term of imprisonment to which a person has been sentenced or which, or part of which, he has served, consecutive terms and terms which are wholly or partly concurrent shall be treated as a single term.

(3)   Nothing in this Part shall require the Secretary of State to release a person who is serving—
(a)   a sentence of imprisonment for a term; and
(b)   one or more sentences of imprisonment for life,
unless and until he is entitled under this Part to be released in respect of each of those sentences.

(4)   Subsections (2) and (3) of section 31 above shall apply for the purposes of this Part as they apply for the purposes of Part I of this Act.

PART III   CHILDREN AND YOUNG PERSONS

Children's evidence

Competence of children as witnesses.
52.—(1)   After section 33 of the 1988 Act there shall be inserted the following section—

"Evidence given by children.

33A.—(1) A child's evidence in criminal proceedings shall be given unsworn.

(2) A deposition of a child's unsworn evidence may be taken for the purposes of criminal proceedings as if that evidence had been given on oath.

(3) In this section 'child' means a person under fourteen years of age."

(2) Subsection (1) of section 38 of the 1933 Act (evidence of child of tender years to be given on oath or in certain circumstances unsworn) shall cease to have effect; and accordingly the power of the court in any criminal proceedings to determine that a particular person is not competent to give evidence shall apply to children of tender years as it applies to other persons.

Notices of transfer in certain cases involving children.

53.—(1) If a person has been charged with an offence to which section 32(2) of the 1988 Act applies (sexual offences and offences involving violence or cruelty) and the Director of Public Prosecutions is of the opinion—

(a) that the evidence of the offence would be sufficient for the person charged to be committed for trial;

(b) that a child who is alleged—

(i) to be a person against whom the offence was committed; or

(ii) to have witnessed the commission of the offence,

will be called as a witness at the trial; and

(c) that, for the purpose of avoiding any prejudice to the welfare of the child, the case should be taken over and proceeded with without delay by the Crown Court,

a notice ("notice of transfer") certifying that opinion may be served by or on behalf of the Director on the magistrates' court in whose jurisdiction the offence has been charged.

(2) A notice of transfer shall be served before the magistrates' court begins to inquire into the case as examining justices.

(3) On the service of a notice of transfer the functions of the magistrates' court shall cease in relation to the case except as provided by paragraphs 2 and 3 of Schedule 6 to this Act or by section 20(4) of the Legal Aid Act 1988.

(4) The decision to serve a notice of transfer shall not be subject to appeal or liable to be questioned in any court.

(5) Schedule 6 to this Act (which makes further provision in relation to notices of transfer) shall have effect.

(6) In this section "child" means a person who—

(a) in the case of an offence falling within section 32(2)(a) or (b) of the 1988 Act, is under fourteen years of age or, if he was under that age when any such video recording as is mentioned in section 32A(2) of that Act was made in respect of him, is under fifteen years of age; or

(b) in the case of an offence falling within section 32(2)(c) of that Act, is under seventeen years of age or, if he was under that age when any such video recording was made in respect of him, is under eighteen years of age.

(7) Any reference in subsection (6) above to an offence falling within paragraph (a), (b) or (c) of section 32(2) of that Act includes a reference to an offence which consists of attempting or conspiring to commit, or of aiding,

abetting, counselling, procuring or inciting the commission of, an offence falling within that paragraph.

Video recordings of testimony from child witnesses.
54. After section 32 of the 1988 Act (evidence through television links) there shall be inserted the following section—

"*Video recordings of testimony from child witnesses.*
32A.—(1) This section applies in relation to the following proceedings, namely—

(a) trials on indictment for any offence to which section 32(2) above applies;

(b) appeals to the criminal division of the Court of Appeal and hearings of references under section 17 of the Criminal Appeal Act 1968 in respect of any such offence; and

(c) proceedings in youth courts for any such offence and appeals to the Crown Court arising out of such proceedings.

(2) In any such proceedings a video recording of an interview which—

(a) is conducted between an adult and a child who is not the accused or one of the accused ('the child witness'); and

(b) relates to any matter in issue in the proceedings,
may, with the leave of the court, be given in evidence in so far as it is not excluded by the court under subsection (3) below.

(3) Where a video recording is tendered in evidence under this section, the court shall (subject to the exercise of any power of the court to exclude evidence which is otherwise admissible) give leave under subsection (2) above unless—

(a) it appears that the child witness will not be available for cross-examination;

(b) any rules of court requiring disclosure of the circumstances in which the recording was made have not been complied with to the satisfaction of the court; or

(c) the court is of the opinion, having regard to all the circumstances of the case, that in the interests of justice the recording ought not to be admitted;
and where the court gives such leave it may, if it is of the opinion that in the interests of justice any part of the recording ought not to be admitted, direct that that part shall be excluded.

(4) In considering whether any part of a recording ought to be excluded under subsection (3) above, the court shall consider whether any prejudice to the accused, or one of the accused, which might result from the admission of that part is outweighed by the desirability of showing the whole, or substantially the whole, of the recorded interview.

(5) Where a video recording is admitted under this section—

(a) the child witness shall be called by the party who tendered it in evidence;

(b) that witness shall not be examined in chief on any matter which, in the opinion of the court, has been dealt with in his recorded testimony.

(6)   Where a video recording is given in evidence under this section, any statement made by the child witness which is disclosed by the recording shall be treated as if given by that witness in direct oral testimony; and accordingly—

(a)   any such statement shall be admissible evidence of any fact of which such testimony from him would be admissible;

(b)   no such statement shall be capable of corroborating any other evidence given by him;

and in estimating the weight, if any, to be attached to such a statement, regard shall be had to all the circumstances from which any inference can reasonably be drawn (as to its accuracy or otherwise).

(7)   In this section 'child' means a person who—

(a)   in the case of an offence falling within section 32(2)(a) or (b) above, is under fourteen years of age or, if he was under that age when the video recording was made, is under fifteen years of age; or

(b)   in the case of an offence falling within section 32(2)(c) above, is under seventeen years of age or, if he was under that age when the video recording was made, is under eighteen years of age.

(8)   Any reference in subsection (7) above to an offence falling within paragraph (a), (b) or (c) of section 32(2) above includes a reference to an offence which consists of attempting or conspiring to commit, or of aiding, abetting, counselling, procuring or inciting the commission of, an offence falling within that paragraph.

(9)   In this section—

'statement' includes any representation of fact, whether made in words or otherwise;

'video recording' means any recording, on any medium, from which a moving image may by any means be produced and includes the accompanying sound-track.

(10)   A magistrates' court inquiring into an offence as examining justices under section 6 of the Magistrates' Courts Act 1980 may consider any video recording as respects which leave under subsection (2) above is to be sought at the trial, notwithstanding that the child witness is not called at the committal proceedings.

(11)   Without prejudice to the generality of any enactment conferring power to make rules of court, such rules may make such provision as appears to the authority making them to be necessary or expedient for the purposes of this section.

(12)   Nothing in this section shall prejudice the admissibility of any video recording which would be admissible apart from this section."

Further amendments of enactments relating to children's evidence.
55.—(1)   In section 103 of the 1980 Act (evidence of children in committal proceedings) subsection (3)(a) shall cease to have effect and for subsection (5) there shall be substituted the following subsection—

"(5)   In this section 'child' has the same meaning as in section 53 of the Criminal Justice Act 1991."

(2)   In subsection (1) of section 32 of the 1988 Act (evidence through television links)—

(a)   for the words from "on a trial" to "1968" there shall be substituted the words "in proceedings to which subsection (1A) below applies"; and

(b)   for paragraph (b) there shall be substituted the following paragraph—

"(b)   the witness is a child, or is to be cross-examined following the admission under section 32A below of a video recording of testimony from him, and the offence is one to which subsection (2) below applies,".

(3)   After that subsection there shall be inserted the following subsection—

"(1A)   This subsection applies—

(a)   to trials on indictment, appeals to the criminal division of the Court of Appeal and hearings of references under section 17 of the Criminal Appeal Act 1968; and

(b)   to proceedings in youth courts and appeals to the Crown Court arising out of such proceedings."

(4)   After subsection (3) of that section there shall be inserted the following subsections—

"(3A)   Where, in the case of any proceedings before a youth court—

(a)   leave is given by virtue of subsection (1)(b) above for evidence to be given through a television link; and

(b)   suitable facilities for receiving such evidence are not available at any petty-sessional court-house in which the court can (apart from this subsection) lawfully sit,

the court may sit for the purposes of the whole or any part of those proceedings at any place at which such facilities are available and which has been appointed for the purposes of this subsection by the justices acting for the petty sessions area for which the court acts.

(3B)   A place appointed under subsection (3) above may be outside the petty sessions area for which it is appointed; but it shall be deemed to be in that area for the purpose of the jurisdiction of the justices acting for that area."

(5)   In subsection (5) of that section, for paragraphs (a) and (b) there shall be substituted the words "Magistrates' Courts Rules, Crown Court Rules and Criminal Appeal Rules".

(6)   After subsection (5) of that section there shall be inserted the following subsection—

"(6)   Subsection (7) of section 32A below shall apply for the purposes of this section as it applies for the purposes of that section, but with the omission of the references to a person being, in the cases there mentioned, under the age of fifteen years or under the age of eighteen years."

(7)   After section 34 of the 1988 Act there shall be inserted the following section—

"Cross-examination of alleged child victims.

34A.—(1)   No person who is charged with an offence to which section 32(2) above applies shall cross-examine in person any witness who—

(a)   is alleged—

(i)   to be a person against whom the offence was committed; or

    (ii)   to have witnessed the commission of the offence; and
    (b)   is a child, or is to be cross-examined following the admission under section 32A above of a video recording of testimony from him.

    (2)   Subsection (7) of section 32A above shall apply for the purposes of this section as it applies for the purposes of that section, but with the omission of the references to a person being, in the cases there mentioned, under the age of fifteen years or under the age of eighteen years."

Responsibilities of parent or guardian

Attendance at court of parent or guardian.
56.   Subsection (1) of section 34 (attendance at court of parent or guardian) of the 1933 Act shall cease to have effect and after that section there shall be inserted the following section—

"Attendance at court of parent or guardian.
34A.—(1)   Where a child or young person is charged with an offence or is for any other reason brought before a court, the court—
    (a)   may in any case; and
    (b)   shall in the case of a child or a young person who is under the age of sixteen years,
require a person who is a parent or guardian of his to attend at the court during all the stages of the proceedings, unless and to the extent that the court is satisfied that it would be unreasonable to require such attendance, having regard to the circumstances of the case.

    (2)   In relation to a child or young person for whom a local authority have parental responsibility and who—
    (a)   is in their care; or
    (b)   is provided with accommodation by them in the exercise of any functions (in particular those under the Children Act 1989) which stand referred to their social services committee under the Local Authority Social Services Act 1970,
the reference in subsection (1) above to a person who is a parent or guardian of his shall be construed as a reference to that authority or, where he is allowed to live with such a person, as including such a reference.
    In this subsection 'local authority' and 'parental responsibility' have the same meanings as in the Children Act 1989."

Responsibility of parent or guardian for financial penalties.
57.—(1)   After subsection (1A) of section 55 of the 1933 Act (power to order parent or guardian to pay fine etc. instead of child or young person) there shall be inserted the following subsection—
    "(1B)   In the case of a young person who has attained the age of sixteen years, subsections (1) and (1A) above shall have effect as if, instead of imposing a duty, they conferred a power to make such an order as is mentioned in those subsections."

    (2)   After subsection (4) of that section there shall be inserted the following subsection—
    "(5)   In relation to a child or young person for whom a local authority have parental responsibility and who—

(a)   is in their care; or

(b)   is provided with accommodation by them in the exercise of any functions (in particular those under the Children Act 1989) which stand referred to their social services committee under the Local Authority Social Services Act 1970,

references in this section to his parent or guardian shall be construed as references to that authority.

In this subsection 'local authority' and 'parental responsibility' have the same meanings as in the Children Act 1989."

(3)   For the purposes of any order under that section made against the parent or guardian of a child or young person—

(a)   section 18 and 21 above; and

(b)   section 35(4)(a) of the 1973 Act (fixing amount of compensation order), shall have effect (so far as applicable) as if any reference to the financial circumstances of the offender, or (as the case may be) to the means of the person against whom the compensation order is made, were a reference to the financial circumtances of the parent or guardian.

(4)   For the purposes of any such order made against a local authority (as defined for the purposes of the Children Act 1989)—

(a)   section 18(1) above, and section 35(4)(a) of the 1973 Act, shall not apply, and

(b)   section 18(3) above shall apply as if the words from "including" to the end were omitted.

Note. Section 57 is printed as amended by the CJA 1993, sch. 3, para. 5.

Binding over of parent or guardian.
58.—(1)   Where a child or young person ("the relevant minor") is convicted of an offence, the powers conferred by this section shall be exercisable by the court by which he is sentenced for that offence; and it shall be the duty of the court, in a case where the relevant minor has not attained the age of 16 years—

(a)   to exercise those powers if it is satisfied, having regard to the circumstances of the case, that their exercise would be desirable in the interests of preventing the commission by him of further offences; and

(b)   where it does not exercise them, to state in open court that it is not satisfied as mentioned in paragraph (a) above and why it is not so satisfied.

(2)   The powers conferred by this section are as follows—

(a)   with the consent of the relevant minor's parent or guardian, to order the parent or guardian to enter into a recognisance to take proper care of him and exercise proper control over him; and

(b)   if the parent or guardian refuses consent and the court considers the refusal unreasonable, to order the parent or guardian to pay a fine not exceeding £1,000.

(3)   An order under this section shall not require the parent or guardian to enter into a recognisance—

(a)   for an amount exceeding £1,000; or

(b)   for a period exceeding three years or, where the relevant minor will attain the age of 18 years in a period shorter than three years, for a period exceeding that shorter period;

and section 120 of the 1980 Act (which relates to the forfeiture of recognisances) shall apply in relation to a recognisance entered into in pursuance of such an order as it applies to a recognisance to keep the peace.

(4)   A fine imposed under subsection (2)(b) above shall be deemed, for the purposes of any enactment, to be a sum adjudged to be paid by a conviction.

(5)   In fixing the amount of a recognisance under this section, the court shall take into account among other things the means of the parent or guardian so far as they appear or are known to the court; and this subsection applies whether taking into account the means of the parent or guardian has the effect of increasing or reducing the amount of the recognisance.

(6)   A parent or guardian may appeal to the Crown Court against an order under this section made by a magistrates' court.

(7)   A parent or guardian may appeal to the Court of Appeal against an order under this section made by the Crown Court, as if he had been convicted on indictment and the order were a sentence passed on his conviction.

(8)   A court may vary or revoke an order made by it under this section if, on the application of the parent or guardian, it appears to the court, having regard to any change in the circumstances since the order was made, to be in the interests of justice to do so.

Note. Section 58 is printed as amended by the CJA 1993, sch. 3, para. 6.

Detention etc. pending trial

Detention at a police station.
59.   In section 38 of the Police and Criminal Evidence Act 1984 (duties of custody officer after charge), for subsections (6) and (6A) there shall be substituted the following subsections—

"(6)   Where a custody officer authorises an arrested juvenile to be kept in police detention under subsection (1) above, the custody officer shall, unless he certifies—

(a)   that, by reason of such circumstances as are specified in the certificate, it is impracticable for him to do so; or

(b)   in the case of an arrested juvenile who has attained the age of 15 years, that no secure accommodation is available and that keeping him in other local authority accommodation would not be adequate to protect the public from serious harm from him,

secure that the arrested juvenile is moved to local authority accommodation.

(6A)   In this section—

'local authority accommodation' means accommodation provided by or on behalf of a local authority (within the meaning of the Children Act 1989);

'secure accommodation' means accommodation provided for the purpose of restricting liberty;

'sexual offence' and 'violent offence' have the same meanings as in Part I of the Criminal Justice Act 1991;

and any reference, in relation to an arrested juvenile charged with a violent or sexual offence, to protecting the public from serious harm from him shall be construed as a reference to protecting members of the public from death or serious personal injury, whether physical or psychological, occasioned by further such offences committed by him."

Remands and committals to local authority accommodation.
60.—(1)   For section 23 of the 1969 Act there shall be substituted the following section—

"Remands and committals to local authority accommodation.
23.—(1)   Where—
(a)   a court remands a child or young person charged with or convicted of one or more offences or commits him for trial or sentence; and
(b)   he is not released on bail,
the remand or committal shall be to local authority accommodation; and in the following provisions of this section, any reference (however expressed) to a remand shall be construed as including a reference to a committal.
(2)   A court remanding a person to local authority accommodation shall designate the local authority who are to receive him; and that authority shall be—
(a)   in the case of a person who is being looked after by a local authority, that authority; and
(b)   in any other case, the local authority in whose area it appears to the court that he resides or the offence or one of the offences was committed.
(3)   Where a person is remanded to local authority accommodation, it shall be lawful for any person acting on behalf of the designated authority to detain him.
(4)   Subject to subsection (5) below, a court remanding a person to local authority accommodation may, after consultation with the designated authority, require that authority to comply with a security requirement, that is to say, a requirement that the person in question be placed and kept in secure accommodation.
(5)   A court shall not impose a security requirement except in respect of a young person who has attained the age of fifteen, and then only if—
(a)   he is charged with or has been convicted of a violent or sexual offence, or an offence punishable in the case of an adult with imprisonment for a term of fourteen years or more; or
(b)   he has a recent history of absconding while remanded to local authority accommodation, and is charged with or has been convicted of an imprisonable offence alleged or found to have been committed while he was so remanded,
and (in either case) the court is of opinion that only such a requirement would be adequate to protect the public from serious harm from him.
(6)   Where a court imposes a security requirement in respect of a person, it shall be its duty—
(a)   to state in open court that it is of such opinion as is mentioned in subsection (5) above; and
(b)   to explain to him in open court and in ordinary language why it is of that opinion;

and a magistrates' court shall cause a reason stated by it under paragraph (b) above to be specified in the warrant of commitment and to be entered in the register.

(7)   A court remanding a person to local authority accommodation without imposing a security requirement may, after consultation with the designated authority, require that person to comply with any such conditions as could be imposed under section 3(6) of the Bail Act 1976 if he were then being granted bail.

(8)   Where a court imposes on a person any such conditions as are mentioned in subsection (7) above, it shall be its duty to explain to him in open court and in ordinary language why it is imposing those conditions; and a magistrates' court shall cause a reason stated by it under this subsection to be specified in the warrant of commitment and to be entered in the register.

(9)   A court remanding a person to local authority accommodation without imposing a security requirement may, after consultation with the designated authority, impose on that authority requirements—

(a)   for securing compliance with any conditions imposed on that person under subsection (7) above; or

(b)   stipulating that he shall not be placed with a named person.

(10)   Where a person is remanded to local authority accommodation, a relevant court—

(a)   may, on the application of the designated authority, impose on that person any such conditions as could be imposed under subsection (7) above if the court were then remanding him to such accommodation; and

(b)   where it does so, may impose on that authority any requirements for securing compliance with the conditions so imposed.

(11)   Where a person is remanded to local authority accommodation, a relevant court may, on the application of the designated authority or that person, vary or revoke any conditions or requirements imposed under subsection (7), (9) or (10) above.

(12)   In this section—

'court' and 'magistrates' court' include a justice;

'imprisonable offence' means an offence punishable in the case of an adult with imprisonment;

'relevant court', in relation to a person remanded to local authority accommodation, means the court by which he was so remanded, or any magistrates' court having jurisdiction in the place where he is for the time being;

'secure accommodation' means accommodation which is provided in a community home for the purpose of restricting liberty, and is approved for that purpose by the Secretary of State;

'sexual offence' and 'violent offence' have the same meanings as in Part I of the Criminal Justice Act 1991;

'young person' means a person who has attained the age of fourteen years and is under the age of seventeen years.

(13)   In this section—

(a)   any reference to a person who is being looked after by a local authority shall be construed in accordance with section 22 of the Children Act 1989;

(b)   any reference to consultation shall be construed as a reference to such consultation (if any) as is reasonably practicable in all the circumstances of the case; and

(c)   any reference, in relation to a person charged with or convicted of a violent or sexual offence, to protecting the public from serious harm from him shall be construed as a reference to protecting members of the public from death or serious personal injury, whether physical or psychological, occasioned by further such offences committed by him.

(14)   This section has effect subject to—

(a)   section 37 of the Magistrates' Courts Act 1980 (committal to the Crown Court with a view to a sentence of detention in a young offender institution); and

(b)   section 128(7) of that Act (remands to the custody of a constable for periods of not more than three days),

but section 128(7) shall have effect in relation to a child or young person as if for the reference to three clear days there were substituted a reference to twenty-four hours."

(2)   In section 37 of the 1980 Act (committal of young person to Crown Court for sentence)—

(a)   in subsection (1), for the words "17 years old" there shall be substituted the words "18 years old";

(b)   in subsection (2), for the words "A person committed in custody under subsection (1) above" there shall be substituted the words "Where a person committed in custody under subsection (1) above is not less than 17 years old, he"; and

(c)   after that subsection there shall be inserted the following subsection—

"(3)   Where a person committed in custody under subsection (1) above is less than 17 years old—

(a)   he shall be committed to accommodation provided by or on behalf of a local authority (within the meaning of the Children Act 1989) and

(b)   the court by which he is so committed shall impose a security requirement within the meaning of section 23 of the Children and Young Persons Act 1969."

(3)   In the case of a child or young person who has been remanded or committed to local authority accommodation by a youth court or a magistrates' court other than a youth court, any application under section 25 of the Children Act 1989 (use of accommodation for restricting liberty) shall, notwithstanding anything in section 92(2) of that Act or section 65 of the 1980 Act, be made to that court.

Provision by local authorities of secure accommodation.

61.—(1)   It shall be the duty of every local authority to secure that they are in a position to comply with any security requirement which may be imposed on them under—

(a)   section 23(4) of the 1969 Act (remands and committals to local authority accommodation); or

(b)   section 37(3) of the 1980 Act (committal of young person to Crown Court for sentence).

(2)   A local authority may discharge their duty under subsection (1) above either by providing secure accommodation themselves or by making arrangements with other local authorities for the provision by them of such accommodation.

(3)   The Secretary of State may by regulations make provision as to the co-operation required of local authorities in the provision of secure accommodation.

(4)   The power to make regulations under this section shall be exercisable by statutory instrument which shall be subject to annulment in pursuance of a resolution of either House of Parliament.

(5)   In this section expressions used in section 23 of the 1969 Act have the same meanings as in that section.

Transitory provisions pending provision of secure accommodation.
62.—(1)   In relation to any time before such day as the Secretary of State may by order made by statutory instrument appoint, section 23 of the 1969 Act as substituted by section 60(1) above shall have effect with the following modifications.

(2)   In subsection (1), immediately before the words "the remand" there shall be inserted the words "then, unless he is declared by the court, after consultation with a probation officer or a social worker of a local authority social services department, to be a person to whom subsection (5) below applies".

(3)   For subsections (4) and (5) there shall be substituted the following subsections—

"(4)   Where a court declares a person to be one to whom subsection (5) below applies, it shall remand him—
(a)   to a remand centre, if it has been notified that such a centre is available for the reception from the court of such persons; and
(b)   to a prison, if it has not been so notified.

(4A)   A court shall not declare a person who is not legally represented in the court to be a person to whom subsection (5) below applies unless—
(a)   he applied for legal aid and the application was refused on the ground that it did not appear his means were such that he required assistance; or
(b)   having been informed of his right to apply for legal aid and had the opportunity to do so, he refused or failed to apply.

(5)   This subsection applies to a young person who is male and has attained the age of fifteen, but only if—
(a)   he is charged with or has been convicted of a violent or sexual offence, or an offence punishable in the case of an adult with imprisonment for a term of fourteen years or more; or
(b)   he has a recent history of absconding while remanded to local authority accommodation, and is charged with or has been convicted of an imprisonable offence alleged or found to have been committed while he was so remanded,
and (in either case) the court is of opinion that only remanding him to a remand centre or prison would be adequate to protect the public from serious harm from him."

(4)   In subsection (6)—

(a)   for the words "imposes a security requirement in respect of a young person" there shall be substituted the words "declares a person to be one to whom subsection (5) above applies"; and

(b)   for the words "subsection (5) above" there shall be substituted the words "that subsection".

(5)   In subsections (7) and (9), the words "without imposing a security requirement" shall be omitted.

(6)   After subsection (9) there shall be inserted the following subsection—

"(9A)   Where a person is remanded to local authority accommodation, a relevant court may, on the application of the designated authority, declare him to be a person to whom subsection (5) above applies; and on its doing so, he shall cease to be remanded to local authority accommodation and subsection (4) above shall apply."

(7)   In subsection (12), the definition of "secure accommodation" shall be omitted.

Young offenders

Custodial sentences under 1982 Act.

63.—(1)   Part I of the 1982 Act (treatment of young offenders) shall be amended as follows.

(2)   In section 1A (detention in a young offender institution)—

(a)   in subsection (1), for the words "a male offender under 21 but not less than 14 years of age or a female offender under 21 but not less than 15 years of age" there shall be substituted the words "an offender under 21 but not less than 15 years of age";

(b)   in subsection (2), for the words "section 1B(1) and (2)" there shall be substituted the words "section 1B(2)";

(c)   in subsection (3), the words "and section 1B(3) below" shall cease to have effect and for the words "21 days" there shall be substituted the words "the minimum period applicable to the offender under subsection (4A) below";

(d)   in subsection (4), for the words "21 days" there shall be substituted the words "the minimum period applicable"; and

(e)   after subsection (4) there shall be inserted the following subsection—

"(4A)   For the purposes of subsections (3) and (4) above, the minimum period of detention applicable to an offender is—

(a)   in the case of an offender under 21 but not less than 18 years of age, the period of 21 days; and

(b)   in the case of an offender under 18 years of age, the period of two months."

(3)   In section 1B (special provision for offenders under 17)—

(a)   subsections (1) and (3) shall cease to have effect;

(b)   in subsection (2), for the words "aged 15 or 16" there shall be substituted the words "aged 15, 16 or 17"; and

(c)   for subsections (4) and (5) there shall be substituted the following subsections—

"(4)   A court shall not pass on an offender aged 15, 16 or 17 a sentence of detention in a young offender institution whose effect would be that the offender would be sentenced to a total term which exceeds 12 months.

(5) Where the total term of detention in a young offender institution to which an offender aged 15, 16 or 17 is sentenced exceeds 12 months, so much of the term as exceeds 12 months shall be treated as remitted."

(4) In section 1C (accommodation of offenders in a young offender institution), for the words "under 17" there shall be substituted the words "under 18".

(5) In section 8 (custody for life) and section 9 (detention of persons aged 17 to 20 for default or contempt), for the words "17 years" there shall be substituted the words "18 years".

Custodial sentences under 1933 Act.
64. Section 53(2) of the 1933 Act (punishment of certain grave crimes) shall have effect, in relation to a person who has attained the age of 16, as if the reference to any offence punishable in the case of an adult with imprisonment for 14 years or more, not being an offence the sentence for which is fixed by law, included a reference to an offence under section 14 of the Sexual Offences Act 1956 (indecent assault on a woman).

Supervision of young offenders after release.
65.—(1) Where a person under the age of 22 years ("the offender") is released from a term of detention in a young offender institution or under section 53 of the 1933 Act, he shall be under the supervision of a probation officer or a social worker of a local authority social services department.

(2) The supervision period ends on the offender's 22nd birthday if it has not ended before.

(3) Subject to subsection (2) above, where the offender is released otherwise than on licence under Part II of this Act, the supervision period begins on his release and ends three months from his release.

(4) Subject to subsection (2) above, where the offender is released on licence under Part II of this Act and the licence expires less than three months from his release, the supervision period begins on the expiry of the licence and ends three months from his release.

(5) Where a person is under supervision under this section, he shall comply with such requirements, if any, as may for the time being be specified in a notice from the Secretary of State.

(6) A person who without reasonable excuse fails to comply with a requirement imposed under subsection (5) above shall be liable on summary conviction—

(a) to a fine not exceeding level 3 on the standard scale; or

(b) to an appropriate custodial sentence for a period not exceeding 30 days, but not liable to be dealt with in any other way.

(7) In subsection (6) above "appropriate custodial sentence" means—

(a) a sentence of imprisonment, if the offender has attained the age of 21 years when he is sentenced; and

(b) a sentence of detention in a young offender institution, if he has not attained that age.

(8) A person released from a custodial sentence passed under subsection (6) above shall not be liable to a period of supervision in consequence of his

conviction under that subsection, but his conviction shall not prejudice any liability to supervision to which he was previously subject, and that liability shall accordingly continue until the end of the supervision period.

Supervision orders.
66. For section 15 of the 1969 Act (variation and discharge of supervision orders) there shall be substituted the provisions set out in Schedule 7 to this Act.

Attendance centre orders.
67.—(1) In section 17 of the 1982 Act (maximum number of hours at attendance centre for persons of different ages)—
    (a) subsection (3) shall cease to have effect; and
    (b) in subsection (5), for the words "17 years", in both places where they occur, there shall be substituted the words "16 years".

(2) In section 18 of that Act (discharge and variation of attendance centre orders), after subsection (4) there shall be inserted the following subsection—
    "(4A) The power to discharge an attendance centre order includes power to deal with the offender, for the offence in respect of which the order was made, in any manner in which he could have been dealt with for that offence by the court which made the order if the order had not been made."

(3) In subsection (6)(b) of that section, the words "if the court is satisfied that the offender proposes to change or has changed his residence" shall cease to have effect.

(4) In subsection (3) of section 19 of that Act (breaches of attendance centre orders or attendance centre rules), after the words "that court" there shall be inserted the words "may, without prejudice to the continuation of the order, impose on him a fine not exceeding £1,000 or".

(5) After that subsection there shall be inserted the following subsection—
    "(3A) Section 18 of the Criminal Justice Act 1991 (fixing of certain fines by reference to units) shall apply for the purposes of subsection (3) above as if the failure to attend or the breach of the rules were a summary offence punishable by a fine not exceeding level 3 on the standard scale; and a fine imposed under that subsection shall be deemed for the purposes of any enactment to be a sum adjudged to be paid by a conviction."

(6) After subsection (5) of that section there shall be inserted the following subsection—
    "(5A) In dealing with an offender under subsection (3)(a) or (5) above, the court concerned—
    (a) shall take into account the extent to which the offender has complied with the requirements of the attendance centre order; and
    (b) may assume, in the case of an offender who has wilfully and persistently failed to comply with those requirements, that he has refused to give his consent to a community sentence which has been proposed by the court and requires that consent."

Miscellaneous

Persons aged 17 to be treated as young persons for certain purposes.
68. The following enactments, namely—
    (a) the Children and Young Persons Acts 1933 to 1969;

(b)   section 43(3) of the 1952 Act (remand centres, young offender institutions etc.);

(c)   section 5(2) of the Rehabilitation of Offenders Act 1974 (which provides for rehabilitation periods to be reduced by half for young offenders); and

(d)   the 1980 Act,

shall have effect subject to the amendments specified in Schedule 8 to this Act, being amendments which, for certain purposes of those enactments, have the effect of substituting the age of 18 years for the age of 17 years.

Non-appearance of persons aged 16 or 17: plea of guilty.

69.   In section 12 of the 1980 Act (non-appearance of accused: plea of guilty), after subsection (1) there shall be inserted the following subsection—

"(1A)   The reference in subsection (1) above to the issue of a summons requiring a person to appear before a magistrates' court other than a youth court includes a reference to the issue of a summons requiring a person who has attained the age of 16 at the time when it is issued to appear before a youth court."

Renaming of juvenile courts etc.

70.—(1)   Juvenile courts shall be renamed youth courts and juvenile court panels shall be renamed youth court panels.

(2)   Any reference to juvenile courts or juvenile court panels in any enactment passed or instrument made before the commencement of this section shall be construed in accordance with subsection (1) above.

Amendments to service law.

71.   The enactments mentioned in Schedule 9 to this Act shall have effect subject to the amendments there specified (being amendments to service law corresponding to certain provisions of this Act).

Repeal of certain provisions not brought in force.

72.   The following provisions (none of which has been brought into force), namely—

section 4 of the 1969 Act (prohibition of criminal proceedings for offences by children);

in section 5 of that Act (restrictions on criminal proceedings for offences by young persons), subsections (1) to (7) and, in subsection (9), the definitions of "qualified informant" and "designated";

section 8 of that Act (fingerprinting of suspected young persons); and

in section 37 of the Police and Criminal Evidence Act 1984, subsections (11) to (14) (duties of custody officer as respects young persons),

shall cease to have effect.

PART IV   PROVISION OF SERVICES

Probation services

Inspectors of probation.

73.—(1)   The Secretary of State may appoint such number of inspectors of probation (to be known collectively as "Her Majesty's Inspectorate of Probation") as he may with the approval of the Treasury determine.

(2)   The Secretary of State shall appoint one of the persons so appointed to be Her Majesty's Chief Inspector of Probation.

(3)   It shall be the duty of inspectors of probation—

(a)   to inspect and report to the Secretary of State on the probation service for each probation area, and the activities carried out by or on behalf of that service; and

(b)   to discharge such other functions in connection with the provision of probation or related services (whether or not provided by or on behalf of the probation service for any area) as the Secretary of State may from time to time direct.

(4)   The Secretary of State shall make to or in respect of inspectors of probation such payments by way of remuneration, allowances or otherwise as he may with the approval of the Treasury determine.

Default power where probation committee fails to discharge statutory duty.
74.—(1)   The Secretary of State may make an order under this section if he is of the opinion that, without reasonable excuse, a probation committee—

(a)   is failing properly to discharge any duty imposed on it by or under any enactment; or

(b)   has so failed and is likely to do so again.

(2)   An order under this section shall—

(a)   state that the Secretary of State is of the said opinion; and

(b)   make such provision as he considers requisite for the purpose of securing that the duty is properly discharged by the committee.

(3)   Where an order is made under this section, it shall be the duty of the committee to comply with the provision made by the order.

The inner London probation area.
75.—(1)   Schedule 3 to the 1973 Act (the probation service and its functions) shall be amended as follows.

(2)   In paragraph 1 (probation areas), for sub-paragraphs (3) and (4) there shall be substituted the following sub-paragraph—

"(3)   The Secretary of State—

(a)   shall make provision by an order under sub-paragraph (1) above for combining in one probation area (in this Schedule referred to as 'the inner London probation area') all of the petty sessions divisions of the inner London area; and

(b)   may make provision by such an order for including in that probation area one or more other petty sessions areas."

(3)   In paragraphs 2(3), 4, 5, 6(3), 13(3) and 18(3), for the words "inner London area", in each place where they occur, there shall be substituted the words "inner London probation area".

(4)   In paragraph 2(3), for paragraph (b) there shall be substituted the following paragraph—

"(b)   of such number as may be so specified of justices of the peace for the petty sessions areas of the inner London probation area who are not metropolitan stipendiary magistrates, chosen in such manner as may be so specified by the justices for those areas who are not such magistrates;".

(5)   For paragraph 16 there shall be substituted the following paragraph—

"16.—(1)   Paragraph 15 above shall not apply in relation to expenses incurred by the probation committee for the inner London probation area, but such sums as the Secretary of State may direct to meet the expenses and contributions which, in the case of any other probation area, would be payable by virtue of that paragraph by the local authority—

(a)   shall be paid out of the metropolitan police fund; or

(b)   where the inner London probation area includes one or more petty sessions areas outside the inner London area, shall be partly paid out of that fund and partly defrayed by the local authority or authorities concerned.

(2)   Where paragraph (b) of sub-paragraph (1) above applies, the proportions to be paid or defrayed under that paragraph shall be such as may be agreed between the Receiver for the metropolitan police district and the local authority or authorities concerned or, in default of agreement, as may be determined by the Secretary of State.

(3)   In this paragraph 'the local authority or authorities concerned' means the local authority or authorities in whose area or areas the petty sessions area or areas outside the inner London area is or are situated."

(6)   In paragraph 17 (provision of accommodation by local authorities for the probation service)—

(a)   in sub-paragraph (1), after the words "paragraph 15(1) or (3)" there shall be inserted the words "or 16(1) or (2)"; and

(b)   after sub-paragraph (3) there shall be inserted the following sub-paragraph—

"(4)   The foregoing provisions of this paragraph shall apply as if the Receiver for the metropolitan police district were a local authority and any sums required to be paid out of the metropolitan police fund were required to be defrayed by him; and any contribution received by him under sub-paragraph (3) above shall be paid into that fund."

(7)   At the end of paragraph 19(1), there shall be added the words "and 'inner London probation area' has the meaning given by paragraph 1(3) above".

Court security

Provision of court security officers.

76.—(1)   In relation to each petty sessions area, the committee shall from time to time determine—

(a)   whether court security officers should be provided, that is to say, persons whose duty it is to maintain order in any court-house to which they are for the time being assigned by the committee; and

(b)   if so, how many such officers should be provided, and whether they should be provided by the committee or by the responsible authority.

(2)   As soon as practicable after the making of a determination under subsection (1)(b) above, the committee or, as the case may be, the responsible authority shall provide the required number of court security officers, on such terms and conditions as they may determine—

(a)   by employing persons to act as court security officers; or

(b)   by entering into a contract with another person for the employment by him of persons to act as such officers.

(3)   Before making any determination under subsection (1) or (2) above in relation to a petty sessions area which does not consist of or form part of the inner London area, the committee shall consult with the responsible authority.

(4)   Where, in relation to a petty sessions area which does not consist of or form part of the inner London area, the responsible authority is aggrieved by any determination made by the committee under subsection (1) or (2) above, the authority may, within one month from the receipt by the authority of written notice of the determination, appeal to the Secretary of State, whose decision shall be binding on the committee and the authority.

(5)   Any determination which, in relation to a petty sessions area which consists of or forms part of the inner London area, is made by the committee under subsection (1) or (2) above, other than a determination that court security officers should not be provided for that area, shall not have effect unless it is confirmed, with or without modifications, by the Secretary of State.

(6)   In this section—
"the committee" means—
(a)   in relation to a petty sessions area which consists of or forms part of a non-metropolitan county, a metropolitan district, an outer London borough, the City of London or a joint committee area, the magistrates' courts committee for that county, district, borough, City or area; and
(b)   in relation to a petty sessions area which consists of or forms part of the inner London area, the committee of magistrates;
"the responsible authority" means—
(a)   in relation to a petty sessions area which consists of or forms part of a non-metropolitan county, a metropolitan district, an outer London borough or the City of London, the council of that county, district or borough or, as the case may be, the Common Council of that City; and
(b)   in relation to a petty sessions area which consists of or forms part of the inner London area, the Receiver.

Power and duties of court security officers.
77.—(1)   A court security officer acting in the execution of his duty shall have the following powers, namely—
(a)   to search any person who is in or is seeking to enter the court-house, and any article in the possesion of such a person;
(b)   to exclude or remove from the court-house any person who refuses to permit such a search as is mentioned in paragraph (a) above, or refuses to surrender any article in his possession which the officer reasonably believes may jeopardise the maintenance of order in the court-house;
(c)   to exclude or remove any person from the court-house, or restrain any person in the court-house, where (in either case) it is reasonably necessary to do so in order—
(i)   to maintain order in the court-house;
(ii)   to enable court business to be carried on without interference or delay; or
(iii)   to secure his or any other person's safety.

(2)   The powers conferred by subsection (1)(a) above to search a person shall not be construed as authorising a court security officer to require a person to

remove any of his clothing other than an outer coat, jacket or gloves.

(3) The powers conferred by subsection (1)(b) and (c) above shall include power to use reasonable force, where necessary.

(4) In the execution of his duty, a court security officer shall act in accordance with any general or specific instructions which have been given to him (whether orally or in writing) by a person in authority.

(5) In subsection (4) above "person in authority", in relation to any court-house, means—

(a) a justice of the peace, chief clerk or justices' clerk who is exercising any functions in the court-house; and

(b) any officer or staff employed to assist such a clerk and authorised by him for the purpose.

(6) For the purposes of this section and section 78 below, a court security officer shall not be regarded as acting in the execution of his duty at any time when he is not readily identifiable as such an officer (whether by means of a uniform or badge which he is wearing or otherwise).

Protection of court security officers.

78.—(1) Any person who assaults a court security officer acting in the execution of his duty shall be liable on summary conviction to a fine not exceeding level 5 on the standard scale or to imprisonment for a term not exceeding six months or to both.

(2) Any person who resists or wilfully obstructs a court security officer acting in the execution of his duty shall be liable on summary conviction to a fine not exceeding level 3 on the standard scale.

Duties of responsible authorities.

79.—(1) In section 55(2) (duties of local authorities outside Greater London) of the Justices of the Peace Act 1979 ("the 1979 Act"), for paragraph (b) there shall be substituted the following paragraphs—

"(b) the sums payable under Part II of this Act on account of a person's salary or expenses as justices' clerk for the non-metropolitan county or metropolitan district or any part thereof, the remuneration of any staff employed by the magistrates' courts committee to assist him and the remuneration of any court security officers employed (whether by that committee or the council) under section 76(2)(a) of the Criminal Justice Act 1991, together with—

(i) secondary Class I contributions payable in respect of any such person, staff or officers under Part I of the Social Security Act 1975, and

(ii) state scheme premiums so payable under Part III of the Social Security Pensions Act 1975;

(bb) the sums payable under any contract entered into (whether by the magistrates' courts committee or the council) under section 76(2)(b) of the Criminal Justice Act 1991;".

(2) In section 58(2) of that Act (corresponding arrangements in the inner London area), for paragraph (b) there shall be substituted the following paragraphs—

"(b) the sums payable by way of salary or expenses to justices' clerks and other officers employed by the committee of magistrates and the remuneration of any court security officers employed (whether by that committee or the Receiver) under section 76(2)(a) of the Criminal Justice Act 1991, together with—

    (i)   secondary Class I contributions payable in respect of any such officers under Part I of the Social Security Act 1975, and

    (ii)   state scheme premiums so payable under Part III of the Social Security Pensions Act 1975;

    (bb)   the sums payable under any contract entered into (whether by the committee of magistrates or the Receiver) under section 76(2)(b) of the Criminal Justice Act 1991;".

Prisoner escorts

Arrangements for the provision of prisoner escorts.
80.—(1) The Secretary of State may make arrangements for any of the following functions, namely—

    (a)   the delivery of prisoners to court premises;

    (b)   the custody of prisoners held on such premises (whether or not they would otherwise be in the custody of the court) and their production before the court;

    (c)   the delivery of prisoners so held to a prison or police station;

    (d)   the delivery of prisoners from one prison to another; and

    (e)   the custody of prisoners while they are outside a prison for temporary purposes,

to be performed in such cases as may be determined by or under the arrangements by prisoner custody officers who are authorised to perform such functions.

(2)   Arrangements made by the Secretary of State under this section ("prisoner escort arrangements") may include entering into contracts with other persons for the provision by them of prisoner custody officers.

(3)   Any person who, under a warrant of commitment, is responsible for the performance of any such function as is mentioned in subsection (1) above shall be deemed to have complied with that warrant if he does all that he reasonably can to secure that the function is performed by a prisoner custody officer acting in pursuance of prisoner escort arrangements.

Monitoring etc. of prisoner escort arrangements.
81.—(1) Prisoner escort arrangements shall include the appointment of—

    (a)   a prisoner escort monitor, that is to say, a Crown servant whose duty it shall be to keep the arrangements under review and to report on them to the Secretary of State; and

    (b)   a panel of lay observers whose duty it shall be to inspect the conditions in which prisoners are transported or held in pursuance of the arrangements and to make recommendations to the Secretary of State.

(2)   It shall be the duty of a prisoner escort monitor to investigate and report to the Secretary of State on—

    (a)   any allegations made against prisoner custody officers acting in pursuance of prisoner escort arrangements; and

    (b)   any alleged breaches of discipline on the part of prisoners for whose delivery or custody such officers so acting are responsible.

(3)   Any expenses incurred by members of lay panels may be defrayed by the Secretary of State to such extent as he may with the approval of the Treasury determine.

Powers and duties of prisoner custody officers acting in pursuance of such arrangements.
82.—(1)   A prisoner custody officer acting in pursuance of prisoner escort arrangements shall have the following powers, namely—

(a)   to search in accordance with rules made by the Secretary of State any prisoner for whose delivery or custody he is responsible in pursuance of the arrangements; and

(b)   to search any other person who is in or is seeking to enter any place where any such prisoner is or is to be held, and any article in the possession of such a person.

(2)   The powers conferred by subsection (1)(b) above to search a person shall not be construed as authorising a prisoner custody officer to require a person to remove any of his clothing other than an outer coat, jacket or gloves.

(3)   A prisoner custody officer shall have the following duties as respects prisoners for whose delivery or custody he is responsible in pursuance of prisoner escort arrangements, namely—

(a)   to prevent their escape from lawful custody;

(b)   to prevent, or detect and report on, the commission or attempted commission by them of other unlawful acts;

(c)   to ensure good order and discipline on their part;

(d)   to attend to their wellbeing; and

(e)   to give effect to any directions as to their treatment which are given by a court,

and the Secretary of State may make rules with respect to the performance by prisoner custody officers of their duty under paragraph (d) above.

(4)   It shall also be the duty of a prisoner custody officer who is on any premises in which the Crown Court is sitting to give effect to any order of that Court made under section 34A of the 1973 Act (power of Court to order search of persons before it).

(5)   The powers conferred by subsection (1) above, and the powers arising by virtue of subsections (3) and (4) above, shall include power to use reasonable force where necessary.

(6)   The power to make rules under this section shall be exercisable by statutory instrument which shall be subject to annulment in pursuance of a resolution of either House of Parliament.

Breaches of discipline by prisoners.
83.—(1)   Where a prisoner for whose delivery or custody a prisoner custody officer has been responsible in pursuance of prisoner escort arrangements is delivered to a prison, he shall be deemed, for the purposes of such prison rules as relate to disciplinary offences, to have been—

(a)   in the custody of the governor of the prison; or

(b)   in the case of a contracted out prison, in the custody of its director,

at all times while that officer was so responsible.

(2)   Nothing in subsection (1) above shall enable a prisoner to be punished under prison rules for any act or omission of his for which he has already been punished by a court.

Contracted out prisons

Contracting out of certain prisons.
84.—(1)   The Secretary of State may enter into a contract with another person for the running by him of any prison which—
   (a)   is established after the commencement of this section;
and while such a contract is in force, the prison to which it relates shall be run subject to and in accordance with sections 85 and 86 below, the 1952 Act (as modified by section 87 below) and prison rules.
   (2)   In this Part—
      "contracted out prison" means a prison as respects which such a contract is for the time being in force;
      "the contractor", in relation to such a prison, means the person who has contracted to run it.
   (3)   The Secretary of State may by order made by statutory instrument provide that this section shall have effect as if there were omitted from subsection (1) above either—
      (a)   paragraph (a) and the word "and" immediately following that paragraph; or
      (b)   paragraph (b) and the said word "and"; or
      (c)   the words from "which", in the first place where it occurs, to the end of paragraph (b).
   (4)   An order under subsection (3)(b) or (c) above shall provide that section 87 below shall have effect as if subsection (5) were omitted.
   (5)   No order shall be made under subsection (3) above unless a draft of the order has been laid before and approved by resolution of each House of Parliament.

Note. Section 84 is printed as modified by the Criminal Justice Act (Contracted Out Prisons) Order 1992 (SI 1992/1656).

Officers of contracted out prisons.
85.—(1)   Instead of a governor, every contracted out prison shall have—
      (a)   a director, who shall be a prisoner custody officer appointed by the contractor and specially approved for the purposes of this section by the Secretary of State; and
      (b)   a controller, who shall be a Crown servant appointed by the Secretary of State;
and every officer of such a prison who performs custodial duties shall be a prisoner custody officer who is authorised to perform such duties.
   (2)   Subject to subsection (3) below, the director shall have such functions as are conferred on him by the 1952 Act (as modified by section 87 below) or as may be conferred on him by prison rules.
   (3)   The director shall not—
      (a)   inquire into a disciplinary charge laid against a prisoner, conduct the hearing of such a charge or make, remit or mitigate an award in respect of such a charge; or

(b) except in cases of urgency, order the removal of a prisoner from association with other prisoners, the temporary confinement of a prisoner in a special cell or the application to a prisoner of any other special control or restraint.

(4) The controller shall have such functions as may be conferred on him by prison rules and shall be under a duty—

(a) to keep under review, and report to the Secretary of State on, the running of the prison by or on behalf of the director; and

(b) to investigate, and report to the Secretary of State on, any allegations made against prisoner custody officers performing custodial duties at the prison.

(5) The contractor shall be under a duty to do all that he reasonably can (whether by giving directions to the officers of the prison or otherwise) to facilitate the exercise by the controller of all such functions as are mentioned in or conferred by subsection (4) above.

Powers and duties of prisoner custody officers employed at contracted out prisons.
86.—(1) A prisoner custody officer performing custodial duties at a contracted out prison shall have the following powers, namely—

(a) to search in accordance with prison rules any prisoner who is confined in the prison; and

(b) to search any other person who is in or is seeking to enter the prison, and any article in the possession of such a person.

(2) The powers conferred by subsection (1)(b) above to search a person shall not be construed as authorising a prisoner custody officer to require a person to remove any of his clothing other than an outer coat, jacket or gloves.

(3) A prisoner custody officer performing custodial duties at a contracted out prison shall have the following duties as respects prisoners confined in the prison, namely—

(a) to prevent their escape from lawful custody;

(b) to prevent, or detect and report on, the commission or attempted commission by them of other unlawful acts;

(c) to ensure good order and discipline on their part; and

(d) to attend to their wellbeing.

(4) The powers conferred by subsection (1) above, and the powers arising by virtue of subsection (3) above, shall include power to use reasonable force where necessary.

Consequential modifications of 1952 Act.
87.—(1) In relation to a contracted out prison, the provisions of the 1952 Act specified in subsections (2) to (8) below shall have effect subject to the modifications so specified.

(2) In section 7(1) (prison officers), the reference to a governor shall be construed as a reference to a director and a controller.

(3) Section 8 (powers of prison officers) and section 11 (ejectment of prison officers and their families refusing to quit) shall not apply.

(4) In sections 10(5), 12(3), 13(1) and 19(1) and (3) (various functions of the governor of a prison), references to the governor shall be construed as references to the director.

(5) [Omitted by the Criminal Justice Act (Contracted Out Prisons) Order 1992 (SI 1992/1656).]

(6) In section 13(2) (legal custody of prisoner), the reference to an officer of the prison shall be construed as a reference to a prisoner custody officer performing custodial duties at the prison.

(7) In section 14(2) (cells), the reference to a prison officer shall be construed as a reference to a prisoner custody officer performing custodial duties at the prison.

(8) Section 35 (vesting of prison property in the Secretary of State) shall have effect subject to the provisions of the contract entered into under section 84(1) above.

Intervention by the Secretary of State.
88.—(1) This section applies where, in the case of a contracted out prison, it appears to the Secretary of State—

(a) that the director has lost, or is likely to lose, effective control of the prison or any part of it; and

(b) that the making of an appointment under subsection (2) below is necessary in the interests of preserving the safety of any person, or of preventing serious damage to any property.

(2) The Secretary of State may appoint a Crown servant to act as governor of the prison for the period—

(a) beginning with the time specified in the appointment; and

(b) ending with the time specified in the notice of termination under subsection (4) below.

(3) During that period—

(a) all the functions which would otherwise be exercisable by the director or the controller shall be exercisable by the governor;

(b) the contractor shall do all that he reasonably can to facilitate the exercise by the governor of those functions; and

(c) the officers of the prison shall comply with any directions given by the governor in the exercise of those functions.

(4) Where the Secretary of State is satisfied—

(a) that the governor has secured effective control of the prison or, as the case may be, the relevant part of it; and

(b) that the governor's appointment is no longer necessary as mentioned in subsection (1)(b) above,

he shall, by a notice to the governor, terminate the appointment at a time specified in the notice.

(5) As soon as practicable after making or terminating an appointment under this section, the Secretary of State shall give a notice of the appointment, or a copy of the notice of termination, to the contractor, the director and the controller.

Supplemental

Certification of prisoner custody officers
89.—(1) In this Part "prisoner custody officer" means a person in respect of whom a certificate is for the time being in force certifying—

(a)   that he has been approved by the Secretary of State for the purpose of performing escort functions or custodial duties or both; and

(b)   that he is accordingly authorised to perform them.

(2)   The provisions of Schedule 10 to this Act shall have effect with respect to the certification of prisoner custody officers.

(3)   In this section and Schedule 10 to this Act—

"custodial duties" means custodial duties at a contracted out prison;

"escort functions" means the functions specified in section 80(1) above.

Protection of prisoner custody officers.

90.—(1)   Any person who assaults a prisoner custody officer acting in pursuance of prisoner escort arrangements, or performing custodial duties at a contracted out prison, shall be liable on summary conviction to fine not exceeding level 5 on the standard scale or to imprisonment for a term not exceeding six months or to both.

(2)   Section 17(2) of the Firearms Act 1968 (additional penalty for possession of firearms when committing certain offences) shall apply to offences under subsection (1) above.

(3)   Any person who resists or wilfully obstructs a prisoner custody officer acting in pursuance of prisoner escort arrangements, or performing custodial duties at a contracted out prison, shall be liable on summary conviction to a fine not exceeding level 3 on the standard scale.

(4)   For the purposes of this section, a prisoner custody officer shall not be regarded as acting in pursuance of prisoner escort arrangements at any time when he is not readily identifiable as such an officer (whether by means of a uniform or badge which he is wearing or otherwise).

Wrongful disclosure of information.

91.—(1)   A person who is or has been employed (whether as a prisoner custody officer or otherwise) in pursuance of prisoner escort arrangements, or at a contracted out prison, shall be guilty of an offence if he discloses, otherwise than in the course of his duty or as authorised by the Secretary of State, any information which he acquired in the course of his employment and which relates to a particular prisoner.

(2)   A person guilty of an offence under subsection (1) above shall be liable—

(a)   on conviction on indictment, to imprisonment for a term not exceeding two years or a fine or both;

(b)   on summary conviction, to imprisonment for a term not exceeding six months or a fine not exceeding the statutory maximum or both.

Interpretation of Part IV

92.—(1)   In this Part—

"contracted out prison" and "the contractor" have the meanings given by section 84(2) above;

"court-house" means a petty sessional court-house within the meaning of the 1980 Act or an occasional court-house appointed under section 147 of that Act;

"court security officer" has the meaning given by section 76(1) above;

"prison" includes a young offender institution or remand centre;

"prisoner" means any person who—
    (a) is held in custody in a prison;
    (b) is kept in police detention after being charged with an offence;
    (c) has been committed to detention at a police station under section 128(7) of the 1980 Act; or
    (d) is in the custody of a court;
"prisoner custody officer" has the meaning given by section 89(1) above;
"prisoner escort arrangements" has the meaning given by section 80(2) above.

(2)   Unless the contrary intention appears, expressions used in sections 76 to 79 above which are also used in the 1979 Act have the same meanings as in that Act.

(3)   Sections 80, 81(1) and (2)(a), 82 and 89 to 91 above, subsection (1) above and Schedule 10 to this Act shall have effect as if—

    (a) any reference in section 80(1), 81(1), 82 or 91 above to prisoners included a reference to persons kept in secure accommodation by virtue of a security requirement imposed under section 23(4) of the 1969 Act (remands and committals to local authority accommodation); and

    (b) any reference in section 80(1)(c) to (e) above to a prison included a reference to such accommodation.

PART V   FINANCIAL AND OTHER PROVISIONS

Cash limits

Cash limits for magistrates' courts.
93.—(1) In section 55 of the 1979 Act (duties of local authorities outside Greater London), after subsection (2) there shall be inserted the following subsection—

    "(2A) Nothing in subsection (1) or (2) above shall require a council to incur any expenditure or make any payment which would—

    (a) cause the net cost to it in any year of the matters mentioned in subsection (1) of section 59 of this Act to exceed the amount which, in relation to the council and that year, is for the time being determined by the Secretary of State under subsection (3)(b) of that section; or

    (b) cause its capital expenditure in any year in pursuance of functions under this Part of this Act to exceed the amount which, in relation to the council and that year, is for the time being determined by the Secretary of State under subsection (4)(b) of that section;

and in determining any such net cost as is mentioned in paragraph (a) above there shall be disregarded any such capital expenditure as is mentioned in paragraph (b) above."

(2)   In section 58 of that Act (corresponding arrangements in inner London area), after subsection (2) there shall be inserted the following subsection—

    "(2A) Nothing in subsection (1) or (2) above shall require the Receiver to incur any expenditure or make any payment which would—

    (a) cause the net cost to him in any year of the matters mentioned in subsection (1) of section 59 of this Act to exceed the amount which, in relation to the Receiver and that year, is for the time being determined by the Secretary of State under subsection (3)(b) of that section; or

(b) cause his capital expenditure in any year in pursuance of functions under this Part of this Act to exceed the amount which, in relation to the Receiver and that year, is for the time being determined by the Secretary of State under subsection (4)(b) of that section;

and in determining any such net cost as is mentioned in paragraph (a) above there shall be disregarded any such capital expenditure as is mentioned in paragraph (b) above."

(3) For section 59 of that Act there shall be substituted the following section—

"Grants by Secretary of State to responsible authorities.

59.—(1) The Secretary of State may out of money provided by Parliament pay to the responsible authorities grants towards the net cost to them in any year—

(a) of their functions under this Part or Part II of this Act;

(b) of their functions under any regulations made, or having effect as if made, under section 7 of the Superannuation Act 1972 with respect to court staff or, in the case of the Receiver, his corresponding functions; and

(c) of making payments under section 12 or 53 of this Act;

and in determining any such net cost as is mentioned above there shall be disregarded any such capital expenditure as is mentioned in subsection (2) below.

(2) The Secretary of State may also out of money provided by Parliament pay to the responsible authorities grants towards their capital expenditure in any year in pursuance of their functions under this Part of this Act.

(3) The amount of any grant under subsection (1) above towards the net cost to a responsible authority in any year of the matters mentioned in that subsection shall not exceed 80 per cent. of whichever of the following is the less, namely—

(a) that net cost; and

(b) the amount which, in relation to the authority and that year, is for the time being determined by the Secretary of State.

(4) The amount of any grant under subsection (2) above towards the capital expenditure in any year of a responsible authority in pursuance of its functions under this Part of this Act shall not exceed 80 per cent. of whichever of the following is the less, namely—

(a) that capital expenditure; and

(b) the amount which, in relation to the authority and that year, is for the time being determined by the Secretary of State.

(5) The Secretary of State, with the concurrence of the Treasury, may by statutory instrument make regulations as to the manner in which—

(a) income and expenditure of responsible authorities are to be taken into account in determining the net cost to them in any year of the matters mentioned in subsection (1) above; or

(b) expenditure of such authorities is to be taken into account in determining their capital expenditure in any year in pursuance of their functions under this Part of this Act;

and for the purposes of this section any question as to that net cost or that capital expenditure shall (subject to the regulations) be determined by the Secretary of State.

(6) The Secretary of State may direct that, in determining—

(a) the net cost to a responsible authority in any year of the matters mentioned in subsection (1) above; or

(b) the capital expenditure of such an authority in any year in pursuance of its functions under this Part of this Act,

there shall be taken into account or disregarded, to such extent as may be specified in the direction, such items as may be so specified.

(7) Grants under this section shall be paid at such times, in such manner and subject to such conditions as the Secretary of State may with the approval of the Treasury determine.

(8) In this section—

'court staff' means persons appointed or deemed to have been appointed as justices' clerks, or employed by a magistrates' courts committee to assist a justices' clerk, under Part III of the Justices of the Peace Act 1949 or Part II of this Act;

'responsible authority' means any of the following, namely, the council of a non-metropolitan county, metropolitan district or outer London borough, the Common Council of the City of London and the Receiver.''

(4) In section 70 of that Act (interpretation), before the definition of ''commission area'' there shall be inserted the following definition—

'''capital expenditure' means expenditure for capital purposes (construed in accordance with section 40 of the Local Government and Housing Act 1989);''.

Cash limits for probation services.

94.—(1) After subsection (3) of section 51 of the 1973 Act (expenses and grants payable out of money provided by Parliament) there shall be inserted the following subsection—

"(3A) The amount of any payments under subsection (3) above towards any person's expenditure, or towards any expenditure out of the metropolitan police fund, in any year shall not exceed the appropriate percentage of whichever of the following is the less, namely—

(a) that expenditure; and

(b) the amount which, in relation to that expenditure and that year, is for the time being determined by the Secretary of State;

and in this subsection 'the appropriate percentage', in relation to expenditure of any description, means the percentage which in relation to expenditure of that description is for the time being determined by the Secretary of State.''

(2) In paragraph 3 of Schedule 3 to the 1973 Act (the probation service and its functions)—

(a) for paragraph (a) of sub-paragraph (1) there shall be substituted the following paragraph—

"(a) to appoint such number of probation officers—

(i) as may be determined by them without objection by the responsible authority; or

(ii)   where objection is made, as may be agreed between them and that authority,

to be a sufficient number of such officers for their probation area, subject, in the case of such classes or descriptions of officers as may be prescribed, to the approval of the appointment by the Secretary of State;";

(b)   at the end of that sub-paragraph there shall be inserted the words "and any question as to number arising under paragraph (a) above shall, in default of agreement, be determined by the Secretary of State"; and

(c)   for sub-paragraph (5) there shall be substituted the following sub-paragraph—

"(5)   In this paragraph 'the responsible authority'—

(a)   in relation to a probation area other than the inner London probation area, means the local authority in whose area that probation area is situated; and

(b)   in relation to the inner London probation area, means—

(i)   the Receiver for the metropolitan police district; and

(ii)   where that area includes one or more petty sessions areas outside the inner London area, the local authority or authorities in whose area or areas that petty sessions area or those petty sessions areas is or are situated; and 'supervision order' and 'supervisor' have the meanings assigned to them by section 11 of the Children and Young Persons Act 1969."

(3)   After paragraph 16 of that Schedule there shall be inserted the following paragraph—

"Limits on sums payable under paragraphs 15 and 16

"16A.—(1)   Nothing in paragraph 15 or 16 above shall require a local authority to defray any sums which would cause its expenditure in any year to exceed the amount which, in relation to that expenditure and that year, is for the time being determined by the Secretary of State under section 51(3A)(b) of this Act.

(2)   Nothing in paragraph 16 above shall require there to be paid out of the metropolitan police fund any sums which would cause the expenditure out of that fund in any year to exceed the amount which, in relation to that expenditure and that year, is for the time being so determined.

(3)   In this paragraph 'expenditure' means expenditure under this Schedule."

Miscellaneous

Information for financial and other purposes.

95.—(1)   The Secretary of State shall in each year publish such information as he considers expedient for the purpose of—

(a)   enabling persons engaged in the administration of criminal justice to become aware of the financial implications of their decisions; or

(b)   facilitating the performance by such persons of their duty to avoid discriminating against any persons on the ground of race or sex or any other improper ground.

(2)   Publication under subsection (1) above shall be effected in such manner as the Secretary of State considers appropriate for the purpose of bringing the information to the attention of the persons concerned.

Grants out of money provided by Parliament.
96. In section 51(3) of the 1973 Act (grants payable out of money provided by Parliament), after paragraph (c) there shall be inserted the following paragraph—
> "(cc)   towards the expenditure of any society or individual engaged in supervising or assisting persons on bail;".

Grants by probation committees.
97. In Schedule 3 to the 1973 Act (the probation service and its functions), after paragraph 12 there shall be inserted the following paragraph—
> *"Payment of grants in prescribed cases*
> 12A   A probation committee may, in prescribed cases, make such payments and to such persons as may be prescribed."

PART VI   SUPPLEMENTAL

Expenses etc. under Act.
98. There shall be paid out of money provided by Parliament—
(a)   any sums required by the Secretary of State for making payments under contracts entered into under section 13, 80 or 84 above, or payments to or in respect of inspectors of probation appointed under section 73 above;
(b)   any sums so required for defraying the expenses of the Parole Board, or any expenses incurred by members of lay panels appointed under section 81 above;
(c)   any administrative expenses incurred by the Secretary of State under this Act; and
(d)   any increase attributable to this Act in the sums payable out of money so provided under any other Act.

General interpretation.
99.—(1)   In this Act—
"the 1933 Act" means the Children and Young Persons Act 1933;
"the 1952 Act" means the Prison Act 1952;
"the 1967 Act" means the Criminal Justice Act 1967;
"the 1969 Act" means the Children and Young Persons Act 1969;
"the 1973 Act" means the Powers of Criminal Courts Act 1973;
"the 1979 Act" means the Justices of the Peace Act 1979;
"the 1980 Act" means the Magistrates' Courts Act 1980;
"the 1982 Act" means the Criminal Justice Act 1982;
"the 1983 Act" means the Mental Health Act 1983;
"the 1988 Act" means the Criminal Justice Act 1988;
"child", unless the contrary intention appears, means a person under the age of fourteen years;
"prison rules" means rules made under section 47 of the 1952 Act;
"young person" means a person who has attained the age of fourteen years and is under the age of eighteen years.
(2)   For the purposes of any provision of this Act which requires the determination of the age of a person by the court or the Secretary of State, his

age shall be deemed to be that which it appears to the court or the Secretary of State to be after considering any available evidence.

Minor and consequential amendments.
100. The enactments mentioned in Schedule 11 to this Act shall have effect subject to the amendments there specified (being minor amendments and amendments consequential on the preceding provisions of this Act).

Transitional provisions, savings and repeals.
101.—(1) The transitional provisions and savings contained in Schedule 12 to this Act shall have effect; but nothing in this subsection shall be taken as prejudicing the operation of sections 16 and 17 of the Interpretation Act 1978 (which relate to the effect of repeals).

(2) The enactments mentioned in Schedule 13 to this Act (which include some that are spent or no longer of practical utility) are hereby repealed to the extent specified in the third column of that Schedule.

Short title, commencement and extent.
102.—(1) This Act may be cited as the Criminal Justice Act 1991.

(2) This Act shall come into force on such day as the Secretary of State may by order made by statutory instrument appoint, and different days may be appointed for different provisions or for different purposes.

(3) Without prejudice to the provisions of Schedule 12 to this Act, an order under subsection (2) above may make such transitional provisions and savings as appear to the Secretary of State necessary or expedient in connection with any provision brought into force by the order.

(4) Subject to subsections (5) to (8) below, this Act extends to England and Wales only.

(5) The following provisions of this Act, namely—
    (a) this section;
    (b) sections 16, 17(1) and (2), 24 and 26(3) and (4); and
    (c) Schedule 3, paragraph 6 of Schedule 6, paragraph 5 of Schedule 8, paragraph 15 of Schedule 11 to this Act and, so far as relating to the Social Work (Scotland) Act 1968, Schedule 13,
also extend to Scotland; and section 23(2) above and, in so far as relating to the Criminal Procedure (Scotland) Act 1975, Schedule 13 to this Act extend to Scotland only.

(6) This section, section 16 above, Schedule 3 to this Act, paragraph 16 of Schedule 11 to this Act and, so far as relating to the Social Work (Scotland) Act 1968, Schedule 13 to this Act also extend to Northern Ireland.

(7) An Order in Council under section 81(11) of the 1982 Act may direct that both or either of—
    (a) section 37 of that Act as amended by section 17(1) above; and
    (b) section 32 of the 1980 Act as amended by section 17(2) above,
shall extend, subject to such modifications as may be specified in the Order, to the Isle of Man or any of the Channel Islands.

(8) Nothing in subsection (4) above affects the extent of this Act in so far as it amends or repeals any provision of the Army Act 1955, the Air Force Act 1955, the Naval Discipline Act 1957 or the Armed Forces Act 1991.

SCHEDULES

SCHEDULE 1

AMENDMENTS OF 1973 ACT

PART I PROVISIONS INSERTED AS SECTIONS 1A TO 1C

"Discharge

Absolute and conditional discharge

1A.—(1) Where a court by or before which a person is convicted of an offence (not being an offence the sentence for which is fixed by law) is of opinion, having regard to the circumstances including the nature of the offence and the character of the offender, that it is inexpedient to inflict punishment, the court may make an order either—

(a) discharging him absolutely; or

(b) if the court thinks fit, discharging him subject to the condition that he commits no offence during such period, not exceeding three years from the date of the order, as may be specified in the order.

(2) An order discharging a person subject to such a condition is in this Act referred to as 'an order for conditional discharge', and the period specified in any such order as 'the period of conditional discharge'.

(3) Before making an order for conditional discharge the court shall explain to the offender in ordinary language that if he commits another offence during the period of conditional discharge he will be liable to be sentenced for the original offence.

(4) Where, under the following provisions of this Part of this Act, a person conditionally discharged under this section is sentenced for the offence in respect of which the order for conditional discharge was made, that order shall cease to have effect.

(5) The Secretary of State may by order direct that subsection (1) above shall be amended by substituting, for the maximum period specified in that subsection as originally enacted or as previously amended under this subsection, such period as may be specified in the order.

Commission of further offence by person conditionally discharged.

1B.—(1) If it appears to the Crown Court, where that court has jurisdiction in accordance with subsection (2) below, or to a justice of the peace having jurisdiction in accordance with that subsection, that a person in whose case an order for conditional discharge has been made—

(a) has been convicted by a court in any part of Great Britain of an offence committed during the period of conditional discharge; and

(b) has been dealt with in respect of that offence,

that court or justice may, subject to subsection (3) below, issue a summons requiring that person to appear at the place and time specified therein or a warrant for his arrest.

(2) Jurisdiction for the purposes of subsection (1) above may be exercised—

    (a)   if the order for conditional discharge was made by the Crown Court, by that court;

    (b)   if the order was made by a magistrates' court, by a justice acting for the petty sessions area for which that court acts.

    (3)   A justice of the peace shall not issue a summons under this section except on information and shall not issue a warrant under this section except on information in writing and on oath.

    (4)   A summons or warrant issued under this section shall direct the person to whom it relates to appear or to be brought before the court by which the order for conditional discharge was made.

    (5)   If a person in whose case an order for conditional discharge has been made by the Crown Court is convicted by a magistrates' court of an offence committed during the period of conditional discharge, the magistrates' court—

    (a)   may commit him to custody or release him on bail until he can be brought or appear before the Crown Court; and

    (b)   if it does so, shall send to the Crown Court a copy of the minute or memorandum of the conviction entered in the register, signed by the clerk of the court by whom the register is kept.

    (6)   Where it is proved to the satisfaction of the court by which an order for conditional discharge was made that the person in whose case the order was made has been convicted of an offence committed during the period of conditional discharge, the court may deal with him, for the offence for which the order was made, in any manner in which it could deal with him if he had just been convicted by or before that court of that offence.

    (7)   If a person in whose case an order for conditional discharge has been made by a magistrates' court—

    (a)   is convicted before the Crown Court of an offence committed during the period of conditional discharge; or

    (b)   is dealt with by the Crown Court for any such offence in respect of which he was committed for sentence to the Crown Court,
the Crown Court may deal with him, for the offence for which the order was made, in any manner in which the magistrates' court could deal with him if it had just convicted him of that offence.

    (8)   If a person in whose case an order for conditional discharge has been made by a magistrates' court is convicted by another magistrates' court of any offence committed during the period of conditional discharge, that other court may, with the consent of the court which made the order, deal with him, for the offence for which the order was made, in any manner in which the court could deal with him if it had just convicted him of that offence.

    (9)   Where an order for conditional discharge has been made by a magistrates' court in the case of an offender under eighteen years of age in respect of an offence triable only on indictment in the case of an adult, any powers exercisable under subsection (6), (7) or (8) above by that or any other court in respect of the offender after he has attained the age of eighteen years shall be those which would be exercisable if that offence were an offence triable either way and had been tried summarily.

    (10)   For the purposes of this section the age of an offender at a particular time shall be deemed to be or to have been that which appears to

the court after considering any available evidence to be or to have been his age at that time.

Effect of discharge.

1C.—(1) Subject to subsection (2) below and to section 50 (1A) of the Criminal Appeal Act 1968 and section 108(1A) of the Magistrates' Courts Act 1980, a conviction of an offence for which an order is made under this Part of this Act discharging the offender absolutely or conditionally shall be deemed not to be a conviction for any purpose other than—

(a) the purposes of the proceedings in which the order is made and of any subsequent proceedings which may be taken against the offender under the following provisions of this Act; and

(b) the purposes of section 1(2)(bb) of the Children and Young Persons Act 1969.

(2) Where the offender was of or over eighteen years of age at the time of his conviction of the offence in question and is subsequently sentenced under this Part of this Act for that offence, subsection (1) above shall cease to apply to the conviction.

(3) Without prejudice to the preceding provisions of this section, the conviction of an offender who is discharged absolutely or conditionally under this Part of this Act shall in any event be disregarded for the purposes of any enactment or instrument which—

(a) imposes any disqualification or disability upon convicted persons; or

(b) authorises or requires the imposition of any such disqualification or disability.

(4) The preceding provisions of this section shall not affect—

(a) any right of any offender discharged absolutely or conditionally under this Part of this Act to rely on his conviction in bar of any subsequent proceedings for the same offence; or

(b) the restoration of any property in consequence of the conviction of any such offender; or

(c) the operation, in relation to any such offender, of any enactment or instrument in force at the commencement of this Act which is expressed to extend to persons dealt with under section 1(1) of the Probation of Offenders Act 1907 as well as to convicted persons.

(5) In this section 'enactment' includes an enactment contained in a local Act and 'instrument' means an instrument having effect by virtue of an Act".

PART II   PROVISIONS INSERTED AS SCHEDULE 1A

"SCHEDULE 1A
ADDITIONAL REQUIREMENTS IN PROBATION ORDERS

Requirements as to residence

1.—(1) Subject to sub-paragraphs (2) and (3) below, a probation order may include requirements as to the residence of the offender.

(2)   Before making a probation order containing any such requirement, the court shall consider the home surroundings of the offender.

(3)   Where a probation order requires the offender to reside in an approved hostel or any other institution, the period for which he is so required to reside shall be specified in the order.

Requirements as to activities etc.

2.—(1)   Subject to the provisions of this paragraph, a probation order may require the offender—

(a)   to present himself to a person or persons specified in the order at a place or places so specified;

(b)   to participate or refrain from participating in activities specified in the order—

(i)   on a day or days so specified; or

(ii)   during the probation period or such portion of it as may be so specified.

(2)   A court shall not include in a probation order a requirement such as is mentioned in sub-paragraph (1) above unless—

(a)   it has consulted a probation officer; and

(b)   it is satisfied that it is feasible to secure compliance with the requirement.

(3)   A court shall not include a requirement such as is mentioned in sub-paragraph (1)(a) above or a requirement to participate in activities if it would involve the co-operation of a person other than the offender and the probation officer responsible for his supervision, unless that other person consents to its inclusion.

(4)   A requirement such as is mentioned in sub-paragraph (1)(a) above shall operate to require the offender—

(a)   in accordance with instructions given by the probation officer responsible for his supervision, to present himself at a place or places for not more than 60 days in the aggregate; and

(b)   while at any place, to comply with instructions given by, or under the authority of, the person in charge of that place.

(5)   A place specified in an order shall have been approved by the probation committee for the area in which the premises are situated as providing facilities suitable for persons subject to probation orders.

(6)   A requirement to participate in activities shall operate to require the offender—

(a)   in accordance with instructions given by the probation officer responsible for his supervision, to participate in activities for not more than 60 days in the aggregate; and

(b)   while participating, to comply with instructions given by, or under the authority of, the person in charge of the activities.

(7)   Instructions given by a probation officer under sub-paragraph (4) or (6) above shall, as far as practicable, be such as to avoid any interference with the times, if any, at which the offender normally works or attends a school or other educational establishment.

Requirements as to attendance at probation centre

3.—(1) Subject to the provisions of this paragraph, a probation order may require the offender during the probation period to attend at a probation centre specified in the order.

(2) A court shall not include such a requirement in a probation order unless—

(a)   it has consulted a probation officer; and

(b)   it is satisfied—

(i)   that arrangements can be made for the offender's attendance at a centre; and

(ii)   that the person in charge of the centre consents to the inclusion of the requirement.

(3) A requirement under sub-paragraph (1) above shall operate to require the offender—

(a)   in accordance with instructions given by the probation officer responsible for his supervision, to attend on not more than 60 days at the centre specified in the order; and

(b)   while attending there to comply with instructions given by, or under the authority of, the person in charge of the centre.

(4) Instructions given by a probation officer under sub-paragraph (3) above shall, so far as is practicable, be such as to avoid any interference with the times, if any, at which the offender normally works or attends a school or other educational establishment.

(5) References in this paragraph to attendance at a probation centre include references to attendance elsewhere than at the centre for the purpose of participating in activities in accordance with instructions given by, or under the authority of, the person in charge of the centre.

(6) The Secretary of State may make rules for regulating the provision and carrying on of probation centres and the attendance at such centres of persons subject to probation orders; and such rules may in particular include provision with respect to hours of attendance, the reckoning of days of attendance and the keeping of attendance records.

(7) In this paragraph 'probation centre' means premises—

(a)   at which non-residential facilities are provided for use in connection with the rehabilitation of offenders; and

(b)   which are for the time being approved by the Secretary of State as providing facilities suitable for persons subject to probation orders.

Extension of requirements for sexual offenders

4.—(1) If the court so directs in the case of an offender who has been convicted of a sexual offence—

(a)   sub-paragraphs (4) and (6) of paragraph 2 above; and

(b)   sub-paragraph (3) of paragraph 3 above,

shall each have effect as if for the reference to 60 days there were substituted a reference to such greater number of days as may be specified in the direction.

(2) In this paragraph 'sexual offence' has the same meaning as in Part I of the Criminal Justice Act 1991.

Requirements as to treatment for mental condition etc.

5.—(1) This paragraph applies where a court proposing to make a probation order is satisfied, on the evidence of a duly qualified medical practitioner approved for the purposes of section 12 of the Mental Health Act 1983, that the mental condition of the offender—

(a)   is such as requires and may be susceptible to treatment; but

(b)   is not such as to warrant the making of a hospital order or guardianship order within the meaning of that Act.

(2) The probation order may include a requirement that the offender shall submit, during the whole of the probation period or during such part of that period as may be specified in the order, to treatment by or under the direction of a duly qualified medical practitioner with a view to the improvement of the offender's mental condition.

(3) The treatment required by any such order shall be such one of the following kinds of treatment as may be specified in the order, that is to say—

(a)   treatment as a resident patient in a mental hospital;

(b)   treatment as a non-resident patient at such institution or place as may be specified in the order; and

(c)   treatment by or under the direction of such duly qualified medical practitioner as may be so specified;

but the nature of the treatment shall not be specified in the order except as mentioned in paragraph (a), (b) or (c) above.

(4) A court shall not by virtue of this paragraph include in a probation order a requirement that the offender shall submit to treatment for his mental condition unless it is satisfied that arrangements have been made for the treatment intended to be specified in the order (including arrangements for the reception of the offender where he is to be required to submit to treatment as a resident patient).

(5) While the offender is under treatment as a resident patient in pursuance of a requirement of the probation order, the probation officer responsible for his supervision shall carry out the supervision to such extent only as may be necessary for the purpose of the revocation or amendment of the order.

(6) Where the medical practitioner by whom or under whose direction an offender is being treated for his mental condition in pursuance of a probation order is of the opinion that part of the treatment can be better or more conveniently given in or at an institution or place which—

(a)   is not specified in the order; and

(b)   is one in or at which the treatment of the offender will be given by or under the direction of a duly qualified medical practitioner,

he may, with the consent of the offender, make arrangements for him to be treated accordingly.

(7) Such arrangements as are mentioned in sub-paragraph (6) above may provide for the offender to receive part of his treatment as a resident patient in an institution or place notwithstanding that the institution or place is not one which could have been specified for that purpose in the probation order.

(8) Where any such arrangements as are mentioned in sub-paragraph (6) above are made for the treatment of an offender—

(a)   the medical practitioner by whom the arrangements are made shall give notice in writing to the probation officer responsible for the supervision of the offender, specifying the institution or place in or at which the treatment is to be carried out; and

(b)   the treatment provided for by the arrangements shall be deemed to be treatment to which he is required to submit in pursuance of the probation order.

(9)   Subsections (2) and (3) of section 54 of the Mental Health Act 1983 shall have effect with respect to proof for the purposes of sub-paragraph (1) above of an offender's mental condition as they have effect with respect to proof of an offender's mental condition for the purposes of section 37(2)(a) of that Act.

(10)   In this paragraph 'mental hospital' means a hospital within the meaning of the Mental Health Act 1983 or mental nursing home within the meaning of the Registered Homes Act 1984, not being a special hospital within the meaning of the National Health Service Act 1977.

Requirements as to treatment for drug or alcohol dependency

6.—(1)   This paragraph applies where a court proposing to make a probation order is satisfied—

(a)   that the offender is dependent on drugs or alcohol;

(b)   that his dependency caused or contributed to the offence in respect of which the order is proposed to be made; and

(c)   that his dependency is such as requires and may be susceptible to treatment.

(2)   The probation order may include a requirement that the offender shall submit, during the whole of the probation period or during such part of that period as may be specified in the order, to treatment by or under the direction of a person having the necessary qualifications or experience with a view to the reduction or elimination of the offender's dependency on drugs or alcohol.

(3)   The treatment required by any such order shall be such one of the following kinds of treatment as may be specified in the order, that is to say—

(a)   treatment as a resident in such institution or place as may be specified in the order;

(b)   treatment as a non-resident in or at such institution or place as may be so specified; and

(c)   treatment by or under the direction of such person having the necessary qualifications or experience as may be so specified;

but the nature of the treatment shall not be specified in the order except as mentioned in paragraph (a), (b) or (c) above.

(4)   A court shall not by virtue of this paragraph include in a probation order a requirement that the offender shall submit to treatment for his dependency on drugs or alcohol unless it is satisfied that arrangements have been made for the treatment intended to be specified in the order (including arrangements for the reception of the offender where he is to be required to submit to treatment as a resident).

(5)   While the offender is under treatment as a resident in pursuance of a requirement of the probation order, the probation officer responsible for his supervision shall carry out the supervision to such extent only as may be necessary for the purpose of the revocation or amendment of the order.

(6)   Where the person by whom or under whose direction an offender is being treated for dependency on drugs or alcohol in pursuance of a probation order is of the opinion that part of the treatment can be better or more conveniently given in or at an institution or place which—

(a)   is not specified in the order; and

(b)   is one in or at which the treatment of the offender will be given by or under the direction of a person having the necessary qualifications or experience, he may, with the consent of the offender, make arrangements for him to be treated accordingly.

(7)   Such arrangements as are mentioned in sub-paragraph (6) above may provide for the offender to receive part of his treatment as a resident in an institution or place notwithstanding that the institution or place is not one which could have been specified for that purpose in the probation order.

(8)   Where any such arrangements as are mentioned in sub-paragraph (6) above are made for the treatment of an offender—

(a)   the person by whom the arrangements are made shall give notice in writing to the probation officer responsible for the supervision of the offender, specifying the institution or place in or at which the treatment is to be carried out; and

(b)   the treatment provided for by the arrangements shall be deemed to be treatment to which he is required to submit in pursuance of the probation order.

(9)   In this paragraph the reference to the offender being dependent on drugs or alcohol includes a reference to his having a propensity towards the misuse of drugs or alcohol, and references to his dependency on drugs or alcohol shall be construed accordingly."

Section 14(1)   SCHEDULE 2

ENFORCEMENT ETC. OF COMMUNITY ORDERS

PART I   PRELIMINARY

1.—(1)   In this Schedule "relevant order" means any of the following orders, namely, a probation order, a community service order and a curfew order; and "the petty sessions area concerned" means—

(a)   in relation to a probation or community service order, the petty sessions area for the time being specified in the order; and

(b)   in relation to a curfew order, the petty sessions area in which the place for the time being specified in the order is situated.

(2)   Subject to sub-paragraph (3) below, this Schedule shall apply in relation to combination orders—

(a)   in so far as they impose such a requirement as is mentioned in paragraph (a) of subsection (1) of section 11 of this Act, as if they were probation orders; and

(b)   in so far as they impose such a requirement as is mentioned in paragraph (b) of that subsection, as if they were community service orders.

(3)   In its application to combination orders, paragraph 6(3) below shall have effect as if the reference to section 14(1A) of the 1973 Act were a reference to section 11(1) of this Act.

PART II   BREACH OF REQUIREMENT OF ORDER

Issue of summons or warrant

2.—(1)   If at any time while a relevant order is in force in respect of an offender it appears on information to a justice of the peace acting for the petty sessions area concerned that the offender has failed to comply with any of the requirements of the order, the justice may—

    (a)   issue a summons requiring the offender to appear at the place and time specified in it; or

    (b)   if the information is in writing and on oath, issue a warrant for his arrest.

(2)   Any summons or warrant issued under this paragraph shall direct the offender to appear or be brought before a magistrates' court acting for the petty sessions area concerned.

Powers of magistrates' court

3.—(1)   If it is proved to the satisfaction of the magistrates' court before which an offender appears or is brought under paragraph 2 above that he has failed without reasonable excuse to comply with any of the requirements of the relevant order, the court may deal with him in respect of the failure in any one of the following ways, namely—

    (a)   it may impose on him a fine not exceeding £1,000;

    (b)   subject to paragraph 6(3) to (5) below, it may make a community service order in respect of him;

    (c)   where the relevant order is a probation order and the case is one to which section 17 of the 1982 Act applies, it may make an order under that section requiring him to attend at an attendance centre; or

    (d)   where the relevant order was made by a magistrates' court, it may revoke the order and deal with him, for the offence in respect of which the order was made, in any manner in which it could deal with him if he had just been convicted by the court of the offence.

(2)   In dealing with an offender under sub-paragraph (1)(d) above, a magistrates' court—

    (a)   shall take into account the extent to which the offender has complied with the requirements of the relevant order; and

    (b)   may assume, in the case of an offender who has wilfully and persistently failed to comply with those requirements, that he has refused to give his consent to a community sentence which has been proposed by the court and requires that consent.

(3)   Where a relevant order was made by the Crown Court and a magistrates' court has power to deal with the offender under sub-paragraph (1)(a), (b) or (c) above, it may instead commit him to custody or release him on bail until he can be brought or appear before the Crown Court.

(4)   A magistrates' court which deals with an offender's case under sub-paragraph (3) above shall send to the Crown Court—

    (a)   a certificate signed by a justice of the peace certifying that the offender has failed to comply with the requirements of the relevant order in the respect specified in the certificate; and

(b)   such other particulars of the case as may be desirable;
and a certificate purporting to be so signed shall be admissible as evidence of the failure before the Crown Court.

(5)   A person sentenced under sub-paragraph (1)(d) above for an offence may appeal to the Crown Court against the sentence.

Powers of Crown Court

4.—(1)   Where by virtue of paragraph 3(3) above an offender is brought or appears before the Crown Court and it is proved to the satisfaction of the court that he has failed to comply with any of the requirements of the relevant order, that court may deal with him in respect of the failure in any one of the following ways, namely—

(a)   it may impose on him a fine not exceeding £1,000;

(b)   subject to paragraph 6(3) to (5) below, it may make a community service order in respect of him;

(c)   where the relevant order is a probation order and the case is one to which section 17 of the 1982 Act applies, it may make an order under that section requiring him to attend at an attendance centre; or

(d)   it may revoke the order and deal with him, for the offence in respect of which the order was made, in any manner in which it could deal with him if he had just been convicted by or before the court of the offence.

(2)   In dealing with an offender under sub-paragraph (1)(d) above, the Crown Court—

(a)   shall take into account the extent to which the offender has complied with the requirements of the relevant order; and

(b)   may assume, in the case of an offender who has wilfully and persistently failed to comply with those requirements, that he has refused to give his consent to a community sentence which has been proposed by the court and requires that consent.

(3)   In proceedings before the Crown Court under this paragraph any question whether the offender has failed to comply with the requirements of the relevant order shall be determined by the court and not by the verdict of a jury.

Exclusions

5.—(1)   Without prejudice to paragraphs 7 and 8 below, an offender who is convicted of a further offence while a relevant order is in force in respect of him shall not on that account be liable to be dealt with under paragraph 3 or 4 above in respect of a failure to comply with any requirement of the order.

(2)   An offender who is required by a probation order to submit to treatment for his mental condition, or his dependency on drugs or alcohol, shall not be treated for the purposes of paragraph 3 or 4 above as having failed to comply with that requirement on the ground only that he has refused to undergo any surgical, electrical or other treatment if, in the opinion of the court, his refusal was reasonable having regard to all the circumstances.

Supplemental

6.—(1)   Any exercise by a court of its powers under paragraph 3(1)(a), (b) or (c) or 4(1)(a) or (b) above shall be without prejudice to the continuance of the relevant order.

(2) A fine imposed under paragraph 3(1)(a) or 4(1)(a) above shall be deemed, for the purposes of any enactment, to be a sum adjudged to be paid by a conviction.

(3) The number of hours which an offender may be required to work under a community service order made under paragraph 3(1)(b) or 4(1)(b) above—

(a) shall be specified in the order and shall not exceed 60 in the aggregate; and

(b) where the relevant order is a community service order, shall not be such that the total number of hours under both orders exceeds the maximum specified in section 14(1A) of the 1973 Act.

(4) Section 14(2) of the 1973 Act and, so far as applicable—

(a) the following provisions of that Act relating to community service orders; and

(b) the provisions of this Schedule so far as so relating,

shall have effect in relation to a community service order under paragraph 3(1)(b) or 4(1)(b) above as they have effect in relation to a community service order in respect of an offender.

(5) Where the provisions of this Schedule have effect as mentioned in sub-paragraph (4) above, the powers conferred by those provisions to deal with the offender for the offence in respect of which the community service order was made shall be construed as powers to deal with the offender for the failure to comply with the requirements of the relevant order in respect of which the community service order was made.

Note. Paragraph 6 is printed as amended by the CJA 1993, sch. 3, para. 6.

PART III   REVOCATION OF ORDER

Revocation of order with or without re-sentencing

7.—(1) This paragraph applies where a relevant order is in force in respect of any offender and, on the application of the offender or the responsible officer, it appears to a magistrates' court acting for the petty sessions area concerned that, having regard to circumstances which have arisen since the order was made, it would be in the interests of justice—

(a) that the order should be revoked; or

(b) that the offender should be dealt with in some other manner for the offence in respect of which the order was made.

(2) The court may—

(a) if the order was made by a magistrates' court—

(i) revoke the order; or

(ii) revoke the order and deal with the offender, for the offence in respect of which the order was made, in any manner in which it could deal with him if he had just been convicted by the court of the offence; or

(b) if the order was made by the Crown Court, commit him to custody or release him on bail until he can be brought or appear before the Crown Court.

(3) The circumstances in which a probation order may be revoked under sub-paragraph (2)(a)(i) above shall include the offender's making good progress or his responding satisfactorily to supervision.

(4)   In dealing with an offender under sub-paragraph (2)(a)(ii) above, a magistrates' court shall take into account the extent to which the offender has complied with the requirements of the relevant order.

(5)   An offender sentenced under sub-paragraph (2)(a)(ii) above may appeal to the Crown Court against the sentence.

(6)   Where the court deals with an offender's case under sub-paragraph (2)(b) above, it shall send to the Crown Court such particulars of the case as may be desirable.

(7)   Where a magistrates' court proposes to exercise its powers under this paragraph otherwise than on the application of the offender it shall summon him to appear before the court and, if he does not appear in answer to the summons, may issue a warrant for his arrest.

(8)   No application may be made by the offender under sub-paragraph (1) above while an appeal against the relevant order is pending.

8.—(1)   This paragraph applies where an offender in respect of whom a relevant order is in force—

(a)   is convicted of an offence before the Crown Court; or

(b)   is committed by a magistrates' court to the Crown Court for sentence and is brought or appears before the Crown Court; or

(c)   by virtue of paragraph 7(2)(b) above is brought or appears before the Crown Court.

(2)   If it appears to the Crown Court to be in the interests of justice to do so, having regard to circumstances which have arisen since the order was made, the Crown Court may—

(a)   revoke the order; or

(b)   revoke the order and deal with the offender, for the offence in respect of which the order was made, in any manner in which it could deal with him if he had just been convicted by or before the court of the offence.

(3)   The circumstances in which a probation order may be revoked under sub-paragraph (2)(a) above shall include the offender's making good progress or his responding satisfactorily to supervision.

(4)   In dealing with an offender under sub-paragraph (2)(b) above, the Crown Court shall take into account the extent to which the offender has complied with the requirements of the relevant order.

Revocation of order following custodial sentence

9.—(1)   This paragraph applies where—

(a)   an offender in respect of whom a relevant order is in force is convicted of an offence before a magistrates' court other than a magistrates' court acting for the petty sessions area concerned; and

(b)   the court imposes a custodial sentence on the offender.

(2)   If it appears to the court, on the application of the offender or the responsible officer, that it would be in the interests of justice to do so having regard to circumstances which have arisen since the order was made, the court may—

(a)   if the order was made by a magistrates' court, revoke it; and

(b)   if the order was made by the Crown Court, commit the offender in custody or release him on bail until he can be brought or appear before the Crown Court.

(3)   Where the court deals with an offender's case under sub-paragraph (2)(b) above, it shall send to the Crown Court such particulars of the case as may be desirable.

10.   Where by virtue of paragraph 9(2)(b) above an offender is brought or appears before the Crown Court and it appears to the Crown Court to be in the interests of justice to do so, having regard to circumstances which have arisen since the relevant order was made, the Crown Court may revoke the order.

Supplemental

11.—(1)   On the making under this Part of this Schedule of an order revoking a relevant order, the clerk to the court shall forthwith give copies of the revoking order to the responsible officer.

(2)   A responsible officer to whom in accordance with sub-paragraph (1) above copies of a revoking order are given shall give a copy to the offender and to the person in charge of any institution in which the offender was required by the order to reside.

PART IV   AMENDMENT OF ORDER

Amendment by reason of change of residence

12.—(1)   This paragraph applies where, at any time while a relevant order is in force in respect of an offender, a magistrates' court acting for the petty sessions area concerned is satisfied that the offender proposes to change, or has changed, his residence from that petty sessions area to another petty sessions area.

(2)   Subject to sub-paragraphs (3) and (4) below, the court may, and on the application of the responsible officer shall, amend the relevant order by substituting the other petty sessions area for the area specified in the order or, in the case of a curfew order, a place in that other area for the place so specified.

(3)   The court shall not amend under this paragraph a probation or curfew order which contains requirements which, in the opinion of the court, cannot be complied with unless the offender continues to reside in the petty sessions area concerned unless, in accordance with paragraph 13 below, it either—

(a)   cancels those requirements; or

(b)   substitutes for those requirements other requirements which can be complied with if the offender ceases to reside in that area.

(4)   The court shall not amend a community service order under this paragraph unless it appears to the court that provision can be made for the offender to perform work under the order under the arrangements which exist for persons who reside in the other petty sessions area to perform work under such orders.

Amendment of requirements of probation or curfew order

13.—(1)   Without prejudice to the provisions of paragraph 12 above, but subject to sub-paragraph (2) below, a magistrates' court for the petty sessions area concerned may, on the application of the offender or the responsible officer, by order amend a probation or curfew order—

(a)   by cancelling any of the requirements of the order; or

(b)   by inserting in the order (either in addition to or in substitution for any such requirement) any requirement which the court could include if it were then making the order.

(2)   The power of a magistrates' court under sub-paragraph (1) above shall be subject to the following restrictions, namely—

(a)   the court shall not amend a probation order—

(i)   by reducing the probation period, or by extending that period beyond the end of three years from the date of the original order; or

(ii)   by inserting in it a requirement that the offender shall submit to treatment for his mental condition, or his dependency on drugs or alcohol, unless the amending order is made within three months after the date of the original order; and

(b)   the court shall not amend a curfew order by extending the curfew periods beyond the end of six months from the date of the original order.

(3)   In this paragraph and paragraph 14 below, references to the offender's dependency on drugs or alcohol include references to his propensity towards the misuse of drugs or alcohol.

Amendment of certain requirements of probation order

14.—(1)   Where the medical practitioner or other person by whom or under whose direction an offender is being treated for his mental condition, or his dependency on drugs or alcohol, in pursuance of any requirement of a probation order—

(a)   is of the opinion mentioned in sub-paragraph (2) below; or

(b)   is for any reason unwilling to continue to treat or direct the treatment of the offender,

he shall make a report in writing to that effect to the responsible officer and that officer shall apply under paragraph 13 above to a magistrates' court for the petty sessions area concerned for the variation or cancellation of the requirement.

(2)   The opinion referred to in sub-paragraph (1) above is—

(a)   that the treatment of the offender should be continued beyond the period specified in that behalf in the order;

(b)   that the offender needs different treatment, being treatment of a kind to which he could be required to submit in pursuance of a probation order;

(c)   that the offender is not susceptible to treatment; or

(d)   that the offender does not require further treatment.

Extension of community service order

15.   Where—

(a)   a community service order is in force in respect of any offender; and

(b)   on the application of the offender or the responsible officer, it appears to a magistrates' court acting for the petty sessions area concerned that it would be in the interests of justice to do so having regard to circumstances which have arisen since the order was made,

the court may, in relation to the order, extend the period of twelve months specified in section 15(2) of the 1973 Act.

Supplemental

16.   No order may be made under paragraph 12 above, and no application may be made under paragraph 13 or 15 above, while an appeal against the relevant order is pending.

17.—(1)   Subject to sub-paragraph (2) below, where a court proposes to exercise its powers under this Part of this Schedule, otherwise than on the application of the offender, the court—

(a)   shall summon him to appear before the court; and

(b)   if he does not appear in answer to the summons, may issue a warrant for his arrest;

and the court shall not amend a relevant order under this Part of this Schedule unless the offender expresses his willingness to comply with the requirements of the order as amended.

(2)   This paragraph shall not apply to an order cancelling a requirement of a relevant order or reducing the period of any requirement, or substituting a new petty sessions area or a new place for the one specified in a relevant order.

18.—(1)   On the making under this Part of this Schedule of an order amending a relevant order, the clerk to the court shall forthwith—

(a)   if the order amends the relevant order otherwise than by substituting a new petty sessions area or a new place for the one specified in the relevant order, give copies of the amending order to the responsible officer;

(b)   if the order amends the relevant order in the manner excepted by paragraph (a) above, send to the clerk to the justices for the new petty sessions area or, as the case may be, for the petty sessions area in which the new place is situated—

(i)   copies of the amending order; and

(ii)   such documents and information relating to the case as he considers likely to be of assistance to a court acting for that area in exercising its functions in relation to the order;

and in a case falling within paragraph (b) above the clerk to the justices for that area shall give copies of the amending order to the responsible officer.

(2)   A responsible officer to whom in accordance with sub-paragraph (1) above copies of an order are given shall give a copy to the offender and to the person in charge of any institution in which the offender is or was required by the order to reside.

Section 16   **SCHEDULE 3**

RECIPROCAL ENFORCEMENT OF CERTAIN ORDERS

PART I   TRANSFER OF COMMUNITY ORDERS TO SCOTLAND OR NORTHERN IRELAND

Probation orders: Scotland

1.—(1)   Where a court considering the making of a probation order is satisfied that the offender resides in Scotland, or will be residing there when the order comes into force, section 2 of the 1973 Act (probation orders) shall have effect as if after subsection (1) there were inserted the following subsection—

"(1A)   A court shall not make a probation order in respect of any offender unless it is satisfied that suitable arrangements for his supervision can be made by the regional or islands council in whose area he resides, or will be residing when the order comes into force."

(2)   Where a probation order has been made and—

(a)   a magistrates' court acting for the petty sessions area specified in the order is satisfied that the offender proposes to reside or is residing in Scotland; and

(b)   it appears to the court that suitable arrangements for his supervision can be made by the regional or islands council in whose area he proposes to reside or is residing,

the power of the court to amend the order under Part IV of Schedule 2 to this Act shall include power to amend it by requiring him to be supervised in accordance with arrangements so made.

(3)   Where a court is considering the making or amendment of a probation order in accordance with this paragraph, Schedule 1A to the 1973 Act (additional requirements in probation orders) shall have effect as if—

(a)   any reference to a probation officer were a reference to an officer of the regional or islands council in whose area the offender resides or will be residing when the order or amendment comes into force;

(b)   the reference in paragraph 2(5) to the probation committee for the area in which the premises are situated were a reference to the regional or islands council for that area;

(c)   paragraph 3 (requirements as to attendance at probation centre) were omitted; and

(d)   the reference in paragraph 5(3) to a mental hospital were a reference to a hospital within the meaning of the Mental Health (Scotland) Act 1984, not being a State hospital within the meaning of that Act.

(4)   A probation order made or amended in accordance with this paragraph shall—

(a)   specify the locality in Scotland in which the offender resides or will be residing when the order or amendment comes into force; and

(b)   specify as the appropriate court for the purposes of subsection (2) of section 183 or 384 of the Criminal Procedure (Scotland) Act 1975 a court of summary jurisdiction (which, in the case of an offender convicted on indictment, shall be the sheriff court) having jurisdiction in the locality specified under paragraph (a) above.

Probation orders: Northern Ireland

2.—(1)   Where a court considering the making of a probation order is satisfied that the offender resides in Northern Ireland, or will be residing there when the order comes into force, section 2 of the 1973 Act shall have effect as if after subsection (1) there were inserted the following subsection—

"(1A)   A court shall not make a probation order in respect of any offender unless it is satisfied that suitable arrangements for his supervision can be made by the Probation Board for Northern Ireland."

(2)   Where a probation order has been made and—

(a)   a magistrates' court acting for the petty sessions area specified in the order is satisfied that the offender proposes to reside or is residing in Northern Ireland; and

(b)   it appears to the court that suitable arrangements for his supervision can be made by the Probation Board for Northern Ireland,

the power of the court to amend the order under Part IV of Schedule 2 to this Act shall include power to amend it by requiring him to be supervised in accordance with arrangements so made.

(3)   Where a court is considering the making or amendment of a probation order in accordance with this paragraph, Schedule 1A to the 1973 Act shall have effect as if—

(a)   any reference to a probation officer were a reference to a probation officer assigned to the petty sessions district in Northern Ireland in which the offender resides or will be residing when the order or amendment comes into force;

(b)   the reference in paragraph 2(5) to the probation committee for the area in which the premises are situated were a reference to the Probation Board for Northern Ireland;

(c)   references in paragraph 3 to a probation centre were references to a day centre within the meaning of section 2B of the Probation Act (Northern Ireland) 1950; and

(d)   the reference in paragraph 5(3) to treatment as a resident patient in a mental hospital were a reference to treatment (whether as an in-patient or an out-patient) at such hospital as may be specified in the order, being a hospital within the meaning of the Health and Personal Social Services (Northern Ireland) Order 1972, approved by the Department of Health and Social Services for Northern Ireland for the purposes of section 2 of the Probation Act (Northern Ireland) 1950.

(4)   A probation order made or amended in accordance with this paragraph shall specify the petty sessions district in Northern Ireland in which the offender resides or will be residing when the order or amendment comes into force.

Community service orders: Scotland

3.—(1)   Where a court considering the making of a community service order is satisfied that the offender resides in Scotland, or will be residing there when the order comes into force, section 14 of the 1973 Act shall have effect as if for subsection (2A) there were substituted the following subsection—

"(2A)   A court shall not make a community service order in respect of any offender unless—

(a)   the court has been notified by the Secretary of State that arrangements exist for persons who reside in the locality in Scotland in which the offender resides, or will be residing when the order comes into force, to perform work under community service orders made under section 1 of the Community Service by Offenders (Scotland) Act 1978; and

(b)   it appears to the court that provision can be made for him to perform work under those arrangements."

(2)   Where a community service order has been made and—

(a)   a magistrates' court acting for a petty sessions area for the time being specified in it is satisfied that the offender proposes to reside or is residing in Scotland;

(b)   the court has been notified by the Secretary of State that arrangements exist for persons who reside in the locality in Scotland in which the offender proposes to reside or is residing to perform work under community service orders made under section 1 of the Community Service by Offenders (Scotland) Act 1978; and

(c)   it appears to the court that provision can be made for him to perform work under the community service order under those arrangements,
it may amend the order by specifying that the unpaid work required to be performed by the order be so performed.

(3)   A community service order made or amended in accordance with this paragraph shall—

(a)   specify the locality in Scotland in which the offender resides or will be residing when the order or amendment comes into force; and

(b)   require the regional or islands council in whose area the locality specified under paragraph (a) above is situated to appoint or assign an officer who will discharge in respect of the order the functions in respect of community service orders conferred on the local authority officer by the Community Service by Offenders (Scotland) Act 1978.

Community service orders: Northern Ireland

4.—(1)   Where a court considering the making of a community service order is satisfied that the offender resides in Northern Ireland, or will be residing there when the order comes into force, section 14 of the 1973 Act shall have effect—

(a)   in the case of an offender aged sixteen, as if the reference in subsection (1A) to 240 hours were a reference to 120 hours; and

(b)   in any case, as if for subsection (2A) there were substituted the following subsection—

"(2A)   A court shall not make a community service order in respect of any offender unless it appears to the court that provision can be made by the Probation Board for Northern Ireland for him to perform work under the order."

(2)   Where a community service order has been made and—

(a)   a magistrates' court acting for a petty sessions area for the time being specified in it is satisfied that the offender proposes to reside or is residing in Northern Ireland; and

(b)   it appears to the court that provision can be made by the Probation Board for Northern Ireland for him to perform work under the order,
it may amend the order by specifying that the unpaid work required to be performed by the order be so performed and, where the offender is aged sixteen, by making any such reduction in the aggregate number of hours specified in the order as is required by sub-paragraph (1)(a) above.

(3)   A community service order made or amended in accordance with this paragraph shall—

(a)   specify the petty sessions district in Northern Ireland in which the offender resides or will be residing when the order or amendment comes into force; and

(b)   require the Probation Board for Northern Ireland to select an officer who will discharge in respect of the order the functions in respect of community service orders conferred on the relevant officer by the Treatment of Offenders (Northern Ireland) Order 1976.

Combination orders: Scotland

5.   Paragraphs 1 and 3 above shall apply in relation to combination orders—
(a)   in so far as they impose such a requirement as is mentioned in paragraph (a) of subsection (1) of section 11 of this Act, as if they were probation orders; and
(b)   in so far as they impose such a requirement as is mentioned in paragraph (b) of that subsection, as if they were community service orders.

General

6.—(1)   Where a community order is made or amended in any of the circumstances specified in this Schedule, the court which makes or amends the order shall send three copies of it as made or amended to the home court, together with such documents and information relating to the case as it considers likely to be of assistance to that court.
(2)   Where a community order is made or amended in any of the circumstances specified in this Schedule, then, subject to the following provisions of this paragraph—
(a)   the order shall be treated as if it were a corresponding order made in the part of the United Kingdom in which the offender resides, or will be residing at the relevant time; and
(b)   the legislation relating to such orders which has effect in that part of the United Kingdom shall apply accordingly.
(3)   Before making or amending a community order in those circumstances the court shall explain to the offender in ordinary language—
(a)   the requirements of the legislation relating to corresponding orders which has effect in the part of the United Kingdom in which he resides or will be residing at the relevant time;
(b)   the powers of the home court under that legislation, as modified by this paragraph; and
(c)   its own powers under this paragraph,
and an explanation given in accordance with this sub-paragraph shall be sufficient without the addition of an explanation under section 2(3) or 14(5) of the 1973 Act.
(4)   The home court may exercise in relation to the community order any power which it could exercise in relation to a corresponding order made by a court in the part of the United Kingdom in which the home court exercises jurisdiction, by virtue of the legislation relating to such orders which has effect in that part, except the following, namely—
(a)   in the case of a probation order or a combination order, a power conferred by section 186(2)(b), 187, 387(2)(b) or 388 of, or paragraph 1 of Schedule 5 to, the Criminal Procedure (Scotland) Act 1975;
(b)   in the case of a probation order, a power conferred by section 4(3)(d) or (4B)(d) or 6 of, or paragraph 1 of Schedule 2 to, the Probation Act (Northern Ireland) 1950; and

(c)   in the case of a community service order—

(i)   a power conferred by section 4(2)(b) or 5(1)(c) or (d) of the Community Service by Offenders (Scotland) Act 1978;

(ii)   a power conferred by Article 9(3)(a) or (b) or 5(b) or 10 of the Treatment of Offenders (Northern Ireland) Order 1976; or

(iii)   a power to vary the order by substituting for the number of hours of work specified in it any greater number than the court which made the order could have specified.

(5)   If at any time while legislation relating to corresponding orders which has effect in Scotland or Northern Ireland applies by virtue of sub-paragraph (2) above to a community order made in England and Wales—

(a)   it appears to the home court—

(i)   if that court is in Scotland, on evidence on oath from the local authority officer concerned; and

(ii)   if it is in Northern Ireland, upon a complaint being made to a justice of the peace acting for the petty sessions district for the time being specified in the order,

that the offender has failed to comply with any of the requirements of the legislation applicable to the order; or

(b)   it appears to the home court on the application of the offender or—

(i)   if that court is in Scotland, of the local authority officer concerned; and

(ii)   if it is in Northern Ireland, of the probation officer concerned,

that it would be in the interests of justice for a power conferred by paragraph 7 or 8 of Schedule 2 to this Act to be exercised,

the home court may require the offender to appear before the court which made the order.

(6)   Where an offender is required by virtue of sub-paragraph (5) above to appear before the court which made the community order, that court—

(a)   may issue a warrant for his arrest; and

(b)   may exercise any power which it could exercise in respect of the community order if the offender resided in England and Wales,

and any enactment relating to the exercise of such powers shall have effect accordingly, and with any reference to the responsible officer being construed as a reference to the local authority or probation officer concerned.

(7)   Where an offender is required by virtue of paragraph (a) of sub-paragraph (5) above to appear before the court which made the community order—

(a)   the home court shall send to that court a certificate certifying that the offender has failed to comply with such of the requirements of the order as may be specified in the certificate, together with such other particulars of the case as may be desirable; and

(b)   a certificate purporting to be signed by the clerk of the home court shall be admissible as evidence of the failure before the court which made the order.

(8)   In this paragraph—

"corresponding order", in relation to a combination order, means a probation order including such a requirement as is mentioned in subsection

(5A) of section 183 or 384 of the Criminal Procedure (Scotland) Act 1975;
"home-court" means—

(a)   if the offender resides in Scotland, or will be residing there at the relevant time, the sheriff court having jurisdiction in the locality in which he resides or proposes to reside; and

(b)   if he resides in Northern Ireland, or will be residing there at the relevant time, the court of summary jurisdiction acting for the petty sessions district in which he resides or proposes to reside;

"the local authority officer concerned", in relation to an offender, means the officer of a regional or islands council responsible for his supervision or, as the case may be, discharging in relation to him the functions assigned by the Community Service by Offenders (Scotland) Act 1978;

"the probation officer concerned", in relation to an offender, means the probation officer responsible for his supervision or, as the case may be, discharging in relation to him the functions conferred by Part III of the Treatment of Offenders (Northern Ireland) Order 1976;

"the relevant time" means the time when the order of the amendment to it comes into force.

PART II   TRANSFER OF CORRESPONDING ORDERS FROM SCOTLAND

Probation orders

7.—(1)   The Criminal Procedure (Scotland) Act 1975 shall be amended as follows.

(2)   In each of sections 183 and 384 (which provide, respectively, for probation orders in solemn and in summary proceedings), in subsection (1A) for the words "by the local authority in whose area he resides or is to reside" there shall be substituted the following paragraphs—

"(a)   in a case other than that mentioned in paragraph (b) below, by the local authority in whose area he resides or is to reside; or

(b)   in a case where, by virtue of section 188(1) of this Act, subsection (2) of this section would not apply, by the probation committee for the area which contains the petty sessions area which would be named in the order".

(3)   In each of sections 188 and 389 (which provide, respectively, for probation orders relating to persons residing in England being made in solemn and in summary proceedings)—

(a)   in subsection (1)—

(i)   for the words "that the offender shall perform unpaid work" there shall be substituted the words "which, while corresponding to a requirement mentioned in paragraph 2 or 3 of Schedule 1A to the Powers of Criminal Courts Act 1973, would if included in a probation order made under that Act fail to accord with a restriction as to days of presentation, participation or attendance mentioned in paragraph 2(4)(a) or (6)(a), or as the case may be 3(3)(a), of that Schedule;

(ii)   for the word "17" there shall be substituted the word "16"

(iii)   the word "and", where it secondly occurs, shall cease to have effect; and

(iv)   at the end there shall be added the words "; and where the order includes a requirement that the probationer perform unpaid work for a number of hours, the number specified shall not exceed one hundred.";

(b)   in subsection (2)—

(i)   for the words "that the probationer has attained the age of 17 years and proposes to reside in or is residing in England" there shall be substituted the following paragraphs—

"(a)   that the probationer has attained the age of 16 years;

(b)   that he proposes to reside, or is residing, in England; and

(c)   that suitable arrangements for his supervision can be made by the probation committee for the area which contains the petty sessions area in which he resides or will reside"; and

(ii)   after the word "section", where it secondly occurs, there shall be inserted the words "or to vary any requirement for performance of unpaid work so that such hours as remain to be worked do not exceed one hundred";

(c)   in subsection (3)—

(i)   in paragraph (a), for the words "section 3(2) of" and "section 3 of" there shall be substituted, respectively, the words "paragraph 5(3) of Schedule 1A to" and "paragraph 5 of Schedule 1A to"; and

(ii)   in paragraph (b), for the words "subsections (4) to (6) of section 3 of" there shall be substituted the words "sub-paragraphs (5) to (7) of paragraph 5 of Schedule 1A to";

(d)   in subsection (4), for the words from "the Powers" to the end of the proviso there shall be substituted the words "Schedule 2 to the Criminal Justice Act 1991 shall apply to the order—

(a)   except in the case mentioned in paragraph (b) below, as if that order were a probation order made under section 2 of the Powers of Criminal Courts Act 1973; and

(b)   in the case of an order which contains requirement such as is mentioned in subsection (5A) of section 183 or 384 of this Act, as if it were a combination order made under section 11 of the said Act of 1991:

Provided that Part III of that Schedule shall not so apply; and sub-paragraphs (3) and (4) of paragraph 3 of that Schedule shall so apply as if for the first reference in the said sub-paragraph (3) to the Crown Court there were substituted a reference to a court in Scotland and for the other references in those sub-paragraphs to the Crown Court there were substituted references to the court in Scotland."; and

(e)   in subsection (5), for the words from "for which" to "this section" there shall be substituted the words "named in a probation order made or amended under this section that the person to whom the order relates".

(4)   Sections 189 and 390 (which make further provision as to probation orders in, respectively, solemn and summary proceedings) shall cease to have effect.

Community service orders

8.   Section 6 of the Community Service by Offenders (Scotland) Act 1978 (community service orders relating to persons residing in England and Wales) shall be amended as follows—

(a)   in subsection (1)(a), for the words from "for paragraphs" to the end of paragraph (b) as substituted in section 1(2) of that Act there shall be substituted the words ", in subsection (2), paragraph (b) were omitted and for paragraph (d) there were substituted the following paragraph—"; and

(b)   in subsection (2), paragraph (b) shall cease to have effect.

Supervision requirements

9.   Section 72 of the Social Work (Scotland) Act 1968 (supervision of children moving to England and Wales or to Northern Ireland) shall be amended as follows—

(a)   in subsection (1)(b), for the words "to a juvenile court acting for the petty sessions area" there shall be substituted the following sub-paragraphs—

"(i)   in the case of residence in England and Wales, to a youth court acting for the petty sessions area (within the meaning of the Children and Young Persons Act 1969);

(ii)   in the case of residence in Northern Ireland, to a juvenile court acting for the petty sessions district (within the meaning of Part III of the Magistrates' Courts (Northern Ireland) Order 1981).";

(b)   in subsection (1A)—

(i)   for the words "The juvenile court in England or Wales" there shall be substituted the words "A youth court";

(ii)   after the word "12" there shall be inserted the words ", 12A, 12AA, 12B or 12C"; and

(iii)   paragraph (a), and the word "and" immediately following that paragraph, shall cease to have effect;

(c)   in subsection (2), for the words "The juvenile court in Northern Ireland" there shall be substituted the words "A juvenile court";

(d)   in subsection (3), after the words "by a" there shall be inserted the words "youth court or, as the case may be"; and

(e)   subsection (4) shall cease to have effect.

PART III   TRANSFER OF PROBATION ORDERS FROM NORTHERN IRELAND

10.—(1)   Where, in the case of an offender of or over the age of 16 years, a court in Northern Ireland considering the making of a probation order is satisfied that the offender resides in England and Wales, or will be residing there when the order comes into force, section 1 of the Probation Act (Northern Ireland) 1950 (probation orders) shall have effect as if after subsection (1) there were inserted the following subsection—

"(1A)   A court shall not make a probation order in respect of any offender unless it is satisfied that suitable arrangements for his supervision can be made by the probation committee for the area which contains the petty sessions area in which he resides or will reside."

(2)   Where a probation order has been made by a court in Northern Ireland and—

(a)   a court of summary jurisdiction acting for the petty sessions district in Northern Ireland for the time being specified in the order is satisfied that the offender has attained the age of 16 years and proposes to reside or is residing in England and Wales; and

(b)   it appears to the court that suitable arrangements for his supervision can be made by the probation committee for the area which contains the petty sessions area in which he resides or will reside,

the power of the court to amend the order under Schedule 2 to the Probation Act (Northern Ireland) 1950 shall include power to amend it by requiring him to be supervised in accordance with arrangements so made.

(3)   Where a court is considering the making or amendment of a probation order in accordance with this paragraph, sections 2, 2A and 2B of the Probation Act (Northern Ireland) 1950 shall have effect as if—

(a)   any reference to a probation officer were a reference to a probation officer assigned to the petty sessions area in England and Wales in which the offender resides or will be residing when the order or amendment comes into force;

(b)   the reference in section 2(2) to treatment (whether as an in-patient or an out-patient) at such hospital as may be specified in the order, being a hospital within the meaning of the Health and Personal Social Services (Northern Ireland) Order 1972, approved by the Department of Health and Social Services for Nothern Ireland for the purposes of that section were a reference to treatment as a resident patient in a mental hospital within the meaning of paragraph 5 of Schedule 1A to the 1973 Act;

(c)   the reference in section 2A(5) to the Probation Board for Northern Ireland were a reference to the probation committee for the area in which the premises are situated; and

(d)   references in section 2B to a day centre were references to a probation centre within the meaning of paragraph 3 of Schedule 1A to the 1973 Act.

(4)   A probation order made or amended in accordance with this paragraph shall specify the petty sessions area in England and Wales in which the offender resides or will be residing when the order or amendment comes into force.

11.—(1)   Where a probation order is made or amended in any of the circumstances specified in paragraph 10 above, the court which makes or amends the order shall send three copies of it as made or amended to the home court, together with such documents and information relating to the case as it considers likely to be of assistance to that court.

(2)   Where a probation order is made or amended in any of the circumstances specified in paragraph 10 above, then, subject to the following provisions of this paragraph—

(a)   the order shall be treated as if it were a probation order made in England and Wales; and

(b)   the provisions relating to such orders of the 1973 Act and Schedule 2 to this Act (except paragraphs 9 and 10) shall apply accordingly.

(3)   Before making or amending a probation order in the circumstances specified in paragraph 10 above the court shall explain to the offender in ordinary language—

(a)   the requirements of the 1973 Act relating to probation orders;

(b)   the powers of the home court under that Act and Schedule 2 to this Act, as modified by this paragraph; and

(c)   its own powers under this paragraph,
and an explanation given in accordance with this sub-paragraph shall be sufficient without the addition of an explanation under section 1(5) of the Probation Act (Northern Ireland) 1950.

(4)   The home court may exercise in relation to the probation order any power which it could exercise in relation to a probation order made by a court in England and Wales by virtue of the 1973 Act, except a power conferred by paragraph 3(1)(d), 4(1)(d), 7(2) or 8(2) of Schedule 2 to this Act.

(5)   If at any time while the 1973 Act applies by virtue of sub-paragraph (2) above to a probation order made in Northern Ireland it appears to the home court—

(a)   on information to a justice of the peace acting for the petty sessions area for the time being specified in the order, that the offender has failed to comply with any of the requirements of the 1973 Act applicable to the order; or

(b)   on the application of the offender or the probation officer, that it would be in the interests of justice for the power conferred by paragraph 1 of Schedule 2 to the Probation Act (Northern Ireland) 1950 to be exercised,
the home court may require the offender to appear before the court which made the order.

(6)   Where an offender is required by virtue of sub-paragraph (5) above to appear before the court which made the probation order, that court—

(a)   may issue a warrant for his arrest; and

(b)   may exercise any power which it could exercise in respect of the probation order if the offender resided in Northern Ireland,
and section 4(2) to (7) of the Probation Act (Northern Ireland) 1950 shall have effect accordingly.

(7)   Where an offender is required by virtue of paragraph (a) of sub-paragraph (5) above to appear before the court which made the probation order—

(a)   the home court shall send to that court a certificate certifying that the offender has failed to comply with such of the requirements of the order as may be specified in the certificate, together with such other particulars of the case as may be desirable; and

(b)   a certificate purporting to be signed by the clerk of the home court shall be admissible as evidence of the failure before the court which made the order.

(8)   In this paragraph "home court" means, if the offender resides in England and Wales, or will be residing there at the time when the order or the amendment to it comes into force, the court of summary jurisdiction acting for the petty sessions area in which he resides or proposes to reside.

SCHEDULE 4

INCREASE OF CERTAIN MAXIMA

PART I   SUBSTITUTION OF OTHER AMOUNTS

(1) Provision	(2) General description	(3) Present amount	(4) New amount
In Schedule 5A to the Army Act 1955 and the Air Force Act 1955, paragraph 11(2).	Maximum amount of compensation order.	£2,000	£5,000
Section 23(3) of the Attachment of Earnings Act 1971.	Maximum judge's fine in High Court or county court.	£100	£250
Section 27(3) of the 1973 Act	Maximum fine for failure to comply with suspended sentence supervision order.	£400	£1,000
Section 8(1) of the Armed Forces Act 1976.	Maximum fine awarded by Standing Civilian Courts.	£2,000	£5,000
Section 40(1) of the 1980 Act.	Maximum amount of compensation order.	£2,000	£5,000
Section 63(3)(a) of that Act.	Maximum fine for disobedience of order other than for payment of money.	£2,000	£5,000
Section 97(4) of that Act.	Maximum fine for refusal to give evidence.	£1,000	£2,500
Section 12(2) of the Contempt of Court Act 1981.	Maximum fine for contempt in face of magistrates' court.	£1,000	£2,500
Section 14(2) of that Act.	Maximum fine for contempt in an inferior court.	£1,000	£2,500
Section 55(2) of the County Courts Act 1984.	Maximum fine for neglecting witness summons.	£400	£1,000
Section 118(1) of that Act.	Maximum fine for contempt of court.	£1,000	£2,500
Section 10(1) and (2) and 21(5) of the Coroners Act 1988.	Maximum coroner's fine for refusal to give evidence etc.	£400	£1,000

PART II SUBSTITUTION OF LEVELS ON STANDARD SCALE

(1) Provision	(2) General description	(3) Present amount	(4) Level on standard scale
Section 33(1)(a) of the 1980 Act.	Maximum fine on summary conviction of offence tried in pursuance of section 22 of that Act (certain offences triable either way to be tried summarily if value involved is small).	£1,000	Level 4
Section 34(3)(b) of that Act.	Maximum fine on summary conviction where statute provides no express power to fine.	£400	Level 3

PART III SUBSTITUTION OF STATUTORY MAXIMUM

(1) Provision	(2) General description	(3) Present amount
Section 6(8) of the Whaling Industry (Regulation) Act 1934.	Maximum fine on summary conviction for failure to keep or falsify records.	£1,000
Section 9(1) of that Act.	Maximum fine on summary conviction for forgery of certain documents.	£1,000
Section 11(1)(c) of the Sea Fisheries (Conservation Act 1967.	Maximum fine on summary conviction for an offence under section 1, 2, 4(7), or (7A), 4A(7) or (8), 6(5) or (5A)(b) or 7(3) of that Act.	£1,000
Section 16(1A) of that Act.	Maximum fine on summary conviction for assaulting or obstructing officer exercising enforcement powers.	£1,000
Section 5(4) of the Sea Fisheries Act 1968.	Maximum fine on summary conviction for contravening order regulating fishing operations.	£1,000

PART IV   PROVISIONS SUBSTITUTED FOR SCHEDULE 6A TO 1980 ACT

"SCHEDULE 6A

FINES THAT MAY BE ALTERED UNDER SECTION 143

Enactment	Maximum fine
CHILDREN AND YOUNG PERSONS ACT 1969 (c. 54)	
Section 15(3)(a) (failure to comply with supervision order)	£1,000
Section 15(5)(b) and (c) (failure to comply with supervision order)	£5,000
ATTACHMENT OF EARNINGS ACT 1971 (c. 32)	
Section 23(3) (judge's fine)	£250
POWERS OF CRIMINAL COURTS ACT 1973 (c. 62)	
Section 27(3) (failure to comply with suspended sentence supervision order)	£1,000
MAGISTRATES' COURTS ACT 1980 (c. 43)	
Section 63(3)(a) (disobedience of orders other than payment of money)	£5,000
Section 97(4) (refusal to give evidence etc.)	£2,500
CONTEMPT OF COURT ACT 1981 (c. 49)	
Section 12(2) (contempt in face of magistrates' court)	£2,500
Section 14(2) (contempt in an inferior court)	£2,500
CRIMINAL JUSTICE ACT 1982 (c. 48)	
Section 19(3) (failure to comply with attendance centre order or attendance centre rules)	£1,000
COUNTY COURTS ACT 1984 (c. 28)	
Section 55(2) (neglect or refusal to give evidence)	£1,000
Section 118(1) (contempt in face of court)	£2,500
CORONERS ACT 1988 (c. 13)	
Sections 10(1) and (2) and 21(5) (refusal to give evidence etc.)	£1,000
CRIMINAL JUSTICE ACT 1991 (c. 53)	
In Schedule 2, paragraphs 3(1) and 4(1) (failure to comply with probation, community service, curfew or combination order)	£1,000".

PART V

[Repealed by the CJA 1993, sch. 3, para. 1(2), and sch. 6, part I.]

Section 37(7).   SCHEDULE 5

THE PAROLE BOARD

Membership

1.   The Board shall consist of a chairman and not less than four other members appointed by the Secretary of State.

2.   The Board shall include among its members—
    (a)   a person who holds or has held judicial office;
    (b)   a registered medical practitioner who is a psychiatrist;
    (c)   a person appearing to the Secretary of State to have knowledge and experience of the supervision or after-care of discharged prisoners; and
    (d)   a person appearing to the Secretary of State to have made a study of the causes of delinquency or the treatment of offenders.

3.   A member of the Board—
    (a)   shall hold and vacate office in accordance with the terms of his appointment;
    (b)   may resign his office by notice in writing addressed to the Secretary of State;
and a person who ceases to hold office as a member of the Board shall be eligible for reappointment.

Remuneration and allowances

4.   There shall be paid to the members of the Board such remuneration and allowances as the Secretary of State may with the consent of the Treasury determine.

5.   The expenses of the Board under paragraph 4 above and any other expenses incurred by the Board in discharging its functions under Part II of this Act shall be defrayed by the Secretary of State.

Reports

6.   The Board shall as soon as practicable after the end of each year make to the Secretary of State a report on the performance of its functions during that year; and the Secretary of State shall lay a copy of the report before Parliament.

Section 53(5).   SCHEDULE 6

NOTICE OF TRANSFER: PROCEDURE IN LIEU OF COMMITTAL

Contents of notice of transfer

1.—(1)   A notice of transfer shall specify the proposed place of trial; and in selecting that place the Director of Public Prosecutions shall have regard to the considerations to which a magistrates' court committing a person for trial is required by section 7 of the 1980 Act to have regard when selecting the place at which he is to be tried.

(2)   A notice of transfer shall specify the charge or charges to which it relates and include or be accompanied by such additional material as regulations under paragraph 4 below may require.

Remand

2.—(1)   If a magistrates' court has remanded in custody a person to whom a notice of transfer relates, it shall have power, subject to section 4 of the Bail Act 1976 and regulations under section 22 of the Prosecution of Offences Act 1985—

(a)   to order that he shall be safely kept in custody until delivered in due course of law; or

(b)   to release him on bail in accordance with the Bail Act 1976, that is to say, by directing him to appear before the Crown Court for trial.

(2)   Where—

(a)   a person's release on bail under paragraph (b) of sub-paragraph (1) above is conditional on his providing one or more sureties; and

(b)   in accordance with subsection (3) of section 8 of the Bail Act 1976, the court fixes the amount in which a surety is to be bound with a view to his entering into his recognisance subsequently in accordance with subsections (4) and (5) or (6) of that section,

the court shall in the meantime make an order such as is mentioned in paragraph (a) of that sub-paragraph.

(3)   If the conditions specified in sub-paragraph (4) below are satisfied, a court may exercise the powers conferred by sub-paragraph (1) above in relation to a person charged without his being brought before it in any case in which by virtue of subsection (3A) of section 128 of the 1980 Act it would have the power further to remand him on an adjournment such as is mentioned in that subsection.

(4)   The conditions referred to in sub-paragraph (3) above are—

(a)   that the person in question has given his written consent to the powers conferred by sub-paragraph (1) above being exercised without his being brought before the court; and

(b)   that the court is satisfied that, when he gave his consent, he knew that the notice of transfer had been issued.

(5)   Where a notice of transfer is given after a person to whom it relates has been remanded on bail to appear before a magistrates' court on an appointed day, the requirement that he shall so appear shall cease on the giving of the notice unless the notice states that it is to continue.

(6)   Where that requirement ceases by virtue of sub-paragraph (5) above, it shall be the duty of the person in question to appear before the Crown Court at the place specified by the notice of transfer as the proposed place of trial or at any place substituted for it by a direction under section 76 of the Supreme Court Act 1981.

(7)   If, in a case where the notice states that the requirement mentioned in sub-paragraph (5) above is to continue, a person to whom the notice relates appears before the magistrates' court, the court shall have—

(a)   the powers and duties conferred on a magistrates' court by sub-paragraph (1) above but subject as there provided; and

(b)   power to enlarge, in the surety's absence, a recognisance conditioned in accordance with section 128(4)(a) of the 1980 Act so that the surety is bound to secure that the person charged appears also before the Crown Court.

Witnesses

3.   For the purposes of the Criminal Procedure (Attendance of Witnesses) Act 1965—

(a)   any magistrates' court for the petty sessions area for which the court from which a case was transferred sits shall be treated as examining magistrates; and

(b)   a person indicated in the notice of transfer as a proposed witness shall be treated as a person who has been examined by the court.

Regulations

4.—(1)   The Attorney General—

(a)   shall by regulations make provision requiring a copy of a notice of transfer, together with a statement of the evidence on which any charge to which it relates is based, to be given—

(i)   to any person to whom the notice of transfer relates; and

(ii)   to the Crown Court sitting at the place specified by the notice of transfer as the proposed place of trial; and

(b)   may by regulations make such further provision in relation to notices of transfer, including provision as to the duties of the Director of Public Prosecutions in relation to such notices, as appears to him to be appropriate.

(2)   The power to make regulations under this paragraph shall be exercisable by statutory instrument subject to annulment in pursuance of a resolution of either House of Parliament.

Applications for dismissal

5.—(1)   Where a notice of transfer has been given, any person to whom the notice relates may, at any time before he is arraigned (and whether or not an indictment has been preferred against him), apply orally or in writing to the Crown Court sitting at the place specified by the notice of transfer as the proposed place of trial for the charge, or any of the charges, in the case to be dismissed.

(2)   The judge shall dismiss a charge (and accordingly quash a count relating to it in any indictment preferred against the applicant) which is the subject of any such application if it appears to him that the evidence against the applicant would not be sufficient for a jury properly to convict him.

(3)   No oral application may be made under sub-paragraph (1) above unless the applicant has given the Crown Court mentioned in that sub-paragraph written notice of his intention to make the application.

(4)   Oral evidence may be given on such an application only with the leave of the judge or by his order; and the judge shall give leave or make an order only if it appears to him, having regard to any matters stated in the application for leave, that the interests of justice require him to do so.

(5)   No leave or order under sub-paragraph (4) above shall be given or made in relation to oral evidence from a child (within the meaning of section 53 of this Act) who is alleged—

(a)   to be a person against whom an offence to which the notice of transfer relates was committed; or

(b)   to have witnessed the commission of such an offence.

(6)   If the judge gives leave permitting, or makes an order requiring, a person to give oral evidence, but that person does not do so, the judge may disregard any document indicating the evidence that he might have given.

(7)   Dismissal of the charge, or all the charges, against the applicant shall have the same effect as a refusal by examining magistrates to commit for trial, except that no further proceedings may be brought on a dismissed charge except by means of the preferment of a voluntary bill of indictment.

(8)   Crown Court Rules may make provision for the purposes of this paragraph and, without prejudice to the generality of this sub-paragraph, may make provision—

(a)   as to the time or state in the proceedings at which anything required to be done is to be done (unless the court grants leave to do it at some other time or stage);

(b)   as to the contents and form of notices or other documents;

(c)   as to the manner in which evidence is to be submitted; and

(d)   as to persons to be served with notices or other material.

Reporting restrictions

6.—(1)   Except as provided by this paragraph, it shall not be lawful—

(a)   to publish in Great Britain a written report of an application under paragraph 5(1) above; or

(b)   to include in a relevant programme for reception in Great Britain a report of such an application,

if (in either case) the report contains any matter other than that permitted by this paragraph.

(2)   An order that sub-paragraph (1) above shall not apply to reports of an application under paragraph 5(1) above may be made by the judge dealing with the application.

(3)   Where in the case of two or more accused one of them objects to the making of an order under sub-paragraph (2) above, the judge shall make the order if, and only if, he is satisfied, after hearing the representations of the accused, that it is in the interests of justice to do so.

(4)   An order under sub-paragraph (2) above shall not apply to reports of proceedings under sub-paragraph (3) above, but any decision of the court to make or not to make such an order may be contained in reports published or included in a relevant programme before the time authorised by sub-paragraph (5) below.

(5)   It shall not be unlawful under this paragraph to publish or include in a relevant programme a report of an application under paragraph 5(1) above containing any matter other than that permitted by sub-paragraph (8) below where the application is successful.

(6)   Where—

(a) two or more persons were jointly charged; and
(b) applications under paragraph 5(1) above are made by more than one of them,
sub-paragraph (5) above shall have effect as if for the words "the application is" there were substituted the words "all the applications are".

(7) It shall not be unlawful under this paragraph to publish or include in a relevant programme a report of an unsuccessful application at the conclusion of the trial of the person charged, or of the last of the persons charged to be tried.

(8) The following matters may be contained in a report published or included in a relevant programme without an order under sub-paragraph (2) above before the time authorised by sub-paragraphs (5) and (6) above, that is to say—
(a) the identity of the court and the name of the judge;
(b) the names, ages, home addresses and occupations of the accused and witnesses;
(c) the offence or offences, or a summary of them, with which the accused is or are charged;
(d) the names of counsel and solicitors engaged in the proceedings;
(e) where the proceedings are adjourned, the date and place to which they are adjourned;
(f) the arrangements as to bail;
(g) whether legal aid was granted to the accused or any of the accused.

(9) The addresses that may be published or included in a relevant programme under sub-paragraph (8) above are addresses—
(a) at any relevant time; and
(b) at the time of their publication or inclusion in a relevant programme.

(10) If a report is published or included in a relevant programme in contravention of this paragraph, the following persons, that is to say—
(a) in the case of a publication of a written report as part of a newspaper or periodical, any proprietor, editor or publisher of the newspaper or periodical;
(b) in the case of a publication of a written report otherwise than as part of a newspaper or periodical, the person who publishes it;
(c) in the case of the inclusion of a report in a relevant programme, any body corporate which is engaged in providing the service in which the programme is included and any person having functions in relation to the programme corresponding to those of the editor of a newspaper;
shall be liable on summary conviction to a fine not exceeding level 5 on the standard scale.

(11) Proceedings for an offence under this paragraph shall not, in England and Wales, be instituted otherwise than by or with the consent of the Attorney General.

(12) Sub-paragraph (1) above shall be in addition to, and not in derogation from, the provisions of any other enactment with respect to the publication of reports of court proceedings.

(13) In this paragraph—
"publish", in relation to a report, means publish the report, either by itself or as part of a newspaper or periodical, for distribution to the public;
"relevant programme" means a programme included in a programme service (within the meaning of the Broadcasting Act 1990);

"relevant time" means a time when events giving rise to the charges to which the proceedings relate occurred.

Avoidance of delay

7.—(1) Where a notice of transfer has been given in relation to any case—

(a) the Crown Court before which the case is to be tried; and

(b) any magistrates' court which exercises any functions under paragraph 2 or 3 above or section 20(4) of the Legal Aid Act 1988 in relation to the case,

shall, in exercising any of its powers in relation to the case, have regard to the desirability of avoiding prejudice to the welfare of any relevant child witness that may be occasioned by unnecessary delay in bringing the case to trial.

(2) In this paragraph "child" has the same meaning as in section 53 of this Act and "relevant child witness" means a child who will be called as a witness at the trial and who is alleged—

(a) to be a person against whom an offence to which the notice of transfer relates was committed; or

(b) to have witnessed the commission of such an offence.

Procedures for indictment of offenders

8.—(1) In subsection (2) of section 2 of the Administration of Justice (Miscellaneous Provisions) Act 1933 (procedures for indictment of offenders), after paragraph (aa), there shall be inserted the following paragraph—

"(ab) the offence is specified in a notice of transfer under section 53 of the Criminal Justice Act 1991 (violent or sexual offences against children); or".

(2) In paragraph (iA) of the proviso to that subsection—

(a) after the words "paragraph (aa)" there shall be inserted the words "or (ab)"; and

(b) for the words "regulations under section 5(9) of the Criminal Justice Act 1987" there shall be substituted the words "regulations under the relevant provision".

(3) At the end of that proviso there shall be inserted the words "and in paragraph (iA) above 'the relevant provision' means section 5(9) of the Criminal Justice Act 1987 in a case to which paragraph (aa) above applies, and paragraph 4 of Schedule 6 to the Criminal Justice Act 1991 in a case to which paragraph (ab) above applies".

Legal aid

9. In section 20(4) of the Legal Aid Act 1988 (power of magistrates' court to grant legal aid for Crown Court proceedings), in paragraph (b), after the word "cases)" there shall be inserted the words "or section 53 of the Criminal Justice Act 1991 (transfer of certain cases involving children)".

Section 66. SCHEDULE 7

PROVISIONS SUBSTITUTED FOR SECTION 15 OF 1969 ACT

"Variation and discharge of supervision orders.

15.—(1) If while a supervision order is in force in respect of a supervised person it appears to a relevant court, on the application of the supervisor or the supervised person, that it is appropriate to make an order under this subsection, the court may make an order discharging the supervision order or varying it—

(a) by cancelling any requirement included in it in pursuance of section 12, 12A, 12AA, 12B, 12C or 18(2)(b) of this Act; or

(b) by inserting in it (either in addition to or in substitution for any of its provisions) any provision which could have been included in the order if the court had then had power to make it and were exercising the power.

(2) The powers of variation conferred by subsection (1) above do not include power—

(a) to insert in the supervision order, after the expiration of three months beginning with the date when the order was originally made, a requirement in pursuance of section 12B(1) of this Act, unless it is in substitution for such a requirement already included in the order; or

(b) to insert in the supervision order a requirement in pursuance of section 12A(3)(b) of this Act in respect of any day which falls outside the period of three months beginning with the date when the order was originally made.

(3) If while a supervision order made under section 7(7) of this Act is in force in respect of a person it is proved to the satisfaction of a relevant court, on the application of the supervisor, that the supervised person has failed to comply with any requirement included in the supervision order in pursuance of section 12, 12A, 12AA, 12C or 18(2)(b) of this Act, the court—

(a) whether or not it also makes an order under subsection (1) above, may order him to pay a fine of an amount not exceeding £1,000 or, subject to section 16A(1) of this Act, may make an attendance centre order in respect of him; or

(b) in the case of a person who has attained the age of eighteen, may (if it also discharges the supervision order) make an order imposing on him any punishment, other than a sentence of detention in a young offender institution, which it could have imposed on him if it—

(i) had then had power to try him for the offence in consequence of which the supervision order was made; and

(ii) had convicted him in the exercise of that power.

(4) If while a supervision order is in force in respect of a person it is proved to the court under subsection (3) above that the supervised person has failed to comply with any requirement included in the supervision order in pursuance of section 12A(3)(a) of this Act directing the supervised person to participate in specified activities, the court may, if it also discharges the supervision order, make an order imposing on him any sentence which it could have imposed on him if it—

(a) had then had power to try him for the offence in consequence of which the supervision order was made; and

(b) had convicted him in the exercise of that power.

(5) In a case falling within subsection (3)(b) or (4) above where the offence in question is of a kind which the court has no power to try, or has no power to try without appropriate consents, the sentence imposed by virtue of that provision—

(a)   shall not exceed that which any court having power to try such an offence could have imposed in respect of it; and

(b)   where the case falls within subsection (3)(b) above and the sentence is a fine, shall not in any event exceed £5,000; and

(c)   where the case falls within subsection (4) above, shall not in any event exceed a custodial sentence for a term of six months and a fine of £5,000.

(6)   A court may not make an order by virtue of subsection (4) above unless the court which made the supervision order made a statement under subsection (1) of section 12D of this Act; and for the purposes of this subsection a certificate under that section shall be evidence of the making of the statement to which it relates.

(7)   Section 18 of the Criminal Justice Act 1991 (fixing of certain fines by reference to units) shall apply—

(a)   for the purposes of subsection (3)(a) above as if the failure to comply with the requirement were a summary offence punishable by a fine not exceeding level 3 on the standard scale; and

(b)   for the purposes of subsection (3)(b) and (4) above as if the failure to comply with the requirement were a summary offence punishable by a fine not exceeding level 5 on that scale;

and a fine imposed under any of those provisions shall be deemed for the purposes of any enactment to be a sum adjudged to be paid by a conviction.

(8)   In dealing with a supervised person under subsection (3) or (4) above, the court shall take into account the extent to which that person has complied with the requirements of the supervision order.

(9)   If a medical practitioner by whom or under whose direction a supervised person is being treated for his mental condition in pursuance of a requirement included in a supervision order by virtue of section 12B(1) of this Act is unwilling to continue to treat or direct the treatment of the supervised person or is of opinion—

(a)   that the treatment should be continued beyond the period specified in that behalf in the order; or

(b)   that the supervised person needs different treatment; or

(c)   that he is not susceptible to treatment; or

(d)   that he does not require further treatment,

the practitioner shall make a report in writing to that effect to the supervisor.

(10)   On receiving a report under subsection (9) above, the supervisor shall refer it to a relevant court; and on such a reference, the court may make an order cancelling or varying the requirement.

(11)   In this section 'relevant court' means—

(a)   in the case of a supervised person who has not attained the age of eighteen, a youth court;

(b)   in the case of a supervised person who has attained that age, a magistrates' court other than a youth court.

(12)   The provisions of this section shall have effect subject to the provisions of section 16 of this Act."

Section 68. **SCHEDULE 8**

AMENDMENTS FOR TREATING PERSONS AGED 17 AS YOUNG PERSONS

Children and Young Persons Act 1933 (c. 12)

1.—(1) Section 31 of the 1933 Act shall be renumbered as subsection (1) of that section and after that provision as so renumbered there shall be inserted the following subsection—

"(2) In this section and section 34 of this Act, 'young person' means a person who has attained the age of fourteen and is under the age of seventeen years."

(2) In section 46(1) and (1A), 48(2) and 99(1) of that Act, for the words "the age of seventeen" there shall be substituted the words "the age of eighteen".

(3) In section 107(1) of that Act, for the definition of "young person" there shall be substituted the following definition—

"'young person' means a person who has attained the age of fourteen and is under the age of eighteen years."

Prison Act 1952 (c. 52)

2. In section 43(3) of the 1952 Act (remand centres, young offender institutions etc.), for the words "aged 17 years" there shall be substituted the words "aged 18 years".

Children and Young Persons Act 1963 (c. 37)

3. In section 29(1) of the Children and Young Persons Act 1963, for the words "the age of seventeen" there shall be substituted the words "the age of eighteen".

Children and Young Persons Act 1969 (c. 54)

4.—(1) Section 29 of the 1969 Act shall be renumbered as subsection (1) of that section and after that provision as so renumbered there shall be inserted the following subsection—

"(2) In this section 'young person' means a person who has attained the age of fourteen and is under the age of seventeen years."

(2) In section 70(1) of that Act, for the definition of "young person" there shall be substituted the following definition—

"'young person' means a person who has attained the age of fourteen and is under the age of eighteen years;".

Rehabilitation of Offenders Act 1974 (c. 53)

5. In section 5(2) of the Rehabilitation of Offenders Act 1974 (which provides for rehabilitation periods to be reduced by half for young offenders)—

(a) in paragraph (a), for the words "seventeen years of age" there shall be substituted the words "eighteen years of age"; and

(b) in the heading to Table A, for the words "under 17" there shall be substituted the words "under 18".

Magistrates' Courts Act 1980 (c. 43)

6.—(1) Part I of the 1980 Act (criminal jurisdiction and procedure) shall be amended as follows—

(a) for the words "the age of 17", in each place where they occur, there shall be substituted the words "the age of 18 years";

(b) in section 22(9), for the words "under 17" there shall be substituted the words "under 18";

(c) in section 36(1), for the words "17 years of age" there shall be substituted the words "18 years of age"; and

(d) in section 38 for the words "17 years old" there shall be substituted the words "18 years old".

(2) In section 81(1), (3) and (8) of that Act, for the words "the age of 17" there shall be substituted the words "the age of 18".

(3) In sections 96A, 135(3) and 136(4) of that Act, for the words "aged 17" there shall be substituted the words "aged 18".

Section 71.   SCHEDULE 9

AMENDMENTS TO SERVICE LAW

Army Act 1955 (c. 18) and Air Force Act 1955 (c. 19)

1. In section 71A of the Army Act 1955 and the Air Force Act 1955 (life custody for young offenders), in subsections (1B) and (4)(a), for the words "17 years" there shall be substituted the words "18 years".

2. In section 71AA of those Acts (young service offenders: custodial orders)—

(a) in subsection (1), for the words "not exceeding" there shall be substituted the words "which—

(a) shall be not less than the appropriate minimum period, that is to say—

(i) in the case of an offender who has attained eighteen years of age, the period of 21 days; or

(ii) in the case of an offender who is under that age, the period of two months; and

(b) shall not exceed";

(b) subsection (1A) and, in subsection (1), the words "subject to subsection (1A) below" shall cease to have effect;

(c) before subsection (1B) there shall be inserted the following subsection—

"(1AA) The court shall not make a custodial order committing an offender aged 17 to be detained for a period exceeding twelve months or for a period such that the continuous period for which he is committed to be detained under that order and any one or more other custodial orders exceeds twelve months."; and

(d) in subsection (6A), for the words "Section 15 of the Criminal Justice Act 1982" there shall be substituted the words "Section 65 of the Criminal Justice Act 1991".

3. For subsection (2) of section 93 of those Acts (evidence on oath in court-martial) there shall be substituted the following subsections—

"(1B) A witness before a court-martial—

(a) shall be examined on oath if he has attained the age of fourteen; and

(b) shall give evidence unsworn if he is under that age.

(2) Unsworn evidence admitted by virtue of subsection (1B)(b) above may corroborate evidence (sworn or unsworn) given by any other person."

4. In paragraph 10 of Schedule 5A to those Acts (civilian offenders: custodial orders)—

(a) in sub-paragraph (1), for the words from "detained" to "and in this sub-paragraph" there shall be substituted the words "detained for a period, to be specified in the order, which—

(a) shall not be less than the appropriate minimum period, that is to say—

(i) in the case of an offender who has attained the age of 18, the period of 21 days; or

(ii) in the case of an offender who is under 18 years of age, the period of two months;

(b) shall not exceed the maximum period for which he could have been sentenced to imprisonment if he had attained the age of 21; and

(c) if the order is made by a Standing Civilian Court, shall not exceed six months.

and in this sub-paragraph".

(b) in sub-paragraph (1A), for the words "17 years" there shall be substituted the words "18 years"; and

(c) in sub-paragraph (6A), for the words "Section 15 of the Criminal Justice Act 1982" there shall be substituted the words "Section 65 of the Criminal Justice Act 1991".

Naval Discipline Act 1957 (c. 53)

5. In section 43A of the Naval Discipline Act 1957 (life custody for young offenders), in subsections (1B) and (4)(a), for the words "17 years" there shall be substituted the words "18 years".

6. In section 43AA of that Act (young service offenders: custodial orders)—

(a) in subsection (1), for the words "not exceeding" there shall be substituted the words "which—

(a) shall be not less than the appropriate minimum period, that is to say—

(i) in the case of an offender who has attained eighteen years of age, the period of 21 days; or

(ii) in the case of an offender who is under that age, the period of two months; and

(b) shall not exceed";

(b) subsection (1A) and, in subsection (1), the words "subject to subsection (1A) below", shall cease to have effect; and

(c) before subsection (1B) there shall be inserted the following subsection—

"(1AA) The court shall not make a custodial order committing an offender aged 17 to be detained for a period exceeding twelve months or for a period such that the continuous period for which he is committed to be detained under that order and any one or more other custodial orders exceeds twelve months."; and

(d)   in subsection (6A), for the words "Section 15 of the Criminal Justice Act 1982" there shall be substituted the words "Section 65 of the Criminal Justice Act 1991".

7.   For subsections (2) and (3) of section 60 of that Act (evidence on oath in court-martial) there shall be substituted the following subsections—
    "(2)   A witness before a court-martial—
        (a)   shall be examined on oath if he has attained the age of fourteen; and
        (b)   shall give evidence unsworn if he is under that age.
    (3)   Unsworn evidence admitted by virtue of subsection (2)(b) above may corroborate evidence (sworn or unsworn) given by any other person."

8.   In paragraph 10 of Schedule 4A to that Act (civilian offenders: custodial orders)—
    (a)   in sub-paragraph (1), for the words from "detained" to "and in this sub-paragraph" there shall be substituted the words "detained for a period, to be specified in the order, which—
        (a)   shall be not less than the appropriate minimum period, that is to say—
            (i)   in the case of an offender who has attained the age of 18, the period of 21 days; or
            (ii)   in the case of an offender who is under 18 years of age, the period of two months; and
        (b)   shall not exceed the maximum period for which he could have been sentenced to imprisonment if he had attained the age of 21;
    and in this sub-paragraph";
    (b)   in sub-paragraph (1A), for the words "17 years" there shall be substituted the words "18 years"; and
    (c)   in sub-paragraph (6A), for the words "Section 15 of the Criminal Justice Act 1982" there shall be substituted the words "Section 65 of the Criminal Justice Act 1991".

Section 89.   SCHEDULE 10

CERTIFICATION OF PRISONER CUSTODY OFFICERS

Preliminary

1.   In this Schedule—
"certificate" means a certificate under section 89 of this Act;
"the relevant functions", in relation to a certificate, means the escort functions or custodial duties authorised by the certificate.

Issue of certificates

2.—(1)   Any person may apply to the Secretary of State for the issue of a certificate in respect of him.

(2)   The Secretary of State shall not issue a certificate on any such application unless he is satisfied that the applicant—

(a)   is a fit and proper person to perform the relevant functions; and

(b)   has received training to such standard as he may consider appropriate for the performance of those functions.

(3)   Where the Secretary of State issues a certificate, then, subject to any suspension under paragraph 3 or revocation under paragraph 4 below, it shall continue in force until such date or the occurrence of such event as may be specified in the certificate.

(4)   A certificate authorising the performance of both escort functions and custodial duties may specify different dates or events as respects those functions and duties respectively.

Suspension of certificate

3.—(1)   This paragraph applies where at any time it appears—

(a)   in the case of a prisoner custody officer acting in pursuance of prisoner escort arrangements, to the prisoner escort monitor for the area concerned; or

(b)   in the case of such an officer performing custodial duties at a contracted out prison, to the controller of that prison,
that the officer is not a fit and proper person to perform the escort functions or, as the case may be, custodial duties.

(2)   The prisoner escort monitor or controller may—

(a)   refer the matter to the Secretary of State for a decision under paragraph 4 below; and

(b)   in such circumstances as may be prescribed by regulations made by the Secretary of State, suspend the officer's certificate so far as it authorises the performance of escort functions or, as the case may be, custodial duties pending that decision.

(3)   The power to make regulations under this paragraph shall be exercisable by statutory instrument which shall be subject to annulment in pursuance of a resolution of either House of Parliament.

Revocation of certificate

4.   Where at any time it appears to the Secretary of State that a prisoner custody officer is not a fit and proper person to perform escort functions or custodial duties, he may revoke that officer's certificate so far as it authorises the performance of those functions or duties.

False statements

5.   If any person, for the purpose of obtaining a certificate for himself or for any other person—

(a)   makes a statement which he knows to be false in a material particular; or

(b)   recklessly makes a statement which is false in a material particular, he shall be liable on summary conviction to a fine not exceeding level 4 on the standard scale.

Section 100.   SCHEDULE 11

MINOR AND CONSEQUENTIAL AMENDMENTS

Children and Young Persons Act 1933 (c. 12)

1.   In section 38(2) of the 1933 Act (false evidence by child) for the words "as aforesaid" there shall be substituted the words "unsworn in any proceedings for an offence by virtue of section 52 of the Criminal Justice Act 1991".

Criminal Justice Act 1967 (c. 80)

2.—(1)   Section 67 of the 1967 Act (remand time to be taken into account in computing sentences) shall be amended as follows.

(2)   In subsection (1A)(c)—

(a)   after the word "remanded" there shall be inserted the words "or committed"; and

(b)   after the words "section 23 of the Children and Young Persons Act 1969" there shall be inserted the words "or section 37 of the Magistrates' Courts Act 1980".

(3)   For subsection (5) there shall be substituted the following subsection—

"(5)   This section applies—

(a)   to sentences of detention in a young offender institution; and

(b)   to determinate sentences of detention passed under section 53(2) of the Children and Young Persons Act 1933 (sentences for serious indictable offences),

as it applies to sentences of imprisonment."

(4)   In subsection (6)—

(a)   after the word "being", in the second place where it occurs, there shall be inserted the words "remanded or";

(b)   for the words "committed to the care of a local authority" there shall be substituted the words "remanded or committed to local authority accommodation"; and

(c)   after the words "the said section 23" there shall be inserted the words "or 37".

Criminal Appeal Act 1968 (c. 19)

3.   In section 10(2) of the Criminal Appeal Act 1968 (appeal against sentence in other cases dealt with by Crown Court), for paragraph (b) there shall be substituted the following paragraph—

"(b)   having been made the subject of an order for conditional discharge or a community order within the meaning of Part I of the Criminal Justice Act 1991 (other than a supervision order within the meaning of that Part) or given a suspended sentence, appears or is brought before the Crown Court to be further dealt with for his offence."

4.   In section 50(1A) of that Act (right of appeal of probationer etc.), for the words "Section 13" there shall be substituted the words "Section 1C" and the words "a probation order or" shall cease to have effect.

Civil Evidence Act 1968 (c. 64)

5.   In section 11(5)(a) of the Civil Evidence Act 1968 (convictions as evidence in civil proceedings), for the words "section 13" there shall be substituted the words "section 1C" and the words "probation or" shall cease to have effect.

Children and Young Persons Act 1969 (c. 54)

6.—(1)   In subsection (1) of section 12D of the 1969 Act (duty of court to state in certain cases that requirement is in place of custodial sentence), in paragraph (ii), for sub-paragraphs (a) to (c) there shall be substituted the following sub-paragraphs—

"(a)   the offence of which he has been convicted, or the combination of that offence and one other offence associated with it, was so serious that only a supervision order containing such a requirement or a custodial sentence can be justified for that offence; or

(b)   that offence was a violent or sexual offence and only a supervision order containing such a requirement or such a sentence would be adequate to protect the public from serious harm from him;".

(2)   After that subsection there shall be inserted the following subsection—

"(1A)   Sub-paragraphs (a) and (b) of subsection (1)(ii) above shall be construed as if they were contained in Part I of the Criminal Justice Act 1991."

Note. The CJA 1993, s. 66(7), provides as follows:

In subsection (1) of section 12D of the Children and Young Persons Act 1969 (duty of court to state in certain cases that requirement is in place of custodial sentence), in paragraph (ii)(a) for the words "other offence" there shall be substituted "or more offences".

7.—(1)   In subsection (4) of section 16 of that Act (provisions supplementary to section 15), for the words "a court" there shall be substituted the words "a youth court".

(2)   In subsection (6)(b) of that section, for the words "subsection (5)" there shall be substituted the words "subsection (10)".

(3)   In subsection (10) of that section, for the words "paragraph (b) of subsection (2A) and paragraph (a) of subsection (4)" there shall be substituted the words "paragraph (a) of subsection (3)".

8.—(1)   In subsection (1) of section 16A of that Act (application of sections 17 to 19 of the 1982 Act), for the words "section 15(2A)(b) and (4)(a)" there shall be substituted the words "section 15(3)(a)".

(2)   In subsection (2) of that section, for the words "each of those paragraphs" there shall be substituted the words "section 15(3)(a) of this Act".

Vehicles (Excise) Act 1971 (c. 10)

9.   In section 9(5) of the Vehicles (Excise) Act 1971 (additional liability for keeping unlicensed vehicle), for the words "Part I of the Criminal Justice Act

1948" there shall be substituted the words "section 1C of the Powers of Criminal Courts Act 1973" and the words "placing him on probation or" shall cease to have effect.

Powers of Criminal Courts Act 1973 (c. 62)

10.   In section 11(2) of the 1973 Act (substitution of conditional discharge for probation) for the words "section 8 of this Act" there shall be substituted the words "paragraph 7 of Schedule 2 to the Criminal Justice Act 1991".

11.   In section 12 of that Act (supplementary provisions as to probation and discharge)—
(a)   in subsection (2), for the words "section 2(7) and paragraph 1 of Schedule 1" there shall be substituted the words "section 2(4)";
(b)   in subsection (4), for the words "section 2 or 7" there shall be substituted the words "section 1A or 2".

12.   In section 14 of that Act (community service orders)—
(a)   in subsection (4), for the words "section 17(5) of this Act" there shall be substituted the words "Part IV of Schedule 2 to the Criminal Justice Act 1991";
(b)   in subsection (5)(b), for the words "section 16" there shall be substituted the words "Part II of Schedule 2 to the Criminal Justice Act 1991"; and
(c)   in subsection (5)(c), for the words "section 17" there shall be substituted the words "Part III and IV of that Schedule".

13.   In section 15(2) of that Act (obligations of person subject to community service order), for the words "section 17(1) of this Act" there shall be substituted the words "paragraph 15 of Schedule 2 to the Criminal Justice Act 1991".

14.   In section 31(3C) of that Act (maximum periods of imprisonment in default of payment of Crown Court fine), for the words "five days" there shall be substituted the words "seven days".

15.   In section 58 of that Act (application to Scotland), for the words "sections 8(4), 10, 13, 17C, 25(3), 29(7)" there shall be substituted the words "sections 1C, 25(3) and 29(7)".

16.   In section 59 of that Act (application to Northern Ireland), for the words "Sections 17C and 29(7)" there shall be substituted the words "Section 29(7)".

17.—(1)   In paragraph 2(2)(a) of Schedule 3 to that Act (the probation service and its functions), the word "several" shall cease to have effect.
(2)   In paragraph 8(1) of that Schedule, after the words "any person" there shall be inserted the words "and to make reports on such matters".

Juries Act 1974 (c. 23)

18.—(1)   In Schedule 1 to the Juries Act 1974, Group B (which disqualifies from jury service persons concerned with the administration of justice) shall be amended as follows.

(2)   After the entry relating to a shorthandwriter in any court, there shall be inserted the following entry—
  "A court security officer within the meaning of Part IV of the Criminal Justice Act 1991."

(3)   After the entry relating to governors, chaplains, medical officers and other officers of penal establishments and members of boards of visitors for such establishments, there shall be inserted the following entry—
  "Prisoner custody officers within the meaning of Part IV of the Criminal Justice Act 1991."

Solicitors Act 1974 (c. 47)

19.   In section 43(7) of the Solicitors Act 1974 (control of employment of certain clerks), for the words "placing a person on probation or discharging him" there shall be substituted the words "discharging a person" and for the words "section 13" there shall be substituted the words "section 1C".

Rehabilitation of Offenders Act 1974 (c. 53)

20.   In section 1(4) of the Rehabilitation of Offenders Act 1974 (rehabilitated persons and spent convictions)—
  (a)   for the words "section 13" there shall be substituted the words "section 1C";
  (b)   the words "put on probation or" shall cease to have effect; and
  (c)   for the words "placing the person concerned on probation or discharging him" there shall be substituted the words "discharging the person concerned".

Bail Act 1976 (c. 63)

21.   In section 4(3) of the Bail Act 1976 (general right to bail of accused persons and others), for the words "section 6 or section 16 of the Powers of Criminal Courts Act 1973 (breach of requirement of probation or community service order)" there shall be substituted the words "Part II of Schedule 2 to the Criminal Justice Act 1991 (breach of requirement of probation, community service, combination or curfew order)".

22.—(1)   Paragraph 8 of Schedule 1 to that Act (restrictions on the imposition of bail conditions) shall be amended as follows.

(2)   In sub-paragraph (1), after the words "(4) to (7)" there shall be inserted the words "(except subsection (6)(d))" and the words from "or, in the case" to the end shall cease to have effect.

(3)   After sub-paragraph (1) there shall be inserted the following sub-paragraph—
  "(1A)   No condition shall be imposed under section 3(6)(d) of this Act unless it appears to be necessary to do so for the purpose of enabling inquiries or a report to be made."

(4)   In sub-paragraph (2) for the words "Sub-paragraph (1) above also applies", there shall be substituted the words "Sub-paragraphs (1) and (1A) above also apply".

(5) In sub-paragraph (3), for the words "sub-paragraph (1)" there shall be substituted the words "sub-paragraph (1A)".

Licensed Premises (Exclusion of Certain Persons) Act 1980 (c. 32)

23. In section 1(2) of the Licensed Premises (Exclusion of Certain Persons) Act 1980 (exclusion orders), for paragraph (b) there shall be substituted the following paragraph—

"(b) where the offence was committed in England and Wales, notwithstanding the provisions of sections 1A and 1C of the Power of Criminal Courts Act 1973 (cases in which absolute and conditional discharges may be made, and their effect), in addition to an order discharging him absolutely or conditionally;".

24. [Repealed by the CJA 1993, sch. 6, part I.]

25. In section 20(2)(b) of that Act (procedure where summary trial appears more suitable), for the words from "on obtaining information" to the end there shall be substituted the words "is of such opinion as is mentioned in subsection (2) of that section".

26. In section 81(3)(a) of that Act (enforcement of fines imposed on young offenders), for the words "section 19(1) of the Criminal Justice Act 1948" there shall be substituted the words "section 17(1) of the Criminal Justice Act 1982".

27.—(1) In subsection (2) of section 143 of that Act (power to alter sums specified in certain provisions), paragraph (i) shall cease to have effect and after paragraph (o) there shall be inserted the following paragraph—

"(p) section 58(2) and (3) of the Criminal Justice Act 1991 (recognisance from parents or guardians);".

(2) For subsection (3) of that section there shall be inserted the following subsection—

"(3) In subsection (1) above the 'relevant date' means—

(a) the date of the coming into force of section 17 of the Criminal Justice Act 1991 (increase of certain maxima); or

(b) where the sums specified in a provision mentioned in subsection (2) above have been substituted by an order under subsection (1) above, the date of that order."

28. In paragraph 2(2) of Schedule 4 to that Act (maximum periods of imprisonment in default of payment of magistrates' court fine), for the words "five days" there shall be substituted the words "seven days".

Contempt of Court Act 1981 (c. 49)

29.—(1) Section 12(2) of the Contempt of Court Act 1981 (offences of contempt of magistrates' court) shall have effect as if the reference to any officer of the court included a reference to any court security officer assigned to the court-house in which the court is sitting.

(2) In this paragraph "court security officer" and "court-house" have the meanings given by section 92(1) of this Act.

Criminal Justice Act 1982 (c. 48)

30.   For subsection (5) of section 1 of the 1982 Act (general restrictions on custodial sentences) there shall be substituted the following subsections—

"(5)   No court shall commit a person under 21 years of age to be detained under section 9 below unless it is of the opinion that no other method of dealing with him is appropriate; and in forming any such opinion, the court—

(a)   shall take into account all such information about the circumstances of the default or contempt (including any aggravating or mitigating factors) as is available to it; and

(b)   may take into account any information about that person which is before it.

(5A)   Where a magistrates' court commits a person under 21 years of age to be detained under section 9 below, it shall—

(a)   state in open court the reason for its opinion that no other method of dealing with him is appropriate; and

(b)   cause that reason to be specified in the warrant of commitment and to be entered in the register."

31.—(1)   In subsection (1) of section 1A of that Act (detention in a young offender institution), for paragraph (b) there shall be substituted the following paragraph—

"(b)   the court is of the opinion that either or both of paragraphs (a) and (b) of subsection (2) of section 1 of the Criminal Justice Act 1991 apply or the case falls within subsection (3) of that section,".

(2)   In subsection (4) of that section, for the words "section 15(11) below" there shall be substituted the words "section 65(6) of the Criminal Justice Act 1991".

32.   In section 3(1) of that Act (restrictions on imposing custodial sentences on persons under 21 not legally represented), for paragraphs (a) and (b) there shall be substituted the following paragraph—

"(a)   pass a sentence of detention in a young offender institution under section 1A above;".

33.   In section 13 of that Act (conversion of sentence of detention in a young offender institution to imprisonment), after subsection (5) there shall be inserted the following subsection—

"(6)   This section applies to a person who is serving a sentence of custody for life under section 8(2) above, or is detained under section 53 of the Children and Young Persons Act 1933, as it applies to a person serving a sentence of detention in a young offender institution."

34.   In section 17(1) of that Act (attendance centre orders), for the words "section 6 of the Powers of Criminal Courts Act 1973" there shall be substituted the words "Part II of Schedule 2 to the Criminal Justice Act 1991".

Repatriation of Prisoners Act 1984 (c. 47)

35—(1)   In section 2 of the Repatriation of Prisoners Act 1984 (transfer of prisoners out of United Kingdom), in subsection (4)(b), for sub-paragraph (i) there shall be substituted the following sub-paragraph—

"(i) release on licence under section 33(1)(b) or (2), 34(3) or 35(1) or (2) of the Criminal Justice Act 1991;".

(2) In section 3 of that Act (transfer of prisoners into United Kingdom), after subsection (8) there shall be inserted the following subsection—

"(9) The provisions contained by virtue of subsection (1)(c) above in a warrant under this Act shall, in the case of a prisoner to whom section 48 of the Criminal Justice Act 1991 (discretionary life prisoners transferred to England and Wales) applies, include provision specifying the relevant part of his sentence within the meaning of section 34 of that Act (duty of Secretary of State to release discretionary life prisoners)."

(3) In paragraph 2 of the Schedule to that Act (operation of certain enactments in relation to prisoners transferred into United Kingdom)—

(a) in sub-paragraph (1), for the words from "section 60" to "of that section" there shall be substituted the words "section 33(1)(b) or (2), 34(3) or (5) or 35(1) of the Criminal Justice Act 1991 whether the prisoner has at any time served a particular proportion or part of his sentence specified in that provision,"; and

(b) in sub-paragraph (2), for the words "one third" there shall be substituted the words "any particular proportion or part".

(4) In paragraph 3 of that Schedule, for the words "section 61 of the Criminal Justice Act 1967" there shall be substituted the words "section 35(2) of the Criminal Justice Act 1991".

Prosecution of Offences Act 1985 (c. 23)

36. In section 22(11) of the Prosecution of Offences Act 1985 (time limits in relation to preliminary stages of criminal proceedings), after the definition of "appropriate court" there shall be inserted the following definition—

"'custody' includes local authority accommodation to which a person is remanded or committed by virtue of section 23 of the Children and Young Persons Act 1969, and references to a person being committed to custody shall be construed accordingly;".

Criminal Justice Act 1988 (c. 33)

37. In section 34 of the Criminal Justice Act 1988 (abolition of requirement of corroboration for unsworn evidence of children), subsection (1) shall cease to have effect and, in subsection (3), for the words "section 38 of the Children and Young Persons Act 1933" there shall be substituted the words "section 52 of the Criminal Justice Act 1991".

Road Traffic Offenders Act 1988 (c. 53)

38.—(1) In subsection (1) of section 46 of the Road Traffic Offenders Act 1988 (combination of disqualification and endorsement with probation orders and orders for discharge), for the words "section 13(3)" there shall be substituted the words "section 1C(3)" and the words "placed on probation or" shall cease to have effect.

(2) In subsection (2) of that section, for the words "section 13(1)" there shall be substituted the words "section 1C(1)" and the words "placed on probation or" shall cease to have effect.

Extradition Act 1989 (c. 33)

39.   In section 20(2)(b)(i) of the Extradition Act 1989 (restoration of persons not tried or acquitted), for the words "section 7(1)" there shall be substituted the words "section 1A(1)".

References to juvenile courts

40.—(1)   Without prejudice to the generality of section 70(2) of this Act, in the enactments specified in sub-paragraph (2) below, for the words "juvenile court" or "juvenile courts", in each place where they occur, there shall be substituted the words "youth court" or, as the case may require, "youth courts".
(2)   The enactments referred to in sub-paragraph (1) above are as follows—
(a)   in the 1933 Act, section 45 to 49, 56 and 108(4) and Schedule 2;
(b)   in the Education Act 1944, section 40;
(c)   in the Children Act 1948, section 4B;
(d)   in the Adoption Act 1958, sections 43, 47 and 48;
(e)   in the Children and Young Persons Act 1963, sections 3, 18, 23, 26, 28, 29 and 57;
(f)   in the Administration of Justice Act 1964, section 12;
(g)   in the 1969 Act, sections 1 to 3, 7, 10, 15, 16, 20A to 22 and 70(1) and Schedule 4;
(h)   in the Criminal Justice Act 1972, section 51(1);
(i)   in the 1973 Act, section 46;
(j)   in the Adoption Act 1976, sections 34 and 37;
(k)   in the 1979 Act, sections 35(3), 37(1), 38(2) and 58(1) and (5);
(l)   in the Child Care Act 1980, sections 5 to 7, 12C to 12E, 21A, 67 and 79(2);
(m)   in the Foster Children Act 1980, sections 11(1), 12(1) and 14;
(n)   in the 1980 Act, sections 12(1), 29, 104 and 106;
(o)   in the 1982 Act, section 16(2) and in Schedule 3, the entry relating to section 49(2) of the 1933 Act;
(p)   in the Administration of Justice Act 1985, section 61;
(q)   in the Legal Aid Act 1988, sections 3(4), 19(3) and (5), 27(3) and (4), 28(3) and (7), 30(2) and in Schedule 3, paragraphs 9 and 10; and
(r)   in the Children Act 1989, section 90(1) and Schedule 14.

References to juvenile court panels

41.—(1)   Without prejudice to the generality of section 70(2) of this Act, in the enactments specified in sub-paragraph (2) below, for the words "juvenile court panel" or "juvenile court panels", in each place where they occur, there shall be substituted the words "youth court panel" or, as the case may require, "youth court panels".
(2)   The enactments referred to in sub-paragraph (1) above are as follows—
(a)   in the 1933 Act, Schedule 2;
(b)   in the 1973 Act, in Schedule 3, paragraph 2(3);
(c)   in the 1979 Act, section 35(3);
(d)   in the Child Care Act 1980, section 12E(5); and
(e)   in the 1980 Act, section 146.

Section 101(1).   **SCHEDULE 12**

TRANSITIONAL PROVISIONS AND SAVINGS

Custodial and community sentences

1.   Each of sections 1 to 13 of this Act shall apply in relation to offenders convicted (but not sentenced) before the commencement of that section as it applies in relation to offenders convicted after that commencement.

2.   Neither subsection (2) of section 8 of this Act, nor the repeal by this Act of section 13 of the 1973 Act, shall affect the operation of section 13 in relation to persons placed on probation before the commencement of that subsection or, as the case may be, that repeal.

3.   An establishment which immediately before the commencement of Part II of Schedule 1 to this Act is a day centre within the meaning of section 4B of the 1973 Act shall be treated as if, immediately after that commencement, it had been approved by the Secretary of State as a probation centre within the meaning of paragraph 3(7) of Schedule 1A to that Act.

4.   Paragraph 6 of Schedule 11 to this Act shall apply in relation to offenders convicted (but not sentenced) before the commencement of that paragraph as it applies to offenders convicted after that commencement.

Community orders: supplemental

5.—(1)   Paragraphs 3 and 4 of Schedule 2 to this Act shall apply in relation to pre-existing failures to comply with the requirements of probation orders or community service orders as if, in sub-paragraph (1)(a), for "£1,000" there were substituted "£400".

(2)   In this paragraph "pre-existing", in relation to either of those paragraphs, means occurring before the commencement of that paragraph.

Financial penalties

6.   None of sections 17 to 20 of this Act shall apply in relation to offences committed before the commencement of that section.

Increase of certain penalties

7.   Neither of subsections (3) and (4) of section 26 of this Act shall apply in relation to offences committed before the commencement of that subsection.

Early release: general

8.—(1)   In this paragraph and paragraphs 9 to 11 below—
   "existing licensee" means any person who, before the commencement of Part II of this Act, has been released on licence under section 60 of the 1967 Act and whose licence under that section is in force at that commencement;
   "existing prisoner" means any person who, at that commencement, is serving a custodial sentence;
and sub-paragraphs (2) to (7) below shall have effect subject to those paragraphs.

(2)   Subject to sub-paragraphs (3) to (7) below, Part II of this Act shall apply in relation to an existing licensee as it applies in relation to a person who is released on licence under that Part; and in its application to an existing prisoner, or to an existing licensee who is recalled under section 39 of this Act, that Part shall apply with the modifications made by those sub-paragraphs.

(3)   Section 40 of this Act shall not apply in relation to an existing prisoner or licensee.

(4)   In relation to an existing prisoner whose sentence is for a term of twelve months, section 33(1) of this Act shall apply as if that sentence were for a term of less than twelve months.

(5)   In relation to an existing prisoner or licensee whose sentence is for a term of—

(a)   more than twelve months; and

(b)   less than four years or, as the case may require, such other period as may for the time being be referred to in section 33(5) of this Act,

Part II of this Act shall apply as if he were or had been a long-term rather than a short-term prisoner.

(6)   In relation to an existing prisoner or licensee whose sentence is for a term of more than twelve months—

(a)   section 35(1) of this Act shall apply as if the reference to one half of his sentence were a reference to one-third of that sentence or six months, whichever is the longer; and

(b)   sections 33(3) and 37(1) of this Act shall apply as if the reference to three-quarters of his sentence were a reference to two-thirds of that sentence.

(7)   In relation to an existing prisoner or licensee—

(a)   whose sentence is for a term of more than twelve months; and

(b)   whose case falls within such class of cases as the Secretary of State may determine after consultation with the Parole Board,

section 35(1) of this Act shall apply as if the reference to a recommendation by the Board included a reference to a recommendation by a local review committee established under section 59(6) of the 1967 Act.

(8)   In this paragraph "custodial sentence" means—

(a)   a sentence of imprisonment;

(b)   a sentence of detention in a young offender institution;

(c)   a sentence of detention (whether during Her Majesty's pleasure, for life or for a determinate term) under section 53 of the 1933 Act; or

(d)   a sentence of custody for life under section 8 of the 1982 Act.

9.—(1)   This paragraph applies where, in the case of an existing life prisoner, the Secretary of State certifies his opinion that, if—

(a)   section 34 of this Act had been in force at the time when he was sentenced; and

(b)   the reference in subsection (1)(a) of that section to a violent or sexual offence the sentence for which is not fixed by law were a reference to any offence the sentence for which is not so fixed,

the court by which he was sentenced would have ordered that that section should apply to him as soon as he had served a part of his sentence specified in the certificate.

(2)   In a case to which this paragraph applies, Part II of this Act except section 35(2) shall apply as if—

(a)   the existing life prisoner were a discretionary life prisoner for the purposes of that Part; and

(b)   the relevant part of his sentence within the meaning of section 34 of this Act were the part specified in the certificate.

(3)   In this paragraph "existing life prisoner" means a person who, at the commencement of Part II of this Act, is serving one or more of the following sentences, namely—

(a)   a sentence of life imprisonment;

(b)   a sentence of detention during her Majesty's pleasure or for life under section 53 of the 1933 Act; or

(c)   a sentence of custody for life under section 8 of the 1982 Act.

(4)   A person serving two or more such sentences shall not be treated as a discretionary life prisoner for the purposes of Part II of this Act unless the requirements of sub-paragraph (1) above are satisfied as respects each of those sentences; and subsections (3) and (5) of section 34 of this Act shall not apply in relation to such a person until after he has served the relevant part of each of those sentences.

10.   Prison rules made by virtue of section 42 of this Act may include provision for applying any provisions of Part II of this Act, in relation to any existing prisoner or licensee who has forfeited any remission of his sentence, as if he had been awarded such number of additional days as may be determined by or under the rules.

Early release of young persons detained under 1933 Act

11.   In relation to an existing prisoner or licensee whose sentence is a determinate sentence of detention under section 53 of the 1933 Act—

(a)   Part II of this Act shall apply as if he were or had been a life rather than a long-term or short-term prisoner;

(b)   section 35(2) of this Act shall apply as if the requirement as to consultation were omitted; and

(c)   section 37(3) of this Act shall apply as if the reference to his death were a reference to the date on which he would (but for his release) have served the whole of his sentence.

Early release of prisoners serving extended sentences

12.—(1)   In relation to an existing prisoner or licensee on the passing of whose sentence an extended sentence certificate was issued—

(a)   section 33(3) of this Act shall apply as if the duty to release him unconditionally were a duty to release him on licence; and

(b)   section 37(1) of this Act shall apply as if the reference to three-quarters of his sentence were a reference to the whole of that sentence.

(2)   In this paragraph "extended sentence certificate" means a certificate issued under section 28 of the 1973 Act stating that an extended term of imprisonment was imposed on an offender under that section.

Early release of fine defaulters and contemnors

13.   Part II of this Act shall apply in relation to any person who, before the commencement of that Part, has been committed to prison or to be detained under section 9 of the 1982 Act—

(a)   in default of payment of a sum adjudged to be paid by a conviction; or

(b)   for contempt of court or any kindred offence,

as it applies in relation to any person who is so committed after that commencement.

Responsibilities of parent or guardian

14.   None of sections 56 to 58 of this Act shall apply in relation to offences committed before the commencement of that section; and the repeals of subsections (7)(c), (7B) and (7C) of section 7 of the 1969 Act shall not apply in relation to offences committed before the commencement of those repeals.

Remands and committals of children and young persons

15.—(1)   In this paragraph—

"section 23" means section 23 of the 1969 Act as substituted by section 60(1) of this Act;

"the modifications" means the modifications of section 23 set out in section 62 of this Act;

"remand or committal" means a remand of a child or young person charged with or convicted of one or more offences, or a committal of a child or young person for trial or sentence.

(2)   Section 23 as it has effect with the modifications shall not apply in relation to any remand or committal which is in force immediately before the commencement of sections 60 and 62 of this Act.

(3)   Subject to sub-paragraphs (4) and (5) below, section 23 as it has effect without the modifications shall not apply in relation to any remand or committal which is in force immediately before the day appointed under section 62(1) of this Act.

(4)   Any person who, in pursuance of any such remand or committal, is held in a remand centre or prison shall be brought before the court which remanded or committed him before the end of the period of 8 days beginning with the day so appointed.

(5)   Where any person is brought before a court under sub-paragraph (4) above, section 23 as it has effect without the modifications shall apply as if the court were just remanding or committing him as mentioned in subsection (1)(a) of that section.

16.—(1)   Subsection (2)(a) of section 60 of this Act shall not apply in any case where proceedings for the offence in question have begun before the commencement of that section.

(2)   Subject to sub-paragraphs (3) and (4) below, subsection (2)(b) and (c) of that section shall not apply in relation to any committal under section 37 of the 1980 Act which is in force immediately before that commencement.

(3)   Any person less than 17 years old who, in pursuance of any such committal, is held in a remand centre or prison shall be brought before the court

which committed him before the end of the period of 8 days beginning with that commencement.

(4)   Where any person is brought before a court under sub-paragraph (3) above, section 37 of the 1980 Act shall apply as if the court were just committing him under that section.

Custodial sentences for young offenders

17.—(1)   Subject to sub-paragraph (2) below, section 63 of this Act shall apply in relation to young offenders convicted (but not sentenced) before the commencement of that section as it applies in relation to young offenders convicted after that commencement.

(2)   Subseections (2), (3) and (5) of that section shall not apply in any case where proceedings for the offence in question have begun before that commencement and the offender is aged 17 at the date of his conviction.

(3)   For the purposes of the provisions substituted by subsection (3)(c) of that section, any sentence of detention in a young offender institution which, as that commencement, is being served by an offender aged 17 shall be disregarded.

18.   Section 64 of this Act shall not apply in any case where the offence in question was committed before the commencement of that section and the offender is aged 16 at the date of his conviction.

Supervision of young offenders after release

19.   Section 65 of this Act shall not apply in relation to any person under the age of 22 years who, before the commencement of that section, is released from a term of detention in a young offender institution or under section 53 of the 1933 Act; and the repeal by this Act of section 15 of the 1982 Act shall not affect the operation of that section in relation to any such person who is so released.

Supervision orders

20.—(1)   In relation to pre-existing failures to comply with the requirements of supervision orders, section 15 of the 1969 Act as substituted by Schedule 7 to this Act shall apply as if—

   (a)   in subsection (3)(a), for "£1,000" there were substituted "£100";

   (b)   in subsection (5)(b), for "£5,000" there were substituted "£2,000"; and

   (c)   in subsection (5)(c), for "£5,000" there were substituted the words "£2,000 in the case of a person who has attained the age of 18 years and £400 in the case of a person who has not attained that age".

(2)   In this paragraph "pre-existing" means occurring before the commencement of section 66 of this Act and that Schedule.

Attendance centre orders

21.—(1)   Subsection (2) of section 67 of this Act shall not apply in relation to attendance centre orders made before the commencement of that section.

(2)   Subsection (4) of that section shall not apply in relation to pre-existing failures to attend in accordance with an attendance centre order or pre-existing breaches of rules made under section 16(3) of the 1982 Act.

(3)   In this paragraph "pre-existing" means occurring or committed before that commencement.

Provisions for treating persons aged 17 as young persons

22.—(1)　Paragraphs 1, 3, 4 and 6 of Schedule 8 shall not apply in any case where proceedings for the offence in question have begun before the commencement of that Schedule.

(2)　Paragraph 5 of that Schedule shall apply in relation to any sentence imposed on any person who was convicted before that commencement and was aged 17 at the date of his conviction.

Renaming of juvenile courts etc.

23.　In relation to any time before the commencement of section 70 of this Act, references in any other provision of this Act, or in any enactment amended by this Act, to youth courts shall be construed as references to juvenile courts.

Supplemental

24.　For the purposes of this Schedule proceedings for an offence shall be regarded as having begun as follows—

(a)　in the case of an offence triable only summarily, when a plea is entered;

(b)　in the case of an offence triable only on indictment, when the magistrates' court begins to inquire into the offence as examining magistrates;

(c)　in the case of an offence triable either way, when the magistrates' court determines to proceed with the summary trial of the offence or, as the case may be, to proceed to inquire into the offence as examining justices.

Section 101(2).　　　　　　　**SCHEDULE 13**

REPEALS

Chapter	Short title	Extent of repeal
2 & 3 Vict. c. 47.	The Metropolitan Police Act 1839.	Section 11.
23 & 24 Geo. 5 c. 12.	The Children and Young Persons Act 1933.	Section 34(1). Section 38(1).
15 & 16 Geo. 6 & 1 Eliz. 2 c. 52.	The Prison Act 1952.	Section 25.
3 & 4 Eliz. 2 c. 18	The Army Act 1955.	In section 71AA(1), the words "subject to subsection (1A) below" and "being not less than 21 days and". Section 71AA(1A). Section 93(2A).
3 & 4 Eliz. 2 c. 19.	The Air Force Act 1955.	In section 71AA(1), the words "subject to subsection (1A) below" and "being not less than 21 days and". Section 71AA(1A). Section 93(2A).

Chapter	Short title	Extent of repeal
5 & 6 Eliz. 2 c. 53.	The Naval Discipline Act 1957.	In section 43AA(1), the words "subject to subsection (1A) below" and "being not less than 21 days and". Section 43AA(1A). Section 60(3A).
1967 c. 80.	The Criminal Justice Act 1967.	Sections 59 to 64. In section 67(6), the words "remanded or", in the first place where they occur, and the words "section 23 of the Children and Young Persons Act 1969 or". Schedule 2.
1968 c. 19.	The Criminal Appeal Act 1968.	In section 50(1A), the words "a probation order or".
1968 c. 49.	The Social Work (Scotland) Act 1968.	In section 72, in subsection (1A), paragraph (a) and the word "and" immediately following that paragraph, and subsection (4).
1968 c. 64.	The Civil Evidence Act 1968.	In section 11(5)(a), the words "probation or".
1969 c. 54.	The Children and Young Persons Act 1969.	In section 3, the words "disregarding section 4 of this Act", in each place where they occur. Section 4. In section 5, subsections (1) to (7) and, in subsection (9), the definitions of "qualified informant" and "designated". In section 7, in subsection (7), the words "is found guilty of homicide" and paragraph (c), and subsections (7B) and (7C). Section 8. Section 10(1)(a). In section 12AA, subsections (7), (8) and (12). In section 34(1), in paragraph (a), the word "4," and paragraph (b).

Chapter	Short title	Extent of repeal
		In Schedule 4, paragraphs 2 and 3.
1971 c. 10.	The Vehicles (Excise) Act 1971.	In section 9(5), the words "placing him on probation or".
1971 c. 23.	The Courts Act 1971.	In Schedule 8, in paragraph 57(1)(a), the reference to subsection (2) of section 10.
1972 c. 19.	The Criminal Justice Act 1972.	Section 35.
1973 c. 62.	The Powers of Criminal Courts Act 1973.	Sections 5 to 10. Section 13. In section 14, in subsection (1), the words "instead of dealing with him in any other way" and, in subsection (3), the words "(i) or (ii)". Sections 16 to 17C. Sections 20 and 20A. Sections 28 and 29. In section 30(1), the words "(such as the power to make a probation order)". In section 42(2)(a), the words from "subject to" to "twelve months)". Section 45. Section 48. In section 57(1), the definition of "supervising court". Schedule 1. In Schedule 3, in paragraph 2(2)(a), the word "several".
1974 c. 53.	The Rehabilitation of Offenders Act 1974.	In section 1(4), the words "put on probation or".
1975 c. 21.	The Criminal Procedure (Scotland) Act 1975.	In section 403, the proviso to subsection (4) and, in subsection (6), the words "the proviso to subsection (4) of this section shall not apply, but". In Schedule 9, paragraph 50.
1976 c. 63.	The Bail Act 1976.	In Schedule 1, in paragraph 8(1), the words from "or, in the case" to the end.

Chapter	Short title	Extent of repeal
1977 c. 45.	The Criminal Law Act 1977.	Section 47. In Schedule 12, in the entry relating to the Children and Young Persons Act 1969, paragraph 3.
1980 c. 43.	The Magistrates' Courts Act 1980.	In section 24(4), the words from "but this subsection" to the end. Section 35. In section 36(2), the words from "but this subsection" to the end. Section 103(3)(a). Section 37(1A). In section 108(1A), the words "a probation order or". Section 143(2)(i). In Schedule 3, paragraph 5.
1982 c. 48.	The Criminal Justice Act 1982.	In section 1, subsections (3) to (4A). In section 1A(3), the words "and section 1B(3) below". In section 1B, subsections (1) and (3). Section 2. Section 15. Section 17(3). In section 18(6)(b), the words from the beginning to "residence". Section 33. In section 48, subsections (1)(c) and (2). Section 62. Schedule 5. In Schedule 11, paragraph 6(a)(v). In Schedule 13, Part I. In Schedule 14, paragraphs 23(a), 25 and 32.
1983 c. 20.	The Mental Health Act 1983.	In section 50(3), the words from "and that period" to the end.

Chapter	Short title	Extent of repeal
1984 c. 60.	The Police and Criminal Evidence Act 1984.	In section 37, subsections (11) to (14).
1988 c. 33	The Criminal Justice Act 1988.	Section 34(1). In section 123, subsections (2) and (3). Section 131(2). In Schedule 8, in paragraph 3(1)(c), the words "1(3) and". In Schedule 10, in Part II, the words "section 15(1)", "section 15(1) and (5) and" and "section 15(1)(a) and", and Part III. In Schedule 15, paragraph 22(1). In Schedule 16, the entry relating to section 41(8) of the Administration of Justice Act 1970.
1988 c. 38.	The Legal Aid Act 1988.	In section 20(4), the word "or" immediately following paragraph (b).
1988 c. 53.	The Road Traffic Offenders Act 1988.	In section 46, in subsections (1) and (2), the words "placed on probation or".
1989 c. 41.	The Children Act 1989.	In Schedule 12, paragraphs 21 and 24. In Schedule 13, paragraph 53(1).
1989 c. 42.	The Local Government and Housing Act 1989.	Section 189.
1991 c. 62.	The Armed Forces Act 1991.	In section 3(1), the words from "and after the words" to the end. In section 5, subsections (2)(b) and (9). In Schedule 2, paragraph 3.

National Standards for the Supervision of Offenders in the Community (1992)

(Extracts)

1 INTRODUCTION

1.1 Why national standards?

The supervision of offenders in the community is a crucial part of any comprehensive response to crime. For *offenders* supervision can *restrict liberty* and make very real *mental and physical demands*. Effective supervision can help offenders *stay out of trouble* and become *responsible members of the community*. For *probation and social services staff*, supervision is *challenging and skilful*, requiring *professional social work in the field of criminal justice*.

2.   Supervision in the community can, therefore, represent both a demanding and a constructive sentence of the criminal court. Increasingly, the value and importance of community sentences are being recognised. This is reinforced through the sentencing framework of the Criminal Justice Act 1991.

3.   The *objective of these national standards* is to strengthen the supervision of offenders in the community, building on the skill and experience of practitioners and service managers:

■   by setting a clear framework of *expectations and requirements* for supervision, understood by those carrying out the task and by others;

■   by enabling *professional judgment* to be exercised within a framework of *accountability*;

■   by encouraging *imagination, initiative* and *innovation*, and the development of *good practice*; and

■   by ensuring that supervision is delivered *fairly, consistently* and *without discrimination*, and that positive steps are taken to ensure that is the case.

1.2 What is the status of these standards?

4.   These standards are issued jointly by the Home Office, Department of Health and Welsh Office as required standards of practice for probation services and social services departments in England and Wales, in relation to the supervision of offenders in the community and the preparation of reports for the criminal courts. Services are expected to follow the guidance and requirements in

the standards or – should that become impossible at any stage – to ensure locally that sentencers are made aware of the situation. Relevant inspections by HM Inspectorate of Probation and, where appropriate, the social services inspectorates will have regard to the satisfactory attainment of the standards.

5.   It should be emphasised that the standards seek to encourage good practice but avoid unnecessary prescription. In many respects, the standards lay down expected norms rather than outright requirements, with the clear onus on practitioners and managers to record and justify any necessary departures from these norms in individual cases. It is recognised that the attainment of the standards by probation and social services is dependent on the cooperation of others with whom they work.

1.3   Who are these national standards for?

6.   National standards are relevant to:

■ **PROBATION STAFF AND LOCAL AUTHORITY SOCIAL WORKERS**, as a clear and consistent statement of *what is required* of them, for their own guidance; as a common framework for developing and sharing *good practice*; and as a basis for *demonstrating accountability and achievement*;

■ **PROBATION COMMITTEES (OR BOARDS) AND LOCAL AUTHORITIES**, who exercise an important function as employers of the staff in each service, ensuring that their service delivers effective performance and the efficient use of resources;

■ **THE VOLUNTARY SECTOR**, with whom probation and social services work in partnership. Probation and social services should ensure that work they request of the voluntary sector or others meets these standards when it forms part of the supervision required by the courts;

■ **SENTENCERS**, who can be assured as to the basis on which *reports* to the court are prepared, how *supervision* is undertaken, and when offenders who behave unacceptably will be *returned to court* under breach proceedings;

■ **OTHER CRIMINAL JUSTICE AGENCIES AND PROFESSIONS** with whom social and probation services work, such as the Crown Prosecution Service, the legal profession, court clerks and administrators, the police, the Prison Service and the Parole Board, to improve inter-agency understanding and cooperation;

■ **OFFENDERS, DEPENDANTS AND OTHER SERVICE USERS**. The standards set an important framework of requirements on – and safeguards for – this group. They are entitled to be treated fairly, courteously and without discrimination. Individuals should be informed of their rights, of what is available to them and what is expected of them in return, and of the material facts about their progress under supervision and what is intended in their case. They should have access to a fair and effective complaints system if they are dissatisfied with the service they receive;

■ **THE GENERAL PUBLIC**, including the victims of crime, who have an important interest in the efficient use of resources, in protection from crime and in the effectiveness and results of supervision;

■ **CENTRAL GOVERNMENT**, who similarly wish to see *efficient, effective and accountable* supervision. National standards are an important means of *defining the framework* within which individual services should operate and of evaluating performance.

7.   The standards are written in plain language, giving clear instructions to practitioners and facilitating informed discussion with others on a common basis of understanding.

. . .

2 PRE-SENTENCE REPORTS

2.1 Introduction

This national standard sets out the requirements for probation officers and social workers preparing pre-sentence reports (PSRs) as required under the Criminal Justice Act 1991 (the 1991 Act). In doing so, it also sets out expectations that others – particularly sentencers – may have in respect of PSRs, and notes the contribution required of others for the necessary arrangements to be effective.

Role of the pre-sentence report
2.   A pre-sentence report is a report in writing, made or submitted by a probation officer or a social worker of a local authority social services department, with a view to *assisting the court in determining the most suitable method of dealing with an offender.* Under the 1991 Act, a PSR *must be considered* before the following types of sentence are imposed:

■ *custody*, except in indictable only offences when the court considers a PSR unnecessary; or where the sentence is prescribed in law;
■ *certain more demanding community sentences*: community service orders; combination orders; or probation or supervision orders with specified additional requirements.

In addition, a PSR may be of value in advising the court about suitability for community sentences for which a PSR is not required by law, and in seeking to ensure that supervision, if ordered, is able to start promptly and effectively.
3.   A PSR should address:

■ the *current offence(s)* in the proceedings, summarising the facts and assessing the seriousness of and the offender's attitude to the offence(s);
■ *relevant information about the offender* setting the current offence in context, including his or her previous offending, and strengths and problems; and
■ a *conclusion* and, where relevant, *a proposal for the most suitable community sentence.*

4.   PSRs and proposals for community sentences must be free of discrimination on the ground of race, gender, age, disability, language ability, literacy,

religion, sexual orientation or any other improper ground. All probation services and social services departments must have a stated *equal opportunities policy* and ensure that this is effectively implemented, monitored and reviewed. Effective action to prevent discrimination (*anti-discriminatory practice*) requires significantly more than a willingness to accept all offenders equally or to invest an equal amount of time and effort in different cases. The origin, nature and extent of differences in circumstances and need must be properly understood and actively addressed *by all concerned* – for example, by staff training, by monitoring and review and by making extra effort to understand and work most effectively with an offender from a different cultural background. The requirements for PSRs in the 1991 Act are themselves an important means of ensuring that sentencers are consistently well informed about offenders being sentenced in a broad range of cases.

5.   The information needed from a probation officer or a social worker, and the contribution to be made by a PSR, will differ greatly from case to case, for example, with respect to the seriousness and type of offence, the offender's motivation and personal situation, and any community sentence to be proposed. Such factors are considered more fully later in this standard. It is inherent in PSR writing that complexities such as drug misuse may not at first be apparent and may only be discovered (if at all) while the PSR is being prepared. It is, therefore, the *professional duty of the report writer to assess what is the correct amount of detail to be investigated and included in a PSR. More* detail than is necessary should be avoided as being wasteful of time and resources, and may obscure the most important points from the sentencer; *less* should also be avoided as risking failure to bring material information to the sentencer's attention. A *practical* judgment is necessary, drawing on professional skill and experience.

Role of the report writer

6.   The sentencer in a criminal case has sole responsibility, after a finding of guilt, for imposing sentence and, therefore, for judging the seriousness of the offence(s) committed. In reaching that view, the sentencer will take into account information contained in a PSR.

7.   It is essential that advice and information in a PSR is provided *impartially* by the report writer. Thus the PSR must present a balanced picture, drawing fairly on both aggravating and mitigating factors in a case. This does not, however, preclude the report writer from presenting facts or advice relevant to a particular sentence (for example, in supporting a programme of community supervision and drawing attention to likely negative consequences of custody for the offender or his or her family, or in the case of a violent or sexual offence, including evidence of risk to the public of serious harm from the offender, as a result of which the sentencer may impose custody) *provided* the distinct role of the sentencer is respected.

2.2   Report preparation

8.   This section of the national standard describes the process of preparing a PSR, including:

- *evaluating seriousness of the current offence(s)* (paragraphs 9 to 13, and Annex 2.A);
- *conducting enquiries* (paragraphs 14 to 16);
- *assessing what, if any, community sentence might best address the offender's behaviour and reduce the risk of further offending* (paragraphs 17 to 24, and Annex 2.B); and
- *writing the PSR, including the format of the report* (paragraphs 25 to 27).

Evaluating seriousness

9.   In preparing a PSR, the report writer should first consider the seriousness of the offence(s) at issue and the likely range of penalties, since this has a large bearing on the style and detail of the report that should be prepared. Such assessment need not usually be lengthy or detailed, since the prosecutor will have given the facts to the court. Report writers should, therefore, have a working understanding of the law and practice of sentencing (in particular, the close relationship between seriousness and the sentence to be imposed, under sections 1 to 7 of the 1991 Act, and some knowledge of more important sentencing guidelines), though expert legal understanding is not necessary. Statutory sentencing criteria are summarised in Annex 2.A.

10.   Whereas the sentencer is required to make the judgment on seriousness and sentence, the report writer is required to make a provisional assessment, intended to ensure that the PSR is properly focused and addresses only those outcomes that are broadly likely. Near the boundary between two classes of sentence, for example, between community sentences and custody, it will be appropriate for the report writer to recognise that more than one sentencing outcome may result, and to provide information relevant to both (or all) of these. Such considerations have implications for the content of PSRS, and are also examined in more detail in Annex 2.A.

11.   It is emphasised that in all cases an *individual* approach is required in assessing seriousness and in deciding on the enquiries to be made and the appropriate content of a PSR. In addition, information coming to light as the PSR is prepared may revise earlier assessments.

12.   When requesting a PSR on adjournment, a sentencer may give a preliminary indication of his or her view of the seriousness of the offence and the sentence which may be appropriate. Such a view will set a starting-point for the preparation of the report. Nevertheless, the report writer should prepare a complete PSR in accordance with this standard and should be vigilant about including information which may assist the sentencer in reaching a final view on sentencing.

13.   Some probation services use offence seriousness scales to help report writers assess seriousness and likely sentence. Where these reflect sentencing practice before the 1991 Act, they will not be a reliable guide to practice after implementation. In due course, Court of Appeal judgments on the assessment of seriousness under the 1991 Act will inform report writers in dealing with these issues. Existing Court of Appeal guidance on aggravating and mitigating factors will also be of assistance, as will the court's interpretation of the similar provisions covering young offenders in the 1982 and 1988 Criminal Justice Acts. Whether based on practice before or after the 1991 Act, seriousness scales can

only give a rough guide to the gravity of an offence, and cannot take into account all the relevant circumstances: the seriousness of an offence depends on a wide range of factors, including the harm caused by the offence and the culpability of the offender.

Conducting enquiries

14.   As discussed in paragraphs 5 and 11, above, the extent of investigation is itself a matter to be decided during the preparation of a PSR. In all cases, however, it is necessary to refer at least to the facts of the *offences(s)* involved, including a recognition of aggravating and mitigating factors, referring to prosecution papers and/or accounts given in court: the starting-point is normally the material disclosed to defence solicitors by way of advance information (for all cases in the Crown Court and for cases triable either way in the magistrates' courts). Where more detail is necessary, this may, for example, be obtained during the required interview of the offender herself or himself (see below), or from statements of co-defendants, witnesses or victims.

15.   The *offender* should be interviewed to obtain information about him or her *relevant to the offence, to the likelihood of reoffending and to the possible sentence* – again with regard to the level of detail necessary for the report. This may require more than one interview with the offender. Relevant information may include the offender's explanation for the offence, acceptance of responsibility and feelings of guilt or remorse, attitudes, motivation, criminal history, relationships (e.g. family, friends and associates), strengths and skills, and personal problems, such as drug or alcohol misuse, or financial, housing, employment, medical or psychiatric problems. In the case of a violent or sexual offence, evidence of risk to the public of serious harm from the offender may also be relevant.

16.   Careful encouragement is necessary on the part of the report writer for the offender to acknowledge certain problems material to offending, such as drug or alcohol misuse, particularly where the offender may fear adverse consequences (e.g. a custodial rather than a community sentence). Addressing such issues may form part of a more general harm reduction strategy, e.g. in the case of drug misuse. The report writer must give clear information to the offender before interviewing him or her about possible disclosure of the report and must avoid giving assurances about likely sentence (see also paragraph 24, below, in relation to communication to prisons).

Assessment for community sentence

17.   Where a community sentence is being considered by the report writer, the most important general criteria are those laid down for such a sentence in section 6(2) of the 1991 Act, i.e. that in the opinion of the court:

■   first that the *particular order(s) are those most suitable for the offender* (section 6(2)(a)); and

■   second that the *restrictions on liberty imposed by the order(s) are commensurate with the seriousness of the offence* (section 6(2)(b)).

18.   A wide range of community sentences is available under the 1991 Act. An example of a possible framework for the guidance of report writers (as well as a possible basis for explaining to sentencers how different types of community order relate to each other) is given in Annex 2.B. The concept of restriction on liberty cannot be interpreted too precisely, not least because of the different basis on which different community orders (e.g. probation and community service) operate. The degree to which a particular order restricts the offender's liberty (in response to the seriousness of the offence) depends on the nature and length of the order imposed by the court.

19.   The selection of a particular order or orders for mention in a PSR should be in accordance with the principles set out in the 1991 Act and should:

■   be made with reference to the *range of community sentences and programmes available locally* (e.g. operated by the statutory or independent sector) and the type of offender for whom they are most suited;

■   fit the individual *criteria laid down for the particular order(s) proposed*, both in legislation and in guidance for their application (e.g. advice in the targeting sections of the national standards for supervision, probation, community service and combination orders, the regime at local attendance or probation centres, etc.);

■   be matched to the individual *offender's personality, needs, ability, etc.*, as assessed by the report writer and others she or he has consulted (see paragraph 20, below). Risk of reoffending scales may also be helpful;

■   appear to stand a *realistic prospect of successful completion* by the offender, including securing his or her informed consent and compliance.

Where a proposal for a community sentence would depart from the normal expectations set out in the relevant national standard (e.g. in relation to the programme of supervision or the regime for enforcement of the order(s)), this should be drawn explicitly to the sentencer's attention in the PSR. Where, in the case of a violent or sexual offence, there is evidence of risk to the public of serious harm from the offender, the report writer should consider whether there are any community sentence options available which might be effective in reducing the risk of serious harm and should include details of any such options in the report.

20.   *Specialist advice or assessment* will be necessary if the report writer considers that specialist provision through the statutory or independent sector (e.g. for mental disorder or drug or alcohol misuse) would help to reduce offending, for example, through a probation order with additional requirements. It may be necessary to establish such referral mechanisms in advance, e.g. a panel of drug misuse specialists, in relation to both offenders in the community and those remanded in custody. In addition, the PSR may be a suitable stage to begin detailed *planning for supervision* that might follow – for example, to prepare on a provisional basis the supervision plan required in the probation, supervision and combination order national standards.

21.   Under section 4 of the 1991 Act, *where the offender is or appears to be mentally disordered*, the court is normally required, if considering a custodial sentence, to obtain both a PSR and a medical report and to consider the likely effect of such a sentence on the offender's mental condition and on any treatment

which may be available for it. In such cases, the report writer should include any relevant information about that condition and should draw attention to possible sources of treatment in the community and to the likely impact of a custodial sentence.

22.   Where a PSR is being prepared on a *child or young person*, the report writer must have regard for the welfare of the individual in accordance with section 44 of the Children and Young Persons Act 1933. Relevant issues are likely to include:

■   the *division of responsibility for PSR preparation* between social and probation services (particularly for 16 and 17-year-olds);
■   *determination of the young offender's stage of development* (and in the case of 16 and 17-year-olds, suitability for juvenile or adult community sentences).

Reference should be made, as appropriate, to Home Office Circular 30/1992, also numbered LAC(92)5 and Welsh Office Circular 21/92, on young people and the youth court.

23.   A PSR written on a *child or young person* must also take account of any 'care plan' prepared for that individual under the Children Act 1989 and must address the child or young person's *relations with her or his parent(s) or guardian* and the degree to which they are responsible for the child or young person and should be involved in any supervision. Under the 1991 Act, the parents of children and young persons can be and in the case of those under 16 should normally be:

■   ordered to attend court with their children;
■   ordered to pay any financial penalties imposed on their children; and
■   bound over to look after their convicted children property.

In dealing with children and young persons, the implications of these powers should be fully considered.

24.   Under section 46 of the 1973 Act, the offender should be given a copy of the report – or, in the case of a young offender, his or her parent(s) or guardian may be given a copy. Information contained in a PSR should be limited to that which is relevant to sentencing. Nevertheless, information collated when a PSR is prepared (for example, in respect of the offender's needs and problems, and suggestions for programmes to address these) can be of value to the offender, and to prison staff in planning and supervising custody, if that is imposed. Such information should, therefore, be sent to the prison: normally by copying the PSR, but if, exceptionally, that is not appropriate or sufficient, then in an alternative or supplementary report prepared for the purpose.

Writing a PSR

25.   In writing a PSR, the report writer must be clear as to what level of detail is appropriate (in accordance with paragraph 5, above), what facts and suggestions to include and to exclude, and what conclusions she or he considers justified. Before signing the report, the writer must be satisfied that it meets the requirements of this standard and of local instructions, for example, with respect

to quality control. Particular care may be appropriate in preparing a PSR where more than one class of sentence may be at issue, e.g. near the boundary between community sentence and custody.

26.   A PSR should be clear, concise, free of jargon and exclude unnecessary detail. Where possible, it should be no more than two pages long. Nevertheless, sentencers will generally expect some interpretation and analysis of factual information collected, particularly in respect of statements or action by the offender; a clear indication of the source of main facts and whether they have been verified; and coherent, logical argument in support of conclusions drawn – particularly where such conclusions envisage a sentence significantly different from that which might be expected by the sentencer. The needs of the particular sentencer may justify some adaptation of the PSR, for example, to explain more fully a community programme where the sentencer is unfamiliar with the area or with local service provision.

27.   As far as possible, PSRs should follow a similar layout of sections and headings, in particular comprising:

■   *introduction* – identifying the document as a PSR in accordance with section 3(5) of the 1991 Act and with this standard and giving the court, the date of the hearing, the date of the report, the full name, address, date of birth and age of the defendant or offender and the offence(s) charged or convicted; then a summary of the sources drawn on to prepare the report. This may be on a pre-printed form;

■   *current offence(s)* – summarising the facts and seriousness of the offence(s), including aggravating and mitigating factors known to the report writer and the offender's attitude to the offence(s);

■   *relevant information about the offender* – such as previous offending and response to supervision, motivation, strengths, personal problems, and (in the case of a violent or sexual offence) evidence of risk of serious harm to the public (see paragraph 15, above);

■   *conclusion* and, whenever relevant, a *proposal for the most suitable community sentence*, under which, were the court to choose that course, the report writer considers the offender could most appropriately be supervised and the risk of future offending be reduced. The report should, finally, be *signed* by the writer.

2.3   Court work

28.   This section of the standard contains *advice and requirements as to court work and the preparation of PSRs in relation to the Crown Court (principally by the probation service) and magistrates' and youth courts.* At the Crown Court there is a need to ensure as few and as short adjournments as possible for PSRs to be prepared: the standard requires probation services to be able to prepare some PSRs at court, and to seek a common understanding locally with the judiciary about the commissioning of PSRs (paragraphs 29 to 32). The preparation of reports in relation to magistrates' and youth courts is described in paragraph 33.

Crown Court

29. Pilot arrangements in five Crown Court centres have demonstrated that given effective cooperation between all participants and some capacity to write PSRs at court, it is possible to provide an effective report-writing sevice for a broad range of cases, including the preparation of some reports, in writing, on the day they are requested. In preparing reports for the Crown Court, the *objectives* should be:

■ *to avoid, as far as possible, adjournments for reports*, by preparing PSRs in advance of trial whenever sufficient notice of a guilty plea to the principal charge(s) in a case is given;

■ where adjournment for a PSR is necessary, *to prepare the report as expeditiously as possible*, especially where the offender is remanded in custody, the trial judge wishes the report to be available quickly or there is any other reason for urgency, consistent with the requirements of this standard;

■ *to seek to operate these arrangements on a basis of mutual understanding* with the judiciary and others in the criminal justice system, respecting, for example, trial judges' wishes and the professional advice of report writers as to the length of time needed for reports to be prepared to the requirements of this standard.

30.   Annex 2.C comprises a model understanding, or *statement of preferred practice*, as a basis for such work. The procedures specified there, as far as they apply to probation, should be followed by probation services and report writers; in addition, probation management should seek the cooperation of the judiciary (through the resident judge) in adopting such a statement of preferred practice locally.

31.   Probation services should make some provision *at each Crown Court centre* to write quickly PSRs which do not require a lengthy adjournment. The staffing and capacity of this provision should have regard for the expected number of reports which may be suitable for urgent preparation by court rather than field teams. Staff in Crown Court teams should, as far as possible, be experienced officers able to speak confidently in court and explain to sentencers the minimum time in which a satisfactory PSR could be prepared, while also being responsive to the needs of others involved in court proceedings.

32.   The importance of avoiding unnecessary adjournments for PSRs and minimising the length of those that do take place arises particularly from the substantial cost and disruption that can otherwise result, for example, for sentencers, legal representatives and remand prisons. Delay is also undesirable for offenders, particularly where they are remanded in custody but may subsequently receive a community sentence (wherever possible, a PSR requested on adjournment on a remand prisoner should, therefore, be completed in seven days). The *role of other participants* in securing the timely completion of PSRs is clearly acknowledged (see paragraphs 36 and 37, below). Nevertheless, ingenuity and flexibility in *working methods adopted by probation services* are also important in achieving the same result – for example, in sharing duties between PSR writing and other court liaison tasks, using fax machines and word

processors to allow PSRs to be written more quickly, and making the most of opportunities to conduct interviews with remand prisoners while they are being held at court.

Magistrates' and youth courts
33.   The preparation of PSRs in magistrates' and youth courts differs from the preparation of reports in the Crown Court: most significantly because it will normally be impracticable to provide dedicated PSR-writing teams in magistrates' or youth courts and, therefore, to respond very quickly to requests for short notice reports. Nevertheless, all reports should be prepared as expeditiously as possible – particularly, for example, in more straight-forward cases and those where the offender is remanded in custody awaiting sentence. The preparation of such reports (by field teams) will benefit from arrangements for disclosure of information by CPS and for prompt access to remand prisons. Such issues could usefully be discussed with magistrates and justices' clerks in probation liaison meetings, and could be the subject of a statement of preferred practice as to the preparation of reports (see paragraph 30, above).

. . .

ANNEX 2.A   REPORT WRITER'S ASSESSMENT OF SERIOUSNESS: RELATIONSHIP TO SENTENCING AND IMPLICATIONS FOR PSRs

Relationship to sentencing

The figure below illustrates the relationship between the provisional assessment of seriousness by the PSR writer, and the judgment by the sentencer.

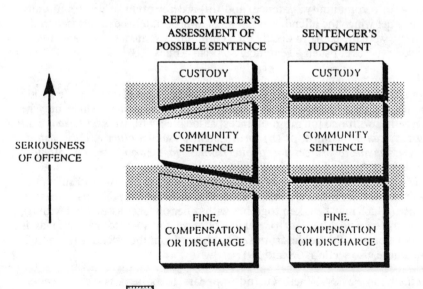

'OVERLAP', i.e. where PSR writer considers that more than one class of sentence might be imposed by the sentencer.

Implications for PSRs

Fine, compensation or discharge
Statutory criteria: A *fine, compensation order or discharge* are the primary disposals available to the court unless the court considers the offence(s) too serious to be dealt with by such a penalty alone.

Implications for PSRs Where a PSR has been asked for and it appears to the report writer that a fine, compensation order or discharge may be appropriate, the PSR should include information about the seriousness of the offence, including aggravating and mitigating circumstances.

Community sentence
Statutory criteria A *community sentence* (i.e. one including a probation order, community service order, combination order, curfew order, supervision order or attendance centre order) *may only be imposed if the offence* (which may be taken together with one [or more offences] associated with it) *is serious enough* to warrant such a sentence.
   The particular community sentence must be that which is *most suitable for the offender*; and the *restrictions on liberty imposed* by the order(s) must be *commensurate with the seriousness* of the offence (which may be taken together with other offences associated with it) (section 6, Criminal Justice Act 1991).

Implications for PSRs Where a community sentence appears to be a possible outcome, the PSR should include (i) information relevant to the determination of the seriousness of the offence(s), including aggravating and mitigating circumstances; (ii) information about the offender, especially as relevant to suitability for a community sentence; and (iii) a description of the community sentence under which the offender might most appropriately be supervised in the community, were the court to decide on a community sentence, with any advice on the likely success of such a sentence. See also Annex 2.B.

Custody
Statutory criteria Other than where the penalty is fixed by law (e.g. life imprisonment), *custody may only be imposed if* (a) the *offence* (which may be taken together with one [or more offences] associated with it) *is so serious that only custody can be justified*; or (b) *for a violent or sexual offence, only custody would be adequate to protect the public from serious harm from the offender* (section 1, 1991 Act).
   The *length of a custodial sentence* (other than one fixed by law, and subject to the maximum for the offence) shall be (a) commensurate with the seriousness of the offence (which may be taken together with other offences associated with it); or (b) in the case of a violent or sexual offence, for such longer term as is necessary to protect the public from serious harm from the offender (section 2, 1991 Act; note also sections 28 and 29).

Implications for PSRs Where custody appears to be a possible sentencing outcome, the PSR should include relevant information on (i) the seriousness of relevant offence(s), including aggravating and mitigating circumstances; and (ii) in the case of a violent or sexual offence, any evidence of risk of serious harm to the public from the offender. The PSR may include information on the likely consequences of custody (e.g. for future offending, or on the offender's family).

ANNEX 2.B   RELATING COMMUNITY SENTENCES TO THE SENTENCING FRAMEWORK OF THE CRIMINAL JUSTICE ACT 1991

NOTE: The diagram below offers a *possible* model for representing the range of community sentences available locally (middle area), taking into account the criteria for sentencing in the Criminal Justice Act 1991. The possibility of custody, and of a fine, compensation order or discharge (shaded areas) must also be taken into account.

The diagram relates to the national standard on pre-sentence reports in respect of guidance prepared by the CPO or Director of Social Services (paragraph 34); assessment of individual cases by report writers (paragraph 18); and explanation of the available range of community sentences to local sentencers and others (paragraph 36).

The model is *not* intended to be prescriptive: if used, it will in any event have to be adapted to local structures and programmes of supervision.

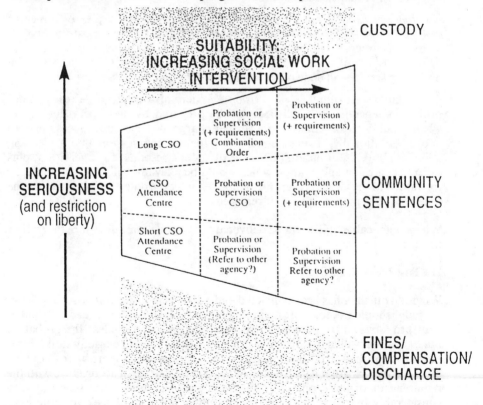

ANNEX 2.C   MODEL STATEMENT OF PREFERRED PRACTICE: PREPARATION OF PRE-SENTENCE REPORTS FOR THE CROWN COURT

In operating the probation service national standard on pre-sentence reports (PSRs) at (X) Crown Court, (Y) Probation Service have agreed the following arrangements with the Resident Judge as the preferred basis of operation.

1.   Pre-trial PSRs

A PSR will normally be prepared pre-trial in the following circumstances:

Guilty pleas.   Where there is a clear indication of a guilty plea at the point of committal in the magistrates' court, a full, written PSR will be provided in advance for the Crown Court hearing.

Mixed pleas.   If there is a plea of guilty to the more serious offence, a full, written PSR will be provided in advance for the Crown Court hearing. However, where the plea of guilty applies only to the minor offence, no pre-trial report will be prepared at that stage.

Not guilty pleas.   Where a defendant indicates a not guilty plea or a plea of guilty only to a lesser offence at the point of committal in the magistrates' court, no pre-trial report will be prepared. However, if given sufficient notice by defence lawyers of a change of plea prior to the Crown Court hearing, the probation service will endeavour to provide a full, written PSR pre-trial.

Defendants under statutory supervision.   Where an offender is already under probation supervision, a full PSR will be prepared by the supervising officer where a guilty plea is entered to a further charge in the circumstances outlined above. Additionally, if an offender faces further charges but is not pleading guilty as above, information about the offender's response to supervision, plus other background information which would be relevant, will, if appropriate, be forwarded to the Crown Court probation team by the date of trial, to reduce the time needed to prepare a PSR, if required.

Where practicable, PSRs will be delivered to the court *the day before* the trial or hearing.

2.   Post-conviction PSRs

Where an offender has been convicted and a PSR is required but is not available, the judge should ask for a probation officer to be called (if not already present in court) to advise how quickly a PSR could be prepared. Unless the probation officer is already able to advise the judge, the case should be briefly stood down so that the probation officer may assess the situation and report back as to how quickly it appears that a satisfactory PSR can be written in accordance with the requirements of the probation service national standard. That time can vary considerably from case to case the probation service will seek to write each report as expeditiously as possible, particularly where the defendant is in custody or the report is otherwise needed urgently. In appropriate cases only, this may be later the same day, but in other cases considerably longer may be required. Once the officer has reported back, the date should be set for the PSR to be available and sentencing to take place.

Probation officers will do all that they can to try to ensure that proceedings are not delayed unnecessarily. It will assist this process if prosecution and defence representatives are asked to make available to the probation officer any relevant documents and other information which could help with the report.

Unforeseen delays
Where a date has been agreed for the preparation of a PSR, the probation service will do all they can to complete the report in time for the agreed resumed hearing. On occasion, unforeseen delays may arise – for example, when unexpected complexities come to light while the report is being written – and in such cases the probation service will notify the Crown Court administrator at the earliest possible opportunity, preferably before the resumed hearing, to report the facts and seek a postponement.

3   PROBATION ORDERS

3.1   Introduction

Legislation
Probation orders are made under sections 2 and 3 of the Powers of Criminal Courts Act 1973 (the 1973 Act), as amended by the Criminal Justice Act 1991 (the 1991 Act.) A probation order may be made on an offender aged 16 years or over and requires the person to be under the supervision of a probation officer for a period of not less than six months nor more than three years. Certain additional requirements may be included in a probation order, including those specified in schedule 1A to the 1973 Act (as inserted by part II of schedule 1 to the 1991 Act). The offender must consent to the making of the order.

2.   This national standard is applicable to the operation both of probation orders and of the probation element of *combination orders* (and, where appropriate, should be read in conjunction with the national standard on combination orders). This standard should also be applied, as far as is appropriate, to the supervision of offenders under a *suspended sentence supervision order* (see paragraph 10, below).

Objectives
3.   The statutory purpose of supervision under a probation order, as defined in section 2(1) of the 1973 Act (as substituted by section 8(1) of the 1991 Act), is:

■   to secure the rehabilitation of the offender;
■   to protect the public from harm from the offender; and/or
■   to prevent the offender from committing further offences.

4.   Effective probation order supervision requires high standards both from probation services and from individual probation staff and should generally entail establishing a professional relationship, in which to advise, assist and befriend the offender with the aim of:

■ securing the offender's cooperation and compliance with the probation order and enforcing its terms;
■ challenging the offender to accept responsibility for his or her crime and its consequences;
■ helping the offender to resolve personal difficulties linked with offending and to acquire new skills; and
■ motivating and assisting the offender to become a responsible and law-abiding member of the community.

. . .

3.2 Targeting

7.   When proposing probation order supervision in a PSR, a probation officer should have regard to:

■ the *seriousness* of the offence and whether, under current sentencing guidelines, (i) it is serious enough to justify a community sentence (section 6(1) of the 1991 Act); and if so, whether (ii) the degree of *restriction on liberty* inherent in a proposed probation order (including any additional requirements) properly reflects the seriousness of the offence (section 6(2)(b));
■ the *suitability of probation order supervision for the offender* (section 6(2)(a) of the 1991 Act) bearing in mind the objectives of supervision set out in legislation and in this standard. Does the offender, for example, have personal problems to do with attitudes, skills, motivation or relationships which influence his or her offending and which might be addressed through probation order supervision? How might this offender respond to such supervision? How well might he or she meet the requirements of the order? Will the offender give his or her informed consent to the making of the order?

8.   A PSR must be considered by the sentencer before a probation order with any of the additional requirements listed in schedule 1A to the 1973 Act is imposed. In addition, a PSR may be of value in advising the court about suitability for community sentences for which a PSR is not required by law, and in seeking to ensure that supervision, if ordered, is able to start promptly and effectively (see paragraph 18, below). Where a PSR that proposes probation order supervision is being prepared, the opportunity should be taken, if possible, to begin drawing up the supervision plan which will be required if such an order is made (see paragraphs 19 and 20, below).

16 and 17-year-olds
9.   The 1991 Act lowers the minimum age for a probation order from the 17th to the 16th birthday. As a consequence, the new youth court (which replaces the juvenile court) will be able to impose probation orders. Under the 1991 Act, courts will have available to them the full range of juvenile and adult community sentences in dealing with 16 and 17-year-old offenders, including

both probation and supervision orders. As paragraph 14 of the supervision order national standard makes clear, the supervision order may often in practice be the more suitable form of supervision for 16 and 17-year-olds. Such supervision can assist the young person's development into adulthood, whereas the probation order is more appropriate for someone who is already an adult.

Suspended sentence supervision orders

10.   All suspended sentences of imprisonment constitute *custodial sentences* and as such must satisfy the criteria in the 1991 Act that the offence (or the offence together with one other associated with it) is so serious that *only* a custodial sentence can be justified, and will normally require a PSR to be considered by the sentencer. In exceptional cases, a court may decide to suspend a custodial sentence for offenders aged 21 and over, and the Crown Court may require supervision, i.e. as a *suspended sentence supervision order (SSSO)*. A SSSO may not include additional requirements and may not be as adaptable to the particular needs of the offender as a probation order, with which it may not be combined. On breach of a SSSO the offender may be fined; and on commission of a further imprisonable offence during the currency of the order the court may reactivate the custodial sentence. *As far as is appropriate, supervision of an offender under a SSSO should be conducted in accordance with this national standard on probation order supervision.*

3.3   Supervision

11.   This section of the standard sets requirements for the supervision of an individual offender under a probation order, within the objectives set out above. It defines the *role of the supervising officer* and requires:

- *prompt commencement* of supervision after the order is made – normally within five working days;
- the drawing up and regular review of a *supervision plan*;
- *frequent appointments* with the offender: where practicable and appropriate, 12 (and a minimum of six) in the first three months;
- accurate and timely *record keeping*, including the reason for any departure from expected standards of supervision;
- prompt and effective action to *enforce* the order, including *breach action* where behaviour is unacceptable.

Role of the supervising officer

12.   The probation officer responsible to the court for the supervision of a probation order (the '*supervising officer*') should ensure that supervision is conducted in accordance with this national standard and with regard to local practice guidance issued by her or his probation service. Where the offender is under 18, the conduct of supervision should have regard for the welfare of the young person in accordance with section 44 of the Children and Young Persons Act 1933.

13.   One of the keys to the effective supervision of probation orders is for those responsible for service delivery (at case, team and senior management

level) to manage workloads effectively, taking the initiative to allocate effort and priorities in accordance with the proper assessment of each case and with good monitoring information, and working to achieve the objectives of supervision in a planned and coordinated way with other agencies. Effort should be focused where it is needed and will have maximum effect, and where the intervention in the life of the offender is appropriate and justified. The supervising officer in each individual case (in appropriate consultation with line management and colleagues) is pivotal in applying such an approach properly within the case, and between that and other cases. Factors that may particularly be considered include:

- the seriousness of the offence(s) committed by the offender and the requirements of the order;
- the risk to the community;
- the offender's particular needs and response to supervision so far; and
- information about the target group, availability, effectiveness and cost of specialist programmes run by the service (see paragraph 33, below) and other resources that could be deployed.

14.   Varying forms of supervision may be engaged during an order and these can be specified as a requirement of the order and should be included in the supervision plan. It is important that full use is made of such resources to the extent that is appropriate. While it may be relevant to address wider problems, the *primary focus of the order on the offender should be kept fully in mind*. Imagination and flexibility are important in devising effective individual programmes of supervision. This can include:

- *direct intervention by the supervising probation officer*. This may be *face to face* with the offender *individually* or in *group work* (most often at a probation office, but *home visits* should also be considered and used, where appropriate, as an aid to understanding the offender's behaviour and gauging progress), or *working with others* in relation to the offender (e.g. resolving difficulties over housing, financial management or employment);
- *referral to a specialist probation team or facility* (e.g. a probation centre or drug or alcohol group), or an independent-sector or other project providing supervision in partnership with the probation service;
- *referral to* (or other involvement with) various *resources or opportunities in the community*, including employment, training, education, health, social services, housing and community groups.

15.   Where the probation order includes a condition for *treatment of the offender's mental condition or drug or alcohol dependency*, the role of the supervising officer is likely to include liaising with the relevant services or agencies to ensure that the offender receives the treatment ordered by the court. While the offender receives treatment as a resident, direct supervision is not required, but the officer retains responsibility for revocation or amendment of the order. Where treatment is on a non-residential basis, the supervising officer is responsible for supervision in the normal manner, but must work closely with those providing treatment for the offender.

16.   The supervising officer should draw to the attention of his or her line manager, in an appropriate manner, issues which are material to the effectiveness of supervision, such as opportunities for improvement, or a lack of resources or expertise to undertake adequate supervision. Line managers should ensure that they are aware of such issues.

Commencement

17.   The *initial appointment* between a probation officer (normally the supervising officer) and the offender should, whenever possible, be arranged for a date *within five working days of the making of the order*. If practicable, the appointment should be made before the offender leaves court.

18.   At their first meeting, the supervising officer (or other probation officer) should:

■   give the offender *written information* setting out what he or she can expect from the probation service during the period of supervision under the probation order; what is expected of the offender; the consequences of unacceptable behaviour, including the possibility of breach; and procedures for discharge or amendment of the order (including the offender's right to apply), and for complaint about his or her treatment under the order. The information should be available in English and, where relevant and practicable, in other languages;

■   *explain* this to the offender, together with any particular requirements which form part of the offender's probation order;

■   if possible, *serve the offender with a copy of the order*, which the offender should sign;

■   *establish that the offender has given her or his informed consent to the order* (or, if not, and the offender states that she or he refuses or withdraws consent, take appropriate action, if necessary by returning the offender to court).

It is recognised that achieving these requirements can only be possible with the effective cooperation of court staff, e.g. in providing copies of orders promptly, and that prompt commencement and effective supervision are more difficult where an order is made where no PSR has been obtained.

Supervision plan

19.   If possible *within two weeks of sentence* (and with in a maximum of four weeks), an individual *supervision plan* should be drawn up in writing for each offender, normally by the supervising officer in consultation with the offender. It should be based upon the requirements of the order (including any additional requirements) drawing, where appropriate, on the assessment and any outline proposals for supervision contained in PSR, to meet the objectives of probation order supervision set out in this standard. The plan should:

■   identify the offender's motivation and pattern of offending, his or her relevant problems and needs, the risk of reoffending or serious harm to the public, and the requirements of the order; and

■ set out an individual programme designed to tackle these elements, identifying the resources that will or may be employed (including probation, community and other resources), setting out the nature and frequency of contact during the order (in accordance with this standard) which is considered most appropriate, and identifying a time-scale for achieving each objective in the programme.

20. It is important that the plan should, wherever possible, be *agreed* with the offender and *signed* by both the offender and the supervising officer. A *copy* should normally be given to the offender (see paragraph 22, below) and another should be held on file. The *plan should be reviewed* with the offender, and progress recorded and the plan amended as necessary after *every three months* from the start of the order (and more frequently, if appropriate), with a *final review* on completion of the order. The early stages should, therefore, focus particularly on a plan of work to be undertaken; later stages should focus increasingly on the degree of achievement of that plan. As initially, further copies of the plan should be given to the offender and held on file. Towards the end of the order, early termination should be considered where good progress has been made (see paragraph 28, below).

Frequency of contact
21. The appropriate frequency of contact will vary both from case to case and during the period of a probation order. The most frequent contact should generally be made *early* in an order as a basis for a prompt and concerted effort to secure lasting change. *Where practicable and appropriate, 12 appointments should be made for an offender to see the supervising officer (or a person operating under his or her direction) in the first three months of an order; six in the next three months; and thereafter at least one each month to the completion of supervision. Where this is not practicable and appropriate, a minimum level of six appointments in the first three months and one appointment monthly, thereafter, must be observed.*

Record keeping
22. *Up-to-date records* must be kept of appointments and contact with the offender during the order, of the supervision plan and of any other information material to effective supervision, in accordance with rule 31 of the Probation Rules 1984. *Where a judgment is taken to depart from an expected requirement of this standard, that departure, and the reasons for it, should be clearly recorded.* It is generally good practice for information held on an individual to be shared with her or him, unless there are good reasons for not doing so. In the case of a young person, information should normally be shared with her or his parent(s) if, in consultation with the offender, that is considered appropriate. Confidentiality of records and all other information about the offender should otherwise be maintained having regard to the need to protect the public and the need to cooperate with sentencers, CPS, prisons or other agencies for the proper functioning of the criminal justice system as a whole.

Enforcement
23. In enforcing a probation order effectively, the supervising officer should:

■   *seek to secure and maintain the offender's consent to and compliance with the order* so that the objectives of supervision may be achieved; but also

■   *recognise where this cannot be achieved and take appropriate action.* Consideration of the objectives of supervision should, however, remain of primary concern during any procedure undertaken to enforce the order.

24.   Securing and maintaining the offender's consent and compliance requires consistent action on several fronts by those responsible for supervision: clear instruction and explanation to the offender, e.g. as to required standards of behaviour; seeking to motivate and assist the offender to comply with the order; and anticipating difficulties and, where possible, pre-empting infringements by some timely encouragement or advice.

25.   Any apparent failure to comply with the requirements of the order must be followed up promptly, normally within two working days, seeking an explanation from the offender. The apparent failure, the offender's explanation (or lack of one), the supervising officer's opinion of whether the explanation (or lack of one) is acceptable and the likely consequences for the effectiveness of supervision must be recorded. (The personal circumstances and characteristics of the offender may affect the acceptability of the explanation or lack of one, for example, where an offender's chaotic or impulsive lifestyle, or substantial difficulties being faced, affect the degree of premeditation behind the apparent failure to comply.) *If the explanation (or lack of one) is not considered acceptable, the incident must formally be recorded as an instance of failure to comply with the order.* If breach action is not being taken, the offender should be warned (orally, confirmed in writing on the second or subsequent occasion) of the likely consequences of further failure to comply with the order. Following up apparent failure to comply can be an important opportunity to strengthen the offender's consent to and compliance with the order (see paragraphs 23 and 24, above). In addition, failure to comply may reveal a need for change in the supervision being undertaken.

26.   Breach action under schedule 2 to the 1991 Act may be appropriate immediately in some instances of failure to comply, such as failure to notify a change of address when it is clear that the intention was to avoid carrying out the order; stated refusal to comply with the order; or withdrawal of consent. In other cases, the supervising officer may consider that the purpose of the order is best served by giving a warning in the first and second instances, as above, but *breach action should normally be taken after no more than three instances of failure to comply with the order.* Further continuation without breach action, in limited circumstances only, may only take place if agreed with a Senior Probation Officer as being strongly in the interest of the objectives of the order. Practice guidance reflecting discussion with sentencers may help to clarify where this may be appropriate (see paragraphs 31 and 34, below). In these considerations earlier instances of non-compliance may normally be disregarded if they took place more than six months before (but all become relevant if breach proceedings are begun). All instances of failure to comply, decisions made and action taken should be noted on case records.

27.   When breach proceedings are undertaken, the supervising officer has an important role in the separate processes of proving the breach and advising the

court on further action. The supervising officer should be clear as to what course of action in his or her professional opinion he or she would advise the court to follow, such as reinforcement of the order with a warning about future conduct; amendment of the terms of the order, e.g. a change in additional requirements; imposition of a fine, CSO or attendance centre order; substitution of a different community order; or whether further continuation of any community order is impracticable or unjustified. This should be contained, as required, in an oral or written report to the court, which should also include an account of the offender's response to supervision so far and the extent to which the offender has successfully completed the order (i.e. has successfully discharged the sentence imposed on him or her – paragraphs 3(2)(a) and 4(2)(a) of schedule 2 to the 1991 Act; this becomes relevant if the court considers dealing with the offender for the original offence). The supervising officer should also consider whether the offender's behaviour amounts to wilful and persistent failure to comply with the requirements of the order, which can be taken as refusal to consent to a community sentence (paragraph 3(2)(b) or 4(2)(b) of the schedule). If the supervising officer considers it likely to be expedient and appropriate, a (further) pre-sentence report may be prepared prior to the breach hearing.

Early termination
28. *Early termination* of an order should be considered where the offender has made good progress in achieving the objectives set out for the order and where there is not considered to be a significant risk of reoffending and/or of serious harm to the public. An application for early termination should not normally be sought before halfway through the term of the order, but such action should be considered by two-thirds of the term unless there are clear reasons for not doing so.

. . .

ANNEX 3.A   PROBATION CENTRES: APPROVAL

Paragraph 3 of schedule 1A to the 1973 Act (as inserted by part II of schedule 1 to the 1991 Act) provides for attendance at a *probation centre* to be specified as an additional requirement of a probation order. Paragraph 3(3)(a) provides for attendance to be required on a maximum of 60 days, though paragraph 4(1) enables this to be increased to the full length of the probation order in the case of an offender convicted of a sexual offence.

2. Paragraph 3(7)(b) *requires a probation centre to be approved by the Secretary, of State, for the time being, as providing facilities suitable for persons subject to probation orders.* Under paragraph 3 of schedule 12 to the 1991 Act, a day centre under (the former) section 4B of the 1973 Act immediately prior to commencement of the new provision for Secretary of State approval (i.e. approved by the Probation Committee, as required by rule 44(4) of the Probation Rules 1984) is deemed to be so approved immediately after commencement. The CPO must ensure that his or her service does not agree to a probation order requiring attendance at a probation centre which does not have the necessary approval.

3.   A broad range of intensity and type of programme is possible at a probation centre within the framework set by the probation order national standard and paragraphs 3 and 4 of schedule 1A. Probation centres are nevertheless capable of providing one of the most demanding programmes of supervision, at highest unit cost and with greatest restriction on liberty (therefore appropriate for some of the most serious offenders given a community sentence). Particular care is, therefore, necessary in addressing the requirements of the national standard – generally, and in respect of the requirements for programmes (paragraphs 32 and 33).

4.   While Secretary of State approval is for a probation *centre* (rather than a particular programme, of which more than one may be operated there), the range and content of the programme(s) to be offered will be considered in examining any application for approval. *Where a probation service decides to operate a programme* forming part of a probation centre requirement under paragraph 3 of schedule 1A *so as to require 20 or more full days' attendance or 40 or more half days*, the *normal expectation* should be that a *full day's attendance* comprises at least six hours at the centre or attendance elsewhere in accordance with instructions given by, or under the authority of, the person running the centre; a *half day's attendance* comprises, similarly, three hours' attendance; and that a *broad-ranging programme* is provided to address offending behaviour, personal difficulties relevant to offending, and constructive use of leisure time. Where these expectations are *not* to be met, specific justification should be made in the application for approval. (It is noted that attendance may only be required on a maximum of 60 days under a probation order, whether full days' attendance or not, except in the case of sex offenders, whose required attendance may be extended to the full length of the order under paragraph 4 of schedule 1A).

. . .

4   SUPERVISION ORDERS

4.1   Introduction

This national standard applies to the supervision by social services departments and probation services of supervision orders made in the criminal courts.

Legislation

2.   Supervision orders may be made on an offender aged 10 to 17, inclusive, under the Children and Young Persons Act 1969 (the 1969 Act), as amended by the Criminal Justice Act 1991 (the 1991 Act) and other legislation. Section 7(7) of the 1969 Act is the primary supervision order making power: the child or young person may be placed under the supervision of a social services department or a probation officer for a period of up to three years. Section 14 requires the supervisor to advise, assist and befriend the supervised person. Sections 12, 12A, 12AA, 12B, 12C and 18(2)(b) provide for certain additional requirements to be included in the order. Annex 4.A to this standard summarises the terms of these requirements.

3. Section 44 of the Children and Young Persons Act 1933 (the 1933 Act) sets out the principle that all courts must have regard to the welfare of children and young persons who appear before them. The 1991 Act brings 17-year-olds, for most purposes, within the definition of 'young persons' (now aged 14 to 17, inclusive), and provides that children (those aged 10 to 13, inclusive) and young persons should be dealt with in the youth court. As the youth court will, therefore, deal with almost all cases involving those under 18, the principle of section 44 of the 1933 Act will be of particular importance to that court and, because the order can only be made on a offender under 18, to the operation of all supervision orders.

4. This standard applies to all ages for which a supervision order is available to the courts. In relation to 16 and 17-year-olds, the standard should be read in conjunction with the corresponding national standard on probation order supervision, since both forms of supervision can be ordered by the courts for offenders of those ages.

Objectives

5. The *objectives* that should be pursued by probation services or social services departments in operating a supervision order are:

■ to encourage and assist the child or young person in her or his development towards a responsible and law-abiding life, thereby promoting the welfare of the offender and seeking:

■ to protect the public from harm from the offender; and

■ to prevent the offender from committing further offences.

6. Effective operation of supervision orders requires high standards from services, from individual members of staff and from others involved in supervision, e.g. through partnerships with the voluntary sector. This should entail establishing a professional relationship, in which to advise, assist and befriend the offender with the aim of:

■ enabling and encouraging the child or young person to understand and accept responsibility for his or her behaviour and its consequences;

■ helping the child or young person to resolve personal difficulties linked with offending and to acquire new skills; and

■ securing the child or young person's cooperation and compliance with the supervision order and enforcing its terms.

. . .

4.2 Targeting

9. When proposing supervision order supervision in a PSR, a probation officer or social worker should have regard to:

■ the *seriousness of the offence* and whether, under current sentencing guidelines, (i) it is serious enough to justify a community sentence (section

6(1) of the 1991 Act); and if so, whether (ii) the degree of *restriction on liberty* inherent in a proposed supervision order (including any additional requirements) properly reflects the seriousness of the offence (section 6(2)(b));

■ the *suitability of supervision order supervision for the offender* (section 6(2)(a) of the 1991 Act) having regard for the welfare of the child or young person and bearing in mind the objectives of supervision set out in this standard. Does the offender, for example, have personal problems to do with attitudes, stage of development, skills, motivation or relationships which influence her or his offending and which might be addressed through such supervision? How might this offender respond to such supervision? How well and how willingly might she or he meet the requirements of the order?

10.   A PSR must be considered by the sentencer before a supervision order with any of the additional requirements in sections 12, 12A, 12AA, 12B or 12C of the 1969 Act is imposed. In addition, a PSR may be of value in advising the court about suitability for community sentences for which a PSR is not required by law, and in seeking to ensure that supervision, if ordered, is able to start promptly and effectively (see paragraph 24, below). Where a PSR that proposes a supervision order is being prepared, the opportunity should be taken, if possible, to begin drawing up the supervision plan which will be required if such an order is made (see paragraphs 25 and 26, below).

11.   A young person or the parent or guardian of a child must consent to the inclusion in a supervision order of any requirement under section 12A(3) of the 1969 Act; a young person must consent to the inclusion of any requirement under section 12B(l). In such cases, informed consent should be obtained by making clear the demands of the requirement and what will be expected of the offender. While consent is not required to other forms of supervision order, every effort should be made to gain the acceptance by the offender, and his or her family, of what is proposed.

10–15-year-olds

12.   The needs of the youngest offenders for whom a community sentence is justified under the criteria in paragraph 9, above, are likely to be varied. The younger the offender, the more important is the welfare requirement under the 1933 Act (see paragraph 3, above,) in determining the most suitable community sentence. The supervision order is a very flexible community sentence. A wide range of requirements may be attached to it. It is, therefore, often likely to offer the best way of matching the intervention justified by the seriousness of the offence to the particular needs of the young offender.

16 and 17-year-olds

13.   An important issue when considering a 16 or 17-year-old offender for supervision is whether to propose to the court in a PSR a supervision order or a probation order. The starting-point should be whether *any* form of supervision appears to be appropriate, given the criteria of seriousness and suitability set out in paragraph 9, above, and in the probation order national standard. Both supervision orders and probation orders, operated to the relevant national

standard, represent a significant restriction on liberty and a significant invest-ment of skilled effort: inappropriate use of these orders is likely to be wasteful and to prevent intervention in more relevant cases, and may even be counter-productive.

14.   While both a supervision order and a probation order are intended to assist an offender to become more responsible and to keep out of trouble, the clearest distinguishing feature is that the supervision order is also intended to help a young person to develop into an adult, whereas a probation order is more appropriate for someone who is already emotionally, intellectually, socially and physically an adult. Since many 16 and 17-year-olds are still very much in the stage of transition into adulthood, the supervision order may often in practice be the more suitable form of supervision.

15.   Paragraph 9 of the joint circular on young people and the youth court in relation to the 1991 Act (Home Office Circular 30/1992, also numbered LAC (92)5 and Welsh Office Circular 21/92, dated 20 March 1992) listed several factors likely to be relevant to this consideration, including the young person's continuing dependence on or independence from parents, and whether he or she is leading a stable, independent life with his or her own family responsibilities. Other considerations may include how the young person would be influenced by other offenders currently subject to supervision orders or probation orders whom he or she may meet at group sessions, and whether assistance is currently being received or is needed from social services.

4.3 Supervision

16.   This section of the standard sets out requirements for the supervision of an individual offender under a supervision order, within the objectives set out above. It defines the *role of the supervising officer* and requires:

■ prompt commencement of supervision after the order is made – normally within 5 working days;
■ the drawing up and regular review of a *supervision plan*;
■ *frequent appointments* with the offender: where practicable and appropriate, 12 (and a minimum of six) in the first three months;
■ accurate and timely *record keeping*, including the reason for any departure from expected standards of supervision;
■ prompt and effective action to *enforce* the order, including *breach action* where behaviour is unacceptable.

Role of the supervising officer

17.   The probation officer or social worker responsible to the court for the operation of a supervision order (the '*supervising officer*') should ensure that supervision is conducted in accordance with this national standard and with regard to local practice guidance issued by his or her service. In operating a supervision order, the supervising officer should have constant regard for the welfare of the child or young person and should gear the supervision towards the patient and careful approach that is particularly required with young people. The tasks set out in this section must be accomplished, but it cannot be assumed, for example, that instructions are perceived by a child or young person as

carrying the same force as they would be by an adult. The supervision must reflect the needs and stage of development of the individual offender.

18.   One of the keys to the effective operation of supervision orders is for those responsible for service delivery (at case, team and senior management level) to manage workloads effectively, taking the initiative to allocate effort and priorities in accordance with the proper assessment of each case and with good monitoring information, and working to achieve the objectives of supervision in a planned and coordinated way with other agencies (see paragraph 37, below). Effort should be focused where it is needed and will have maximum effect, and where the intervention in the life of the young person is appropriate and justified. The supervising officer in each individual case (in appropriate consultation with line management and colleagues) is pivotal in applying such an approach properly within the case, and between that and other cases. Factors that may particularly be considered include:

- the seriousness of the offence(s) committed by the offender and the requirements of the order;
- the risk to the community;
- the offender's particular needs and response to supervision so far; and
- information about the target group, availability, effectiveness and cost of specialist programmes (see paragraph 42, below) and other resources that could be deployed.

19.   Varying forms of supervision may be engaged during an order and these may be specified as a requirement of the order and should be included in the supervision plan. It is important that full use is made of such resources to the extent that is appropriate. While it may be relevant to address wider problems involving others, such as working with parents to resolve difficult relationships, the *primary focus of the order on the young offender should be kept fully in mind.* Imagination and flexibility are important in devising effective individual programmes of supervision. This can include:

- *direct intervention by the supervising officer* working face to face with the offender, for example, at the probation/social services office or the offender's home;
- *direct intervention by the supervising officer with others*, particularly with the offender's family, but also with others, such as the school, careers office, housing department, social security office, employment or training provider or local education authority;
- *cooperation with or referral to others who will work with the young offender*, particularly the youth service or schools; also employment or training, offender groups, independent-sector projects or workers, reparation or mediation projects or other community resources. The voluntary sector, in particular, has often worked in partnership with probation or social services in supervising young offenders. Where any such referral forms an integral part of the planned intervention with the young offender, the supervising officer should ensure that she or he properly informs the other party of what is intended, and reviews progress and outcome adequately.

20.   Consistent with the provisions of both the Children Act 1989 and the Criminal Justice Act 1991, the supervising officer should seek to work in *partnership with the young offender and his or her parent(s) or guardian,* and as far as is appropriate, to involve the parent(s) or guardian at all stages of the supervision of the order. Unless there is a good reason for doing otherwise, parents should be encouraged to take responsibility for their children and to support them during the period of supervision. Where the offender is in the care of the local authority, the supervising officer should work closely with those social services staff having responsibility for him or her.

21.   The supervising officer should draw to the attention of her or his line manager, in an appropriate manner, issues which are material to the effectiveness of supervision, such as opportunities for improvement, or a lack of resources or expertise to undertake adequate supervision. Line managers should ensure that they are aware of such issues.

Commencement

22.   The *initial appointment* between a probation officer or social worker (normally the supervising officer) and the offender should, whenever possible, be arranged for a date within *five working days of the making of the order.* If practicable, the appointment should be made before the offender leaves court.

23.   At their first meeting the supervising officer (or other probation officer or social worker) should:

■   give the offender *written information* setting out what he or she can expect from the probation service or social services department during the period of supervision under the order; what is expected of the offender; the consequences of unacceptable behaviour, including the possibility of breach; and procedures for the discharge or variation of the order (including the offender's right to apply), and for complaint about his or her treatment under the order. The information should be available in English and, where relevant and practicable, in other languages;

■   *explain* this to the offender, together with any particular requirements which form part of the order;

■   if possible, *serve the offender with a copy of the order,* which the offender should sign;

■   *establish that the offender is aware of what the order will entail and is able and willing to cooperate* (or, if not, take appropriate action, ultimately by returning the offender to court);

■   at the initial appointment or as soon as possible thereafter, provide similar information to and seek similar commitment from, as appropriate, the *offender's parent(s)* or others who it appears will be material to the supervision.

24.   It is recognised that achieving these requirements can only be possible with the effective cooperation of court staff, e.g. in providing copies of orders promptly, and that prompt commencement and effective supervision are more difficult where an order is made where no PSR has been obtained.

Supervision plan

25.   If possible, *within two weeks of sentence* (and within a maximum of four weeks), an individual *supervision plan* should be drawn up in writing for each offender, normally by the supervising officer in consultation with the child or young person and, if appropriate, her or his parent(s). It should be based upon the requirements of the order (including any additional requirements) drawing, where appropriate, on the assessment and any outline proposals for supervision contained in the PSR, to meet the objectives of supervision set out in this standard. The plan should:

■   identify the offender's motivation and pattern of offending, her or his relevant problems and needs, the risk of reoffending or serious harm to the public, and the requirements of the order; and
■   set out an individual programme designed to tackle these elements, identifying the people and resources that will or may be employed (e.g. including, as appropriate, parent(s), school, and voluntary and statutory agencies), setting out the nature and frequency of contact during the order (in accordance with this standard) which are considered most appropriate, and identifying a time-scale for achieving each objective in the programme.

26.   It is important that the plan should, wherever possible, be *agreed* with the offender and *signed* by both the offender and the supervising officer. A *copy* should be given to the offender and another should be held on file. A copy should also normally be given to others closely involved in the supervision, e.g. parent(s) and/or a voluntary sector worker (see paragraph 28, below). The *plan should he reviewed* with the offender and, where appropriate, the parent(s), progress recorded and the plan amended as necessary after *every three months* from the start of the order (and more frequently, if appropriate), with a *final review* on completion of the order. The early stages should, therefore, focus particularly on a plan of work to be undertaken; later stages should focus increasingly on the degree of achievement of that plan. As initially, further copies of the plan should be given to the offender and others involved and held on file. Early termination of the order should be considered where good progress has been made (see paragraph 35, below). Where the child or young person is subject to a residence requirement under a supervision order, regulations under the Children Act 1989 apply to the review of the case.

Frequency of contact

27.   The appropriate frequency of contact will vary both from case to case and during the period of a supervision order. The most frequent contact should generally be made *early* in an order as a basis for a prompt and concerted effort to secure lasting change. *Where practicable and appropriate, 12 appointments should be made for an offender to see the supervising officer (or a person operating under his or her direction) in the first three months of an order; six in the next three months; and thereafter at least one each month to the completion of supervision. Where this is not practicable and appropriate, a minimum level of six appointments in the first three months and one appointment monthly, thereafter, must be observed.*

Record keeping
28.   *Up-to-date records* must be kept of appointments and contact with the offender during the order, of the supervision plan and of any other information material to effective supervision. *Where a judgement is taken to depart from an expected requirement of this standard, that departure, and the reasons for it, should be clearly recorded.* It is generally good practice for information held on an individual to be shared with him or her, unless there are good reasons for not doing so, and with his or her parent(s) if, in consultation with the individual, that is considered appropriate. Confidentiality of records and all other information about the offender should otherwise be maintained having regard to the need to protect the public and the need to cooperate with sentencers, CPS, prisons or other agencies for the proper functioning of the criminal justice system as a whole.

Enforcement
29.   In enforcing a supervision order the supervising officer should:

■   *seek to secure and maintain consent to and compliance with the order by the offender and others involved* so that the objectives of supervision may be achieved; but also
■   *recognise where this cannot be achieved and take appropriate action.* Consideration of the objectives of supervision should, however, remain of primary concern during any procedure undertaken to enforce the order.

30.   Seeking to secure and maintain the child or young person's consent and compliance (even where the offender's consent to the making of the order was not required) is important to effective supervision and demands consistent action on several fronts by those responsible for the order: clear instruction and explanation to the offender, e.g. as to required standards of behaviour; seeking patiently to motivate and assist the child or young person to comply with the order; and anticipating difficulties and, where possible, pre-empting infringements by some timely encouragement or advice. The process of enforcement should encourage the child or young person to accept some discipline, but should retain the degree of flexibility demanded by the individual's age, stage of development and degree of responsibility for her or his actions. Any action taken to enforce the order should take full account of the welfare of the child or young person.
31.   Under section 15 of the 1969 Act (as substituted by schedule 7 to the 1991 Act), the supervising officer (or supervised person) may apply to discharge any supervision order or vary it by inserting or cancelling an additional requirement in the order. Other procedures under section 15 can occur if the offender fails to comply with an additional requirement included under sections 12, 12A, 12AA, 12C or 18(2)(b).
32.   Any apparent failure to comply with one of those requirements must be followed up promptly, normally within two working days, seeking an explanation from the offender. The apparent failure, the offender's explanation (or lack of one), the supervising officer's opinion of whether the explanation (or lack of

one) is acceptable and the likely consequences for the effectiveness of supervision must be recorded. (The personal circumstances and characteristics of the offender may affect the acceptability of the explanation or lack of one, e.g. by indicating the degree of premeditation behind the apparent failure to comply.) *If the explanation (or lack of one) is not considered acceptable, the incident must formally be recorded as an instance of failure to comply with a requirement of the order.* If breach action is not being taken, the offender should be warned (orally, confirmed in writing on the second or subsequent occasion) of the likely consequences of further failure to comply with the requirement. It is desirable that the child or young person should be accompanied by a parent or other adult when being dealt with under any enforcement procedure. Following up apparent failure to comply can be an important opportunity to strengthen the offender's consent to and compliance with the order (see paragraphs 29 and 30, above). In addition, failure to comply may reveal a need for change in the supervision being undertaken.

33.   Breach action may be appropriate immediately in some instances of failure to comply, such as failure to notify a change of address when it is clear that the intention was to avoid carrying out the order; stated refusal to comply with the order; or withdrawal of consent (where this is required). In other cases, the supervising officer may consider that the purpose of the order is best served by giving a warning in the first and second instances, as above, but *breach action should normally be taken after no more than three instances of failure to comply with a requirement of the order.* Further continuation without breach action, in limited circumstances only, may only take place if agreed with a Team Manager or Senior Probation Officer as being strongly in the interests of the objectives of the order. Practice guidance reflecting discussion with sentencers may help to clarify where this may be appropriate (see paragraphs 41 and 43, below). In these considerations, earlier instances of non-compliance may normally be disregarded if they took place more than six months before (and this period may be reduced, to a minimum of three months, where that is considered essential to have adequate regard for the child or young person's age and stage of development: if so, the decision and reasons for it should be recorded on the case file). However, all previous instances of failure to comply become relevant if breach proceedings are begun. All instances of failure to comply, decisions made and action taken should be noted on case records.

34.   When breach proceedings are undertaken, the supervising officer has an important role in the separate processes of proving the breach and advising the court on further action. The supervising officer should be clear as to what action he or she would advise the court to take, such as reinforcement of the order with a warning about future conduct; variation of the terms of the order, e.g. a change in additional requirements; or imposition of a fine or attendance centre order; or whether further continuation is impracticable or unjustified. This should be contained, as required, in an oral or written report to the court, which should also include an account of the offender's response to supervision so far and the extent to which the offender has successfully completed the order. If the supervising officer considers it likely to be expedient and appropriate, a (further) PSR may be prepared prior to the breach hearing.

Early termination
35.   Early termination of an order should be considered where the offender has made good progress in achieving the objectives set out for the order and where there is not considered to be a significant risk of reoffending and/or of serious harm to the public. An application for early termination should normally be considered by two-thirds of the term of the order unless there are clear reasons for not doing so.

. . .

5   COMMUNITY SERVICE ORDERS

5.1   Introduction

Legislation
Community service orders (CSOs) are made under section 14 of the Powers of Criminal Courts Act 1973 (the 1973 Act), as amended by section 10 of the Criminal Justice Act 1991 (the 1991 Act). A CSO may be made on an offender aged 16 years or over and requires the person to perform unpaid work of 40 to 240 hours duration. Before making the order the court must be satisfied that the offender is a suitable person to perform community service and that such work can be made available locally. The court must consider a pre-sentence report (PSR) before imposing a CSO and the offender must consent to the making of the order.
2.   This national standard is derived from the earlier CS national standard which came into force on 1 April 1989 (Home Office Circular 18/1989), which is now withdrawn. The standard is applicable to the operation both of CSOs and of the CS element of *combination orders* (and where appropriate, should, therefore, be read in conjunction with the national standard on combination orders). Similarly, the previous Community Service Orders Rules, SI 191/1989, are being replaced with new CSO Rules appropriate to this present standard.

Objectives
3.   *The main purpose of a CSO is to reintegrate the offender into the community through:*

■ *positive and demanding unpaid work*, keeping to disciplined requirements; and
■ *reparation to the community* by undertaking socially useful work which, if possible, makes good damage done by offending.

4.   The operation of CSOs represents a valuable opportunity for probation services to engage offenders constructively with the local community, to promote the rehabilitation of offenders generally.

. . .

5.2 Targeting

7.   Under section 7(3) of the 1991 Act, a PSR must be considered by the court before imposing a CSO. Careful assessment at the PSR stage will have important advantages in satisfying the court as to the suitability of the offender for a CSO and in securing the offender's informed consent to the order. When proposing a CSO in a PSR, a probation officer should have regard to:

- the *seriousness of the offence* and whether, under current sentencing guidelines, (i) it is serious enough to justify a community sentence (section 6(1) of the 1991 Act); and if so, whether (ii) the degree of *restriction of liberty* inherent in a proposed CSO properly reflects the seriousness of the offence (section 6(2)(b)), taking into account the length of the order;
- the *suitability of a CSO for the offender* (section 6(2)(a) of the 1991 Act) bearing in mind the requirements and objectives of CS work set out in the legislation and in this standard. Would the offender be likely to keep successfully to the requirements and discipline expected of him or her, taking into account, for example, the offender's age (especially if 16 or 17) and stage of development? (If a significant amount of social work intervention is required and if justified by the seriousness of the offence, a supervision, probation or combination order is likely to be more appropriate.) Does the offender's current offence, offending history or likely risk to the public mean that placement on a CS scheme would be unacceptable? Will the offender give her or his informed consent to the making of the order?

5.3 Supervision

8.   This section of the standard sets requirements in relation to the *operation of local CS schemes*, including:

- *arranging work placements*, and
- *referral arrangements*, e.g. at the PSR stage,

and then sets out requirements for the *supervision of individual offenders* under CSOs including:

- *prompt commencement* of work after the order is made – normally within 10 working days;
- *the management of community service*;
- *work rate* – a minimum of five hours per week during the order, with a normal maximum of 21 hours in any one week;
- acceptable *standards of performance and behaviour*;
- accurate and timely *record keeping* (including guidance on *reckoning of hours worked*); and
- *enforcement*.

Arranging work placements

9.   Probation services should arrange a variety of CS work placements for offenders: these should be *demanding* in the sense of being physically, emotion-

ally or intellectually taxing; *of benefit to the community*; and, if possible, *personally fulfilling* for offenders and designed to *secure public support for the supervision of offenders in the community*. Many imaginative and innovative approaches to CS work are possible – and are to be encouraged – consistent with ensuring good-quality placements that are sustainable and well managed, that can demonstrate the worth of CS work, and that have regard for the perception of CS by those outside the probation service. Possible examples of work placements could include work for elderly people or people with disabilities, environmental projects, improvements to the appearance or amenities of a neighbourhood and crime prevention initiatives.

10.　Offenders should be encouraged to recognise the damage their offending has done and to see CS work as a means of making amends. Efforts should be made to avoid requirements of the order conflicting with the offender's responsibilities, and CS work should be available at weekends and in the evenings to provide for employed offenders. The order must, however, restrict the offender's liberty and is not intended to be arranged for his or her convenience. Appropriate equipment, instructions (for example, in relation to health and safety) and protective clothing should be provided where appropriate.

11.　Probation services should avoid CS work impacting adversely on local employment. Offenders should, therefore, not be instructed to carry out work under a CSO which would normally be done by employees and, where appropriate, trade unions should be consulted about particular CS schemes.

12.　CS work may be undertaken in individual placements (where an offender works under appropriate supervision on her or his own) or group placements (with two or more offenders working together). *Individual placements* emphasise to the offender her or his personal responsibility and sense of integration within the community. Supervision is normally undertaken by the person or organisation providing the placement. *Group placements* permit greater uniformity of CS work; since they are normally supervised by probation staff, provide an opportunity to ensure directly that standards of performance and behaviour are met; allow offenders to participate in a team-based project, emphasising cooperation with others; and may well provide a more visible result from CS work. *Both* types of placement should be made available by probation services and should be used in the most appropriate manner within CS schemes and in individual cases (see paragraph 21, below).

13.　Individuals and organisations that agree to provide CS placements (beneficiaries) should be adequately informed, in writing, as to the purpose of CS work; what is expected of them as providers (including insurance arrangements); what is expected of offenders working for them under CSOs; and their informed consent should be obtained before CS placements begin. Where appropriate, the views of beneficiaries on the benefits (or disadvantages) of the work undertaken should be invited.

14.　Each (potential) CS placement or project should be *assessed* considering:

- length of each work session;
- amount of supervision needed;
- risk to all persons or property;

- types of work involved (including skills required and health and safety implications);
- demands imposed by the work (physical, emotional and intellectual);
- benefit to the community and to offenders placed there from the work;
- approximate duration of the project and degree of continuity from week to week;
- how much the project will be affected by bad weather; and
- facilities for dealing with offenders with disabilities and offenders with responsibilities for children.

Particular care should be maintained over the supervision of offenders given access to private property.

Referral

15.   In assessing the suitability of an offender for CS work, procedures should have regard to:

- the need to minimise court delays;
- enabling offenders to start the order promptly, in suitable work;
- ensuring offenders are clear about the requirements of, and give their informed consent to, the order; and
- maximising opportunities for the courts to impose CSOs on appropriate offenders, particularly those who have committed the most serious offences for which a community sentence might be appropriate.

16.   In assessing an offender's suitability for CS work, the probation service should consider and record information about the offender's employment, domestic circumstances, physical and mental ability, skills, trustworthiness, current offence(s), offending history and response to previous CS or other community sentences, and likely risk to the public. The probation service should not adopt unduly narrow criteria when assessing suitability for CS. An unacceptable risk of repeat offending or a need for significant social work intervention may indicate that CS is unsuitable, but a previous failure should not preclude consideration for a further CSO, particularly where arrangements can be made to anticipate similar difficulties recurring.

17.   The probation service should make particular efforts to find suitable work for people with disabilities, for women offenders and single parents, and for offenders from minority ethnic, racial or other groups (see paragraph 5, above). Under paragraph 10(3)(d) of schedule 3 to the 1973 Act, probation committees are entitled to defray offenders' special expenses (e.g. child-minding fees) incurred in performing CS and are encouraged to do so, within available resources, where this would help to prevent discrimination.

Commencement

18.   The first work session under a CSO should, whenever possible, be arranged to take place within *10 working days of the making of the order*. If practicable, the arrangement should be made before the offender leaves court. However, work should not begin unless sufficient information about the

offender (especially his or her criminal record) is available to those arranging the work to show that it can be performed without undue risk to the public (delay may, for example, arise when CS was not anticipated in the PSR).

19.   At the first appointment (either the first work session or a CS assessment, whichever is appropriate) a member of probation staff should:

■   give the offender *written information* setting out *what she or he can expect from the probation service* during the operation of the CSO; *what is expected of the offender*, such as possible work requirements, how to contact the CS scheme and what to do if ill; the *consequences of lateness, failure to attend and unacceptable behaviour*, including the possibility of breach, and what evidence is required when unavoidable reasons for absence arise; and how to make a *complaint* about her or his treatment under the order and *how to seek variation* of its terms. The information should be available in English and, where relevant and practicable, in other languages;
■   *explain* this information to the offender;
■   if possible, *serve the offender with a copy of the order*, which the offender should be asked to sign; and
■   *establish that the offender has given his or her informed consent to the order* (or, if not, and the offender states that he or she refuses or withdraws consent, take appropriate action, if necessary by returning the offender to court).

20.   Achieving these requirements can only be possible with the effective cooperation of court staff, e.g. in notifying the probation service of the order and providing a copy promptly (as required under section 14(6) of the 1973 Act), and of others, e.g. in providing details of criminal records. Court duty probation staff must, similarly, notify the appropriate CS scheme (which may be in another probation area) very quickly of CSOs that have just been made and assist, if practicable, in arranging an early commencement date.

Management of CS
21.   The management of a CSO should, as far as practicable, be devised to be appropriate for the individual offender. Early in the order the CS scheme should, therefore, identify the offender's characteristics, abilities and needs (see paragraph 16, above), and select suitable CS placements accordingly, in consultation with the offender. The opportunity should be taken, where possible, to motivate the offender, to help her or him to see the consequences of offending and to make amends, and to increase the offender's skill and experience, e.g. in relation to possible future employment. Full use should also be made of both individual and group placements, as most appropriate (see paragraph 12, above).

22.   Progress and future plans should be reviewed at appropriate intervals during the order. At the conclusion of the order, the offender should be invited to express his or her views on the benefits (or disadvantages) of the work undertaken, and if the offender wishes, the relevant officer should discuss his or her own conclusions with the offender. The information should also be recorded on the case file.

Work rate

23.   Schemes should aim to ensure a minimum work rate of five hours per week throughout the order, calculated as an average over the whole of the order starting from the first work session attended. Normally, no more than 21 hours should be worked in any one week unless there are special circumstances, e.g. that the average hours worked have fallen below five per week. Work should not, however, conflict with the offender's entitlement to welfare benefits and, if unemployed, CS placements should not prevent the offender from being readily available to seek or take up employment.

Standards of performance and behaviour

24.   Throughout CS placements (and any related supervision, e.g. on travel to or from a site) offenders should be expected to report on time as directed; to behave acceptably, without disrupting work or giving offence to others; and to work effectively, as reasonably directed by the supervisor and within each offender's ability. Offenders should also abide by the rules of the workplace. Alcohol should not be consumed during CS work, including breaks. Offenders should be made fully aware of these required standards, and reminded when appropriate. Where unacceptable behaviour or performance occurs, the offender may be sent home and hours worked that day may, if appropriate, not be recorded. This should, for example, be done where an offender arrives later than is allowed under local guidance (which should not exceed half an hour) without reasonable excuse.

Recording and reckoning of hours worked

25.   Each probation service should have a standard form on which to record hours worked by each offender. In the case of work not supervised by the probation service, a person must be nominated to maintain the record. Offenders must be told how and by whom hours are recorded. The probation service must keep an *up-to-date record* of the hours worked by each offender, and should provide her or him with a *weekly report* detailing the hours worked that week; a brief comment (e.g. 'satisfactory'); total hours worked under the order; and hours remaining to be worked.

26.   On the principle that offenders should be treated fairly and that some travel time should be the offender's own responsibility, travel time to or from CS placements in excess of half an hour, which the probation service accepts as actually and reasonably incurred, should normally be credited as time worked under the order. Such time should be shown separately on records of hours worked (paragraph 25, above) and should be kept within a reasonable overall proportion of the hours worked under the order as a whole.

27.   Where bad weather prevents the performance of work, the supervisor should determine whether to require the offenders to remain in the expectation of a resumption of work; to make alternative arrangements for work; or if neither of those is practicable, to discharge the offender(s) for the day. Lengthy periods waiting for weather to clear should be avoided. In such circumstances, offenders should be credited with the time spent on site.

Enforcement

28.   In enforcing a CSO effectively, the probation service should:

■ *seek to secure and maintain the offender's consent to and compliance with the order* so that the objectives of the order may be achieved; but also
■ *recognise where this cannot be achieved and take appropriate action.* Consideration of the objectives of the order should, however, remain of primary concern during any procedure undertaken to enforce it.

29. Securing and maintaining the offender's consent and compliance requires consistent action on several fronts by those responsible for the order: clear instruction and explanation to the offender, e.g. as to required standards of work and behaviour; seeking to motivate and assist the offender to comply with the order; finding suitable CS placements and recognising good work; and anticipating difficulties and, where possible, pre-empting infringements by some timely encouragement or advice. Although a CSO is not primarily an order requiring social work supervision to the extent, for example, of a probation order, *some* application of such skills may make all the difference to successful completion of a CSO and is encouraged.

30. Any apparent failure to comply with the requirements of a CSO, such as lateness, failure to attend, or unacceptable performance or behaviour, must be followed up promptly, normally within two working days, seeking an explanation from the offender. The apparent failure, the offender's explanation (or lack of one), the relevant officer's opinion of whether the explanation (or lack of one) is acceptable and the likely consequences for successful completion of the CSO must be recorded. (The personal circumstances and characteristics of the offender may affect the acceptability of the explanation or lack of one, for example, by indicating the degree of premeditation behind the apparent failure to comply.) *If the explanation (or lack of one) is not considered acceptable, the incident must formally be recorded as an instance of failure to comply with the order.* If breach action is not being taken, the offender should be warned (orally, confirmed in writing on the second or subsequent occasion) of the likely consequences of further failure to comply with the order. Following up apparent failure to comply can be an important opportunity to strengthen the offender's consent to and compliance with the order (see paragraphs 28 and 29, above). In addition, failure to comply may reveal a need to change the CS placements being given.

31. An offender claiming absence through sickness should be asked to provide a medical certificate signed by a doctor (though at the discretion of the relevant officer, self-certification may be accepted on limited occasions). The cost of obtaining a certificate should be reimbursed. It is recognised that securing such evidence depends on the cooperation of others. Arrangements with a local doctor (for a fee or retainer) may make this easier. Where there is frequent absence on medical grounds, further evidence should be sought, e.g. from the offender's GP or an independent medical examination (at the expense of the probation service). In the case of long-term sickness or disability, a change in the type of work, or an application to revoke the CSO, may be appropriate.

32. Breach action under schedule 2 to the 1991 Act may be appropriate immediately in some instances of misbehaviour or failure to comply. In other cases, the relevant officer may consider that the purpose of the order is best served by giving a warning in the first and second instances, as above, but *breach*

action should normally be taken after no more than three instances of failure to comply with the order. Further continuation without breach action, in limited circumstances only, may only take place if agreed with a Senior Probation Officer or equivalent grade as being strongly in the interests of the objectives of the order. Practice guidance reflecting discussion with sentencers may help to clarify where this may be appropriate (see paragraphs 35 and 36, below). In these considerations, earlier instances of non-compliance may normally be disregarded if they took place more than six months before (but all become relevant if breach proceedings are begun). All instances of failure to comply, decisions made and action taken should be noted on case records.

33.   Except in cases of gross misconduct or refusal to comply, offenders subject to CSOs should normally be allowed to continue working when breach action is pending, provided that they confirm that they will accept all the requirements of the order. (This is consistent with seeking to secure the offender's successful completion of the order.) It should be explained to the offender that the court *may* nevertheless revoke the order, but *may* take good – or bad – conduct in the meantime into account when hearing the breach. If a further instance of unacceptable behaviour takes place pending beach, the offender should normally be suspended from further CS work until after the breach hearing.

34.   When breach proceedings are undertaken, the probation service has an important role in the separate processes of proving the breach and of advising the court on future action. Such advice should encompass the possibility of reinforcement of the order with a warning about future conduct; imposition of a fine or additional CS hours; substitution of a different community order; or whether further continuation of any community order is impracticable or unjustified. This should be contained, as required, in an oral or written report to the court, which should also include an account of the offender's response to supervision so far and the extent to which the offender has successfully completed the order (i.e. has successfully discharged the sentence imposed on him or her – paragraph 3(2)(a) or 4(2)(a) of schedule 2 to the 1991 Act; this becomes relevant if the court considers dealing with the offender for the original offence). The relevant officer should also consider whether the offender's behaviour amounts to wilful and persistent failure to comply with the requirements of the order, which can be taken as refusal to consent to a community sentence (paragraph 3(2)(b) or 4(2)(b) of the schedule). If the relevant probation officer considers it likely to be expedient and appropriate, a (further) PSR may be prepared prior to the breach hearing.

. . .

6   COMBINATION ORDERS

6.1   Introduction

Legislation
Section 11 of the Criminal Justice Act 1991 (the 1991 Act) provides for a community order to be known as a *combination order* combining *probation* and

community service (CS). The probation element may be of one to three years duration; the CS element of 40 to 100 hours. The combination order is available only for offences punishable with imprisonment, and is subject to the general criteria for community sentencing set out in section 6 of the 1991 Act as well as (separately) for probation and for CS. In principle, the full range of additional requirements available for probation orders is available also for combination orders. The court must consider a pre-sentence report (PSR) before imposing a combination order and the offender must consent to the making of the order.

2.   The probation element of a combination order may, therefore, be all but the shortest (6–12 month) duration of probation orders; and the *CS* element may be up to (just over) 40% of the maximum for a community service order (CSO), as shown diagrammatically below:

	6 mths	12 mths		3 yrs
PROBATION				

	40 hrs	100 hrs		240 hrs
COMMUNITY SERVICE				

░░░░ Possible range under a combination order

3.   The legislation provides that, as far as is practicable, the probation element of a combination order shall be dealt with as if it were a probation order; and the CS element as if it were a community service order. Similarly, much of the operation of the probation element of a combination order is dealt with in the national standard on probation order supervision, and much of the operation of the CS element by the national standard on CSOs. This standard, therefore, addresses those aspects of combination order supervision *not* adequately dealt with in the other standards. This includes coordinating supervision of the two parts of the order, *recognising that a combination order is a single order of the court, relating to a single offender, supervised by a single probation service*. Nevertheless, much of this standard is *also* relevant to the *coordination of separate probation orders and CSOs* imposed on the same offender, eg following conviction for different offences.

Objectives
4.   The statutory purpose of a combination order, as defined in section 11(2) of the 1991 Act, is:

■   to secure the rehabilitation of the offender;
■   to protect the public from harm from the offender; and/or
■   to prevent the offender from committing further offences.

5.   The operation of a combination order should seek to achieve the aims of probation order supervision, set out in paragraph 4 of the probation order national standard, while additionally assisting the reintegration of the offender

into the community through the carrying out of positive and demanding community service work.

. . .

6.2 Targeting

7.   In addressing a combination order in a PSR, it is important for the probation officer to consider:

■ the *seriousness of the offence*. Given the considerable restriction on liberty inherent in a combination order, such an order will be appropriate for amongst the most serious offenders likely to be given a community sentence, as a consequence of section 6(2)(b) of the 1991 Act. In practice, this may well mean that combination orders feature most frequently in Crown Court rather than magistrates' court cases;
■ the *suitability of a combination order for the offender* in accordance with section 6(2)(a) of the 1991 Act. Due regard should be given to assessing in the PSR the offender's suitability for *probation* (i.e. that the offender needs the type of supervision and professional intervention provided under a probation order, as defined in the relevant legislation and national standard); his or her suitability for *CS* (i.e. that the offender is suitable to perform such work and that provision can be made); *and* that the offender has a reasonable prospect (with suitable encouragement and support) of completing the order satisfactorily.

8.   In practice, a combination order is likely to be most appropriate for an offender who has:

■ committed an offence which is amongst the most serious for which a community sentence may be imposed;
■ clearly identified areas of need that have contributed to the offending and which can be dealt with by probation supervision; and
■ a realistic prospect of completing such an order, including both the probation and CS elements.

9.   Amongst those offenders who might *not* be well suited to a combination order would be those whose lifestyle is particularly chaotic, for example, as a result of drug or alcohol misuse, and who might therefore have particular difficulty in keeping to a programme of CS work; or offenders with well-ordered lifestyles who have little need of (or alternatively little prospect of responding to) probation supervision. Combination orders that include demanding additional requirements within the probation element are particularly onerous and are likely to be difficult to complete, especially for younger offenders. In *all* cases, particularly those outlined in this paragraph, it is, therefore, essential for a probation officer to make a careful assessment with reference to the criteria of seriousness and suitability, above, before proposing a combination order in a PSR.

6.3 Supervision

Supervision and coordination

10. As with a probation order, one probation officer should be identified as the *supervising* officer given overall responsibility for a combination order. This person should keep herself or himself informed of the general progress under the order and should be consulted by others, as necessary, where key decisions need to be made. An *initial appointment* with a named probation officer, normally the supervising officer, should take place within five working days of the making of the order, to begin probation supervision (as under the probation order standard),   and   to   ensure   that   arrangements   are   made   for the CS element to begin, normally within 10 working days of the making of the order. Where the commencement of one element of the order is deferred, the reason for the delay should be recorded on the case records.

11. Although there must be a single supervising officer, many different arrangements are possible for supervising a combination order within the requirements in paragraph 10, above, including:

■   a field probation officer supervising the probation element (and the combination order as a whole), and a probation ancillary supervising the CS element;
■   a field probation officer supervising the probation element and a specialist probation officer in a CS team supervising the CS clement, either of whom might be the supervising officer; or
■   one probation officer supervising the whole order, for example, in a field team (especially in a rural area) or a specialist combination order team (especially in an urban area).

It is for the CPO to determine how combination order supervision is conducted in his or her area, in accordance with what is most suitable for local circumstances.

12. Officers supervising the probation and CS elements of combination orders carry the same responsibilities as do officers supervising probation orders and CSOS. Where responsibility is split between officers, each has a responsibility to ensure that an overall view can be and is taken of the offender's progress through the combination order as a whole. This responsibility applies particularly to the supervising officer in overall charge, but also to any others involved, who should inform her or him of significant developments. There should, therefore, be routine contact between officers to exchange relevant information; and important developments (particular improvements and successes, or problems and unacceptable behaviour) should be notified promptly. The supervising officer should *review the order as a whole* on the cycle required for the review of probation orders (i.e. three-monthly), in consultation with the other officer(s) involved; similarly the *supervision plan* required for probation orders should in the case of a combination order address the order as a whole.

13. Such effective coordination is necessary not only for the information of the staff (or teams) concerned, but also so that joint issues of relevance for the offender and ways of maximising the effectiveness of the order can be considered

– for example, for the probation element to reinforce the CS element or to help to secure compliance or, if appropriate, for the CS element to build on work being undertaken in the probation element.

Enforcement
14.   The dual principle of seeking to secure the offender's consent to and compliance with the order, but, where that cannot be achieved, recognising the situation and taking appropriate action, applies to combination orders as it does to probation orders and community service orders. Securing and maintaining the offender's consent and compliance requires consistent action on several fronts by those responsible for the order: clear instruction and explanation to the offender, e.g. as to required standards of work and behaviour; seeking to motivate and assist the offender to comply with the order; finding suitable CS placements and recognising good work; and anticipating difficulties and, where possible, preempting infringements by some timely encouragement or advice.

15.   The decision on whether to institute breach proceedings should be taken by the supervising officer. If different people are supervising each element of the order, they should be in touch with each other *prior* to the commencement of breach proceedings. Any report to the court in such proceedings should address the offender's progress under both parts of the order.

16.   Enforcement should, as far as practicable, be dealt with in respect of each element according to the relevant individual standard. An offender should, therefore, be breached under a combination order where justified by the normal criteria for breach of a probation order or a CSO: separate totals of infringements should, therefore, be kept for each element of the combination order. Particularly in borderline cases, it may however be helpful to have regard to the offender's performance under the order as a whole.

17.   If, following breach action, the court wishes to resentence the offender to either a probation order or a CSO, it must first revoke the combination order as a whole.

Early termination
18.   Early termination may be considered for a combination order *after* completion of the CS element of the order in accordance with the criteria for early termination of probation orders (paragraph 28 of the probation order national standard).

. . .

7   MANAGEMENT OF APPROVED PROBATION AND BAIL HOSTELS

7.1   General

This national standard deals with the management of approved probation and bail hostels. It should be read in conjunction with the national standards for *probation order supervision* and for *supervivion before and after release from custody*, since many residents at approved hostels will also be subject to probation supervision or post-release supervision; and also with the *Approved Bail and Probation Hostel Rules*. This national standard for the management of approved hostels applies equally to approved hostels run by probation committees and those which have a voluntary management committee so that whenever the term 'committee' is used in this standard, this should be taken as referring to the area probation committee or the managing committee, as appropriate, unless specified otherwise.

2.   This standard provides a set of fundamental requirements for the management of approved hostels in England and Wales. Its purpose is to reinforce the confidence of the courts and the public in approved hostels, to provide a structure for the development of good practice in each probation area; and to promote efficient and effective standards of service delivery.

3.   The area probation committee should satisfy itself that this standard is complied with in the hostels it provides. The managing committee should do the same for the voluntary-managed hostels for which it is responsible.

7.2   Purpose of approved hostels

4.   The purpose of approved hostels is to provide an enhanced level of supervision to enable certain bailees and offenders to remain under supervision in the community. Hostel residents should be expected to go to work or to attend projects, training courses or treatment facilities *in the community*. It follows that approved hostels should have close links with, and form part of, the probation committee's area strategy for the supervision of bailees and offenders in the community.

5.   Approved hostels should be reserved for those who require this enhanced supervision and are not meant simply as accommodation. They should provide a supportive and structured environment within which their residents can be supervised effectively. But it should be clearly understood that approved hostels are *not secure* and so cannot provide the same degree of protection from the risks posed by the most serious offenders as do most Prison Service establishments.

6.   Chief Probation Officers (CPOS) should encourage judges, magistrates and representatives of other criminal justice agencies in their areas to visit approved hostels so that they may see for themselves how the hostels operate, what they have to offer and the kind of residents for which they are best suited.

7.   Hostel staff should develop a regime in consultation with their committee and the local probation service. This should provide a structured and supportive environment which will seek to:

■   promote a responsible and law-abiding lifestyle, and respect for others;
■   create and maintain a constructive relationship between the hostel's staff and residents;
■   facilitate the work of the probation service and other agencies aimed at reducing the risk that residents will offend or reoffend in future;
■   assist the residents to keep or find employment and to develop their employment skills;
■   encourage and enable residents to use the facilities available in the local community and to develop their ability to become self-reliant in doing so;

■ enable the residents to move on successfully to other appropriate accommodation at the end of the period of residence;
■ establish and maintain good relations with neighbours and the community
   in general.

This should be set out in a published statement of aims and objectives.

8.   The committee should have in place an equal opportunities policy to
ensure fair treatment for all staff and residents, and equal access to the facilities
provided. A statement setting out the policy should be prominently displayed on
the premises and consideration should be given as to whether it should be made
available in appropriate ethnic minority languages. The implementation of the
policy should be monitored regularly by the committee, and action taken where
necessary to remedy discrimination on the ground of race, gender, age,
disability, language ability, literacy, religion, sexual orientation or any other
improper ground. The committee should ensure that adequate provision is made
for dietary and religious needs of residents and staff.

7.3   Safety and housing legislation

9.   Committees should also satisfy themselves that hostels meet the appropriate standards of housing, health and safety, food and hygiene and other relevant
legislation. Their responsibilities extend to both the staff and the residents of the
hostel. In all rostering of staff, the safety of staff and of hostel residents should be
a high priority. In the context of this paragraph, the hostel includes its grounds
and any cluster properties and their grounds.

8   SUPERVISION BEFORE AND AFTER RELEASE FROM CUSTODY

8.1   Introduction

This standard covers the supervision by the probation service and social services
departments of offenders both before and after release from custody. It focuses
primarily on the role of the home probation officer who will be responsible for
supervising offenders on licence following their release. The standard relates to
those offenders sentenced to 12 months or more (excluding life sentence
prisoners) and young offenders serving less than 12 months who are also
supervised under section 65 of the Criminal Justice Act 1991. It also applies to
young offenders serving determinate sentences under section 53 of the Children
and Young Persons Act 1933, including those accommodated in communinity
homes by local authority social services or by the Youth Treatment Service. It
does *not* apply to offenders sentenced to custody before implementation of part
II of the Criminal Justice Act 1991 on 1 October 1992, but the good practice
elements contained in the standard could be applied to those cases. In the case of
offenders sentenced to less than 12 months, who will be released automatically at
the half-way point of sentence, existing voluntary throughcare arrangements
will continue to apply. References in this standard to probation services should
be taken to include corresponding social services staff and functions, as
appropriate.

2. Good throughcare practice will be crucial to effective supervision following release. It should aim to enhance the ability of offenders to resettle in the community whilst giving access to help and resources which assist them to maintain themselves in the community without offending. Whilst throughcare is primarily the responsibility of the Prison Service, the probation service has a key contribution to make. Effective throughcare will require close cooperation between the Prison and probation services.

3. Sentence planning will coordinate the provision of services to offenders and will seek to identify ways in which the offender will attempt to tackle his/her offending behaviour. It will be the responsibility of the Prison Service to bring forward sentence planning for all prisoners, although it will initially only be comprehensively available for young adult offenders and those serving sentences of four years and over.

Early release of prisoners under the Criminal Justice Act 1991

4. Sections 32 to 51 of the Criminal Justice Act 1991 introduce a new set of arrangements for the early release of sentenced prisoners to replace the existing systems of parole and remission of sentence. They come into effect at the same time as the Act's provisions on sentencing, namely 1 October 1992.

5. The new arrangements are based on the recommendations of the Committee under Lord Carlisle of Bucklow's chairmanship which reviewed the present parole and remission systems and whose report was published in 1988 (Cm 532). The report pointed out that the present parole system erodes the distinction between the amounts of time spent in custody under sentences of different lengths and creates an unacceptable disparity between the sentence given and what the sentence means in practice.

6. The Act therefore introduces a wholly new concept, namely that of a sentence served partly in custody and partly in the community with the offender being liable to recall to custody right up to the end of sentence. There are two schemes for the release of determinate prisoners based on sentence length. Offenders sentenced to 12 months and over and up to four years will be released automatically halfway through their sentence and then supervised up to the three-quarter point and liable for recall up to the end of sentence. Those sentenced to four years and over will be subject to a discretionary release system operating from the halfway point of sentence up to the two-thirds, with the Parole Board considering the suitability of release, and if released, will be supervised to the three-quarter point and be liable to recall up to the end of sentence. Those discretionary offenders not released before the two-thirds point will be released automatically at that stage of sentence and will be supervised to the three-quarter point. They are also liable for recall up to the end of sentence. Some sex offenders in both automatic and discretionary categories will be supervised to the very end of sentence at the direction of the sentencing judge. . . .

7. The automatic conditional release (ACR) scheme has no discretionary elements and will be administered entirely by Prison Service establishments at local level. It will be the responsibility of establishments to issue the licence, which is signed by the Governor on behalf of the Home Secretary. There is provision for the Governor to approve special licence conditions on the

recommendation or with the agreement of the supervising officer. Probation managers (see paragraph 17, below) should ensure that systems are in place to ensure that any additional conditions recommended are restricted to those listed at Annex 8.A.

8.   For offenders in the discretionary release category, the Home Secretary will retain formal responsibility for all parole decisions. However, he will delegate that responsibility to the Parole Board for those sentenced to under seven years. The Criminal Justice Act 1991 contains powers for the Home Secretary to raise or lower the seven year threshold for delegated decision-making by the Board, subject to Parliamentary approval.

9.   Proceedings to be taken in the event of a breach of licence conditions are different for the two categories of offender. For those serving under four years released under the ACR scheme, breach proceedings are dealt with through the magistrates' courts, who have the power to impose a fine of up to £1,000, order a return to custody for a maximum of six months or the outstanding period of the licence if that is less, or both. For those on discretionary release (including those released automatically at the two-thirds point), the Home Secretary, on recommendation of the Parole Board, may recall offenders to prison if they are in breach of their licence conditions.

Objectives of the supervision period of the sentence –
– In custody

10.   To be effective, a programme of supervision in the community following the custodial part of the sentence has to be drawn up in close cooperation between the Prison, probation or other supervising services. Planning for release should therefore start as soon as sentence is passed. A supervising officer should be allocated throughout the offender's sentence. He or she should visit the offender in custody as often as is practicable and take an active role in sentence planning. The supervising officer should be involved, along with the seconded prison probation officer and Prison Service grade, in drawing up the initial sentence plan and should contribute to the regular assessments and updates of the plan and reviews of the offender's progress. This is the most effective means of providing continuity of supervision by ensuring that work done with the offender in custody is carried on to the community part of sentence and by ensuring that the probation officer supervising the offender on release is fully involved in planning decisions about what happens to the offender during the custodial part of sentence.

11.   The seconded officer has a key role in ensuring the effective delivery of offender throughcare. This is achieved not only by focusing on the social work task and tackling the offending behaviour of inmates but also by the linking role of the post, bridging the prison and outside probation service.

12.   Contracts between CPOs and Governors will provide the framework for the delivery of more effective throughcare arrangements and will define more clearly the role and status within the institution of seconded staff. The emphasis on continuity of supervision requires that closer working relationships must be forged between the prison, the seconded and the supervising probation officer in order to achieve this objective.

– In the community
13.   The objectives of supervising offenders on licence in the community are analogous to those offenders under a probation order. Those objectives are:

(i)   protection of the public
(ii)   prevention of reoffending;
(iii)   successful reintegration in the community.

14.   The supervising officer should have clear regard to these objectives throughout the community part of sentence. Ensuring effective supervision requires high professional standards both from the probation services and from individual probation staff and should generally entail establishing a professional relationship, in which to advise, assist and befriend the offender with the aim of:

(i)   enforcing the conditions of the licence and securing the offender's cooperation and compliance with those conditions;
(ii)   challenging the offender to accept responsibility for his or her crime and gaining their cooperation in avoiding offending in the future;
(iii)   helping the offender to resolve personal difficulties linked with offending and acquire new skills;
(iv)   motivating and assisting the offender to change for the better and to become a responsible and law-abiding member of the community; and
(v)   assessing the risk of the offender reoffending and/or of presenting a danger to the public, and responding appropriately.

15.   This standard requires that a visit to the offender's home address should take place within five working days of the first interview following release from prison whilst the probation order supervision standard does not contain such stringent requirements. This is mainly to reflect the fact that the offence which led to the imposition of a prison sentence will have been more serious and that more serious offenders will require more intensive supervision, particularly at the outset, in order to achieve the primary objective of supervision, i.e. protection of the public. A home visit can help impress upon the offender that he/she is still serving part of the sentence so that he/she is in no doubt as to the demands imposed by the supervision period and serves the practical purpose of being a check on his/her successful resettlement into the community. In cases where the home visit appears to the supervising officer to be problematic (e.g. for reasons of potential violence or of confidentiality in relation to other members of the household), the officer and the line manager should review all possible options. This might include two officers visiting, or negotiating visits at a particular time. The assumption should be that a visit will be made but, in exceptional cases, where there are serious concerns about safety, the line manager may agree otherwise. The reasons should be recorded on file.
16.   Supervision programmes should be adapted carefully to the individual circumstances of each offender, for example, to respond to employment difficulties or racial disadvantage. The work of probation services must be free of discrimination on the ground of race, gender, religion, disability, sexual orientation or any other improper ground. All probation services must have a

stated *equal opportunities policy* and ensure that this is effectively implemented, monitored and reviewed. Effective action to prevent discrimination (*anti-discriminatory practice*) requires significantly more than an equal willingness to accept all offenders equally or to invest an equal amount of time and effort in different cases. The origin, nature and extent of differences in circumstances and need must be properly understood and actively addressed *by all concerned* – for example, by staff training, by monitoring and review and by making extra effort to understand and work most effectively with an offender from a different cultural background.

17.   The provision of effective supervision in each area is primarily the responsibility of the probation committee and should be achieved through their Chief Probation Officer (CPO). All probation committees must ensure that supervision is provided in their area in accordance with this national standard and with regard to any guidance associated with this standard. References in the standard to 'probation manager' means either a Senior Probation Officer or Chief Probation Officer grade (i.e. CPO or above). It is for each probation service to determine who should undertake this role. Similar arrangements will be required of social services.

18.   Joint Circular Instruction 17/1992 and Home Office Circular 49/1992 require the supervising officer to complete and return to the establishment from which the offender is released a feedback report covering details of the offender's period under supervision in the community. The report will be sent by the establishment to the supervising officer one month before the end of the supervision period for return as soon as possible. It is important that these reports are completed and returned to enable establishments to identify the effectiveness of work undertaken and help given in custody and to assess what additional or different work or assistance would have been helpful. The feedback report is an important part of the process of forming closer links between the Prison and probation services and will help establishments to assess and improve their programmes of custodial activities.

19.   All reports should be prepared on the basis that they are intended to be open documents which may be disclosed to and discussed with the offender. Supervising officers should ensure that information recorded is factual and that, where opinions are offered, they are firmly grounded on facts.

. . .

8.5   Enforcement of licence

Objectives of enforcement
59.   There are two main objectives of enforcement of licence conditions. These are:

■   *to secure compliance with the requirements of the licence;*
■   *to recognise where that cannot be secured and to take appropriate action.*

Consideration of the objectives of supervision (see paragraph 14, above) should, however, remain of primary concern during any procedure taken to enforce the licence.

60. The requirements of a licence and the need to attend appointments should be made clear, and the consequences of any failures to comply fully explained to the offender. . . . When these requirements are not complied with action must be taken promptly and an explanation sought for each apparent failure either to attend an appointment or comply with a licence condition, and recorded on the case file.

61. It will be for the supervising officer to decide whether the explanation is acceptable and this must be recorded. The personal circumstances and characteristics of the offender may affect the acceptability of the explanation, for example, where an offender's chaotic or impulsive lifestyle, or substantial difficulties being faced, affects the degree of premeditation behind the apparent failure to comply. If no explanation is given, this fact should be recorded. If the supervising officer considers that the explanation is not acceptable, the incident must be recorded as a prima facie breach of the licence.

Failure to report/attend an appointment

62. When an offender fails to report within the specified period following release . . ., the supervising officer should contact the relevant prison to confirm that release took place. If it did, the supervising officer should inform the probation manager of the failure to report and pay a visit to the offender's address. It is for the probation manager to decide in cases where the home visit appears to the supervising officer to be problematic (e.g. for reasons of potential violence) whether the visit should include two officers or take place at a particular time (see paragraph 15). Where an offender on discretionary release fails to report, the Parole Board via the Parole Unit should be informed with a recommendation as to further action.

63. In a case where an offender fails to attend a first or subsequent appointment, the supervising officer may consider that the purpose of supervision is best served by giving an oral or written warning. Alternatively he/she may decide immediately to institute action against the offender. If an offender fails to attend an appointment on a second occasion a written warning should be issued or action begun. Breach action should be instituted after the third instance. Further continuation without breach [action], in limited circumstances only, may take place if approved by the probation manager as being in the best interests of the objectives of supervision. In these considerations, earlier instances of non-compliance may normally be disregarded if they took place more than six months before (but all become relevant if breach action is begun). All instances of failure to comply, decisions made and action taken should be noted on case records.

64. If medical reasons are repeatedly given for failure to comply, a doctor's certificate should be sought at an early stage. If necessary the offender should be asked to undergo an independent medical examination at the expense of the probation service.

Failure to comply with other licence conditions

65. If the offender fails to comply with any other licence conditions the supervising officer should start the action outlined at paragraphs 60 and 61, above, as soon as possible and within two working days at most.

Addition or deletion of additional licence conditions

66.   For offenders in the automatic conditional release category, the supervising officer must apply to the Governor at the prison establishment from which the offender was discharged in order to add or delete a licence condition (. . . this should be limited to the conditions set out in Annex 8.A). The supervising officer should provide a full account of the reason for the request, including details of the offender's behaviour under supervision, and also forward a copy of the original licence. If the request is approved by the Governor, the establishment will issue a fresh licence and send it (in duplicate) to the supervising officer. The supervising officer must then serve the licence to the offender, explaining in what way it has been altered and giving reasons for the change, signing and dating it to that effect. The offender should be asked to sign the licence. If he or she refuses to sign or accept the licence, then the supervising officer should certify the licence to the effect that he or she has explained the alterations but that the offender was unwilling to sign or accept it. Three copies of the licence should then be returned to the establishment, one for its own retention, one to be forwarded by the establishment to the National Identification Bureau and one to the Chief Constable covering the supervising probation or social services area.

67.   For offenders in the discretionary release category, including those released automatically at two-thirds point of sentence, the supervising officer must apply to the Parole Unit in order to add or delete a licence condition. The application should be in the same form as that for offenders in the automatic conditional release category outlined at paragraph 66, above. Because the original licence is issued by the Governor of the establishment from which the offender is released, any changes agreed by the Parole Board have to go to the Governor so that a fresh licence can be issued. Two copies of the new licence will be forwarded to the supervising officer who must then follow the procedures for serving the licence and returning three copies to the establishment as detailed in paragraph 66.

8.6   Breach action and recall to prison

68.   Proceedings to be taken in the event of breach of licence conditions are different for the two categories of offender as detailed below (see also paragraph 9 in the introduction).

Offenders on automatic conditional release

69.   For the breach action to succeed the court will need to be satisfied that a licence condition has not been adhered to.

70.   Necessary breach action should be instituted in court in the usual way, taking care to assemble the evidence should a not guilty plea be submitted. Following a plea of guilty or a finding of guilt, a report should be submitted to the court which should contain a recommendation about how reasonable it would be for the offender to continue under supervision, whether a financial penalty should be imposed, or whether he/she should be returned to prison. The report should include reference to the offender's behaviour on supervision subsequent to the instigation of breach action. In cases where the offender continues to fail to comply with licence conditions after breach action has been

lodged but before the breach is heard by the magistrates' court, the report should be updated accordingly.

Offenders on discretionary release

71.   As with offenders on automatic conditional release, breach must normally be tied to licence conditions. But other factors should be taken into consideration, these include:

■   situations where the offender's behaviour is such that further serious offences are likely to be committed;
■   it appears that the safety of the public may be at risk;
■   the offender's behaviour, although not involving a direct risk to the safety of the public, seems likely to bring the licence system into disrepute, or to create general difficulty in the supervision of offenders if action is not seen to be taken.

In taking forward such action the supervising officer must provide full details to support the recall and may wish to refer to the Parole Board's criteria for the recall of determinate sentenced prisoners (Annex D to Circular Instruction 26/1992 and Home Office Circular 85/1992: The Discretionary Conditional Release Scheme).

72.   Where the probation manager determines that recall proceedings should be instigated, a Chief Probation Officer grade should submit a written report with a recommendation to the Parole Board via the Parole Unit. The report should contain as much relevant background information as possible, say whether recall is considered to be necessary and indicate whether the offender has previously received written warnings from the probation service.

73.   It will be for the Parole Board to decide whether the offender's behaviour is sufficiently serious to justify suspension of the licence and recall to prison or whether to issue a formal warning.

8.7   Emergency recall

74.   Emergency recall is available only for those offenders on discretionary release (that is offenders sentenced to four years or over) during the period under supervision on licence. It should be considered where any of the criteria in paragraph 71 are met and the risk to the safety of the public appears so great as to justify immediate action to recall the offender to prison.

75.   Where the probation manager determines that there is a case for emergency recall, a request for the offender's licence to be revoked should be made through the Chief Probation Officer grade to the Parole Unit by telephoning (during office hours). . . . After 5.00 p.m. the duty officer should be contacted . . . . The telephone call should be followed up by the submission of a written report on the same day or by the next working day detailing why emergency recall was considered to be essential. The Parole Unit will decide on action to be taken and notify the Chief Probation Officer of the outcome.

ANNEX 8.A   EXTRA LICENCE CONDITIONS

Recommendations to the prison governor (in automatic or discretionary conditional release cases) or the Parole Board (in discretionary conditional release cases) *must* be limited to appropriate choices from those listed below (see ... [paragraph] 66 in the national standard):

While under supervision you must:

(i)   attend upon a duly qualified psychiatrist/psychologist/medical practitioner for such care, supervision or treatment as that practitioner recommends; (where known, the practitioner should be named, subject to their agreement)

(ii) not engage in any work or other organised activity involving a person under the age of . . ., either on a professional or voluntary basis

(iii) reside at (name and address, e.g. hostel) and must not leave to live elsewhere without obtaining the prior approval of your supervising officer; thereafter you must reside as directed by your supervising officer

(iv) not reside in the same household as any child under . . . years of age

(v)   not seek to approach or communicate with your wife/former wife/daughter/son/children/grandchildren/other persons or any members of their family (persons must be named) without the prior approval of your supervising officer/and (name of the appropriate social services department)

(vi) comply with any requirements reasonably imposed by your supervising officer for the purpose of ensuring that you address your alcohol/drug/sexual/gambling/solvent abuse/anger/debt/ offending behaviour problems at (name of course/centre where appropriate)

Index